2004

Taming the Sovereigns

Institutional Change in International Politics

It is commonly claimed that international politics has recently entered a new era, following the end of the Cold War and then the events of September 11. In this book, Kalevi Holsti asks what we mean by 'change' in international politics. How do we identify it? How do we distinguish between significant and unimportant changes? Do we really live in a new era or do we see more continuity than transformation in the texture of international politics? Combining theoretical and empirical argument, Holsti investigates eight major international institutions including the state, sovereignty, territoriality, international law, diplomacy, trade, and war. Having identified the types of change these institutions have undergone during the past three centuries, Holsti analyzes the sources of those changes and speculates on their consequences. This is a major book, likely to have lasting influence in the study of international politics.

KALEVI J. HOLSTI is Research Associate at the Centre for International Relations and University Killam Professor, Political Science (Emeritus), at the University of British Columbia. He is the author of *The State, War, and the State of War* (1995), *Peace and War: Armed Conflicts and International Order, 1648–1989* (1991), *Change in the International System* (1991), *The Dividing Discipline* (1985), *Why Nations Realign* (1983), and *International Politics: A Framework for Analysis* (1967) (7 editions).

CAMBRIDGE STUDIES IN INTERNATIONAL RELATIONS: 94

Taming the Sovereigns

Cambridge Studies in International Relations is a joint initiative of Cambridge University Press and the British International Studies Association (BISA). The series will include a wide range of material, from undergraduate textbooks and surveys to research-based monographs and collaborative volumes. The aim of the series is to publish the best new scholarship in International Studies from Europe, North America and the rest of the world.

CAMBRIDGE STUDIES IN INTERNATIONAL RELATIONS

Series list continues after index

Taming the Sovereigns

Institutional Change in
International Politics

K. J. Holsti

CAMBRIDGE
UNIVERSITY PRESS

PUBLISHED BY THE PRESS SYNDICATE OF THE UNIVERSITY OF CAMBRIDGE
The Pitt Building, Trumpington Street, Cambridge, United Kingdom

CAMBRIDGE UNIVERSITY PRESS
The Edinburgh Building, Cambridge, CB2 2RU, UK
40 West 20th Street, New York, NY 10011-4211, USA
477 Williamstown Road, Port Melbourne, VIC 3207, Australia
Ruiz de Alarcón 13, 28014 Madrid, Spain
Dock House, The Waterfront, Cape Town 8001, South Africa

http://www.cambridge.org

First published 2004

Printed in the United Kingdom at the University Press, Cambridge

Typeface Palatino 10/12.5 pt   *System* LATEX 2$_\varepsilon$ [TB]

A catalogue record for this book is available from the British Library

Library of Congress Cataloguing in Publication data

Holsti, K. J. (Kalevi Jaakko), 1935–
Taming the sovereigns : institutional change in international politics /
K. J. Holsti.
        p.   cm. – (Cambridge studies in international relations ; 94)
Includes bibliographical references and index.
ISBN 0 521 83403 1 (hbk.) – ISBN 0 521 54192 1 (pbk.)
1. International relations.   2. World politics.   3. National state.
4. Sovereignty.   I. Title.   II. Series.
JZ1310.H65   2004   327.1′01–dc21   2003047255

ISBN 0 521 83403 1 hardback
ISBN 0 521 54192 1 paperback

For Karina, Dan, and Peter

Contents

Tables

Preface

When a layperson asks scholars and theorists of international relations "What do you do?" the answer is more likely to puzzle than to enlighten. The idea that there are big pictures to describe, generalizations to establish, and essential characteristics to discover, explain, and debate eludes those who are more likely to see the field as one involving expertise on the latest world crisis. Even media people, when telephoning to ask an academic if they will comment on the new crisis in Bhutan or Tuvalu, are not easily put off by the answer that the "expert" knows nothing more about those places than is already available in a reasonably competent newspaper. An expert in International Relations is supposed to know everything about everywhere in the immediate sense. Theory simply will not do because it does not explain or provide adequate background to a series of events in location a at time b. Few laypeople are interested in questions about relative gains, international norms, the construction and change of identities, prisoner's dilemmas, agent–structure debates, and the like.

However, when the question of change comes into the discussion, everyone has opinions and immediately the conversation between the layperson and the theorist becomes engaged. One conversation might go as follows:

IR PERSON: The main lines of American foreign policy have certainly changed since the events of September 11, 2001.
LAYPERSON: I don't agree. States always follow their national interest, as they define it. The Americans, whether under Eisenhower or George W. Bush, place their country first, and the rest be damned. If others share American interests, then there might be alliances; but absent those interests, the alliances will fall apart.

IR PERSON: You imply that international relations is a game of clashing national interests and that the texture and rules of the game remain the same regardless of historical context.

LAYPERSON: Yes, that's it. It's just like all people are and always have been. I come first, I do what I want and no one tells me what to do . . . aside from paying taxes.

IR PERSON: I'm not certain the personal analogy holds very well, but even if it does, we can debate about the extent to which you are as self-centered as you claim. Aren't there certain rules in your house that you must observe in order to maintain domestic harmony? And next time you drive to work, consider why you drive on the right (or left in England and Japan) side of the road.

LAYPERSON: Of course there are rules, but in the case of those of the household, I set them up in the first place. They reflect my interests. As for the highway, I drive on the right because I am accustomed to do so (I always have trouble driving in the UK). I do it also because I am not suicidal. I follow my interest in self-preservation.

IR PERSON: But surely major events or trends can change rules. The rules in your household are probably not the same as they would have been fifty years ago. Driving rules have also changed to keep pace with technological innovations.

LAYPERSON: OK, OK; you have a point. Some things do change, but I still think that in international politics, states do only what serves their immediate interests. That was the case three hundred years ago and it remains so.

Change is a mighty engine for debate. It is the hidden stuff of arguments in pubs, formal academic seminars, newspaper editorials, and at least implicitly, in countless treatises on international politics, international relations, and "global politics." This should not be surprising. Our attitudes about the possibilities of change in the realms we inhabit are based on more general opinions about life and the social world. Conservatives, liberals, and radicals disagree on many issues, but the most fundamental one is the possibility and desirability of social or political change. Conservatives' images of the world tend to highlight "eternal truths," to which the radicals reply that that is exactly the problem: the present world and its antecedents are not the worlds we wish to live in any longer. We must therefore change them.

In the more rarified contexts of intellectual debates among theorists of international relations, a major axis of controversy also revolves around questions of change: where, when, for what reasons, and how. Indeed, most of the great debates in the field, going back to its early years at the beginning of the twentieth century, have been implicitly arguments about change. On one end of the continuum, realists such as Kenneth

Waltz (1979) and Robert Gilpin (1981) insist that the "texture" of international relations in anarchical systems remains essentially the same regardless of historical context or of the properties of the units that constitute the system. At the other end, constructivists insist that identities, and therefore interests, are constantly redefined through social interaction. Relationships can range from close collaboration, even integration, to total war. There is no single variable that determines their character, whether power, interest, anarchy, or structure. All politics are about the social construction of identities through interaction and the development of intersubjective meanings. Change in the character of relationships is thus ubiquitous. The "texture" of international politics never remains the same but depends upon, among other things, the social and cultural context in which they take place.

Agreement between these and other views is not likely because their proponents are wedded to different conceptions of change. But what are they? Curiously, the field is largely bereft of serious analysis of the nature and sources of change. We assume that change is obvious to all, that it needs no analysis on its own terms, and that anyone should be able to identify it when it occurs. But the debates that go on about change suggest that matters are more complicated. We do not all recognize change; we often do not or cannot describe it; and sometimes we do not even "see" it when it is obvious. On the other hand, our openness to novelty, fads, and appearances may seduce us to cry "change" every time something appears different from the previous day. Major events in international relations are particularly prone to be interpreted as markers of fundamental change and of novelty. The ends of major wars are notable times when hope for, and signs of, a better world appear in both public and academic discourses. However, if we are to take the 1930s and the 1950s as main post-war eras, then the hopes of 1919 and 1945 would seem to have been misplaced. Many things changed, but the often cruel "texture" of international politics was not one of them. In contrast, many people today insist that the forces of globalization are changing things for the better, bringing nations and peoples closer together, and thus undermining the traditional bases of warlike behavior. The foundations of national power and welfare today reside in information and knowledge, not conquest of foreign territories, the establishment of empires, or creating trade monopolies. So, things have changed and continue to do so.

I have been puzzled as to why, when the nature, qualities, and sources of change in international politics are so fundamental to academic debates, so few have turned their attention to the phenomenon. What do we mean by change? How do we know it when we see it? What is significant as opposed to insignificant change? On what sorts of foundations do we make assertions about the character and possibility of change in the texture of international politics? There are many other questions that come to mind. This study addresses some of them in the hope that the debates in the field can become more disciplined.

The domains of change

Scholars and laypersons are likely to use the terms "international politics," "international relations," and "global" or "world" politics interchangeably. It is important to identify the scope of the phenomena we address in this study. Many of the debates in the field arise because proponents of one or the other view of the sources, nature, and desirability of change are not talking about the same domain. I take the term *global politics* to mean the main political and sociological processes or trends occurring around the world. One example would be the rise of ethnic, religious, and other forms of political mobilization taking place within countries, and the relations between them in different countries (e.g., the relations between ethnic "liberation" movements such as the Tamils in Sri Lanka, and the Tamil diaspora in many other countries). Another would be the political consequences of the globalization of capital and investment.

International relations, in my view, refer to the structured and organized relations between established entities that may or may not become involved in the major political issues of the day. They include the growing global networks of activists and non-governmental organizations (NGOs) surrounding issues such as human rights, feminism, environmental problems, and the like. There has been a dramatic growth in such networks and organizations, and their role in identifying, promoting, and advocating their preferred solutions to the international agenda has been a notable change in the past two or three decades. This is not a new phenomenon (think of the international anti-slavery network in the nineteenth century), but its dimensions have grown rapidly in more recent history. There are all sorts of fascinating (and sometimes dangerous – the multi-billion-dollar drug trade network) changes taking place in global networks and they rightfully demand scholarly inquiry. Governments are concerned with them, sometimes dealing with them through reasonably effective regulations, and sometimes unable to do much about them. In other instances, governments mobilize them to promote their own purposes.

But networks and non-governmental organizations usually have *particular* sets of activities, purposes, values, and interests to promote. In the broad sense of the term, these are "political." However, most of the time they are not directly involved in the major diplomatic and security issues on the global or regional agendas. Unless they are mobilized by states for state purposes, they are not part of the domain of international politics. However, if they seek to enter that domain through lobbying, fund-raising, or other types of activities that seek to change the agenda of international politics, then they are part of it. Otherwise, they remain mostly isolated in the issue areas that are of primary interest only to them. These networks and organizations have grown rapidly in numbers and members in the past few decades, and they are a phenomenon worthy of systematic examination. But a comparative study of, let us say, the International Association of Taxidermists and the International Ice Hockey Federation would not tell us much about international politics.

International politics take place in the realm inhabited by governments of states and a few other actors such as the Secretary-General of the United Nations or the Commissioner of the European Union. Empirically, it is the domain comprising the ideas, beliefs, practices, and actions of states in their mutual relations. The actors are *public authorities* and their representatives (e.g., diplomats, armed forces officers). The main, though by no means exclusive, issues which these authorities address include peace and security at the local, regional, and global levels, commerce and finance, international development, environmental problems that transcend national borders, and the regulation of hundreds of types of private transnational activities. This is a domain of bargaining, locating solutions to common problems, persuasion, threats, and occasional use of public force. It is the latter phenomenon that distinguishes actors in international politics from the activities of international NGOs and other types of organizations and individuals involved in transnational relations.

This study is confined to the domain of international politics. It is not an exploration of that huge contemporary topic, globalization. It does not examine the many facets and types of changes taking place in global politics or international relations, except where these have a demonstrable impact on the quality and texture of international politics. In some cases, the line between the relationships of public authorities acting on behalf of states and governments and relationships with other types of private actors and associations is not strict, but for analytical purposes it is useful to keep the distinction in mind. Otherwise, the task of analyzing change in all three domains would be Herculean and beyond the competence of a single person. The most notable efforts to erase the lines and to examine the impact of changes in different domains upon each other are represented in the works of James N. Rosenau (1990, 1997, 2003). Yet even Rosenau acknowledges that the domains are separate and distinct. This is implied in his concept of the "Two Worlds of World Politics," one world populated by sovereign state actors, the other by non-sovereign actors.

I am indebted, first, to many undergraduate and graduate students who populated some of my courses at the University of British Columbia. In one of them, I specifically used the concept of international institutions as the framework for the course. Student discussions and essays brought to mind a number of points and conceptual distinctions that in one way or another have found their way into the analysis that follows. Two graduate students, Will Bain and Mark Salter, offered a number of insights that have strengthened the chapter on colonialism. I am also indebted to Mark W. Zacher and Miki Fabry who read one or more chapters in draft form and who made numerous useful suggestions. Robert Jackson, James Mayall, Sasson Sofer, Georg Sørensen, and Mark Zacher and members of the audience made numerous meaningful criticisms and suggestions during a panel centered on a synopsis of this work at the 2002 meetings of the International Studies Association. I continue to find inspiration in the work of Barry Buzan and am pleased to acknowledge his observations on some of the problems introduced in the first chapter. I also acknowledge the helpful and critical comments of the two external reviewers of the original manuscript.

Earlier and abbreviated versions of chapters 1 and 4 appeared, respectively, in Holsti (2002) and (2001).

1 The problem of change in international relations: rhetoric, markers, and metrics

The summer of 2001 in North America was one of unusual political torpor. In Canada, the daily headlines reported on an uncivil war within the opposition party. In the United States, the media had little to report other than a peccadillo involving a Congressman of little note. The presidency was slipping into a mediocrity that even the most ardent critics of George W. Bush could not have predicted at the time of the inauguration.

The attacks of September 11 changed all of this. Symbolic of the humid dog days of summer, the American president on that day was reading a book to a school class, yet another photo opportunity to show his devotion to "compassionate conservatism." Several days later, the president delivered a speech to the joint houses of Congress, inspiring Americans and many others around the world to mobilize in a war against terrorism. The most common comment in speeches at the highest level and among ordinary folks was that the "world will never be the same," "everything is now changed," "we live in a new world," and "forget everything that has happened before; we are now in a new era."

This type of response is typical of armchair analysts following major world events. We would find numerous parallels in the discourses surrounding the end of the two World Wars of the twentieth century. Having suffered almost immeasurable losses in such disasters, people could be excused for regenerating hope and emphasizing important lessons that would eventually lead to a "new world," "peace in our time," the war having been a "war to end all wars," and similar utopias. At a cost of eight million and fifty million lives, respectively, there was understandably a determination to create new worlds and to banish past practices that had given rise to such horrors. A major assault on our normal lives and on our pictures of the world naturally engenders confusion between how the world is and how we hope it might be. To declare a "new world order" or "new era" is as much an expression of aspiration as it is an empirical statement. The media of course quote such statements repeatedly because they prove that a story is worth the time and attention of reporters and commentators.

Those whose professional lives are dedicated to describing, interpreting, and theorizing about international politics are not immune to such sentiments. Political scientists, diplomatic historians, and experts in the field of International Relations have been no less enthusiastic discoverers of trends, ideas, and events that presage our entry into a new era, or that indicate a "revolution" in the typical patterns of relations between states and other types of political actors. They are among the most vehement critics of "old" ways of thinking and seeing, and insist that our intellectual furniture must be redesigned so that we can better describe and explain the novelties of the world.

But there is more than just change in the theoretical air. Increasingly, scholars of International Relations are claiming fundamental *transformations*. We live not in an era of marginal alterations and adaptations, of growth and decline, but in an era of discontinuity with the past. James Rosenau speaks (1990: ch. 1) of "post-international politics" and (1997: 7) of a contemporary "epochal transformation." Yoshikazu Sakamoto (1994: 15, 16) characterizes the contemporary scene as a *new era* involving fundamental transformations. Rey Koslowski and Friedrich Kratochwil (1994: 215–48) argue that the end of the Cold War constituted a "transformation" of the international system – not a change within the system but a change of system. The 1998 annual meetings of the International Studies Association were resplendent with papers and panel titles bearing the term "Post-Westphalian" order, suggesting that recent trends and events have transcended some of the foundational practices and principles of international politics as we have known and studied them over the past three centuries.

Post-modernists join a variety of positivist-oriented critics in claiming that the main conceptual categories of traditional renderings of the field – for example, sovereignty and anarchy – are no longer consistent with the observed facts of international life. R. B. J. Walker (1993: x), for example, charges that mainstream versions of IR theory "remain caught within the discursive horizons that express spatiotemporal configurations of another era." The late Susan Strange, although of the positivist persuasion, argued (1996: 3) that "social scientists, in politics and economics especially, cling to obsolete concepts and inappropriate theories. These theories belong to a more stable and orderly world than the one we live in." The result is "one-eyed social science" (p. 195). For others, traditional concepts are mere "discursive strategies" used to play or support the game of power politics (George, 1995). In these views, we are living in an era of profound change, but our ways of seeing the world have not changed. Few of the assumed characteristics of, say, nineteenth-century international politics remain with us any longer. We continue to employ the older conceptual apparatus at our intellectual peril. It is thus incumbent upon us to accomplish an intellectual "jailbreak" (Rosenau, 1990: ch. 2), to move beyond ritual invocations of concepts that once had theoretical and descriptive uses, but that are no longer able to capture those things that are truly new and novel in the world. We need, in brief, to reconfigure our conceptual equipment and to look at the world in new ways. Today, traditional analytic concepts act as ontological blinders (Deibert, 1997: 169) rather than as aids to understanding. Overall, then, the conceptual foundations of the field of International Relations have not kept up with changes in the real world. The essential critique against "old" theories of International Relations is that they neither describe nor explain the phenomenon of change.

The great debates in the genealogy of International Relations have revolved one way or another around the question of historical change: its sources, types, and possibilities. Realism, as perhaps the most influential rendering of the diplomatic, security, and military domains of social life, has an essentially materialist and monochromatic view of change. The only change that really matters in international politics is the relative capabilities of states. These alter over lengthy periods of time, depending upon mostly domestic factors such as industrial and population growth, the relative allocation of national resources between defense, consumption, and investment (Gilpin, 1981), and technological innovation. The patterns of change, accounted solely on a national basis, result in balances and imbalances of power, with the consequences of increasing or decreasing the probabilities of system-wide war. Theorists continue to debate whether it is balances or imbalances (hegemony) that promote peace. Over the centuries, the eternal minuet of rising and falling powers shows patterns, often associated with the outbreak of major wars. Thanks to the universal law of uneven economic development, this pattern is not likely to change; only the cast of characters changes and so humankind is doomed to repetition until the world either ends up as a universal monarchy or disintegrates into a "new medievalism."

Critics rightly point out that such a narrow conception of change fails to acknowledge the importance of other *sources* of change (such as ideas and revolutions), other *types* of change (such as the growth of non-state actors and international civil society), and other *consequences* of change (such as global governance). Realism not only is based on faulty logic (the assumption that anarchy necessarily leads to conflict), but fails to acknowledge the critical importance of developments in the vast domain outside state-to-state relations. The essential concepts of realism indeed act as blinders to a vast array of significant developments.

What about liberal and constructivist characterizations of international politics? The problem here is that there are so many brands of liberalism that no brief sketch can do justice to the variety and subtle differences between them. For our purposes – which are to outline different conceptions of change and how to identify them – all we need to acknowledge is that liberal theories of international politics place change at the core of their descriptive and normative tasks. States may be self-centered and pursue their interests, but their leaders are also capable of learning, sometimes through trial and error, and frequently from crises such as wars. Learning comes not only through surviving horrible experiences, as Kant suggested, but also through the promotion, popularization, and adoption of *ideas* and *norms* by various entrepreneurs, including "international civic society" and "epistemic communities." One of the main lessons learned is that state interests can be maximized through collaborative ventures, including the establishment and support of international institutions. Moreover, the foundations of state interest lie in the values and aspirations of national societies and, increasingly, of the vast networks of transnational associations and groups. The *scope* of change is thus much broader than in realism, and so are its possibilities.

Liberal and constructivist approaches to international politics have an implicit bias toward a progressive view of history. Learning seems always to be in the direction of improvement of the human condition, quite overlooking the fact that people like Lenin and Hitler learned quite different lessons about the kinds of changes that were required to reshape the world according to ideological blueprints.

Critics of liberal approaches to international relations point out, however, that despite their open-mindedness towards various kinds of change and their emphasis on ideas, beliefs, and norms as crucial explanations for altering state behaviour, liberals and many constructivists remain wedded to a state-centric view of the world, accept anarchy as the organizing principle upon which interstate relations are based, and continue to employ terms such as power, coercion, sovereignty, and nationalism in their analyses. Liberals and

4

constructivists have not incorporated into their maps of the world such important trends as the compression of time and space, the declining importance of borders, shifting loyalties of people away from the state toward other micro- and macro-organizations and movements, the "hollowing out" of the state, and other similar trends. The purview of liberals and most constructivists remains too narrow to appreciate what is really going on in the world.

Writers on globalization – although they hardly have a unified theory or even a corpus of agreed-upon concepts – emphasize the enormity of changes that are taking place at both the micro (individual and group) and macro (transnational) levels. They have produced a massive literature chronicling all the sociological and technological changes that are the basis of the argument for global transformation. We cannot review that literature, for it is far too vast and undisciplined to warrant any sort of generalization. However, this literature attacks the narrow, materialist, and limited possibility of change characteristic of realism, and implicitly chastizes the liberals and most constructivists for being too timid in recognizing the scope of the revolution that is going on around the world. Like many liberals and constructivists, this literature exudes a *desire* for change. It is strong on assertion but weak on historical depth.[1] For this reason, it is distinct from post-modernist and critical approaches to international politics, both of which (along with some others) celebrate the new lack of certainty.

Post-modernists and many critical theorists join the stream of criticism against IR "orthodoxy" but interpret the intellectual predicament somewhat differently. Rosenau, Strange, and others arguing for "intellectual jailbreaks," do not go far enough because they remain wedded to positivism and to the idea that the trained observer can through a variety of rigorous procedures encapsulate the amazing complexity of the world into totalizing theoretical projects. The world, they claim, cannot be rendered intelligible through grand theoretical projects that attempt to distil complexity, paradox, irony, and change into neat theoretical packages and categories. Rather, we now have to acknowledge that everything is in flux, paradox prevails, and we can only know what we ourselves experience (cf., Ashley and Walker, 1990; George, 1995).[2]

---

[1] Most of the analysts who see globalization as bringing forth a "new era," "new world," or such like forget that their predecessors in the 1920s and 1930s said almost exactly the same thing, making inferences from the innovations of telephones and other electronic gadgetry of that era.

[2] The anti-theoretical stance of many post-modernists and post-structuralists encourages "dissidence" and "resistance" rather than theory. Most definitions of social science include

Generalization is a Western logocentric practice that invariably contains a political program. To know, literally, is to act, and since the record of action on the diplomatic front in the twentieth century and more recently is not one to be proud of, it is probably better not to know in the sense of generalization. Post-modernists, in their profound pessimism and epistemological narcissism, basically claim that change has rendered the pursuit of knowledge as we have known it since Aristotelian times not only a fool's game, but also ethically dangerous. The human mind is incapable of understanding the complexity of the world, and since change is ubiquitous, any attempt to characterize it in general terms is bound to fail.

Analysis of change, then, has become almost a constant in the academic field of international theory. A whole new vocabulary of clichés or analogies has invaded debate. "Globalization," the "global village," "spaceship earth," "interdependence," the "new millennium," "the borderless world," and the like, suggest that we have entered, or are entering, a new era or epoch in which contemporary ideas, practices, institutions, and problems of international politics are qualitatively different from their predecessors. But popular monikers, while evocative of things that are different, do not substitute for rigorous analysis. Lacking in all of this claim of novelty is a consensus not only on *what* has changed but also on *how we can distinguish* minor change from fundamental change, trends from transformations, and growth or decline from new forms. The intellectual problems are both conceptual and empirical. The remainder of this chapter addresses two questions: (1) what types of markers can we use to identify change?; and (2) what do we mean by change?

Markers of change

Change, like beauty and good skiing conditions, is in the eye of the beholder. From a micro perspective, the international events recorded in today's headlines constitute change because they are not identical to yesterday's news. The media, to perhaps a greater extent than ever before,

terms such as explanation, generalization, construction, and the like. These are not possible in an approach which assumes that knowledge can come only from direct experience. Sandra Harding (1986: 164) sums up this view: "coherent theories in an incoherent world are either silly and uninteresting or oppressive and problematic, depending on the degree of hegemony they manage to achieve. Coherent theories in an *apparently* coherent world are even more dangerous, for the world is always more complex than such unfortunately hegemonic theories can grasp."

run on a 24-hour cycle that militates against notions of continuity, that emphasizes novelty, and that encourages pessimistic framing of issues for analysis (cf., Patterson, 1998). To a historian of civilizations, on the other hand, today's events do not even appear on the intellectual radar screen. They are not noted because nothing in those events suggests any sort of fundamental alteration of the persisting dynamics and patterns of power, achievement, authority, status, and the nature of social institutions. Somewhere between these micro (media) and macro (philosophical) extremes, observers may note certain types of markers where, typically, things appear to be done differently to the way they were previously. There is of course no objective marker that suggests that one type of change is more obvious than the other. The only question is the uses to which different conceptions of change are put. To CNN, the daily headlines are all that matters. The 24-hour period becomes the main analytical unit marking one set of events from another. But CNN's operating idea of change is of no use to the historian of civilizations, or even to most theorists of international politics, for the vast majority of daily headlines do not suggest something that is fundamentally new. Micro change almost never indicates macro transformation. Yet, as the works of the French historian Fernand Braudel indicate, grass-roots-level actions and activities can be imaginatively aggregated to produce a multi-layered narrative of change with historical and philosophical import. At the bottom layer is the pattern of daily activities – not the great events of kings and warriors but the lives of the ordinary people – that produce or account for trends over a period of time. These combine over the *longue durée* into patterned structures spanning centuries (cf., Braudel, 1988).

A simple move away from daily events, whether at the individual or systemic levels, to more extended time periods – an alteration of perspective – does not solve the problem of change, however. It is not only units of time or levels of activity that encapsulate change. When we speak of change, we normally employ certain types of "markers" that identify its domain.

Trends

Trends record one kind of change, usually of a quantitative character. They also specify the domain of change, that is, the area or types of activity among a million possibilities. World population grows, the membership in the United Nations increases, communications networks and the messages they carry proliferate and speed up (space and time are compressed), the volume of international trade grows at a much faster rate than total economic production, and the number of people travelling abroad increases annually. Moving in the other direction, world equality (as measured by relative wealth) declines, the number of nuclear warheads declines, and the incidence of interstate wars declines. What are we to make of these well-chronicled trends? That they are noticeable or that they occur over a relatively short period of time does not necessarily make them theoretically significant. For the stock market player, the day's events or the week's economic trends may be a key component of buy or sell decisions. But for the theorist of international politics, mere quantitative change in a particular domain of international communication over a relatively short period of time will probably be of little interest unless those trends have a demonstrable major impact on how diplomatic, military, or commercial things are typically done. The change must have significant *consequences* in another domain, in our case the domain of international politics. Otherwise the claim of change is no more than one observer's arbitrary judgment that things in a quantitative sense are not the same as they used to be. We have many notable trends over the past half-century, but their implications are by no means obvious. The theorist's claim to novelty thus remains no more than a claim: population, international trade, number of sovereign states, number of intergovernmental organizations (IGOs) and NGOs, investment flows, citizen competence, and the like may increase. But individually or collectively, what is their import? This is the Hegelian and Marxist problem: at what point does quantitative change lead to qualitative consequences (cf., Jones, 1981: 20)? If the United Nations, with 51 founding members, ultimately has 300 members in 2050, can we say it is the same organization? If global literacy rates reach the 75 percent mark by the end of this century, compared with 10 percent at the beginning of the nineteenth century, is this merely a quantitative change? Surely there must be some *consequences* – social, economic, political, and the like – that transform mere quantities into qualities. It is not the quantities that are so important; it is our designation of a meaning to them, usually a meaning that connects causes – quantitative changes – to consequences, or qualitative (type) changes.

Many contemporary clichés about international life implicitly make a quantitative/qualitative distinction, but without specifying at what point and how quantitative changes have produced new patterns, practices, and institutions – that is, new types. Absent a discussion of how we attribute meaning to quantities, we have no way of knowing when change becomes significant, or, more important, when it is or becomes transformational. Is the proliferation of communications networks of major significance? The concept of the "global village" suggests that at some point this quantitative growth in the media has led to new types of politics. But unless this novelty can be demonstrated, the idea remains a cliché rather than a useful analytic concept. All the problems of simple quantitative analysis emerge here. It can be argued, for example, that an increase in message volume between people says nothing about content. How does one compare a cryptic six-word e-mail message today with a twelve-page handwritten letter of the 1930s? Which is likely to have a greater impact on the reader, and in what ways? How do we interpret the well-known statistic that about 200 million people in the world regularly use the world wide web against the less well-known statistic that one-half of the world (three billion souls) have never made a telephone call? If you choose the first you will infer very different characteristics of the world than if you choose the second. Thus, inferring system-wide trans-formations from increases or decreases of selective quantitative trends in a single domain is a tricky business indeed. Few of the advocates of the "new" international politics (or new paradigm, or whatever) have made a convincing case that all the quantitative changes since 1945 or 1989 – to pick arbitrary dates – somehow constitute a revolution, a new era, or a transformation in the world.

Trends are relative to the scales against which they are measured. And these are often arbitrary and reflect political bias. Take one example. In February 2003, the space shuttle *Columbia* disintegrated shortly before its scheduled landing in Florida. Seven astronauts lost their lives. In consequence, American media shifted their attention from the problems of Iraq to a full coverage of the tragedy. That focus lasted for more than a week, leading to hundreds of different kinds of stories about the astronauts and their families, the American space program, locating the sources of the disaster, memorial services, and the like. In contrast, in July 1988 the American cruiser *Vincennes* shot down an Iranian commercial airliner with the loss of 290 civilian lives. That incident barely made the headlines in the United States (in contrast to the stories in the Middle East), and was quickly forgotten. It has never been mentioned as just one of many American actions that have served as the fount of terrorist and revenge incidents. The scales in these two incidents were entirely different. The first dealt with the death of heroes and had numerous consequences. The second concerned the civilians of a foreign, hostile regime, and were thus of little significance. Our scales, then, are not merely quantitatively arbitrary, but also qualitatively constructed. This is one reason why it is so difficult to pin down the meaning of change: we have no consensus on the scales to use in measuring trends.

Great events

Others favor "great events" as the main markers of change. Change is not an accumulation of many little acts, seen as trends. What matters are not straight-line variations in the quantities of standard practices or social interactions, but huge interruptions in typical patterns. Change of true significance, many argue, tends to be dramatic and compressed. The practices, ideas, and institutions of international politics assume reasonably fixed patterns over the long haul, until a major historical event – usually cataclysmic – changes them. Lord Bolinbroke defined epochs in terms of chains of events (indicating regular patterns) being so broken "as to have little or no real or visible connection with that which we see continue" (quoted in Ruggie, 1993: 148). Historians often use the device of a major discontinuity to organize their narratives. Since 1800 to 1900 would be a purely arbitrary designation of the "nineteenth century," most historians prefer the period 1815 to 1914. The markers of change here are the end of one great period of European war and the beginning of another. An era or period is configured around major events that ostensibly caused major disruptions or changes of previous patterns. They are also the sources of entirely new patterns. James Der Derian (1997: 66) has termed these "monster years," for they mark a critical transition, not just some arbitrary point on a quantitative scale. Notice, however, that the marker is still a chronological artifact and there is no guarantee that major events in fact subsequently alter typical patterns in various social domains including those of international politics.

The problems of major events as markers of change are nicely (if unwittingly) summarized in Ian Clark's *Globalization and Fragmentation: International Relations in the Twentieth Century* (1997). He summarizes a number of historians' use of periodization to characterize the twentieth century. Most use the great events of 1914, 1919, 1939, 1945, and/or 1989–91 as demarcating significant changes, even transformations, rather than continuities. But there is no agreement on these dates. That they all contained significant events – they were "monster" years – is beyond dispute, but there is no consensus – indeed there is wide disagreement – as to whether these events actually led to new historical patterns. As with trends, choices tend to be arbitrary.

Did 1919 really constitute some sort of discontinuity? Woodrow Wilson's wartime and post-war perorations would certainly lead one to believe that after 1919 the world had entered some sort of new age that was essentially different from its predecessors. Yet, the record of war, imperialism, and national chauvinism in the 1920s and 1930s would justifiably give rise to skepticism. A major event – the Great War and its subsequent peace conference – may have been notable, but in many respects it did not significantly and irrevocably alter diplomatic and military practices and institutions in the predicted direction, that is, toward a more peaceful and democratic world. Was 1945 a major marker separating significantly different epochs of twentieth-century history? Many analysts have made a compelling case that it was; others have simply assumed it. Yet others, such as Clark himself, vigorously dispute the dichotomization of the twentieth century into two clear-cut parts, with World War II as the critical dividing line. Thus one person's discontinuity or great event is not necessarily a sign of transformation for others. Arbitrary decisions remain, and because this is so, theorists of international relations are not likely to agree on their import.

Significant social/technological innovations

This is a subset of the "great events" category. Like it, it creates significant discontinuities. It only differs in sources. In the "great event" (or "big bang") category, major, purposeful human social activities such as wars suggest dividing lines of change. In this subcategory, material endowments cause the change. After 1945, there was a good deal of talk about the "nuclear revolution," a technological innovation that nullified the Clausewitzian conception of war . . . or so it was believed. The record of war since 1945 is inconsistent with the conclusion, however. The "nuclear revolution" altered the nature of relations between great powers, to be sure, but it did not terminate violence between states. One reason there is a process of nuclear dismantling by some countries is the recognition that for most purposes they are very costly weapons that have become irrelevant to most foreign policy problems. Yet the term "nuclear age" still has some resonance and continues to suggest that those two days in August 1945 ushered in new qualities to international politics.

Today, the computer or more broadly the digital revolution has reputedly replaced the atomic bomb as the main causal agent of change or transformation. The bomb could only alter traditional security thinking – away from how to win wars to how to prevent them – whereas the microelectronic revolution has changed the daily life of several billion people. Its influences are more ubiquitous, and therefore more transformative than nuclear weaponry. Most of the discussion of "globalization," "the global village," or "borderless world" derives specifically from technological innovation. As with great events, however, there is little consensus on the consequences of the innovation. For some, globalization results in the erosion of sovereignty; for others it has strengthened the state. And there are innumerable positions between these two extremes.

Most analysts of technological change locate trends and their consequences in the vast realm of all human interaction. It is a type of "global sociology." Technology has led to the rapid growth of transnational movements and organizations, the active participation of grassroots organizations in international networks, the great increases in the speed of information dissemination, the global spread of a capitalist, US-centered culture, and the like. It has become a matter of faith among many analysts of change that the academic field of International Relations should itself become globalized. It should encompass actors, transactions, and trends far beyond the purview of state-sponsored activities. This "thick" view of the world is naturally sensitive to all types of changes, but it frequently fails to establish a nexus between them and diplomatic and warrior activities. Globalization is supposed to have severe consequences on states, transnational networks, and individuals, but the causal effect is usually only in one direction, *from globalization to networks, states, and individuals*. Reverse relationships have seldom been explored. This of course biases the analysis toward the view that everything is new.

Concepts of change

Markers only identify when, supposedly, change takes place. They do not specify what kinds of change are involved. Theorists in our field, perhaps astonishingly, rarely take the trouble to define what they mean by change, even when disagreements about change are what drive many of the great theoretical debates in the field. But there are several major conceptions of change. These include change as novelty or replacement, change as addition or subtraction, increased complexity, transformation, reversion, and obsolescence.[3] The differences between them are theoretically important, perhaps even crucial in estimating the validity of claims of novelty or transformation.

Change as novelty or replacement

The end of the Cold War stimulated a large industry of projections for the future. Most of these heralded significant changes in the texture, structures, and practices of international politics as we approached a new millennium. For Goldgeier and McFaul (1992), Singer and Wildavsky (1993), and Koslowski and Kratochwil (1994) the end of the Cold War constituted, minimally, a critical change in the way the superpowers relate to each other and, maximally, an entirely new type of international system. They accepted John Mueller's (1989) view that the probabilities of seeing a major power war are significantly declining. If there is such a trend, then obviously one significant pattern of international relations since the sixteenth century – great power war – will terminate. This would be the main marker for the claim that we live in a *new or novel* type of system. For Samuel Huntington (1993), in contrast, war and violence did not end with the Cold War. Only the fault-lines of international conflict have changed from conflicts between states and their encapsulated ideologies, to conflicts between civilizations. Notice that one common practice of international politics, namely war, does not disappear; only the types of actors that engage in it change. Huntington's change is novel in the sense that the parties to war will change, but the other essential features of the international system presumably will remain similar. For Francis Fukuyama (1989), in contrast, we are in the midst of a major historical transformation, where for a variety of ideational and technological reasons, something resembling perpetual peace – the dream of thinkers since at least the duc de Sully in the seventeenth century – will come to pass. This will also be a new world. For Alain Minc (1993), there is yet another novelty, although it hearkens to patterns of the medieval era and is thus a form of reversion. The breakdown of political authority in many Third World states and in the OECD countries is giving rise to *le nouveau moyen age*, an era in which we can expect less safety of life and property than we have seen in almost a millennium. If Minc's

---

[3] This list is not necessarily exhaustive. It does not include the jargon of contemporary debates, such as "shift," "move," or "moment." These terms are so nebulous that they cannot add to conceptual clarity.

prognostication comes to pass, clearly there will have been more than just a quantitative change. Contemporary patterns and structures will be *replaced* by vast sets of novel conditions.

For Mueller and Fukuyama, peace replaces war. For Huntington, civilizational wars replace interstate wars. For Goldgeier and McFaul, Singer and Wildavsky, and Kaplan (1994) the relative stability of the Cold War is replaced by the "coming chaos" characteristic of armed conflict in the Third World. All these authors take a common stand in their implicit notion of change. *A significant change is something new, and that new thing is usually the antithesis of something old.*

This is a *discontinuous* idea of change: new forms replace old ones, so the problem of transformation does not arise. Certainly nothing new develops without a past, but the characteristics of the new may be so fundamentally different from anything preceding it that transformation is not an appropriate word. Replacement means *novelty*. Anthony Giddens (1987: 33–4), though focusing on macro-social phenomena rather than contemporary international politics, adopts the discontinuist view of history on the grand scale when he argues:

> I do not wish to deny the importance of transitions or ruptures in previous eras. I do, however, want to claim that, originating in the West but becoming more and more global in their impact, there has occurred a series of changes of extraordinary magnitude when compared with any other phases in human history. What separates those living in the modern world from all previous types of society, and all previous epochs in history, is more profound than the continuities which connect them to the longer spans of the past . . . [T]he contrasts which can be made will often prove more illuminating than the continuities that may be discerned. It is *the* task of sociology . . . to seek to analyze the nature of that novel world in which, in the late twentieth century, we now find ourselves . . . In a period of three hundred years, an insignificant slither of human history as a whole, *the face of the earth has been wiped clean.* (my italics)

This is not an organic view of historical change. It is not similar to Braudel's concept of the *longue durée*. It is not analysis of trends, of systemic change at the margins, of changes in the distribution of capabilities between states, or of the transformation of old institutions. In elaborating his social theory, Giddens makes it clear that contemporary social formations, and in particular the modern state, have virtually nothing in common with what has preceded. For Giddens, meaningful modern history is the story of discontinuity and replacement, not transformation. And so it is with many current speculations about the character of international politics after the Cold War or the events of 9/11.

Change as addition or subtraction

Most of the changes characterized as "transformation" or novelty are in fact little more than a quantitative growth or decline. A good deal of what goes under the moniker of globalization refers in fact to increases in the volumes and speed of transactions in trade, finance, communications, and technology realms. This sort of change has primarily the quality of more or less of something. This is probably the most common form of change in the literature, although analysts have a tendency to attribute assumed qualitative consequences.

For theories of international politics, addition should not imply replacement. International politics, as Hedley Bull (1977) reminds us, has always contained coexisting Hobbesian, Grotian, and Kantian elements. Thus, if we see more elements of cooperation and "global governance," this does not mean that they have replaced realist patterns of behavior. Regional "pluralistic security communities" (Deutsch, 1954) such as those in Western Europe, South America, and North America have not replaced realist-type regions such as South Asia and the Middle East, but are an addition to them. "International civil society" does not replace national-level political activity; it only complements or adds to it. And most conspicuously, though seldom noted in the literature, the growth of transnational corporations and intra-firm international trade does not replace the business activities of local, regional, and national firms that do not engage in any foreign trade at all. These firms, in fact, make up the vast majority of economic enterprises in the world and will continue to hold this position.

Change as increased/decreased complexity

Change can also be *increased or decreased complexity*. For example, in the institution of diplomacy, the essential practices, ideas, norms, rules and etiquette remain, but activities and agents expand in numbers and tasks, rules become more elaborate, new formats (such as multilateral conferences and routine heads of state meetings) emerge, and the scope of activity expands. But the essential functions remain unchanged. A mechanical analogy of growing complexity is the automobile. The automobile is constituted of several essential elements: wheels, a frame and chassis, the source of power, gearing device, a steering mechanism, and brakes. A driver of a 2003 model car can easily drive a 1930 Model "A" Ford. But the contemporary typical automobile is a much more complex machine, decked out in computers, audio systems, navigation devices, and a whole host of electronic gadgetry that defies fixing by the amateur mechanic. Advertisers may suggest that the latest model is "a new world of driving pleasure," but in fact the driver today is doing essentially what his or her predecessor did seventy-five years ago. In the case of diplomacy, the institution has grown much more complex, but its essential functions, norms, rules, and ideas have not altered to the point of non-recognition.

Change as transformation

Transformation can result from quantitative changes which, when accumulated over a period of time, bring new forms to life. But, logically, the new forms must derive from old patterns. They can partly replace old forms, but by definition they must include residues or legacies of the old. One cannot transform from nothing. In the case of social and political institutions, a transformation is distinguished from obsolescence in the sense that old ideas, practices, and norms may remain reasonably similar over long periods of time, but the functions of the institution change. A good example is monarchy. In the Scandinavian countries, in Japan, and perhaps less so in England, many of the practices of monarchy, as well as protocol, norms, and ideas, remain similar over the centuries, but the functions of the monarchy have changed from ruling, to symbolism and national identity. There has been a transformation of an institution, but not its replacement. The old and the new coexist. This could also be considered a form of dialectical change.

Change as reversion

We must not assume only progressive forms of change. Novelty, complexity, and transformation in human arrangements usually imply some sort of improvement over previous conditions. The transformation of monarchies, for example, implies a progressivist movement from despotic to democratic rule, with monarchies retaining only the symbolic functions of previous eras. But change can also move in the other direction, or move toward more primitive forms. We will argue in chapter 9, for example, that many contemporary wars have reverted to patterns of action more similar to medieval warfare than to that of the eighteenth century.

Change as obsolescence

Finally, typical behaviors, institutions, practices, ideas, norms, and rules can become *obsolete*. They simply disappear and there is no presumption that something new must take their place. Slavery is an old human institution, but except for a few residues in some areas of the world, it has disappeared. In international relations, conquest as a legitimate form of state behavior has been completely de-legitimized and has declined to almost insignificant proportions. As we will see in chapter 8, colonialism as a patterned, legitimate form of rule has also become obsolete.

Much of the International Relations rhetoric of the recent past implicitly adopts the novelty, additive, and transformation types of change, without considering alternatives. This seems natural following great events such as the end of the Cold War or the attacks of September 11, 2001. But previous claims to a "new world order," or "new era," whether in 1815, 1919, 1945, 1989–91, or 2001 have usually turned out to be somewhat premature. Claims of novelty, replacement, or transformation would often better be classified as additions or growing complexity, where elements of the old and the new coexist. In a few cases, reversion would be a better category. Too often our language inappropriately implies novelty and replacement. For example, if we do indeed live in a "Post-Westphalian" order, then there must be few traces of Westphalia remaining in it. We cannot legitimately use the term "Post-Westphalia" if many elements of the Westphalian order survive, as they clearly do. Westphalia must be *obsolete* for a "post" order to replace it. Similarly, if, as Rosenau (1997) suggests, we now live in a new epoch of post-international politics, then the main characteristics of international politics as we knew them for about three centuries must be demonstrated to have disappeared and to have been replaced by other (or new) practices, ideas, and norms. That we have more states, that we communicate more rapidly, or that we trade more within the context of a vastly expanded global population does not automatically entitle us to claim either novelty, transformation, or obsolescence. The problem remains: at what point does additive change produce transformation? Commentators are often too quick to assert qualitative change from mere additions or growing complexity.

17

International institutions as metrics and markers of change

None of the markers of change outlined above is inherently more authoritative than others. The question is: for what use will they be used? Great events or "big bang" markers of change have face validity because they frequently do have significant consequences, although rarely of the system-wide character that many ascribe to them. I have chosen *international institutions* as essential markers of change in the domain of international politics. Why? Because, first, institutions are the context within which the games of international politics are played. They represent patterned (typical) actions and interactions of states, the norms, rules, and principles that guide (or fail to guide) them, and the major ideas and beliefs of a historical era. Second, they are critical to international politics – the relationships between states – whereas global sociological changes have largely indeterminate consequences on the politics between states.[4] International institutions contain the essential rules of coexistence between states and societies. They are of a primary order. We could not have the free flow of information, goods, money, and travel if states and their societies did not allow them, or establish certain rules and regulations upon which they are based. In other words, much of the change in the global social realm depends upon the rules and norms for transactions that states establish among themselves. Institutions are the permissive contexts of many social transactions. It is not the other way around.

Third, an examination of changes in international institutions can avoid many of the determinist-type explanations of change so rampant in the contemporary literature. Institutions change through a variety of means and from numerous sources, including ideas and beliefs. Changes in power relations or technological innovations, while relevant, are only part of the story.

Fourth, institutions, although they do change in significant ways, often survive great events. We can identify institutions and, even though imperfectly, we can measure how and what kinds of changes they have undergone. This will then help us avoid views that little has changed in international politics (cf., Mearsheimer, 1990), when, for example, the institution of colonialism has disappeared and when international trade,

---

[4] There are always consequences, of course, but often they are extremely difficult to identify and measure. For example, what are the consequences on diplomacy and security issues of the increasing use of the internet?

once a major source of wars between all the powers, is today highly institutionalized and thus a domain void of warlike behavior. Similarly, for
those who are convinced that we already live in a "Post-Westphalian"
order, they might ponder why it is that the quintessential element of that
order – sovereignty – continues as the most important foundation of international relationships and why it is that, in using passports, going
through customs, and paying taxes in a foreign country (if they work
there), they are in fact sustaining and strengthening the sovereignty of
states. Institutions, in brief, offer a marker that can *discipline* inquiry
about change in the domain of international politics.

Finally, change in institutions can have much greater impact on the
daily lives of ordinary people than most technological innovations. If
aggressive war and conquest have been de-legitimized, and if behavior
becomes largely consistent with the anti-war norm, then more people
will live without the threat of foreign invasion than at any previous time
in history. That surely is more significant than the fact that millions of
people can spend their time in "chat groups" on the internet or that
events can be reported more quickly today because of the existence of
CNN than was the case one hundred years ago when the attentive world
had to rely on the telegraph and mail. Robert Jackson (2000: 41) reminds
us that the foundational principles of international politics – what we
term today the Westphalian system – did not undergo transformation
as a result of major changes in the social and technological environment
in previous centuries. Diplomatic life in 1775 was not unrecognizable
from its predecessor in, let us say, 1700 despite that major intellectual
upheaval of the eighteenth century, the Enlightenment. Similarly, the
Industrial Revolution, surely a change as momentous as globalization
is today, did not reorder major international institutions, except perhaps
in the domain of war. In our awe of recent technological and commercial
changes, we may forget that this is not the first "revolution" in world
history. Its consequences on the special domain termed international
politics remain to be explored and not explained away as simply representative of a "new era" or "new world."

To choose international institutions as a critical marker of change in
international politics would have appeared bizarre or even blasphemous only several decades ago when realists insisted that international
institutions are merely the instruments of the most powerful and have
no independent influence on the purposes and actions of states. There
is a rapidly expanding literature that suggests otherwise. We need not
review it here, but several random quotations will make the point that

my choice of institutions is not idiosyncratic. Michael Barnett (1996: 159) summarizes the constructivist view of institutions:

> Constructivist approaches acknowledge that states might establish institutions to encourage cooperation [and to facilitate communication], but they differ from rationalist approaches by raising the possibility that institutions might not be the product of conscious design but rather emerge out of patterned interactions that become routinized and institutionalized; represent an important source of state identity, rules, and interests; and encourage order by creating relatively stable expectations and shared norms . . .

Wendt and Duvall (1989: 59–60) suggest that institutions organize and structure behavior; they deeply affect the repertoire of decision-making choices. But they do more. "[A]ctual practices that are institutionally organized and selected in turn constitute the medium through which the social or constitutive side of international institutions is reproduced and/or transformed – thereby completing the circle of structuration (or ordering) of the international system" (62). To Christian Reus-Smit (1997: 557), "Fundamental institutions are those elementary rules of practice that states formulate to solve coordination and collaboration problems associated with coexistence under anarchy." Many others make similar claims and empirical studies of the impact of one institutional component – norms – demonstrate clearly that they have singular effects on both the definition of interests and the organization of state actions (cf., Finnemore, 1996: Finnemore and Sikkink, 1998).

What do we mean by international institutions? I follow Hedley Bull's (1977) use of the term institution which, while not exact, implies the critical importance of ideas, practices, and norms:

> A *society of states* (or international society) exists when a group of states, conscious of certain common interests and common values, form a society in the sense that they conceive themselves to be bound by a common set of rules in their relations with one another, and share in the working of common institutions . . . In international society . . . the sense of common interests . . . does not in itself provide precise guidance as to what behaviour is consistent with these goals; to do this is the function of *rules*. These rules may have the status of international law, of moral rules, of custom or established practice, or they may be merely operational rules or "rules of the game", worked out without formal agreement or even without verbal communication . . . It is not uncommon for a rule to emerge first as an operational rule, then to become established practice, then

to attain the status of a moral principle and finally to become incorporated in a legal convention . . . States communicate the rules
through their official words . . . But they also communicate the rules
through their actions, when they behave in such a way as to indicate that they accept or do not accept that a particular rule is valid.
(1977: 13, 67, 71)

I do not adopt the teleological aspects of this definition, because institutional growth, development, reversion, or obsolescence are not always
accounted for by common purposes or by design.[5] Moreover, Bull does
not adequately emphasize the role of ideas, and he is somewhat unclear
on practices. In the selection of institutions in the subsequent chapters
of this study, three criteria establish their existence. An international
institution comprises, or is indicated by:

1 patterned *practices*, or practices that are routinized, typical, and recurrent. As an example, the exchange of ambassadors between states and
  their functions have become routine practice, whereas in the sixteenth
  century they were diverse, contested, and non-routine.
2 Institutions are based, usually, on coherent sets of *ideas and/or beliefs*
  that describe the needs for the common practices and point out how
  certain social goals can be achieved through them. Ideas refer to un-
  derstandings of what *is*, either in fact or hypothetically (i.e., the theory
  of comparative advantage), as well as to imagined (better) states of
  affairs. Ideas are powerful sources of change and critical tools for mo-
  bilizing political action. In Daniel Philpott's (2001: 47) words, "ideas
  do not freely remake the world in their image, but they are inestimably
  effectual. Ideas are a form of power, and are often a partner to other
  forms of power – and this, in intricate ways."

---

[5] There is no consensus on the meaning of the term *institution*. I use Bull's version because it refers to the importance of ideas and practices as well as to rules. Keohane (1998:
93) uses a narrower conception when he defines them as "rules and standards to govern
specific sets of activities." This term refers only to rules and norms and does not include
ideas, beliefs, and common practices that, as suggested below, are critical to the broader
notion of institutions. An important analysis of the concept of international institutions
is in Wendt and Duvall (1989). They contrast the "English School" notion of institutions –
similar to the idea of *Gemeinschaft* – with the neo-realist notion that is akin to *Gesellschaft*.
Wendt and Duvall emphasize that institutions both regulate practice and are constituted
through practices. "Fundamental" institutions "represent the shared intersubjective un-
derstandings about the . . . preconditions for meaningful state action" (p. 53) and are thus
more than simply the results of calculations of state interests or the desire to reduce transactions costs. Kratochwil (1989: 64) also emphasizes the combination of practices and
norms. For a discussion of the origins of institutions – by design or through customary
practices – see Nicholas Onuf (2002).

Beliefs, usually based on sets of ideas, contain the justifications for those ideas and normative statements regarding the necessity for certain forms of behavior (norms) and/or change in behavior.[6] Using our example of diplomacy again, the essential ideas of diplomacy were set out in a number of seventeenth- and eighteenth-century tracts that not only defined the essential characteristics of the activity, but also advanced arguments as to why diplomacy had to be regularized or routinized, why it was necessary for promoting state, royal, and social interests, and what qualities were essential to the successful diplomat. Ideas and beliefs are expressed in a variety of ways including general discourses taking place in debates, publications, electioneering, academic studies, court decisions, treaties, and the like.

3 Institutions reflect *norms*, and they include rules and etiquette. They prescribe how the critical actors or agents should behave, under what conditions they can do certain things, what types of activities and actions are proscribed, and what protocols and etiquette should be observed in various circumstances. Norms can be identified, but important variables in estimating their influence include how clearly they are specified, their duration, their conversion into the normal thinking habits and moral repertoires of political actors, and their ability to withstand competing or inconsistent values (cf., Legro, 1995). In the case of diplomacy, the most significant norm is free and unfettered communication between sovereigns. The rules include all those associated with immunities, *agrément*, espionage, and rank, and etiquette refers to such matters of precedence, the presentation of credentials, seating, symbolism, and the like.[7]

The question of norms in international relations has commanded increasing interest, with major statements coming from many quarters (cf., Kratochwil, 1989; Checkel, 1997; Hurd, 1999; Alderson, 2000;

---

[6] Neta Crawford (2002; esp. ch.1) offers a thorough discussion of the nature of and linkages between ideas, beliefs, and norms. For an extended discussion of the role of ideas in shaping actor interests, see Philpott (2001), esp. ch. 4. His analysis is an excellent riposte to the materialism of realism and Marxism.

[7] The literature on norms is voluminous and it contains many contested elements. However, they do contain a common core. Three definitions summarize what is a near-consensus. Martha Finnemore (1996: 22) suggests norms are "shared expectations about appropriate behavior held by a community of actors." Jean-Louis Durand (2000) defines a norm as "shared understanding that stipulates the parameters of acceptable collective behavior and that contributes to reducing the uncertainty inherent in anarchy." For Neta Crawford (2002: 40), normative beliefs are "those ideas individuals and groups hold about how they ought to act (or not act) to do what is 'right' or expected. They are prescriptions with justifications attached to them."

Väyrynen, 2000; and Crawford, 2002). These and similar studies investigate the sources of norms, how they disseminate, by which actors
(governments [cf., Howard and Neufeldt, 2000; Philpott, 2001: 67–71;
Ingebritsen, 2002], non-state actors, and other entrepreneurs or couriers
of ideas), the incentives for observing them, and the processes through
which, and how much, they become "internalized" so that they attain
a take-it-for-granted character (cf., Väyrynen, 2000). Norms and rules,
as Friedrich Kratochwil reminds us (1989: 69), are not just constraints
on action, but serve as "reasons" that decision-makers find more or less
persuasive in their calculations. All norms and rules, he suggests, "are
problem-solving devices for dealing with the recurrent issues of social
life: conflict and cooperation." Unlike in the 1940s and 1950s when great
debates of idealists versus realists raised the question of whether norms
were even relevant to the study and practices of international politics,
the whole question of norms and their influence is now squarely in the
empirical domain. It is no longer a question of whether or not they exist
(or are relevant), but where they come from, how they get disseminated,
and how they eventually become part of the ordinary evaluative backgrounds of foreign policy decision-making.

This study will not be concerned specifically with the origins of norms
and their supporting ideas and beliefs, or even with their impact beyond
the somewhat dubious inference that if norms and behavior are reasonably consistent, the explanation for the behavior – particularly if it has
changed significantly – must lie at least in part in the influence of norms
and their more concrete manifestations, in rules.

There seems to be no hierarchy or set causal links between the
three major components of institutions. Actions, ideas/beliefs, and
norms/rules act upon each other in complicated ways. Sometimes actions become so routine that they gain legitimacy as a custom that simultaneously or eventually becomes a norm or rule. Much of what "is"
in international politics has a tendency to become an "ought" or even
more formal rule (cf., Kegley and Raymond, 2002: 4). Naval "rules of the
road" are one example. In other instances, changes in ideas and derivative beliefs are critical in shaping actions and developing new norms.
Chapter 7 on trade is one illustrative case. The development of the liberal
economic "sciences" starting in the late eighteenth century was a critical foundation for the end of mercantilist practices and the development
of rules of trade reciprocity and free trade. Yet, in other circumstances,
governments get together to negotiate standardizing rules because practices are so varied and costly – and even chaotic. The agreements in 1815

regarding diplomatic rank and other questions of diplomatic practice are cases in point. Each chapter that follows attempts to locate the nexus between the various components of institutions, but lack of structured evidence does not often allow authoritative generalizations. In some instances, it will be possible only to demonstrate the importance of patterned actions, norms/rules, and ideas/beliefs, leaving their relative weight to further research.

The purpose of examining each institution is to narrate the kinds of changes they have undergone in the past three hundred years, approximately. The method is essentially comparative and diachronic. Each chapter characterizes an institution in its early years (or in the case of sovereignty, its emergence as a novelty), meaning usually the period between Westphalia and the late eighteenth century, and then comparing it with the institution today. On the basis of the evidence, each chapter closes with a summary evaluation of the type of change involved: novelty or replacement, addition, complexity, transformation, reversion, or obsolescence. This is accompanied by some estimate of the degree of institutionalization, indicated primarily by the "fit" between institutional requirements (patterned actions, norms, rules, etiquette, and ideas) and typical behavior. For example, over the past half-century, trade has become increasingly institutionalized through the articulation of ever more encompassing rules and regulations, while the institution of war, particularly as seen in poorer societies, is tending strongly in the direction of de-institutionalization or reversion.

The six possibilities outlined above – new institutions, additions/subtractions, change as complexity, institutional transformation, reversion, and obsolescence – do not take place simultaneously or in one direction. Each institution has its own historical profile. While some, like diplomacy, were emerging into full institutional status in the eighteenth century, trade in this era resembled a Hobbesian state of nature, where activities were unpatterned, intermittent, often punctuated by war and private violence, and largely devoid of effective norms and rules. International trade became institutionalized to a high degree only after World War II, at almost exactly the same time that colonialism was becoming obsolete.

Foundational and process institutions

We can distinguish *foundational institutions* of the states system from procedural institutions such as diplomacy (cf., Sørensen, 2001: ch. 10).

Foundational institutions have allowed analysts of virtually all persuasions – from realists to liberal institutionalists and constructivists – to claim or assume that there is an international states system (or society of states, to use Bull's term) that is markedly distinguishable from empires, migrant clans and lineages, the complex medieval system of overlapping jurisdictions, leagues of cities, suzerainty systems, and other formats for organizing distinct political communities. Without these foundational institutions and their component principles, political space would be organized on different principles and would feature very different forms of behavior. Foundational institutions define and give privileged status to certain actors. They also define the fundamental principles, rules, and norms upon which their mutual relations are based. Finally, they lead to highly patterned forms of action. The foundational institutions of the Westphalian international system include sovereignty, territoriality, and the fundamental rules of international law.

Procedural institutions are composed of those repetitive practices, ideas, and norms that underlie and regulate interactions and transactions between the separate actors. These institutions refer not to questions of "who are we?", "how do we become?", and "how do we claim status and legitimacy?", but to more instrumental issues of how we behave towards one another in the conduct of both conflict and normal intercourse. They are important in helping us describe the essential characteristics of an international system, but they are of secondary significance compared with the foundational institutions. A procedural institution such as war, for example, could disappear without fundamentally altering the foundational institutions of sovereignty and international law.

What criteria should we use in identifying and selecting international institutions? Hedley Bull's treatment of institutions avoided the issue. He listed a variety without specifying them in any particular order, why he chose them, why he excluded others, and the relationships between them. Two of his choices – balance of power and the great powers – do not meet all the three criteria or essential components of international institutions, namely patterned actions, ideas, and norms/rules. The notion of "great power" refers to a status, not to an institution. The concept was first specified in the Treaty of Châtillon (1814) and repeated in the special status of the great powers in the League of Nations Covenant and the United Nations Charter. There is thus the *idea* of the great power, and perhaps even some norms prescribing appropriate behavior for states that enjoy that status, but it does not meet the criterion of patterned practices. One can make the case that the Concert of Europe significantly guided great power practices at least until 1854 (cf., Holsti, 1992) and that these were largely consistent with the special responsibilities accorded (or demanded) by the great powers at Vienna. But for most of the latter part of that century and until 1914, practices increasingly diverged and systematically broke the norms of 1815. In the 1930s, the great powers were the problem, not the solution to international peace and security. The same occurred after 1948, approximately. The great powers, led by the Soviet Union, systematically violated the norms of great power responsibility for maintaining international peace and security. Rather than "managing" the international system, they were the main sources of its deep insecurity. More recently, the unilateralist and frequent norm-violating foreign policy of the United States during the George W. Bush administration is inconsistent with the idea of the great powers as having special responsibilities taking into consideration the interests of the international community when making decisions. Bull himself recognized that the great powers did not constitute an institution in his denunciatory analysis of their behavior in the essay "The Great Irresponsibles?" (1980). In brief, there is no pattern to great power behavior; a distinct status does not lead to consistent policy.

As for the balance of power, it meets the criterion of ideas – a developed theory and discourse explaining and guiding action. But its norms and rules are vague and contradictory. There are so many theories and renditions of the concept that it ends up essentially meaningless. As with the idea of great power, balance of power theory is not linked to any consistent or patterned behavior. States have balanced, bandwagoned, and withdrawn through isolationism with about equal frequency and inconsistency. War has not correlated with either balance or imbalance.

The list of foundational institutions includes sovereignty, territoriality, and international law. One could argue that the first two are simply different sides of a single institution of sovereignty. This may be the case, but since they refer to rather unique aspects, I will separate them for analytical reasons. We can at least imagine that some types of states could exist without territory (the Vatican?), and that territory does not have to be exclusive. How should we classify states? States meet all the criteria of institutions, but unlike most international institutions, they are also *agents.*[8] They are the main if not the only creators of institutions and it is primarily their actions that develop and alter them or render them obsolete. The other institutions are not agents, but structures of norms, rules, and ideas that influence the behavior of agents. We cannot "see" institutions, whereas states have authority that everyone experiences in their daily lives. Whatever the case, we cannot ignore states because we could not understand the origins and development of the other institutions without constant reference to state actions and interactions. Moreover, a number of analysts have recently made the case that states are disappearing as effective actors and agents. Such a trend would greatly affect all the other institutions. Indeed, without states to sustain them, most would become obsolete or revert to more primitive forms. We thus need to include a discussion of states, however we conceive of them.

The procedural institutions include diplomacy, trade, colonialism, and war. This list is not exhaustive. It is not difficult to conceive of other institutions, such as the "market," the international monetary system, or foreign aid. Some institutions are clearly subcategories of broader institutional forms. For example, trade and monetary institutions can be conceived as components of a broader category, the "market." Since our main purpose is to explore a metric of change in the international system, however, it is not necessary to discuss every conceivable institution to come up with a general map of institutional change in the international system over the past three centuries. The institutional sketches offered in each of the chapters will allow us to conclude with some general comments about the more critical questions of the nature and extent of change in international politics.

Each sketch has three main purposes: (1) to highlight the interplay of practices, ideas, and norms/rules, and etiquette; (2) to identify the kind of change (of the six outlined above) that is taking or has taken place; and (3), in rudimentary fashion, to outline some of the sources or explanations of those changes.

---

[8] I am grateful to Barry Buzan for raising this issue. We could use the term *statehood* to designate the institution and *state* as the agent. But the term is clumsy and since agency and institutional features are so intermingled, the author could not apply the distinction consistently.

2 States and statehood

Societies and smaller groups throughout history have formed organizations that provide and sustain them with security, access to resources, social rules, and means of continuity. Frequently they also devised, embodied, or sought more ephemeral objectives or qualities such as identity, glory, renown, and reputation. The institutional forms they have taken have varied greatly. Even terms we commonly use to designate polities – tribes, clans, empires, principalities, city-states, protectorates, sultanates, or duchies – would not begin to cover the actual diversity of political forms.

In contemporary parlance, all these actors are "polities" (Ferguson and Mansbach, 1996) in the sense that they have distinct identities, authority structures, and leadership. Such types of polities have probably numbered in the hundreds of thousands throughout recorded history. But most did not survive their leaders' lives, while a few have had a continuous organized history, in the case of the Roman church, of almost two millennia.

Our concern, however, is with states, the only contemporary political organizations that enjoy a unique legal status – sovereignty – and that, unlike other types of polities, have created and modified enduring public international institutions. They are thereby the foundational actors of international relations. Other types of polities may ultimately become states but until they have transformed themselves into public bodies – moral agents representing some sort of community – they do not have the legal standing of states. The Commonwealth of Massachusetts and the British East India Company began as a private colony and a chartered company, but through legal and constitutional means they transformed themselves into public bodies that eventually became parts of the British Empire.

States are both institutions of the international political realm (they fulfil the three criteria outlined in the previous chapter) and the main though not exclusive agents that create and change the institutions in which they operate. The *idea* of the state – statehood – provides its institutional form, while as agents states act. The discussion below does not discriminate between these two interpretations of the state because they are so closely intertwined.

Polities that had many but not all the features of states include the Han Empire, the Greek city-states, the Roman state, the Aztec and Inca empires, the Byzantine Empire, and the Italian city-states. We would not include in this list thousands of polities that once may have been politically and militarily formidable but otherwise lacked most of the critical attributes of statehood. The Visigoths, Lombards, Franks, Vandals, and Huns, for example, are better known for their depredations than for political continuity and the creation of international institutions. Others such as the Cimbri, Knights Templars, Samnites, Taurisci, Tigurini, Carbo, or Frisians, have disappeared into the mists of history. They lacked the essential qualities of statehood that provide polities with both legitimacy and longevity. What are these? A non-inclusive list would contain at least the following: (1) fixed position in space (territoriality); (2) the politics of a public realm (differentiation between private and public realms); (3) institutionalized political organizations (continuity independent from specific leaders or other individuals); (4) and a multiplicity of governmental tasks and activities (multifunctionalism), based on (5) legitimizing authority structures (cf., Morris, 1998).[1]

Nomads do not create states. They may have distinct identities (e.g., the Tuaregs today, the Kingdom of the West Goths a thousand years ago), but otherwise lack state characteristics. Rule is personal, there is little or no differentiation between private and public spheres, political organizations do not become institutionalized, and the polity has no distinct geographic base. The West Goths – who remembers them today? – moved through their brief history from the Baltic area to the Black Sea and ultimately to the Bay of Biscay where they eventually disappeared

---

[1] Christopher Morris (1998) lists the essential characteristics of states as (1) continuity in time and space; (2) transcendence (a particular form of political organization that constitutes a unitary public order distinct from and superior to both ruled and rulers, one that is capable of agency); (3) political organization (institutions through which the state acts, differentiated from other political organizations and associations); (4) sovereignty (the ultimate source of political authority in the territory); and (5) allegiance or loyalty from the permanent inhabitants of the territory that supercedes other loyalties such as those to the clan, commune, bishop, or university.

as a distinct social group. Their failure to continue in time was one result of their lack of a defining territory. Some notion of a home territory or exclusive geographic space is essential to the quality of stateness.[2]

States have a public realm that is continuous and distinct from the private or family interests of those who rule. We call this political differentiation. A kingdom run essentially as a private estate is not a state, although with transformations, as was the case throughout Europe in the fifteenth and sixteenth centuries, it may become one. A public realm of politics indicates a field where numerous interests and causes are promoted, debated, and decided upon. It is the "common weal," or the *res publica* that is also characterized by some sort of legal system that sustains authority, defines public roles, and mediates private disputes.

Political organization is institutionalized in at least two ways: first, governing bodies are designed to endure beyond the life of incumbents. Individual kings, queens, doges, caudillos, princes, sultans, chiefs, or warlords may come and go, but in a state government authority and services are continuous. Continuous authority is usually embodied in an independent legal system. Second, states have highly developed ideas, doctrines, social ideologies, and/or constitutions that grant a comprehensive "right to rule" to certain individuals or bodies. This dimension of legitimacy helps sustain authority and a continuous political existence.

Rule and authority in states are comprehensive and multifunctional. They touch upon many aspects of lives within the community. Similarly, the state has many purposes and interests. They range from providing security for the community to building economic infrastructures and providing for public education. For these services, individuals pay taxes and may be required to provide manpower for the military.

In contrast, non-state polities typically have a primary and often only a single purpose and they do not have authority. They may seek to survive as a group or organization, to maximize profits, to pay shareholders, to organize international sporting activities, or to save souls. The International Olympic Committee may regulate the organization of sports and sporting events with the power to bar individual athletes or certain national organizations from competing in international games. Toyota

---

[2] To this assertion, Ferguson and Mansbach (1999: 79) reply "territory is no more essential to identity than the barnacle is to the boat." Yet, when travelling the first question that one is asked is "Where are you from?" Few ask what is your race, occupation, gender, or age.

Corporation may hire and fire employees, determine their salaries, move them from plant to plant or to different headquarters, pay stockholders dividends, or invest in new technologies. The Catholic Church may oversee the spiritual and social lives of its adherents, request financial contributions, or make pronouncements on public issues as a means of wielding political influence. But none of these polities has authority in the sense that the state possesses it. They cannot tax or imprison their members. They cannot execute public laws. If members disagree with the policies of their leaders, they can simply withdraw from the organization, stop paying dues, and cease attending to its business. Citizens can escape state authority by migrating, but then they can only migrate to another state, to another domain of comprehensive authority. Leaving a social club or a transnational company is not the same as leaving a state.

The distinction between states and other types of polities is implicitly revealed in our use of the term "authority." We commonly speak of the tax, police, or prison authorities. But we do not say the authorities of the Mafia, the IOC, or of the Toyota Corporation. Interestingly, however, we still speak of church authorities. The reason is that until the seventeenth century, the church had many of the attributes of statehood.

Today, political homogeneity in the form of statehood has replaced heterogeneity. We have a few feudal leftovers such as the Principality of Monaco, some pre-colonial entities such as sultanates in the Middle East, several functioning (as opposed to symbolic) kingdoms such as Bhutan, and a couple of remaining colonies (e.g., the Falkland Islands), but ours is a world of states. The progenitors developed in Europe between approximately 1400 and 1700. All existing states copied them. In contrast, no European state modeled itself on Asian, African, or other prototypes (Strayer, 1970: 1–15).

The late seventeenth-century Westphalian state

At the beginning of the fifteenth century, Europe remained dotted with hundreds of different polities, overlapping jurisdictions, a low degree of differentiation between private and public realms, and divided loyalties. No prince could predictably prevail over his feudal barons, independent towns, or even church authorities. To muster military strength he had to rely on purchasing armies or making alliances with subordinates who had their own – though seasonal – military capacities. By 1700, in contrast, most princes could effectively suppress most challenges to their authority, although the costs of doing so were often ruinous (Bean, 1973: 203).

The processes of political and military consolidation around the figure of a king or emperor did not occur along similar trajectories throughout Europe. By 1400 the British kings had effectively subdued or co-opted most land-based barons, but in the mid-seventeenth century they faced extreme challenges or parliamentary constraints to their authority, particularly over issues of taxation. In France, Louis XIV faced a major armed rebellion against his rule (the *fronde*, 1648–53) during the middle of the seventeenth century, yet the absolutist French state was a model for many other princes throughout the continent. Sweden was a unified kingdom by the seventeenth century, as was Denmark. In contrast, in the late seventeenth century Peter the Great in Russia found it necessary to hang publicly hundreds of *boyars*, the landed nobility who resisted his attempts at modernization and centralization. In the early seventeenth century, Spain actually regressed toward earlier political forms (Tilly, 1975: 35). In brief, there was nothing inevitable about the development of the state, and it did not move along a straight trajectory.

Practices: the great power grab

The struggle to establish central authority – to bring to life the various assertions of internal sovereignty – could not be conducted unilaterally by the royal figures. They faced resistance and opposition from a variety of sources, including towns and cities, the landed aristocracy, the church, and the peasantry. In order to prevail they had to make alliances, concede charters and grants of autonomy, buy off the aristocracy, purchase loyalty through the sale of offices, put down rebellions and resistance with force, and, as in the case of Peter's Russia, physically annihilate the opposition. Power and authority during the medieval era had resided in many centers, including the church, local assemblies and councils, and in the various landed estates, towns, duchies, and principalities. In the construction of the Absolutist State, those claiming sovereignty had to curtail the ancient rights and privileges of these bodies. As Tilly (1975: 77) explains, "A large part of the process [of state-making] consisted of the state's abridging, destroying or absorbing rights previously lodged in other political units: manors, communities, provinces, estates. In cases like the state's seizure of control over justice from manorial lords, churches, and communities, the right itself continued in more or less the same form, but under new management."

There was nothing inevitable about the outcome. Some polities, including the great trading cities, were militarily as strong as the monarchs and occasionally defeated them in war. Old traditions required princes to obtain taxes only with the consent of the town councils and/or the landed gentry, and in the efforts to centralize the princes could not rely exclusively on their own estates to finance bureaucratic and military organizations (Braun, 1975: 251). In some instances assemblies and estates granted taxes to the crown only in times of national emergency when the state was threatened by external aggression.

The issue of taxation was thus critical. Until the fifteenth century, approximately, princes could pay for most of the very limited functions of government from income deriving from their own estates. By the seventeenth century, the costs of administration and war had grown dramatically and no royal household had the means to sustain them (Isaacs and Prak, 1996: 223).

The strategies for obtaining the necessary funds and support varied. In France, Richelieu ordered the destruction of all town fortifications, thus rendering them defenseless against royal troops. Louis XIV initiated the "court" at Versailles, an institution widely copied in other centralizing monarchies. This involved "locking up the nobility in the gilded cage of a strictly ordered, controlled, and hierarchical court life, and maintaining discipline by taking [the nobles] into his personal service" (Braun, 1975: 245). Louis systematically tied the nobility to his own person by selling offices, for which there were always many aspirants.[3]

Thus it became a game of shifting coalitions: kings rallying popular support by offering guarantees against cruel and arbitrary local magnates or by challenging their claims to goods, money or services, but not hesitating to crush rebellion when the people were divided or a sufficient military force was at hand; magnates parading as defenders of local liberties against royal oppression, but not hesitating to bargain with the crown when it appeared advantageous. Ultimately, the people paid (Tilly, 1975: 67).

---

[3] The numbers of offices proliferated even beyond Louis XIV's imagination. One of his officials brought his master a list of offices that he proposed to create for sale. Louis was astonished that anyone would want to hold such absurd offices, to which the official replied, "Sire when the King of France creates an office, God immediately creates an idiot to buy it" (quoted in Finer, 1975: 128). Ertman (1997: 103) estimates that at the height of its practice in the sixteenth century the French court had sold approximately 16,000 offices as a means of raising state revenue. For Spain, the figure was about 40,000.

They paid not only with their money but also with their lives. Peasant and urban tax rebellions were a constant feature of the seventeenth-century state. The memoirs of the leading officials of the era – Richelieu, Mazarin, Colbert – underline their daily concerns with predicting either where and when the next revolt was going to take place or how well the troops were quelling an existing revolt – usually by hanging all of its leaders (Ardant, 1975: 167). In the 1640s, rebellion in France was so extensive that Richelieu and Mazarin had to begin thinking about ways of ending French participation in the Thirty Years War. They could no longer bear the military burdens when hundreds of thousands of peasants and townspeople refused to pay taxes.

But by the end of the seventeenth century the centralizing authorities prevailed throughout much of Europe. The polity increasingly had those characteristics we listed as essential for statehood. It was fixed in space and time; the idea of patrimony – the state as a private realm – was in decline everywhere but in France and Spain; governance was becoming increasingly institutionalized as a vehicle distinct from the dynast or dynasty; and the state was well along the way to becoming multifunctional.

We will investigate the territorial aspect of the state in the next chapter. Here it is sufficient to point out that one of the main characteristics of the late seventeenth-century state was its "bordering," that is, the formal delimitation of exclusive areas of legal and other forms of jurisdiction.

The distinction between public and private became clearly drawn in those polities that had effective parliaments and where royal figures were constrained by constitutional provisions.[4] This was the case in late seventeenth-century England, Sweden, Denmark, and Hungary. In Latin Europe, in contrast, the patrimonial royal state was predominant. In it, as Louis XIV's famous declaration, "L'état, c'est moi," suggests, legislative, executive, and judicial powers were concentrated in the royal figure who continued to regard the state as his or her private realm, subject only to personal wishes. Sovereignty, they believed, was a personal attribute, as well as an attribute of their states. Both French and Spanish queens or kings of the era either ignored bodies such as the Cortes or

---

[4] Rodney Bruce Hall (1999) offers an important analysis of the distinction between "territorial-sovereign identity" states (dynastic states) and "national-sovereignty identity" states, or nation-states, as well as the consequences of their differences on their foreign policies. Although it is somewhat overdrawn, he offers an illuminating discussion of the dynastic state as essentially a private realm.

Parlement, or abolished them. They turned the growing bureaucracies into their personal possessions, used as sources of personal revenue as much as administrative mechanisms. They systematically sold offices that then became private sinecures for life. Some even became hereditary. They sold the tax-gathering functions to financiers and to other "tax farmers," who systematically looted their harvest before turning over the remaining sums to the state. In Spain, the crown even sold off towns in its domains to the highest bidder and converted mayoral offices into lifetime sinecures.

All states of the period met the criterion of continuity through time not only by means of hereditary succession but also through bureaucratization. The dynasts created all sorts of administrative formations that were distinct from the royal household. In England, for example, the Tudors established complex executive agencies such as the Privy Council and the Star Chamber. The Great Elector had his Land-oder Krieskommissarien, Kriegskommissarien, Stueuerrat, and Landrat. The French kings had their *intendants*, the Conseil d'Etat, the controleur général des finances, and numerous regional governors.

The late seventeenth-century Westphalian state was multifunctional. It regulated several aspects of private and communal life, including religion, impressment for military or militia service, taxation, currency, commercial activity, the provision of justice and courts systems, and, particularly in the case of France, attempts to standardize French in a realm that was characterized by numerous languages and dialects. In addition to these activities, Louis promulgated ordinances and codes that uniformly regulated throughout his realm such diverse activities as civil and criminal court procedure, the management of forests and rivers, shipping and sailing, and the trade in slaves. The most revolutionary aspect of such ordinances was that the sovereign was *creating* law in a society in which previously it had been based on custom and ancient titles of rights and privileges deriving ultimately from the superhuman agency of the Deity (Poggi, 1978: 72–3). The criterion of a state as a continuous legal entity was thus increasingly met by the seventeenth century. Obedience and loyalty – despite the frequent tax rebellions – became rooted not only in the monarch as a divine representative, but more importantly in respect for the state's right to regulate economic and social relations.

Social surveillance accompanied the development of legal relationships. In most of Europe, local bodies such as the French Parlements and Gardes Bourgoise composed of nobles and clergy, or towns and

35

landed nobles in Prussia, carried out the police functions of society until well into the nineteenth century (Bayley, 1975: 349). But in addition, the growing bureaucracy connected to tax collection gathered all sorts of information about individuals and collective productive facilities. The increasing knowledge of private activities by state agencies was accompanied by the slow disarming of the civilian population.

No account of the growing multifunctionality of the state would be complete without mention of two intertwined "services" that became fully concentrated under central authority. Taxation and the military, each of which fed upon the other in a closed symbiotic relationship, were perhaps the most important characteristics of the seventeenth-century state. As Braun (1975: 254) explains:

> the protective function referred not only to enemies from without, but also to those within the border of the territory. For the maintenance of law and order as well as for the exercise of central power, the princes needed loyal military forces. In order to get and maintain the military and political support of the power elite of the territory, the princes had to pay pensions, annuities and a host of other costly rewards to these groups. The rapid development of the spoils system, nepotism, and favoritism during the formative stage of modern state building was both a factor and a symptom of sociopolitical changes and a heavy financial burden for the ruling houses.

Various studies show that the fiscal requirements of the European royal houses escalated dramatically in the seventeenth century. For France and England, the requirements roughly tripled between the beginning of the century and the end of the Thirty Years War (1648) (Finer, 1975: 128). Bean (1973: 214) estimates that in England real government revenue per capita increased from slightly over one-half pound at the turn of the seventeenth century to about two-thirds of a pound by 1640. In the case of Brandenburg-Prussia, in 1640 central revenues were about one million thalers, of which about one-half came from the Elector's own estates. By 1688, revenues had increased to 3.3 million thalers, of which only about one-seventh derived from the Elector's personal sources of income. The peasantry paid most of the remainder. In terms of expenses, the Elector used between 50 and 70 percent of his revenues to maintain his permanent army of 30,000 soldiers (Finer, 1975: 140).

Most experts now agree that the geopolitical competition and war were the main motors driving the development of bureaucracy and public finance in the seventeenth-century state. Braun (1975: 311) notes that almost every major taxation change in Europe during this epoch was occasioned by the preparation and commissioning of wars. There were four main sources of revenues for these expanding requirements: (1) the personal possessions of the crown, (2) sale of offices, (3) public taxation, and (4) income from colonies. The first was inadequate in relation to the vastly increasing expenditures required to create and sustain permanent bureaucracies and armies. The second, perfected in France and Spain, generated only about 15 percent of the state's needs (Ertman, 1997: 103). The third was the predominant source, but it was never adequate to meet growing needs. Colonies were available only for some countries[5] (particularly Spain). To meet the shortfalls, crowns often mortgaged their kingdoms to private financiers. Most seventeenth-century states were thus fundamentally weak: they had to extort, tax, and borrow to pay for their growing armies and bureaucracies, all with the result that loyalty (except among those with sinecures), legitimacy, and credit-ratings were compromised. They thus had to have myths, ideas, and ideologies to prop up their legitimacy.

Ideas

The extension of state activities in the seventeenth century was accompanied by a number of ideas that explained and justified them. We cannot say that ideas caused the practices or vice versa. Both were closely intertwined. In some cases ideas seemed to precede practices; in others, the reverse was the case. We have to see both ideas and practices as reinforcing each other.

The most important ideas associated with the seventeenth-century state reflected declining patrimonialism. Already in the fifteenth-century Italian city-states the concept of *raison d'état* – the differentiation between the private interests of the ruler and the welfare of the state – developed. Although Machiavelli's great *problematique* in *The Prince* was how leaders can retain power, the text is filled with references to the notion of public responsibility. In seventeenth-century thinking, the prince was not free to do as he pleased. He was constrained by law, by God's intentions, and by the welfare of the body politic. All his or her actions had to be undertaken within the context of an obligation to the state.

To legitimize the great power grabs and taxation for supporting armies and bureaucracies, the monarchs required ideological justifications. Theories of the divine origins of royal rule provided the main ideas. Robert Filmer (1588–1653) developed the most exhaustive

---

[5] The American war of independence was initially a tax revolt, not a revolution.

treatment of the issue, although his ideas were mainly expansions of notions appearing already in the sixteenth century. Royal figures rule by divine right, he suggested, because God granted all social power to Adam, their ancestor. Through succession, kings and queens inherited Adam's authority. The basis of authority is thus laid out in the Bible, not in Roman law or in Greek political philosophy. In France, Jacques-Bénigne Bossuet (1627–1704) set down similar ideas. The primary assertion was that God chooses monarchs and they in turn are responsible only to God. But this is not a license for whim or arbitrary rule. Monarchs may have absolute authority over their subjects but they are under the jurisdiction of God's law. Royal rule must be reasonable and just, since God's will is reasonable and just (Knutsen, 1997: 92–3). British kings of the period, particularly James I (1603–25) and Charles I (1625–49), relied extensively on such ideas during their period of rule.

There were also more secular ideas in play. Thomas Hobbes' notion of the social contract was a popular, though often contested, argument in favor of strong royal rule. This is not the place to survey the argument and its flaws, but only to point out that when Hobbes wrote *Leviathan* in 1651, Europe had just passed through its first "world" war, the Thirty Years War that devastated large swathes of land and population in central Europe.[6] Louis XIV was confronted with the *fronde*, which he did not successfully put down until 1653. Civil discontent wracked the military republic of Oliver Cromwell in England at the same time. Political turbulence, revolution, and war were the main hallmarks of the mid-seventeenth century. These circumstances help explain the popularity of ideas favoring a strong state and the necessity to constrain individual freedom.

Such ideas did not go unchallenged despite their popularity in broad political circles, particularly in the royal ones. All sorts of local bodies, including many representative (though narrowly so) institutions, faced the erosion or royal cancellation of what they considered to be their historical rights. Whether town or city councils, the assemblies of landed estates, or local guilds, the great royal power grab was incompatible with notions of autonomy based on old legal contracts, custom, and partially on Roman law. Although ideas of individual rights became popular in late seventeenth-century England (particularly under the influence of John Locke), these older notions of collective rights were fundamentally

---

[6] Central Europe did not until the late eighteenth century regain the population it had had before the Thirty Years War.

incompatible with doctrines of divine right or of social contracts between an amorphous, unorganized populace and some single authority.

But it may be a paradox that while publicists and ideologues of the royal houses were busy developing theories of absolutism against the claims of local authorities and bodies, another theory of rights was also becoming established. This was the right to private property, another revolutionary concept and one that placed serious constraints on the royal prerogative to tax. It also distinguished the European form of absolutism from its parallels in the Ottoman Empire, Shogun Japan, or Imperial China. The age of absolutist public authority in Europe was, as Perry Anderson suggests (1979: 429), also the age in which 'absolute' private property was progressively consolidated. To the extent that this was the case, absolute rule was inherently limited.

In addition to the basis of their rule, European dynasts also needed ideas to justify and explain the significant increases in seventeenth-century state extraction. The Cameralists and Mercantilists provided them. Reason of state – the long-term welfare of the community – requires public finances and economic leadership. Only the state can provide it, and thus it must become the main productive force. Everything within an organic society requires its own proportionate place in a complex economic and social structure. As Braun (1975: 279) explains:

> The principle of social and economic justice is not guided by equality or uniformity but by the guarantee of a "just" proportion. An organic functional view of a body with different parts and different functions can be recognized as the underlying principle, but all parts and functions are now regulated by and have to serve the same purpose: the reason of state. As the main productive force, the governmental institutions have to perform as a heart: they take blood from the organs and distribute it according to need, that is for the well-being and sound development of the body. Taxation serves as an instrument for extracting blood from the organs; the allocation of revenues is the redistribution of this blood. Both tasks have to be accomplished, however, in the "just" or right proportion.

We see here a notion of a contract: the government can extract, but it can do so only to redistribute what it takes in terms of government functions to provide security from external threats and to protect the life and property of royal subjects. This is a distinctly public view of finances and implies constraints on frivolous spending. The state is an agent of redistribution, not an agent for the personal gain of the monarch. So, despite terms such as absolutism and the venal practices of the Spanish and

French kings of the period, the political vocabulary and discourses of the seventeenth century abound with notions of constraint, obligations, and responsibilities. The distinction between the public and dynastic interests in government was becoming more common, although in France it did not become firmly established until the 1789 revolution.

Seventeenth- and early eighteenth-century ideas about the state also derived from the widespread European curiosity about the Amerindians who had been the object of conquest since the early fifteenth century. Publicists and voyage narrators often described indigenous political arrangements as pre-state, or typifying the state of nature. It was a picture of chaos, cruelty, and disorder, to say nothing of blasphemous social behavior. Europeans now began to adopt notions of historical development, with the Amerindian communities typifying the savage and primitive point in historical development, and the European state as "modern." The state thus became associated with modernity, a progressive form of political organization superior to others. These notions of the primitive and the modern did a great deal to provide legitimacy to the European idea of the state, and thus to state practices (Jahn, 1999: 423–4).

But perhaps the most influential ideas surrounding statehood in the early modern period derived from the logic and political demands of the Reformation. The Lutheran claims against the Roman church constituted a major assault on the bases of Catholic influence (and even authority) throughout Europe. The idea that the princes should have the authority to determine the religion of their subjects (the Peace of Augsburg, 1555), and thus that religion is essentially a *local* affair, undermined the medieval cosmology of a united and organic Christian community. And in order to make claims to freedom of religious choice stick, the Lutheran and Calvinist rulers in the Holy Roman Empire and elsewhere had to mobilize all resources available to turn themselves into powerful states. Daniel Philpott (2001: 108) summarizes how the ideas of the Reformation constituted a powerful foundation for substantiating the emerging state against its competitors:

> Facing armed eradication [from the Counter Reformation] . . . reformers now found even more reason to ally with, and give full sovereignty to, secular rulers, whose armies could protect them. This pursuit of protection was a . . . route through which the theological propositions of the Reformation led their adherents to sovereign statehood. Although physical protection considered in isolation is hardly a theologically laden desideratum, the need of the reformers for it is scarcely

intelligible apart from their heretical beliefs . . . The dynamic is cyclical: Protestant propositions provoked the hostile reaction of Catholic authority, leading the holders of the propositions to seek goals that reinforced their content. Sovereign statehood was the carapace that would stanch the Counter Reformation.

To substantiate this model, Philpott (2001: 110) demonstrates a strong correlation between the claims of the Reformation and the emergence of states: "every polity that came to have an interest in a system of sovereign states had experienced a strong Reformation crisis." Moreover, most of the polities that developed an interest in a states system did so only after Protestantism arrived in their land. The connection between statehood and the Reformation is strong and consistent.

Norms

The main moral and legal canon surrounding the seventeenth-century state was sovereignty, or supreme rule within the realm. It was at once an aspiration, a fragile fact, and a norm in the sense that it provided a standard against which royal behavior and status could be measured and judged. Europe's rulers had been making assertions of sovereignty for several centuries, often without much effect either internally or externally. By the seventeenth century, however, sets of ideas had defined in considerable detail that which was sought, for example, by fourteenth-century kings in their long efforts to free themselves from the competition and control of the church. Henry VIII's final takeover of the church and its properties, his establishment of the Church of England, and the extension of his authority over numerous ecclesiastical matters was a major watershed, one that others sought to emulate later. By the sixteenth century, writers and publicists had begun to enunciate what was appearing in practice: the increased concentration of power and authority around the royal figure. Jean Bodin (1530–96) was among the first to offer a conceptual solution to the wars, revolutions, and general chaos of the times: a clear-cut statement that order must rely upon some continuous and legitimate authority that transcends a particular ruler. Sovereignty, he suggested in his *Six Books on the Commonwealth* (1576), is an "absolute and perpetual power vested in the commonwealth" but exercised by one center, whether a monarch, an assembly, or an aristocracy. Sovereignty does not lie with an individual or group, but is an attribute of the commonwealth. Bodin rejected medieval notions of shared sovereignty – as between landed estates, town assemblies, and territorial princes – and insisted it is indivisible. The essential idea is that there can be no competing authority (as distinct from power) either within or exterior to the realm. The facts may differ, but sovereignty is the norm. Anything that deviates from the norm is thus a violation, an injustice, a wrong, or an error that must be remedied. Sovereignty is not a status or condition that fluctuates (a variable) with the rising and falling fortunes of individual leaders. It is an attribute of a continuous and distinct political community inhabiting a defined realm. It cannot wax and wane, be shared, or diluted. States may be big or small, weak or strong, peaceful or chaotic, but so long as there is exclusive legal authority – the *right* to make and apply laws for the community – there is sovereignty. By the end of the seventeenth century, town assemblies might draft or alter local laws but such initiatives required implicit or explicit royal consent. And, finally, only sovereigns could send diplomatic delegations abroad, establish embassies, and make treaties with other sovereigns.

The Peace of Westphalia

Ideas, practices, and norms of stateness and sovereignty were intermingled in the two treaties negotiated at Osnabrück and Münster that comprised the 1648 Peace of Westphalia. The lengthy document includes a long list of territorial revisions, exchanges of towns, castles, and fortifications, compensation for some of the noble victims of war, a nascent scheme for conflict resolution, the elevation of France and Sweden as guarantors of the treaty, and many other matters. It does not, however, mention the word sovereignty. Yet the 1648 settlement was a watershed because it engraved in Europe's first great multilateral treaty the essential ideas of sovereignty (see chapter 4). The main principle, *cuius regio, eius religio*, of the 1555 Peace of Augsburg, was reiterated and solidified as a *right* of princes to change or retain either version of Christianity for their subjects. By this means, the position of the church on religious issues within each state was further undermined.[7] Thus, two major sources of both power and authority in the medieval world, the Holy Roman Emperor and the papacy, were reduced to the status of onlookers of the affairs of the new states. Other provisions enhanced the sovereigns' right to rule and diminished the importance

---

[7] The pope denounced the Westphalia settlement as "null, void, invalid, unjust, damnable, reprobate, inane, empty of meaning and effect for all time" (quoted in Maland 1966: 16).

of medieval legal formulations. Critical for the conduct of international relations, the treaties established the principle of legal equality and thus set the foundations for an international law *between* states as opposed to the older notion of law, whether religious or natural, *above* states. Law subsequently came to be defined in terms of what the sovereigns consented to through international treaties rather than from some rather vague emanations from God or nature. Monarchs, diplomats, warriors, and philosophers of the day interpreted the Westphalia settlement as a major historical watershed because it sanctified through multilateral means and international consent what the sovereigns had been claiming unilaterally for almost two hundred years: exclusive legal authority within the realm, and legal equality between realms. The era's most renowned analyst of the growing international law, Samuel Pufendorf, wrote in about 1682 that in the treaties the rights of princes "have been expressly and particularly confirm'd and establish'd" (quoted in Rowen, 1968: 75). More than one hundred years later, Jean Jacques Rousseau wrote that the Westphalia settlement "will perhaps forever remain the foundation of our international system" (quoted in Knutsen, 1997: 135).[8]

The late seventeenth-century state in many parts of Europe now contained most of the ingredients of our definition of a state: territoriality (see next chapter), at least the beginning of a distinction between private and public realms (the distinction between dynastic and state interests), the institutionalization of political bodies guaranteeing continuity through time, multifunctional tasks, and legitimate authority. It lacked, nevertheless, a sound basis in a sense of community or loyalty. Individuals may or may not have felt loyalty to the royal figure – most were probably indifferent – but there was little sense of a national community. Hobbes' "commonweal" was made up of atomistic individuals, not of a society as we understand the term today. Indeed, most political thought of the era was highly individualistic, whether discussing political and property rights, or the duties of obedience to the absolute ruler. The nation part of the state, the idea of group solidarity and identity, did not appear widely until the nineteenth century.[9]

---

[8] Students of international relations have taken a renewed interest in the Peace of Westphalia, after ignoring it for the better part of a century. There are three notable examples, with full historical details. See Philpott (2001), Kegley and Raymond (2002), and the dissenting views of Andreas Osiander (2001).

[9] This generalization has many exceptions. There is considerable evidence of community bonds and identity in fifteenth-century Italian city-states, for example.

Nation and state in nineteenth-century Europe: growing complexity

The English and French revolutions of 1688 and 1789 largely destroyed the normative bases of royal rule and substituted for them the novel idea that authority derives ultimately from the people. The ideas of popular sovereignty and rule by consent were truly revolutionary and helped pave the way for the concept of citizenship (resurrected by the French from Roman usage) which in turn was linked to the rights of individuals.

The concept of the citizen, while still individualistic, nevertheless suggests a larger body, a community of citizens. At the time of the French Revolution, those who had been royal subjects automatically became French citizens. Theorists and politicians of the age now portrayed France as a community of citizens transcending the diversity of languages, dialects, religions, and races that existed within the traditional boundaries of the French kingdom.

This community was not, however, a spontaneous emanation from revolutionary citizens. Throughout Europe, the state itself took the lead in creating a sense of national community. It did this through its control of education, through the promotion and/or suppression of local languages and dialects, and through military conscription. It also employed the traditional means of military displays and pomp to inculcate feelings of loyalty. The development of a sense of nationhood took many different forms and occurred in different places at different times. Such a sense of community was probably fairly well established in England by the sixteenth century. In contrast, even as late as the mid-nineteenth century, there was no sense at the village level of an Italian nation. As one astute politician noted after the successful unification of the heterogeneous polities of the peninsula, "we have created Italy. Now we must create Italians" (*The Economist*, December 22, 1990: 43). Parochialism was also the case in Germany, throughout the Balkans, and in central Europe. Nationalism was a project that did not come to full fruition throughout the entire continent until the early twentieth century. We cannot therefore speak of "nation" states as being the predominant political forms of Europe until fairly recently.

Among the other innovations of the nineteenth century, we can add the following:

- a single currency and fiscal system
- a national language(s) that superseded or supplemented local languages

- national armies based on conscription from among the entire male population
- national police organizations to enforce a disarmed public and to engage in various forms of social surveillance and coercion against criminal (and sometimes political) activity
- the greatly expanded social and commercial services provided by the state, to include education and some elementary welfare services, all of which in the seventeenth century had been provided through private means such as extended families and the church
- state leadership in organizing, funding, and regulating industrialization
- the direct involvement of citizens in local, regional, and national governance through legislative and other types of deliberative bodies.

Two other characteristics of the nineteenth-century state were particularly important. Governance became increasingly based on legal means and deliberative processes, and less on royal whims, prejudices, and status considerations that were so prominent in seventeenth- and eighteenth-century rule. By the nineteenth century the business of government was dealt with "in a sober, discursive manner; the state is run increasingly on the basis of matter-of-fact judgement and sophisticated, trained reasoning, and less and less on the basis of brawn, ceremonial pomp, and warlike displays" (Poggi, 1978: 109). These changes had important consequences on feelings of national loyalty and for the legitimacy that allowed states to extract taxes and impose compulsory military service. There was the feeling that such sacrifices – including the loss of life in war – were not just duties or responses to commands from a sovereign, but responsibilities that emerged from a common citizenship and membership in a national community.

The second extraordinary characteristic of the late nineteenth-century state was its militarization. Between 1880 and 1914 most European states built massive military machines costing an ever-increasing proportion of national wealth. Finer (1975: 162) cites a few figures that are symbolic of the trend. British military expenditures in the last decade of the nineteenth century amounted to about £36 million. In the next decade they increased to £876 million, that is, more than a twenty-fold expansion within less than twenty years. In the seventeenth century, armies typically numbered below 100,000. In 1914, France deployed a conscripted military force of 3 million. Casualties in wartime similarly ballooned, ultimately reaching about 8 million in the Great War. These figures tell us something about the willingness of nineteenth-century citizens to bear the burdens of national defense or national grandeur. If tax rebellions and organized resistance to central authority wracked the seventeenth-century state, two centuries later the state found not just willing but enthusiastic support of its military projects. Without a strong sense of nationalism, of the state as embodying a national community, such extractions would be inconceivable.

The contemporary state

The critical importance of states as the main agents of international relations and the essential format for protecting, promoting, and sustaining the national community is revealed in part by their numbers. In the medieval era, there were about five hundred polities with some state-like characteristics (Tilly, 1990: 45). Through the processes of aggregation, integration, marriages, and conquests these units eventually emerged as twenty-one states, principalities, and independent cities in Europe in 1875 (Sharpe, 1989: 227). There was still some political heterogeneity, as feudal leftovers such as Liechtenstein and Monaco had a distinct international status. There were also the multinational Russian, German, Ottoman, and Austro-Hungarian empires. By 1919, these empires collapsed and the feudal leftovers maintained their autonomy but were not recognized as sovereign states.

In the twentieth century there were three major explosions of state-making: the first in 1919, the second in the three decades after World War II, and the third in the early 1990s. In all cases, war was the main engine of historical change. In 1918–19 a number of constituent nationalities within the great empires of central Europe and the Balkans revolted and achieved independence. The new states ran from Finland in the north to Yugoslavia in the south. Now Europe suddenly had eight more states, actually nine since Norway had peacefully seceded from Sweden in 1905. The second great wave of state-making followed World War II. It started in 1947 with India's independence and was essentially completed by 1975 with the withdrawal of Portugal from Angola and Mozambique. Fifty-one governments signed the Charter of the United Nations in 1945. By 1970 the organization had 150 members. During this same period Cyprus, Malta, East Germany, Greenland, and Iceland joined the roster of European states, which, however, had lost Estonia, Latvia, and Lithuania through Soviet conquests in 1940.

After the end of the Cold War, a raft of new states appeared, including thirteen former republics of the Soviet Union. They achieved independence primarily through peaceful means. Yugoslavia, however, broke up into its constituent republics through violence and massive orgies of killing and ethnic cleansing. If we include Russia, Ukraine, Belarus, and the rest of the former Soviet republics, today Europe is composed of fifty-one countries compared with twenty-one in 1875. Worldwide, candidates for future statehood include Montenegro, Palestine, the Faroe Islands, Turkish Cyprus, and Somaliland. Any number of armed secessionist movements in what used to be known as the Third World could push the number higher. United Nations membership will probably reach 200 within the next decade.

Since 1945 the main issue causing wars, conflicts, and crises has been state-creation (K. J. Holsti, 1996). The agenda of the United Nations since 1945 has been littered with cases of violence over the question of who is going to have a state, of what kind, and when. It seems that almost every distinct cultural/language/religious group in the world today is making a case for independent statehood. Statehood has an unprecedented popularity, certainly much more than was the case in the seventeenth century (cf., Hueglin, 1989; Seiler, 1989).

The practices of contemporary statehood

State practices are so many that we cannot make a comprehensive list. That so many are taken for granted tells us something about the continuing importance of this unique form of political organization. For the sake of brevity, let us mention just a few of the typical domestic and external practices that reflect the critical importance of statehood.

We might list first the growing scope of government services (multi-functionality). By the twentieth century, the list of government functions expanded to include education, health, science and technology, welfare, massive infrastructure subvention (airports, highways, and the like), economic regulation in the broadest sense, disaster relief, and sports. The modern citizen is touched in almost all his or her daily activities by services the state provides. We should also emphasize the role of the state as the major vehicle for creating, sustaining, and promoting the sense of a unique political community, that is, the national culture. Schools teach the vernacular language and emphasize national history. Public universities are major institutions for promoting historical research of the nation, national arts, national and regional cultures, and other areas of inquiry that help focus public attention on the unique qualities of being a Russian, Canadian, Japanese, Bangladeshi, Nigerian, or Finn. The state not only helped to create the nation, but also sustains it.

Among the many new and growing functions of the state, moral and ethical leadership, regulation, and instruction are significant. In the European context at the time of the early Westphalian state, religious institutions sustained these tasks. Today, in states where religious and government institutions are separate, they share these functions, but with one big difference: religious institutions do not have enforcement capacity. Most contemporary states set limits, regulate, or otherwise define policies relating to population growth and sexual relations, and to the sale and/or possession of alcohol, tobacco, and drugs. They propagate norms relating to behaviors of citizenship, and define a host of regulations governing other private activities. In states where religious and state institutions are not separated (e.g., Iran) the state may establish regulations that guide the full range of public and private behavior, from codes of dress, through appropriate relationships between the sexes, to what individuals may read or watch on television. As the name implies, in states with totalitarian regimes (e.g., North Korea) there is no realm of "private" behavior; the state regulates every facet of individuals' lives, including what, where, and how much they eat! The state is much more than an administrative or justice-providing institution. It has become the great moral teacher and regulator.

The multifunctional tasks of governments have to be paid for. State practices in the twentieth century included massive intervention in the market economy and dramatic growth of taxation. The standardized universal income tax is an invention of the twentieth century – imposed in most countries as a temporary measure to finance participation in World War I – and has grown to extract prodigious proportions of personal wealth. In a typical OECD country today, government receipts, mostly through taxes, constitute more than 40 percent of the Gross Domestic Product (GDP). In a few, such as Sweden in 1985, the figure reached almost 60 percent. Growth in government expenditures is of similar magnitude. Between 1960 and 1985, government outlay as a proportion of GDP increased by an average of about 50 percent in the Western European countries. In the same period, social security transfers as a proportion of GDP increased typically by more than 100 percent, and in the case of Spain, by almost 600 percent (Puchala, 1993: 75, 80). While under the impact of recession in the early 1990s such growth rates decelerated, the main practices of governments continue to provide for the welfare of citizens and to promote their distinct social and cultural characteristics. Defense spending, a traditional government function, grew as dramatically as spending on welfare during and after the great wars of the century, but it no longer accounts for the majority of public expenditures as it did in the seventeenth century. A typical state today spends less than 5 percent of its GDP and about 20 percent of its government expenditures on defense-related activities.

Several typical practices relating to external relations also bear mentioning because they reflect the high normative and legal status of political independence in the contemporary world. In previous centuries, the collapse of public authority in a territory usually led to foreign annexation, partition, the creation of colonies, or other forms of subjugation. This is no longer the case. States are sacrosanct in a way not seen historically. Rather than colonize or annex Somalia, Liberia, Sierra Leone, or Kampuchea – all recent collapsed states – the international community has sought to resuscitate them. Similarly, contemporary standard practice is to grant official recognition to new states no matter what their internal condition. In the eighteenth and nineteenth centuries, governments granted recognition only when the public authorities of the new states could prove that they had effective control over a population inhabiting a defined territory, and also had the ability to meet treaty obligations and in other ways to carry out international responsibilities. Since 1945, in contrast, most states have usually granted recognition to new states no matter in what condition (cf., Jackson, 1990). The only entrance requirement for new members of the United Nations is that they be "peace-loving," a qualification that is eminently flexible and subjective. To have been a colony almost automatically qualifies a candidate for statehood. The contemporary practice of lowering the standards for recognizing new states is a reflection of the inherent moral quality of statehood and of the general norm of self-determination and self-rule. This helps explain why the community of states has been reproducing itself at the average rate of nearly 2.5 new states each year since 1945.

Ideas

The ways we look at the world, perceive events, and conduct our daily activities – our mental frames of reference – are highly conditioned by statehood and our ideas about states. So are our identities. Nationality and occupation are among the main forms of identity today as anyone learns quickly when traveling abroad. They were not several centuries ago, when religion and family lineage were of greater importance. Our statistics, our political systems, and our plethora of political symbols all derive from "stateness." Most people are roughly familiar with the geography and history of their own country. The further one moves away, however, the more public knowledge dissipates. Even among political elites, knowledge of other countries and cultures is often rudimentary, highly stereotyped, and often just plain wrong.[10] Large numbers of people throughout the world maintain suspicious attitudes toward anything that is "foreign."

The public media sustain these perspectives. Most newspapers in the world have a predominantly national and local focus. For many, 90 percent or more of the coverage is of local and national news. Television and radio news programs – even those entitled "world" or "global" news – typically contain a large majority of local and national news stories. Many contain no foreign news most days. Even in major countries such as the United States, in which communications media are the most diverse, availability of foreign information is scarce. Typical Americans seldom watch foreign movies or television programs, not necessarily because they choose to ignore them but because those who control and distribute films and television programs do not offer them. This intense focus on the national and local implicitly reinforces our conceptions of "stateness."

Another way to underline the critical importance of the contemporary state and its internalizing in our mental maps of the world is to look at the alternatives. A few have commanded significant attention and continue to do so today, but none has offered a successful alternative to the state and to the ideas underlying it. Communists originally believed that the bourgeois state – which they argued was an instrument of class oppression – would eventually disappear through revolution. In official Soviet futurology in the 1920s, states would ultimately give way to a great transnational brotherhood of the working class. After World War I, however, the working classes in Europe did not revolt successfully against the bourgeois state, and subsequently Soviet leaders had to confront the obvious discrepancies between Marxist beliefs about statehood and what was actually going on in the world.

Nazism offered the alternative of states based on race rather than on territory, history, and the other legacies of Westphalia. In Hitler's

---

[10] As illustrated in the story about former American Vice-President Dan Quayle. He was reported to have proposed learning a bit of Latin before undertaking an official tour of Latin America.

worldview, Europe would be reorganized hierarchically along strict racial lines. The Aryans would be supreme, effectively ruling over the inferior Latins and Slavs in colonial-type (or worse) relationships. World War II was in part a war to prevent the implementation of this alternative to the Westphalian state.

In the late 1950s and early 1960s, there was a good deal of talk among Africans about the inappropriateness of Western-style states for African conditions. After all, long before colonial conquest, Africans had had their own polities, many of which had state-like qualities (cf., Warner, 1999). They recognized that the colonial state was an artificial creation, imposed by the colonial authorities, and largely inconsistent with African political and social traditions. One solution was pan-Africanism, the unification of the entire continent into a single state. By the middle 1960s, these ideas were abandoned, and both national liberation movements and indigenous political formations in the colonies embraced the Western concept of the state as the preferred way of politically organizing their multi-ethnic and polyglot societies.

The struggle between state-like ideas and others is currently being played out in some areas of the Arab and Muslim world. Many insist that Western notions of statehood, including the principle of territoriality, were foisted upon the Arab or Muslim societies as a way of keeping them divided from each other. Pan-Arabism was an alternative that promised both greater political influence in the world and greater consistency with traditional Muslim beliefs about the relationship between politics and society. The true community is the *umma*, the community of believers. It should be unified not only in belief, but also in social and political relations.

Debates about the appropriate nature of political community in Islam continue to this day, but practice has effectively settled the issue for the time being. Increasingly since the 1960s Arab and other Islamic leaders have adopted the strategies of state-building and the norms of sovereignty. These have included projects "that were designed to encourage the transfer of both subnational and transnational [e.g., pan-Arabism] identities to the state, and, therefore, to enhance the state's legitimacy and domestic stability" (Barnett, 1996: 164). Like their European predecessors, Arab and other Islamic leaders have created symbols emphasizing distinct state identities, histories, permanence, and cultures at the expense of transcendental ones. Over the years, the vocabulary of Arabism has changed to accommodate notions and ideas that accentuate regional differences and local uniqueness.

None of these alternatives has successfully challenged the ideas and ideology surrounding the Westphalian state and its modern successors. Communism has collapsed and transnational loyalties of the working class never replaced national identities and loyalties. An international order based on a racial hierarchy has no appeal today. Pan-Africanism and pan-Arabism still animate debates but have not prompted political leaders to behave in a manner consistent with their main ideas. In contrast, dozens of secessionist groups, national liberation movements, and peoples have appropriated the ideas and ideology of national self-determination defined in terms of statehood.

The essential component of the doctrine of self-determination is that states ought to be based on nations. The idea was already popular in the mid-nineteenth century, particularly in respect to Poland (incorporated into the Russian Empire) and Hungary. But it gained universal appeal during World War I when Woodrow Wilson announced that the peace following that war ought to apply the principle to the various peoples that made up the German, Austro-Hungarian, Russian, and Ottoman empires. In Paris in 1919, Wilson learned that the application of the principle was much more difficult than its enunciation. He was besieged by dozens of delegations representing "nations" demanding that the great powers recognize them as independent states. Some succeeded, many failed. The mapmakers in Paris also discovered that it was impossible to create ethnically homogeneous states so they came up with the idea of creating fictitious multi-ethnic states such as Czechoslovakia and Yugoslavia, smaller versions of the multi-ethnic empires they had just dismantled. Moreover, the principle was not applied to the victors, some of whom (e.g., the British and Ireland) had their own secessionist movements. Nevertheless, Wilson's ideas became universalized and thus amounted to an emancipation charter for political particularism and format homogeneity. The effect of the Paris Peace Conference and of subsequent League of Nations activities was to consolidate "conceptions of national sovereignty as the 'natural' condition of humankind, via a particular interpretation of the sovereignty-citizenship-nationalism relation" (Giddens, 1987: 259, 258). The idea of national self-determination legitimized the primacy of the nation-state as the universal political form of the current era. That idea continues today and forms the basis of innumerable groups' demands for independence. Indeed, the idea has become a fundamental norm of the contemporary international system because it is no longer characterized simply as a political preference, but as a right. Numerous United Nations resolutions have so depicted it and virtually all public discourse on the plight of minorities or distinct groups such as the Kosovars or the Timorese is conducted as if self-determination is indeed a human right. The problem, of course, is in the definition of "national."

Norms

The predominant norm of statehood today is self-rule. We no longer tolerate one "people" ruling over others, even if it is not in a colonial-type relationship. In the seventeenth and eighteenth centuries there was nothing peculiar about a German from Hanover becoming the king of England, or a Swedish king exercising sovereignty over Lübeck, a German city, or of the Spanish king as sovereign over Naples. This was normal practice. In contrast, the norms of statehood in the Versailles Treaty and the League of Nations Covenant sustain a view of the state as a contiguous entity based on distinct peoples who have self-rule, that is, government by "one's own" (cf., Morris, 1998: 241). Under contemporary international law, a polity that does not have self-rule cannot become a state. It is some sort of dependency, and thus does not have a crucial element of statehood. In terms of international relationships, the principles of the Covenant outlawed territorial revision through armed force and defined the extinguishing of states or the imposition of foreign rule through military means as the ultimate international crime. The whole purpose of the League was to defend the independence and self-government of its members. The theory of collective security in the League Covenant – where an attack on one state is to be considered an attack on all states – raises self-governing statehood to the ultimate political value worthy of protection by collective military means.

Dorothy Jones (1990: 49) nicely summarizes the critical importance of the *idea* of the state as the ultimate grounding for an international organization:

> As for the body of thought from which the principle of self-determination was derived, that was so much a part of the intellectual and emotional milieu of 1919 that its propositions seemed not so much self-evident as natural. *In the beginning was the nation-state, which people saw as good.* From that, the rest followed: the very structure of the League as an association of independent states; the establishment of new states; the preparation of mandated territories for eventual statehood; the guarantees of the political independence and territorial integrity of existing states. Every arrangement for the new international order was grounded on the fact of the state . . .

The essential principles of the League carried forth into the United Nations Charter, which, like its predecessor, is a constitution for the preservation of the Westphalian state and the principle of self-rule. In the years subsequent to its founding in 1945, the UN raised the aspiration or principle of self-determination into an international *right* and thus into a fundamental norm of the contemporary system. Various UN resolutions explicitly stated that no conditions (size, level of development, political legitimacy of the rulers, and the like) were to qualify the right. In addition to the United Nations Charter and subsequent resolutions, it is also encoded in the charters of most regional organizations such as the Organization for African Unity (now the African Union), the Organization of American States (OAS), and the Association of Southeast Asian Nations (ASEAN).

The norms of self-determination and self-rule have helped to create more than 140 new states since 1945, and to de-legitimize all forms of imperial or suzerain-type relationships. The self-ruling state is now universally recognized and assumed to be the "natural" form of political organization. But in some cases the realities of statehood are not consistent with the norms. Some states have collapsed, others, like some of their seventeenth-century predecessors, cannot establish effective authority over their territories, and still others remain states primarily by virtue of outside support. While the state is the predominant form of legitimate authority over distinct societies, it is by no means universally successful.

The problem of weak states

What political characteristics are commonly found in these states? A number of observers have compared the state-making process after 1945 to the pattern of developments in early modern Europe (cf., Tilly, 1990; Ayoob, 1995). While we must remain sensitive to significant historical and cultural differences, there are suggestive points of comparison. The state-making process in Europe, as in the post-1945 world, involved attempts to centralize authority, to extract resources from the population, and to constrain or destroy local rule-making individuals and bodies (cf., Migdal, 1988; Bereciartu, 1994: Young, 1994). This process often undermined or destroyed local authority structures and incumbents, homogenized cultures, imposed national laws to replace local customs, diluted local languages, and not infrequently, as in the Sudan, led to the expropriation of lands and resources of indigenous and other people.

Numerous civil wars, rebellions, armed resistance, and massacres punctuated the state-making process in Europe. They have been no less evident in the transformation of colonies into independent states in the twentieth century.

Unlike their European predecessors, however, most post-1945 states began with democratic constitutions, and with an international set of norms that promoted and sustained self-determination, self-government, and independence. Many of these paraphernalia of popular sovereignty were "delivered" as part of the de-colonization process. But the problem was that many of the colonies-turned-states were in fact fictions. They had the appurtenances of states – flags, armies, capital cities, legislatures, and ambassadors – but they did not have the other requisites of statehood, such as a clear distinction between public and private realms, government institutionalization, and effective multifunctionality. Most had only weak civil societies (Harbeson et al., 1994). Many were polities, but not functioning states as we have defined them. Few populations had deeply ingrained senses of national identity; most, in fact, remained primordial, fixed around clans, tribes, religious groups, or limited geographic regions. The fiat of the "national" government often extended no further than the suburbs of the capital city, beyond which local leaders, based on a variety of claims to legitimacy, ruled. The modern symbol of sovereignty, a monopoly over the legitimate use of force, plus the effective disarmament of society, existed more in rhetoric than in fact.

These and other characteristics of some new states constitute a syndrome that Barry Buzan (1993) has called the *weak state* and Robert Jackson (1990) has termed *quasi-states*. The terms may differ, but the phenomena to which they direct attention are similar. Weak states have all the attributes of sovereignty for external purposes – they are full members of the international community and have exactly the same legal standing as the oldest or most powerful states in the system – but they severely lack the internal attributes of sovereignty.

Weakness is a variable, not a teleological destination or origin. Throughout their history, states move back and forth along a continuum of weakness and strength. The comparative politics literature alludes to the various components of state strength, including capacity to extract resources, degree of social control, the extent to which the public is effectively disarmed, the provision of government services in exchange for tax extractions, and the degree to which national legislation is effectively applied throughout the designated territory. These are all material bases of state strength or weakness. However, the critical dimension of state strength is *legitimacy*, which is an idea or feeling. It is a measure of citizens' attitudes toward the state, whether they withhold or grant the "right to rule" to those who act in the name of the state. Rebels and armed insurgents of various kinds often grant no legitimacy to the incumbent government. They challenge its "right to rule" and take actions to replace incumbents with those who can make a superior claim. Others withdraw legitimacy from the state itself. Either they wish to change the entire constitutional order (not just incumbents), or they wish to secede. Radical Muslim elements in Algeria are an example of the former; contemporary separatists in Quebec, Corsica, or Sri Lanka are examples of the latter. Their purposes differ, but they fundamentally make the same claim: the leaders of the state in which they reside do not have the right to rule, and so they want to rearrange matters either by changing the fundamental contours of the state or by creating a new state. Why?

Weak and failed (or collapsed) states became the object of considerable attention during the 1990s. With the end of the Cold War, analysts began to acknowledge that rebellions, civil wars, and massacres taking place in the Third World and elsewhere were not just the manifestations of great power competition or ideological incompatibilities. Suddenly, observers discovered the phenomenon of "ethnic wars," overlooking the fact that wars within states having nothing to do with Cold War competition had been part of the Third World landscape for many years. Civil wars and wars of secession in Burma, Sudan, Eritrea, Nigeria, and elsewhere long preceded the collapse of the Berlin Wall (Holsti, 1997: 107–9).

Some states have moved from original weakness to collapse. They are the ultimate failures of contemporary statehood. In 1991, Somalia became the symbol of the *collapsed state*, ostensibly a new phenomenon in international politics. Lebanon in 1976, Angola and Mozambique (perhaps more aborted than collapsed states because they began to fall apart immediately upon independence) and Chad between 1980 and 1982 all had the symptoms of the state moving toward collapse.

The critical absent ingredient in a collapsing state is authority. It fragments or evaporates in direct proportion to the loss of government legitimacy in society and its component groups. Rule – to the extent that it exists – is based on coercion, corruption (the purchase of support), or terror. It is no longer a *right*. In the vacuum of legitimacy, all sorts of "governors" appear – warlords, gangs, religious movements, and clans.

The sources of these difficulties are similar to those found in weak seventeenth-century states. They include the lack of distinction between private and public realms. Governors or claimants to authority use the state for their own private purposes, sell offices, and purchase loyalty through patrimonial offerings. Bureaucrats use their positions to enhance their wealth, to provide jobs for their families and friends (mini-patrimonialism), and to impose various forms of illegal taxation. To maintain this arena of privilege, some segments of society are favored, while others are excluded from office and resources, thus setting the stage for rebellion and secession from the state. Rule may also be sustained by playing the "ethnic card," that is, creating social divisions within society that help maintain the loyalty of those who count. The politics of ethnicity range from subtle forms of discrimination and exclusion all the way to expulsions of distinct groups from the state, and to ethnocides and genocides. These conditions and policies have all been common to the great internal wars and secessionist movements of the post-1945 world. They include Sri Lanka, Rwanda, Burundi, Sierra Leone, Liberia, Somalia, Tajikistan, pre-1999 Nigeria, Sudan, and many others (Holsti, 2000).

Some states are in effect "kleptocracies," where individuals use the state apparatus to enrich themselves and to create, in the French seventeenth-century manner, systems of patrimonial rule. Public offices become the primary vehicles for family wealth, and a chain of superior and subordinate officeholders, virtual sinecures, serves as the foundation for rule. As was the case with rulers such as the Somoza family in Nicaragua, the Duvaliers in Haiti, Ferdinand Marcos in the Philippines, and numerous rulers in Africa, billions of dollars gained through the sale of offices, plundering the public treasury, graft, extortion, and pure theft were sent to Swiss banks and invested in Western enterprises. Upon the death, assassination, or forced removal from office of such "leaders," the state apparatus frequently collapsed, followed by civil war, secession, or revolution.

On the other hand, many originally weak states have avoided or overcome the syndrome and today function much as their European forebears. Singapore, Malaysia, Mauritius, Tanzania, Barbados, and Trinidad are prominent examples. But a fair number of former colonies cannot yet sustain the qualities of statehood outlined earlier, including effective control over a defined territory, a clear distinction between public and private realms, political institutionalization, and effective multifunctionality.

One final characteristic of weak states needs emphasis because it is largely an artifact of the twentieth century and finds no predecessors in the state-building enterprise in Europe during the early modern period. Unlike Hobbes' Leviathan, which had the main purpose of maintaining order and providing security for members of the commonwealth, many weak states have been a major threat to their populations. The state, instead of being a vessel of security and national community, has become a menace to parts of its population. Since World War II, more people have been killed by the agents of their own state than by foreign invaders. Where the state is captured by one individual or a political clique that has no foundation in popular legitimacy, opposition to arbitrary rule is often met by widespread oppression and killing. The citizens of Kampuchea, Equatorial Guinea, China, or Uganda in the 1970s, of South Africa at the height of apartheid in the 1980s, or of Rwanda in 1994 and Sudan today faced murderous regimes that in some cases have counted their victims in the hundreds of thousands, and even in millions. Such are the sources of secessionism. The seventeenth century did not have precedents for the many politicides of the past one hundred years.

The state and change: the case for transformation

Where does this historical discussion lead in terms of types of institutional change? Here we evaluate the patterned practices of states, the ideas and beliefs that sustain and justify them, and the norms that guide policies towards other states. Recall the six theoretical types of change: (1) a new institution (novelty and replacement); (2) addition or subtraction; (3) increased or decreased complexity; (4) transformation; (5) reversion; and (6) obsolescence. The beginning parts of this chapter described the early years of this *new* institution. Subsequent parts described the main changes in the nineteenth and twentieth centuries. They can be characterized as increasing *complexity*. This leaves the possibilities of *transformation*, *reversion*, and *obsolescence*. Reversion is not prominent, although there was an example in seventeenth-century Spain and in some more recent collapsed states. This leaves *transformation* and *obsolescence*. There are adherents of each of these possibilities, although most take the position that the trend is toward weakening of the state, which, if it continues, will lead to its obsolescence. These include E. H. Carr, who in 1946 (Carr, 1946: viii) wrote: "The conclusion now seems to impose itself on any unbiassed [sic] observer that the small independent nation-state is obsolete or obsolescent and that no workable international organization can be built on a membership of a multiplicity of nation-states."

Numerous observers have recently made similar projections. We read comments to the effect that sovereignty is "eroding," that the territorial basis of the state is "disappearing" under the onslaught of communications technology and the compression of time and space, that there is a drastic alteration of the forms of governance in the world, with supranational and subnational polities replacing national polities, and the like. Yale Ferguson and Richard Mansbach (1996: 417) suggest there is a "revolt against the prerogatives of the Westphalian state." The literature on this question is notable more for its volume and scope of assertions than for systematic empirical inquiry. Much is claimed, but not much has been verified according to the methodological canons of the social sciences.[11] Yet, the case has become so prominent that it has almost become conventional wisdom. The state is in the process of transformation toward weakness. If present trends continue, the transformation will be toward obsolescence.

Transformationalists approach the problem from two perspectives. The first suggests that the *authority* of the state is "leaking," "moving up," or "evaporating" toward forces, agents, and entities beyond it, including international organizations, transnational associations, the global market, or the global civil society. The second suggests that *individuals within* states are increasingly questioning the authority of the state, withholding loyalty to it, and developing new loyalties toward more accommodating or psychologically satisfying identity groups such as ethnic associations, churches, and regional groupings. The first approach brings to mind the metaphor of a leaking balloon. Its air is dissipating towards the outside, with the encasing ultimately collapsing. The second suggests a crumbling house of cards. The emotional props of the state – legitimacy and loyalty – are eroding, leading eventually to the collapse of the house, or at least to its marginalization compared with other new houses above or within states. Just as the early Westphalian state was challenged by the church

---

[11] Two important exceptions to this observation are Weiss (1998) and Held et al. (1999).

authority above it and by peasant rebellions and the numerous armed dukes, nobles, and pirates within it, so the modern state is eroding in two different directions.

The late Susan Strange, a noted international political economist, presents an exemplary and robust case for the first type of state transformation in her study *The Retreat of the State* (1996). Her main thesis is that state power and authority are "leaking" to globalized markets and their main agents, transnational corporations (TNCs), to international criminals, and to international organizations. She argues (p. 188):

> One hypothesis is that there is not much left of the territorial basis for authority . . . When the shift of power is to other authorities – authorities whose basis is not their command over territory but command over the nature, location and manner of production and distribution of goods and services, this clearly raises some new questions about the nature of sovereignty and the dispersion of power and political control.

Strange examines recent trends in the three sectors to support this basic position. There are numerous interesting and compelling illustrations as, for example, the multi-billion-dollar international drug trade that not only escapes government efforts to curtail it, but actually involves collusion because governments have been unwilling to regulate the banks through which the profits of the trade are "laundered." "The contradiction between the two decisions – that selling drugs is illegal but handling the financial proceeds of the trade is not – is putting the entire system of state authority at risk" (p. 119). International markets and their major TNC operators have the power to "discipline" governments that attempt to follow policies that help the poor or redistribute income within highly inegalitarian societies. The result is that government economic and fiscal policies serve the interests of transnational corporations and other operators of the international financial and productive systems rather than the public welfare. The cases and illustrations are legion. The ones Strange chooses all point to the same conclusion, which is that market power dilutes and diffuses government authority over economy and society (p. 121).

In addition to the cases Strange discusses, we might add the role of the World Bank (IBRD) and International Monetary Fund (IMF), both international organizations that help sustain the globalizing world economy. A weak developing country seeking outside support has little choice but to accept the "conditionality" attached to loans. The list of impositions by international bureaucrats on poor countries is almost endless. It includes limits on credit expansion and ceilings on bank credit for state-run institutions, freezes or reductions in the number of government employees, capping or reducing subsidies on food, gasoline, and fertilizers, increasing payroll taxes, and raising excise taxes on beer and cigarettes, wage restraints, and any number of other policies that fall harshly on the poor (cf., Krasner, 1999: 146). Frequently, officials of the IMF or World Bank become *de facto* finance ministers of weak states and their economies. In Strange's terms, authority to establish national priorities and preferred economic policies has shifted from states to bureaucrats of the IMF or IBRD. Moreover, the policies of the two international financial organizations closely adhere to the economic interests of the largest donors, particularly to those of the United States. However, even modern developed states cannot escape the discipline and power of international markets and their operators. During the 1980s, when the French government sought to sustain or institute policies that emphasized social welfare spending, the markets responded by causing a massive flight of capital, forcing a devaluation of the French franc. Ultimately, the government had to abandon its priorities and to shift them to the demands of international capital. Can we then speak of states as critical agents in the international political realm when the real locus of authority and power today resides outside the country? Overall, in Strange's estimation, the authority of the state is "retreating," a trend that in the long run portends obsolescence.

James Rosenau (1990) has made one of the most interesting arguments regarding the erosion of state authority through shifting loyalties and the appearance of various particularisms – the second approach to state obsolescence or regression. He emphasizes phenomena such as declining loyalties to the state as seen, for example, in resistance to conscription, in tax cheating and evasion, migration, and declining voter participation. Increasingly people judge states not on the basis of presumed authority, but by performance. When states fail to perform according to expectations, people resist, withdraw, or shift their loyalties in other ways. The explanation lies in the increased analytical skills of people gained through universal education, increased literacy, and the availability of new information technologies. If many people no longer submit automatically to state authority, then either loyalty will be directed elsewhere to polities that can effectively challenge the state, or in the extreme, the state may become obsolete or in some other way become transformed. The trend is already well on the way, for authority is escaping both to the outside and within the state. In his words (Rosenau, 1997: 154):

> the numerous shifts in the loci of governance stem from the interactive tensions whereby processes of globalization and localization are simultaneously unfolding . . . In some situations the . . . dynamics are fostering control mechanisms that extend beyond national boundaries and in others the need for the psychic comforts of neighborhood or ethnic attachments is leading to the diminution of national entities and the formation or extension of local mechanisms. The combined effect of the simultaneity of these contradictory trends is that of lessening the capacities for governance located at the level of sovereign states and national societies.

Critique of the state transformation/ obsolescence argument

The arguments for transformation and/or obsolescence are partly persuasive, even if based on highly selected indicators and cases. Five major theoretical difficulties come to mind, however: (1) confusion of influence and power with authority; (2) conceptions of power based on zero-sum assumptions; (3) lack of benchmarks; (4) confusion of the legitimacy of the state with the performance of governments; and (5) setting the bar of state authority too high. There are also a number of empirical difficulties.

Susan Strange joins the company of many who consistently confuse power and authority. No one can deny that global markets discipline and increasingly constrain governments (cf., Sørensen, 2001: 131; Sassen, 2002: 178), that huge transnational enterprises, particularly of the criminal kind, escape government regulation, and that some international organizations greatly influence the priorities and policies of some governments. She argues (1996: 53) that "power . . . is to be gauged by influence over outcomes rather than mere possession of capabilities or control over institutions." Since TNCs, financial markets, criminal groups, and international organizations influence outcomes both between and within states, it follows, according to Strange, that they have authority. Authority flows from power. But this is a fundamental error. If we accept her very broad definition of politics (p. 35) as "any kind of association of individuals for a commonly agreed purpose," then virtually everyone who has power also has authority. School children who join together to boycott a school cafeteria because of the low quality of food, by Strange's definition, have power. Mafia extortionists have power.

Obviously TNCs, many with greater financial holdings than those of the majority of states in the world, have power. And the IMF has the power to withhold financial aid to governments that do not toe the line of financial orthodoxy. But do all of these associated individuals or organizations having a commonly agreed purpose actually have *authority*, as Strange implies? Do the school children have the authority to arrest, try, and imprison their peers who do not support the boycott? Does the Mafia have the authority to execute politicians who are investigating their activities? Do the drug barons have the authority to make binding treaties that will have validity under international law? Do TNCs have the authority and thus the right to establish productive facilities wherever they wish without the consent of states? Or to make and apply law within a state's territory? Authority is a particular type of relationship that presumes a right to rule, to make law, and to enforce it. It is not the same as influence or power. All the cases Strange uses to illustrate her argument of transformation pertain not to authority but only to influence. To claim that TNCs, financial markets, drug cartels, and international organizations all have power in international political relationships and over states is undeniable. But that is not the same as having authority over states and it does not mean that state authority is retreating. It may mean, however, that states are increasingly constrained in their freedom to make policy choices. States may be losing autonomy (although this is also arguable), but this is not the same as losing authority.

A second problem is that Strange assumes a zero-sum quality to power and influence. If TNCs have political influence today, she implies, it must mean that someone has lost it, and that someone is the state. In her view, it does not seem conceivable that both states and transnational actors and agents of various kinds may be increasing their power simultaneously, or that states voluntarily and purposefully increase the stature and possible influence of transnational or international bodies so as to promote their own purposes. Geoffrey Underhill (1997: 4, 9) argues that in the realms of regulation of banking and securities, for example, there is a complex symbiotic relationship between transnational and government agents. He suggests that "states and markets constitute integrated ensembles of governance and should not be conceptualized as opposing and/or competing principles of social organization . . . The states against markets debate is misconceived." Rather, states (excepting those with socialist economies) are embedded in the market and the system of production, and markets are in turn embedded in states as institutions of political authority. Together, they form an integrated mechanism of governance of global socio-economic space, but their interests do not always converge. Sovereignty remains intact, but "state functions are becoming integrated across jurisdictional boundaries in a way which corresponds to the extension of market structures across borders."

States have long been involved in the establishment and sustenance of the world capitalist system, and since World War II they have been primary promoters of the globalization of capital, securities, and finance (Polanyi, 1944). States through various processes and institutions of collaboration regulate some of these markets, although as Underhill demonstrates, they do so in a manner that usually serves the interests of the major economic players. Regulations that promote economic stability, however, may also serve the interests of states and of the general welfare. If we take Rosenau's argument about increased analytical skills of ordinary people seriously, then we can assume that numerous social groups that do not accept the notions of the public interest as defined by private capital will express their points of view as well. In countries such as France, Denmark, Norway, and Canada, public resistance to increased international economic integration offers numerous examples. The public outcry against an internationally negotiated treaty on the rights of foreign investors (MAI) was so vigorous that the signing governments had to abandon the project in 1998.

Moreover, it is often in the interests of private economic actors, or indeed of major global markets, to have strong and effective state regulations. Major global companies such as Disney or Microsoft, as Peter Evans (1997: 78) points out, need strong states to enforce property rights and to establish international regulations against piracy of media materials.

> Intellectual property rights are a specific instance of a general point. In the complex exchange of novel intangibles, authoritative normative structures, which are provided in large measure by the state, become the keystones to efficient exchange. The new institutional economics, with its emphasis on the necessity of governance structures and the pervasive importance of institutional frameworks to any kind of economic transactions, further generalizes the argument that efficient markets can exist only in the context of effective and robust nonmarket institutions.

Many sociological and economic observers have noted that governments have reduced their participation in the private sphere or have abandoned attempts to regulate international markets and the agents that create them. Saskia Sassen (2002: 183, 178), for example, argues that the growth of cross-border activities and global actors operating outside the formal interstate system derogates from the competence of governments and of international law, that the world capital market "is succeeding in imposing itself on important aspects of national economic policy making, though . . . some states are more sovereign than others in these matters," and that it is private actors rather than governments that are erecting regulatory devices. Under the influence of global economic players and the demands of "the market," states have been involved in a major project to downsize themselves. All of this suggests a retrenchment of state multifunctionality, and as with Susan Strange, a zero-sum loss of state authority in favor of non-state actors and global markets.

Many governments have indeed discovered that their extensive penetration of private markets, as indicated through public ownership of telecommunications, airlines, and railroads, power utilities and other types of enterprises, has led to waste, mismanagement, and chronic subsidies borne by taxpayers. But that they should divest themselves of such assets is not the result only of political pressures by national and global corporations or markets. Taxpayers have been equally insistent on major scaling down of direct government ownership and, in some cases, of over-extensive government regulation of private concerns. But if states are divesting themselves of monopolies and other economic facilities, or de-regulating some economic sectors (sometimes with disastrous results), does this imply that they are losing their authority or sovereignty? Any answer is debatable, but that debate at least must acknowledge the critical distinction between autonomy and sovereignty.

Another problem with the state transformation or obsolescence argument is that it offers no benchmarks. What is the standard against which states are supposedly "eroding?" Is it the early modern Westphalian state that was typically on the verge of bankruptcy, deeply in debt to private financiers, forced to sell public offices in order to obtain revenues, and facing external predation from neighboring states whose boundaries were either unknown or highly contested? Is it the typical nineteenth-century state whose functions extended no further than providing national security, a judicial system, and some minor economic regulation and stimulation? Is it the state typical of the 1920s, where now education and a few welfare services were added to the previous limited list of government functions? The "welfare state" – that state which takes upon itself the responsibility for sustaining individuals in security from cradle to grave – is primarily an invention of the 1930s (with German precedents in the previous century), a response to the immense social tragedies attending the world depression. It was not institutionalized in most industrial states until well after the end of World War II. If we use the early twentieth-century state as our benchmark, then by almost any measure the state has grown dramatically in the depth and scope of its activities and continues to do so. If we use 1960 as our standard, then in some states there has been some retrenchment of state activities. But in most states the figures indicate a *slowing down of the rate of growth of state functions but no decline.* Indeed, for most industrial countries, social security transfers as a percentage of GDP actually increased through the 1970s and 1980s (Weiss, 1998: 106). This hardly comprises evidence of the transformation or obsolescence of the state. For every government program that has been downsized, or for every government monopoly that has been privatized, there are dozens of new types of government programs and initiatives (Crouch and Streeck, 1997). Individuals in modern states habitually turn to their governments to solve an extraordinarily wide range of problems, from the personal (e.g., state-sponsored marriage counseling facilities) to the commercial (e.g., government subsidization of sports facilities). Most do not turn to agents or programs outside of the state. The amazing growth of state bureaucracy throughout the twentieth century and early into this one continues unabated and indicates the growing, not lessening, demand for state services.[12] Throughout the OECD world, the proportion of national income comprising government spending has gone up steadily since the beginning of the twentieth century, and even during the recent era of globalization the figures continue to increase (*The Economist*, September 20, 1997: 7). Over the course of the twentieth century the average share of government spending to national income has increased from 8 percent to almost 50 percent, with no diminution as a result of globalization (Wolf, 2001: 185). This indicates an extraordinarily high range of state functions, and a high degree of state institutionalization and acceptance of state authority.

The major exception to the generalization is the case of weak and collapsing states, where individuals facing major natural disasters or

---

[12] Throughout Europe since World War II the growth of the civil service has significantly outstripped the growth of the labor force. For example, between 1960 and 1985 in Germany, the figure for civil service increase was 70 percent compared with 5 percent for the labor force; for Finland, it was 111 percent compared with 17.5 percent; for Belgium, 57 percent compared with 15 percent (*The Economist*, September 20, 1997: 7).

humanitarian emergencies come to rely on international agencies rather than on their own state for relief or protection. In the past decades, international agencies such as the World Health Organization, the United Nations Commission for Refugees, or transnational associations such as Médecins sans frontières have saved millions of lives. They have assumed some of the functions of states. Yet, this does not indicate the end of the Westphalian state as much as the incapacity of some newer and weaker states to provide the services expected of them. The goal of these international organizations or associations is not to replace states, but ultimately to strengthen them. The ultimate purpose of international rescue efforts is the maintenance of statehood.

Rosenau's suggestion that shifting loyalties within the state are evidence of its erosion requires similar interrogation. There is, first, confusion between loyalty to a state and support of a government. Increased political participation, a widespread sense of public confidence, and increasing intellectual skills that enable citizens to judge government performance and sometimes to oust them indicates little about loyalty to the state. In virtually every polity organized as a state, there are opponents of government. In parliamentary systems, they are organized as "the loyal opposition." Millions join political parties that seek to replace incumbents. This is normal. Only in cases of secession do we see the withdrawal of loyalty to the state. Here, separatists and secessionists deny legitimacy to the state and seek to create a state of their own. But this is the key point. They are not denying the legitimacy of statehood as such, but only of a particular state. Millions in the world today seek the goal of separate statehood, whether in Sri Lanka, Kashmir, Punjab, Quebec, Palestine, Kurdistan, and many other places. And, while it is the case that people today may find it somewhat easier to change citizenship than fifty years ago, exiting from one state to another does not indicate erosion of the state. People who leave a state necessarily have to go to another state. The only alternative is a refugee camp or a center for stateless people. We cannot withdraw from statehood and citizenship today. In contrast, three hundred years ago – before the introduction of the concept of citizenship and the issuance of passports – it was easy.

Does the illicit drug trade, estimated to involve purchases and profits close to one trillion dollars annually and directly costing taxpayers hundreds of million dollars to control (not very successfully), indicate the loss of state authority? There is a conceptual problem here as well. First, it is states themselves that have created the problem by making the trade and use of *stupefiants*[13] illegal. The prohibition of alcohol in the Scandinavian countries and the United States in the 1920s led to widespread rum-running and international trafficking in liquor. Efforts to enforce anti-alcohol regulations were generally as ineffective as those in relation to the trade in *stupefiants* today. Only if we assume that states have been, are, and should be omnipotent – a standard against which we can measure – could we successfully argue that the inability to control the trade in *stupefiants* represents a retreat of the state. If the state did for smoking or alcohol what it has done for *stupefiants*, we would have exactly the same problem but on a more massive scale. That a state cannot effectively enforce such bans hardly warrants the conclusion that it is declining, disappearing, or transforming. *The argument sets the bar of state capacity far too high.* The failure to control effectively all trafficking in drugs may be more indicative of impossible goals than of a "retreat" of state authority.

The case for complexity

The types of changes we have seen in the contemporary state have been primarily related to the extension and proliferation of government activities, that is, to growing complexity rather than to transformation. The odds are pretty good that states as we know them will be around for a lot longer than most TNCs, transnational criminal groups, and even international organizations. The state remains the primary agent of international relationships and is the only one that has the quality and status of sovereignty. It is primarily states that create and sustain international institutions such as diplomacy, trade, international law, and the like. It is primarily states, through their practices and the ideas, beliefs, and norms that underlie them, that sustain and change those institutions. Other types of entities (e.g., banks) may create private international institutions of various kinds, but they seek to regulate only a single domain. In many cases, these sets of regulations do not *replace* the activities of states, but supplement them, or are entirely new. Collapsed or failed states show us what life would be like without states. In the absence of other more attractive alternatives, none of which seems to be on the horizon, we remain the inhabitants of an international society of states. They are much more complex than their Westphalian era

---

[13] I prefer the French term for mind-altering drugs because it more clearly indicates the consequences of their use and does not confuse them with legitimate medicines.

predecessors. They have changed significantly, particularly in the bases of legitimacy and loyalty and in the scope of state functions, but their seventeenth- eighteenth- and nineteenth-century territorial, ideological, and normative roots are easily recognizable.

The unique case of the European Union offers obvious exceptions to the generalization. Spain, for example, has ceded some of its autonomy in foreign policy to the EU's "Common Foreign and Security Policy" and to NATO, monetary policy to the European Central Bank, and control of borders to the Schengen Agreement. At the subnational level, the Basque Country and Catalonia are setting up their own police forces and raising their own taxes. Competence for health, education, and social policies has been delegated either to Brussels or to regional governments (Riordan, 2003: 79). This looks dramatic enough, but in part it resembles more unique forms of federalism or of "multilevel governance" (Sørensen, 2001: 88) than a true "hollowing out" of the state. All this is arguable, but whatever the case, the forms and processes of European integration have not become universal prototypes. To date, Europe is *sui generis*.

The case for complexity as the major form of change in the state is not difficult to sustain on an empirical basis. The requirements of statehood – differentiation, territoriality, institutionalization, and continuity, for example – have been met by a large proportion of states in the contemporary international system. Weak or collapsing states are the exception. It is in the area of multifunctionality, however, where the argument for complexity is most compelling. The government of the average state today sustains an immense variety of programs, interests, purposes, and undertakings. This is in stark contrast to the seventeenth-century dynastic state that was organized around only four major tasks: defense, justice, minor amounts of infrastructure development, and economic regulation. The vast area of social welfare was filled by the church, by a few non-religious but private agencies, and by the extended family. The promotion of the arts and culture was a realm of noble and princely activity, that is, a private realm, rather than a matter of the state. This was also the case for education, where it was monopolized by the church. The reader can easily identify scores of other state functions today that did not exist in the dynastic state. Any catalogue of programs organized and funded by national governments in an average country is immense. It ranges from catching rats to exploring outer space.[14]

---

[14] Recent studies have developed interesting and important typologies of states, and demonstrate how state types have important consequences for foreign policy objectives

Explaining change

Accounting for the growth of complexity in the state is no simple manner and would require several treatises, but we can mention briefly at least three major sources: (1) war; (2) economic depression; and (3) ideas such as self-rule, self-determination, and sovereignty.

Charles Tilly (1990: 32) has claimed that "the state makes war and war makes the state." Tilly's aphorism refers to the symbiotic processes by which monarchs of the seventeenth century developed standing armies to protect their realms from external predation and also to monopolize political authority at home. Armed forces cost a great deal, and in order to raise funds to build and sustain them, dynasts had to expand bureaucracies and to tap numerous sources of wealth within their societies. The needs of defense thus led to the growth and development of the state apparatus.

But wars have been a great state-maker in another sense as well. Most pre-1945 states were born and consolidated through violent means, either through revolution or by classical wars between states. Many states disappeared through the same means. To take some prominent examples. Holland (the United Provinces) became independent after a long war of "liberation" from Spain in the mid-seventeenth century. The United States became a state through the same means, as did the countries of South America. Italy and Germany became unified through major wars in the mid-nineteenth century. Cuba fought a lengthy war of independence against Spain, but did not achieve its goal until the Spanish-American war ended. The states of central Europe were born from the ashes of the Great War. And, as we will see in chapter 8, World War II provided a major boost to the independence movements of dozens of British, French, Dutch, American, and Italian colonies. War has been the greatest source and means of state-creation, as well as state-consolidation.

Economic depression was a major source of the profound growing complexity of state tasks in the twentieth century. Some of the ideas and practices of the welfare state appeared in Europe (particularly in

and international problems. Rodney Bruce Hall (1999) distinguishes between territorial-sovereign states and national-sovereign states. Georg Sørensen (2001) explores the sources and consequences of the modern state, the post-colonial state, and the post-modern state. While these typologies are significant for some kinds of analysis, all of the different types, with the possible exception of failed states, meet the criteria of statehood outlined at the beginning of the chapter. Those criteria thus emphasize continuity rather than change, but they also establish the crucial distinctions between states and other types of polities. They are more important for an institutional analysis such as this one.

Germany) already in the 1870s, but the massive extension of state activity in the economic and social realms was primarily a product of the Great Depression of the 1930s. In the twentieth century the welfare state replaced the liberal model of the minimal state that predominated in much of Europe in the nineteenth century. It remains as the most typical form of collective governance, characterized by a huge array of government programs, complicated bureaucracies to administer them, and massive taxation to pay for them.

The ideas of and belief in self-rule and self-determination also account for many of the changes we have characterized as complexity. The implementation of the self-rule principle has given the state a basis in popular legitimacy that it lacked in the seventeenth century. Although we rarely think about it, we accept public authority because it is authority emanating from "our own," that is, government leaders who share our nationality and, for the most part, who were elected to exercise the authority. In the twentieth century, wherever rule was not of "our own," authority has been challenged and in most cases overthrown. The Palestinians, like Indians in the 1940s, Kenyans in the 1950s, and Mozambicans in the 1960s, do not accept "alien" rule, which means that if it is exercised at all, it is usually through coercion and force. Self-rule is the ideological foundation for the vast growth of state tasks in the past century. Citizens demand government services and assent to taxation to pay for them. Governments that are perceived as "occupiers" neither want to provide those services nor would they be likely to obtain tax revenues from recalcitrant populations. The whole idea that the state is a welfare organization rests on the assumption of self-rule.

The state is both a foundational institution and exclusive agent of international political relationships. Unlike its seventeenth-century predecessors, which had to compete (and sometimes failed to do so successfully) with numerous domestic and external agents, many of whom were wealthy and well-armed, its ability to survive in its capacity as the sole legal and sovereign agent in international institutions is not in serious jeopardy today. The state as an agent was never static in terms of practices, norms, and ideas. But as I have sought to demonstrate, those components of an institution are stronger than in previous eras. Statehood has a legal and ideological sanctity that it did not enjoy in previous eras. Entire international organizations have as their main purpose the protection of states, that is, guaranteeing or protecting their independence, territorial integrity, and sovereignty. We define "international security" primarily in terms of the security of states rather than the security of other forms of human association and organization.[15] This situation may of course change but there is not yet sufficient evidence to sustain the argument of state obsolescence. The argument for transformation – less often articulated – would have to compile impressive evidence that the requirements of statehood such as territoriality and differentiation of the public and private are no longer being met by current polities. In the meantime we must recognize that almost two hundred states populate the contemporary world. Some are successful in helping to provide the "good life" for their citizens. Others are barely getting along, while a few have collapsed. But whatever their fortunes, for most people most of the time, the "good life" is made possible primarily within the state and not through other types of organizations.

---

[15] The new emphasis on "human security" might seem to challenge this proposition, but it seems that most of the relevant threats in this new repertoire exist in weak states where authority has collapsed or is waning. In most cases, "human security" cannot be guaranteed or protected in the absence of state authority.

3   Territoriality

One essential attribute of our definition of statehood is fixed territoriality. Like the state itself, this is a relatively new phenomenon, one that is historically unique. The lineal, surveyed borders that separate contemporary states are a practice going back only to the seventeenth century. Territorial limits of most historical empires, traditional kingdoms, city-states, and tribal and lineage groups were mostly floating zones of indeterminate extent. Traditional Chinese conceptions of territory, for example, bore little relation to those that underlie the doctrines of contemporary international law. For them, territory was defined primarily in cultural terms. The Chinese world was one of hierarchy, with the Han civilization in the middle and the barbarians on the peripheries. Since there was constant intermingling and movement of populations, the exact location between centers and peripheries could not be established in lineal terms. Malcolm Anderson (1996: 88) explains:

> Imperial China . . . held the view that the empire had two frontiers, an inner and an outer. The latter was the limit, sometimes fanciful, of Chinese influence or, as in the steppes of central Asia, indicated the limit of temporary Chinese occupation. The outer limits of Chinese influence did not necessarily imply that the Chinese had the intention of occupying the territory up to this frontier. It was a conception of the boundaries of "the Chinese world."

China was typical of pre-modern polities in the sense that its rulers defined themselves primarily in terms of centers rather than peripheries. Pre-modern polities had neither the surveillance capacity to monitor what was going on in their realms nor guards and other means of controlling ingress and egress. For example, the Great Wall was never a border in the contemporary sense, but rather a defensive construction and a base for controlling nomadic peoples. In neither the Roman nor Chinese walls, do we find the predecessors to modern borders. They were the outer extensions of an "in-depth" defensive system (cf., Kratochwil, 1986: 35; Giddens, 1987: 51).

In the historical Muslim societies, the relevant conceptions of space were religious and cultural. The contemporary notion of national boundaries has no parallel in historic Koranic cultures. Dividing lines were conceived more as truce lines in the struggle between the *umma*, or Muslim religious community, and the infidels. Hence, if one looks at the history of the Caliphates and the Ottoman Empire, mental lines representing some notion of borders or frontiers shifted from year to year as the military and proselytizing fortunes of the Muslims waxed and waned. Again, there is no parallel to modern conceptions of territoriality that include the formalized legal and delimited separation of political jurisdictions.

Territorial practices varied as much as conceptions. They ranged from the indifference to and irrelevance of the hinterlands and wastes of a realm, where there was little to struggle about, to unlimited but temporary imperial expansion, as in the case of the Mongol invasions of the Russian steppes, south and central Asia, through Persia, and into central Europe. These empires, with no demarcated limits, seldom outlived the conquerors. More limited conflicts over spatial definition often occurred between more stable polities, such as the Greek city-states.

These historical polities lacked borders for a variety of reasons, including sparse transactions in the peripheries, lack of maps and surveying technology, no clear notions of location, undeveloped administrative and bureaucratic organizations far from the imperial centers, and scarcity of manpower to monitor and control vast frontier regions.[1] For constantly moving polities such as the Mongols of the thirteenth and fourteenth centuries, the culture had no concept of fixed territoriality. It was a moving polity that expanded and contracted according to the fortunes of military conquest, one that ultimately collapsed within several generations after the death of its most famous or infamous leader, Genghis Khan.

---

[1] Many other types of polities had rough notions of territorial limits, but they bore little resemblance to contemporary lines between states. For example, among the ancient Hawaiians, the borders of subchiefdoms (*ali'i*) were often ragged mountain ridges. Where such prominent physical details were not present, the Hawaiians invented other devices for identification. One included the path followed by a stone rolling down a hill, that is, the fall line. Few people knew where it was located, and it was seldom demarcated.

The historical evidence indicates the rarity of norms, rules, or regulations pertaining to territory. There were no conceptions of territorial rights, or of mutually recognized titles to permanent and exclusive possession. Except among the Greeks and Romans, there were no concepts of citizenship. Pre-modern polities had no passports, and ingress and egress by traders, nomads, religious leaders, pirates, and military adventurers was seldom monitored and even more rarely controlled. In the absence of administrative capacity to establish and maintain authority over defined spaces, of notions of territorial rights, and with effective political power concentrated in imperial cities and other centers, territorial limits were among the most poorly defined and most movable of all human arrangements.

The bordering of Europe

The seventeenth-century cartographer Vincenzo Coronelli crafted an immense globe of the world that sits today in the Doge's palace in Venice. It dates from 1620. It portrays all major geographic features of Europe such as mountains and rivers, as well as the main centers of human habitation, that is, the major cities of the era. It also uses traditional designations of geographical regions, such as Gallica, Germania, and Italia. But borders are notable by their absence. There are no lines except for one that was drawn later between France and Spain. An eighteenth-century tourist probably placed it there. During the height of the Thirty Years War (1618–48), another Venetian artist, Menias, prepared a copper engraving *"Nova et Accurata Ducatus Venitian"* that depicted all of northern Italy, southern Germany, Switzerland, and a small part of eastern France. There are no frontiers, only the general regional designations. The Duchy of Tuscany, for example, has no borders. There is only a name imprinted on the map designating a general area.

When we move forward to the late eighteenth century to visit the great galleries of royal estates, we find maps depicting the territories making up the royal kingdoms and principalities of the day. We would see, in fact, formal lines separating one state from the other. They are borders in the modern sense. What happened in the 150 years between Coronelli's or Menias' depiction of the world and Europe, and the maps of the late eighteenth century? How did the states of Europe become territorially defined? How did the borderless European world of the early seventeenth century become transformed into the clearly delineated, bordered states system of the late eighteenth century? Borders are a human institution. They are an invention of the early modern period of European history. Today, we take them for granted, but they were created for very specific purposes having to do with the creation of states and bringing into effect the main ideas associated with statehood and sovereignty.

Sixteenth-century ideas of territoriality

Sixteenth-century Europe was characterized by political heterogeneity. The polities of the era included nascent states, principalities, leagues of cities, empires, church territories, large and small private estates and free cities. Most had functions associated today with the concept of sovereignty: they minted their own coins, they had local laws and law-making bodies, many had their own military establishments, and most had taxing power. The kingdom of France existed as a legal entity, but it was not a unified, territorial whole. The appropriate metaphor is a Swiss cheese. The kingdom was solid enough, but within it resided numerous political jurisdictions that were mini-sovereigns. For example, a local lord, Charles de Nevers, held numerous estates and towns within France and behaved as if he were sovereign over them. He minted his own coins, dispensed justice within his realms, and maintained armed forces. He was literally a sovereign within a sovereign until 1637 (Parrot, 1997). So were the principality of Bearn and the kingdom of Navarre, until they were formally incorporated into France about the time Coronelli was constructing his globe. The papal territories of Avignon and Comtat Venaissin, surrounded by France, did not become part of France until 1791 as the result of military occupation and a later plebiscite. France was by no means untypical. During these same years, Prussia was akin to an archipelago, with three main non-contiguous territories stretching from the Rhine all the way to Poland. The Holy Roman Empire was an extraordinarily complex family association of estates, principalities, and free cities. It was not even mapped as a single entity until 1730 and could not be termed a state in the modern sense until well into the nineteenth century (Vann, 1992; Klingenstein, 1997). Reflecting these characteristics of the polities of the era, maps of the latter part of the sixteenth century were used primarily to record sheep or cattle walks and boundaries of winter grazing locations, town plans, and fortifications – but not political jurisdictions. The first composite maps of whole administrative systems in Italia date only to about 1765 (Marino, 1992: 14).

The European political world in Coronelli's time was constituted of many different types of realms that were not so much prototypes of modern states as legal concepts, personal possessions, and patrimonies. Legal possession of and claims for realms – not specific territories – were based on numerous criteria, including marriage, succession, effective control, the religion of the inhabitants, and for the New World, *terra nullius*. Prior to the eighteenth century, moreover, the owners of these poorly articulated estates were often vassals of two or more superiors. Their exact legal status was thus open to frequent contestation, and often to conquest by those with superior military capabilities.

Formal lines designating distinct and exclusive jurisdictions were almost impossible in such circumstances because territorial distinctions, to the extent that they existed at all, were overlain by "a mass of traditional rights, claims to exercise jurisdiction or to collect dues and taxes of various kinds, which made the modern idea of a frontier scarcely applicable" (Anderson, 1993: 97). When territories were exchanged, ceded, joined through marriage, or conquered, they went as entire local administrative divisions or patrimonies, not as pieces of earth defined by lines drawn on a map. In France, for example, these were *baillages, prévotés, sénéchaussées*, or *communes*. When ownership was changed, the parties always insisted that their new lords would honor all ancient rights and freedoms.

The way centralizing monarchs began to perceive their realms in the late sixteenth and early seventeenth centuries explains in part the rise of clearly delimited borders. The major conceptual transformation was from a realm as a complicated system of often non-contiguous mutual obligations and legal status, to a centralized, contiguous territory in which the royal writ trumped local rights and traditions, as well as personal obligations (e.g., fiefdoms). The re-visioning of territory was the natural concomitant to the claims of sovereignty that kings and lesser figures were beginning to make. Maps helped the rising sovereigns envision their realms in spatial rather than legal terms. As Vann (1992: 162) has pointed out, "[maps reflected] first, a desire to govern more effectively; second, a perceived need for spatial abstraction of their own authority . . . [T]hey were concrete statements of political rights, statements now deemed important to those who felt compelled to define themselves by a marked separation from their neighbors."

Early border practices

The practice of formally demarcating borders began shortly after the end of the Thirty Years War (1648). In that period, the Swedish crown and the Elector of Brandenburg agreed to define the border between Swedish

Pomerania and Brandenburg with boundary stones. The Treaty of the Pyrenees (1659), ending yet another of Louis XIV's wars with Spain, established a commission to demarcate the Franco-Spanish frontier, a task that was not completed until the mid-nineteenth century.[2] The Peace of Ryswick (1697) was the earliest occasion on which a line replaced legal rights in the terms of a treaty (Barber, 1997: 82). At the same time, the Ottoman Empire began to define itself in geographic terms when, after the 1699 Treaty of Carlowitz, it agreed to membership in a joint commission to demarcate its frontiers with the Habsburg Empire. In 1718 the Habsburg emperor Charles IV and the Dutch Republic negotiated a territorial settlement over their contiguous territories in the southern Netherlands. It not only defined lineal borders in the text of a treaty, but also identified them with an attached map (Anderson, 1993: 96). Throughout the remainder of the eighteenth century, all states in Europe surveyed and established territorial limits, tidied up the numerous enclaves that existed on both sides of putative borders, and through exchanges and partitions, generally created the precedents of modern lineal frontiers. By the mid-eighteenth century, approximately, borders were "ceasing to be an area and tending to become a line" (Clark, 1947: 143).

Why borders?

The territorial enclosure of early modern European states was part of the larger transformation of the medieval Christian hierarchical order, with the pope and Holy Roman Emperor sharing nominal authority over the complex jumble of polities, into the independent states system that emerged in the sixteenth and seventeenth centuries. The secular rulers over the diverse realms of Europe had been challenging both papal and lower-level vassals and free cities since the twelfth century, sometimes with doctrinal arguments about sovereignty, and more frequently with bribes, coercion, and armed force. All of this was part of the great project that culminated in the highly centralized, territorially defined polities that we know today as states. Sovereignty claims – supreme legal authority over a defined territory – had been appearing for centuries going

---

[2] Significantly, the border commission initially arranged for the exchange of jurisdictions between some villages in the Cerdanya region, thus creating pockets of French authority within Spain and vice versa. It did not yet imagine a straight line dividing the two kingdoms. For details, see Sahlins (1998) and Anderson (1993: 98).

back to the medieval era, but for the most part they were only claims. In practical terms those who made these claims wanted to hold a monopoly over several functional areas, including the right to create nobles, to issue coins, administer justice, and create and sustain a permanent military establishment. It took several centuries to turn claims into reality. Part of the sovereignty game (see next chapter) was to define more precisely where "national" law would prevail over foreign and local laws and jurisdictions. This implied drawing lines and abolishing the myriad principalities, free cities, duchies, church territories, and private estates that stood as little sovereignties of their own.

Prior to the fifteenth century, rulers could not "see" their realms unless they were very small. They had few ideas about the limits; frontier zones were outside the purview of judicial, administrative, or military control; and as the nascent states tried to convert claims into reality, they needed above all tax revenues. Without maps or censuses, they had little capacity to raise necessary funds except from the core areas of their domains. New surveying techniques and developments in cartography in the sixteenth and seventeenth centuries greatly aided the processes of political centralization. Maps became a major tool in the sovereigns' rise to political predominance. They not only identified the main physical features of the realm, but also helped rulers visualize the Swiss cheese character of their possessions, and thus the necessity to centralize the administrative and judicial systems. If a ruler could "see" the outlying regions of his realms he could form opinions about them and take decisions about specific issues relating to them with less need to defer to the opinions of local assemblies and magnates (Barber, 1997: 83). Maps were also propaganda weapons. They visually demonstrated the comparative physical proportions of the various kingdoms and displayed their prestige.

Maps charted the changing perceptions and requirements of sovereignty (Barber, 1997: 76–7). But because surveys were very expensive in the seventeenth century, only those rulers with necessary finances could afford detailed maps of their realms. Further technological innovations in surveying techniques reduced costs, and in the usual manner that eighteenth-century sovereigns copied each other's practices and pretensions, most sovereigns had demarcated their realms by the late eighteenth century. The first printed map explicitly intended to show all the lands ruled by the Austrian Habsburgs as one distinct unit rather than as a congeries of provinces, church territories, estates, and principalities did not appear until 1730. This was the first public image of the

Habsburg Empire as a separate political unit, as distinct from the old German imperial ideal. Maps had thus become important symbols of sovereignty.

But not all maps were equal in political value. While maps long pre-dated the seventeenth century, their accuracy was notably deficient. Exact location depended upon the development of accurate survey-ing techniques and the conceptual definition of longitude and latitude. While both concepts go back to the times of the Greeks, they were not seriously investigated until the tenth century by the Arab scholar al-Biruni. But his conceptual breakthroughs could not serve cartogra-phy adequately because of the lack of measurement devices. These had to wait until the late seventeenth and early eighteenth century, when the Académie Royale in France and the Royal Academy in the United Kingdom provided the necessary investments for their development (by way of competitions) (O'Connor and Robertson, 1997). Armed with rea-sonably precise technology for identifying location, it was now possible to establish borders with a previously unknown precision – particularly where they did not coincide with prominent physical features such as rivers and coastlines. The 1815 Canada–United States border was among the first to be a straight line based on a latitude, a choice that was not available prior to the eighteenth century.

A third explanation for the development of borders and the territorial enclosure of sovereigns was defense. The invention of the cannon had a great deal to do with the demise of the walled town, garrison, and castle as units of defense. From the fifteenth century to present times, the whole idea of defense changed from protection of distinct points to protection of the entire realm or of major strategic areas that required lin-eal protection. This implied drawing lines and preparing defenses along extensive perimeters. The first lineal frontiers of Europe appeared in the flat regions separating France, the United Provinces, and the Austrian Netherlands. These areas had been scenes of repeated military activities and served as major avenues for attack. Entire areas or lines rather than cities or towns had to be protected.

Territorial practices in seventeenth- and eighteenth-century Europe

Developing cartographic and surveying technologies helped provide visual impressions of political space, but these did not necessarily erase legal claims and ancient titles. Royal figures, for example, did not reduce their search for contiguity or additions to their realms through claims of inheritance or succession. On the contrary, as Europe's population, trade, and commerce began to expand after the disasters of the Thirty Years War, territory became a prime source of revenues necessary to further the great project of state consolidation. Not surprisingly, change of territorial ownership was one of the hallmarks of European diplomacy in the years after Westphalia. It was achieved through at least six major means.

Conquest. The states of the era sought territorial expansion for a variety of reasons, including reaching "natural" (e.g., defensible) frontiers, consolidating disparate territories into a single state, and gaining population for a tax base. Territorial changes resulting from military victory were standard practice. All diplomats simply *assumed* that victory in war would bring territorial gains. No post-war settlement in this era lacks territorial revision. A list of Napoleon's territorial adjustments between 1798 and 1808 – more than thirty in all – is truly startling from today's perspectives. They included, among others, the annexation by the kingdom of Italy (which Napoleon placed under his own crown) of Venetia, Urbino, Macerata, Ancona, and Camerino, the Trentino and south Tyrol. Huge tracts of land were torn away or attached to Napoleon's rearrangements throughout the continent. In some cases, old realms were extinguished; in others, major states such as Prussia were downsized to roughly one-half their previous size (Ellis, 1991: 50–2). In the period between Westphalia and the 1815 Treaty of Vienna, conflicting territorial claims were the source of more than 60 percent of the wars (Holsti, 1991: chs. 3–5, pp. 308–11).

Partition. In order to maintain a rough balance of power on the continent, the great powers collusively partitioned territories amongst themselves. The most famous case was the three partitions of Poland in 1772, 1792, and 1795 by Austria, Prussia, and Russia. The last partition effectively ended the independent existence of a Polish state. The partitions were effected through bilateral and multilateral diplomacy without, of course, the consent of the authorities whose territories were being given away.

Compensation. The great powers of the eighteenth century were also royal powers. The honor, prestige, and status of dynasts were intimately linked with diplomatic practices and wars. Any territorial changes – and they were ubiquitous during the era – reflected not only on the power of governments, but also on their prestige. Hence, it was an unwritten diplomatic rule that if one power made territorial adjustments through conquest or other means, it had an obligation to compensate other powers that made claims. This it did through offering parts of its conquest, or even other territories over which it had no legal jurisdiction. In the Peace of Loeben (1797), Napoleon agreed to deliver Venice (an independent, neutral power over which he had no jurisdiction) to Austria in compensation for his conquest of the Austrian Netherlands (Wight, 1978: 186). The practice of compensation continued well into the nineteenth century. In the Treaty of Berlin formally terminating the Russo-Turkish war in 1878, for example, Austria received Bosnia and Herzegovina and Great Britain received Cyprus as compensation for gains Russia made against the sultan. In the 1915 Treaty of London Great Britain promised compensation to Italy in Somaliland for gains it might make through the war.

Sale. Territory was also for sale. Particularly in colonial areas, it was a commodity. In the late eighteenth century, Spain sold the Louisiana Territory to France, which during Napoleon's rampage across Europe sold it in turn to the new United States (1806). The United States purchased Florida from Spain in 1819. Forty-eight years later the Russian tsar, through the Russian American Company, sold Alaska to the United States for $7 million, a transaction which at the time was roundly condemned by Americans as "Seward's (the American secretary of state's) folly."

Marriage. Since the predominant conception of territory through the seventeenth century was that of a personal possession (the realm as real estate), a royal marriage could combine two distinct territories into a single jurisdiction, or a piece of territory was considered part of a dowry that went along with the owner.

Exchange. Even late into the nineteenth century territory was a diplomatic currency, but one that had to involve equal values. Since the game of international politics was frequently of a zero-sum character, territorial exchanges were carefully crafted to make certain that one party did not gain greater benefits through exchange than the other did. One prominent example was in 1720 when the Duke of Savoy exchanged with the Holy Roman Emperor the kingdom of Sicily for the kingdom of Sardinia. In 1890 Germany received Heligoland from Great Britain in exchange for the latter's protectorates over Zanzibar and Witu.

We might mention a seventh form of territorial change, but it occurred only once in modern European history so it can hardly be termed a practice. This refers to Great Britain's unilateral cession of the Ionian islands to Greece in 1864.[3]

Norms and rules

Rules and norms associated with territory reflected the ideals of dynastic sovereignty. The territorially defined political space was one of *exclusive* legal jurisdiction. In the Treaties of Westphalia, both the pope and the Holy Roman Emperor had been stripped of their claims to temporal jurisdiction over secular concerns of the dynasts and princes. Embarrassing anomalies remained (e.g., Swedish possessions in northern Germany) well into the nineteenth century, but the general rule of a demarcated exclusive territorial jurisdiction was fully accepted as an essential characteristic of sovereignty by the late seventeenth century.

A second rule was conventional rather than legal: delimiting borders is a process involving mutual consent. Except during war (see below), territorial boundaries were to be negotiated. The actual drawing of lines was left to technical experts. In the case of forced annexations or other forms of territorial revision, after the seventeenth century the convention was that the local inhabitants would be granted the right to stay under the new authority or to move into the remaining jurisdictions of the ceding state (Giddens, 1987: 88–9).

Finally, the conventions and rules of the era specified that until a formal disposition of territory was made through a negotiated treaty, there was a regime that involved certain rights and responsibilities of the occupying power.

By the eighteenth century, we can say that territory was beginning to become institutionalized. *Ideas* about territory were distinct from those that prevailed in earlier eras. The *norm* of exclusive territorial jurisdiction critically replaced medieval notions of overlapping jurisdictions. Certain *practices*, all involving the careful delimitation of a bounded realm in precise terms, came into being as part of the state-building process. These practices were extended as well to colonial jurisdictions. And finally, there were numerous derivative rules and norms associated with state jurisdiction and with the change in status of any territories. Yet, because territories were sold, partitioned, exchanged, and conquered with abandon, the institution was weak. Territory had great patrimonial value but little social value. The practices relating to territory were

---

[3] For a detailed account of nineteenth-century territorial revisions, see Crutwell (1937).

more analogous to commerce and conquest than to the modern notion of "territorial integrity" that is a hallmark of all major international security organizations. We turn to the foundational institution of territory in the contemporary era and we can see that the trajectory has been toward increasing strength rather than erosion.

Changing ideas of territory: from the limits of realms to lines of nations

The main change in ideas about territory concerned the basis of claims to them. Prior to the eighteenth century, territories as the personal possessions of dynasts and the diverse polities of the era were constantly subject to challenge. These challenges were primarily of a legal character (who has the better or more just claim to succeed in a particular jurisdiction, or to gain new territory). By the eighteenth century, claims to territory were increasingly phrased in the terminology of *state* requirements such as defense, state-building, creating a contiguous state territory, and the like. "Territory no longer resulted from a claim; the claim resulted from [other] demands for territory" (Holsti, 1991: 92). But of all the different types of aspirations and purposes for which the various claims arose, none denoted a *community or social right* to territory.

Prior to the French Revolution, the common people of European states were subjects of a queen, king, or prince, inhabitants of a village, town, province, *pays*, *Land*, or region, and minimally the denizens of a national political community. Hobbes spoke of a "Common-wealth," without defining it, while others discussed "kingdoms," meaning a particular type of patrimonial family that rightfully ruled over a particular realm. We have seen how territorial change was a prominent feature of these polities. The territorial exchanges, sales, partitions, and compensations could be transacted with a minimum of public outcry or fuss. The royal figure, in a sense, had the right to claim or dispose of possessions as he or she saw fit and the people were not consulted about such matters. Until the late seventeenth and early eighteenth century, the common conception of territory was that of a personal possession of the royal figure, the *dominium* of the monarch. In a few other places, territory was the possession of the state, but symbolized by the monarch. Transfers of territory, whether by conquest, cession, sale, or gift, included not just land, but all of its inhabitants. The new owner could do with them whatever he or she wished, because it was now his or her own estate

(Korman, 1996: 30–1). Even as late as 1815 at the Congress of Vienna, the territorial map of Europe was reconfigured to create a spatial and population balance of power on the continent. Popular sentiment, even if there was an organized expression of it, was not taken into consideration in redrawing the map. The overriding concerns were those of strategy and status.

During the remainder of the century, however, ideas about territory underwent a transformation. The idea of territory as an exclusive, bounded legal realm remained, but a great deal more was grafted on to it. Under the influence of nationalism and Romanticism, a link between a "people" and territory became imprinted in popular discourse. The songs, music, images, poetry, and literature of Romantic nationalism were replete with territorial imagery (Murphy, 1996: 97). How could Bohemia be disassociated from the Moldau? Finnish music, painting, and poetry of the late nineteenth century were filled with the images and moods of the forest and lakes. Wagner's operas involved the tales of conflict, fury, and redemption of mythical Norse figures and gods within a mountainous and wooded landscape that was inescapably Germanic. Nationalists spoke increasingly of the "homeland," "fatherland," or "motherland," concepts that bring forth emotions entirely different from those of the "realm," "common-wealth" or kingdom. Territory was no longer a royal possession, claims against which in the dynastic era were based on inheritance, succession, treaties, and other legal criteria, but a vessel that contains a people with distinct languages, cultures, histories, and (often) religions. The Romantic ideas of territory featured distinctive relationships between geographical characteristics, such as mountains and rivers, and "national character." Territory thus became the most obvious marker of a people and their identity. Moreover, as the republican form of government spread through the continent, territory also became linked to political rights and security. The state provides political goods of increasing diversity (health, education, civil liberties, and the like), and also protection against neighboring predators. Most importantly, the organic connection between geography and a "people" created a moral good in the sense that now the state and its defining territory belong to the people. Popular will thus became the major legitimizing principle for territorial change (cf., Hall, 1999: 169). Robert Jackson and Mark Zacher (1997: 34–5) explain

> [The reluctance to violate the territorial integrity of states is rooted in] the moral idea that states everywhere belong to their populations

whether or not they are democracies. That is the...*norm of self-determination for the civic nation* which does not specify a requirement for a particular form of government – but only that it exists and must be respected. International boundaries are today not only the markers of a state's legal jurisdiction and political control; they are lines that define separate and distinctive nations and peoples which are assumed to have inherent moral value. To interfere with such boundaries without the consent of the peoples involved is to violate the normative doctrine of self-determination based on the civic nation defined by existing state jurisdictions.

The symbolic meaning of territory thus changed radically in the nineteenth century. It developed from concepts of territory similar to a possession and legal realm, to the idea that it is the essential basis and marker of a people's history, culture, identity, and political order. The polity was now a moral good: to challenge ownership of territory was to challenge that good. Peter Taylor (1994: 155) summarizes the shift:

> as a nation the people were deemed to share cultural attributes so that their citizenship was not an arbitrary matter of location . . . It became a collective group with a common destiny. In this way national identity replaced religious identity as the basis for incorporating individuals into the political arena . . . This completely changed the nature of territory, especially the integrity of borders. From being parcels of land transferable between states . . . all territory, including borderlands became inviolate.

The idea of distinct nations also had its political dimensions. What distinguished the French idea of *nation* from the concept of a *royaume* was that the former belonged to the people and the latter to the royal figure. The idea of popular sovereignty created a *stake* for every citizen. It was not just a polity, but *his* or *her* political entity, marked by borders distinguishing it from other entities.

In terms of international relations this meant that territory in Europe could no longer be bartered, exchanged, sold, conquered, or partitioned as in the seventeenth, eighteenth and early nineteenth centuries. A peasant in 1750 could probably not care less about the territorial patrimony of the king. But by 1850, the loss of a province through war was a *national* humiliation or tragedy. Witness the completely different French reactions to the territorial losses of 1815 compared with those of 1871. The downsizing of France to its pre-Napoleonic territorial limits at the Congress of Vienna in 1815 was not a matter of indifference for French elites, but it was accepted with little resistance by the average French citizen. In contrast, the French in general considered the loss of Alsace and Lorraine to Prussia in 1871 a national humiliation and a legitimate basis for a war of revindication. There was no possibility that the French would fail to reincorporate those territories after the German defeat in 1918, even if by so doing they would create all sorts of post-war problems. By the late nineteenth century, popular territorial discourse spoke of "sacred" soil, of the "holy motherland," of *"la patrie,"* and other monikers invoking values that must be defended at all costs. Territory became the very essence of a political and cultural community that is distinct from all others in the world. The people of these spaces no longer identified with a religion, valley, or the village as "their own," but with the entire country. And in order to identify it clearly, it had to be demarcated clearly, even through the most impenetrable mountain ranges, jungles, and deserts. Not one square centimeter of it should be sold or given up without a fight. This transformation of territorial concepts had a profound impact on the texture of international politics throughout the nineteenth century and continues today. As Rodney Bruce Hall (1999: 20) notes:

> In the nationalist era, statesmen were no longer speaking with the voice of a prince, a dynastic house, or of a kingdom or empire – the territorial patrimony of the traditional European conception of sovereignty. Nor did they any longer articulate these interests and goals. The statesmen of nation-states began speaking in the voice of a sovereign people, a collective actor possessed of a collective identity and collective interests and goals . . .

Eighteenth-century territorial practices nevertheless continued into the early twentieth century in the processes of colonization. In the second great era of imperialism (roughly 1880 to 1914), Europeans transplanted their earlier territorial practices outside the continent. They drew lines to separate their colonial spaces from each other. In many instances these lines bore no relationship to indigenous polities, population distributions or movements, settlements, and commerce. In Europe, for example, rivers frequently divided one state from another. On one side were German-speaking peoples, on the other French, Dutch, or Polish. In Africa, on the other hand, the same tribal, clan, or lineage groups usually settled rivers on both sides. Thus, a common European territorial marker – a river – was used to divide a single people into two distinct political jurisdictions. Where there were no "natural" dividing lines, borders were simply straight lines that of course had no meaning at all for nomads or for other highly mobile peoples who had no concept of borders to begin with. As in the Canada–United States border, meridians often served as markers for dividing colonial possessions. In some instances, colonial authorities attempted to draw lines that reflected sociological conditions (cf., Anderson, 1996: 79–80), but on the whole the great border-drawing exercise was an imposition of seventeenth- and eighteenth-century European practices on areas that had no conception of sovereignty, of exclusive territorial jurisdiction, or of states. Throughout colonial history, the Europeans continued their earlier practices of exchanges, partitions, and forced territorial revision. Where the Europeans had difficulties drawing clear lines of demarcation, they resorted to ill-defined "spheres of influence," but there was still the common understanding that such spheres were exclusive. The Russians could have their sphere in Persia, while the British had theirs. There was no overlap between them.

Lest this discussion of ideas as the sources of their changing territorial practices and norms seems overly determinist, it is also important to acknowledge that a host of sociological processes in the nineteenth century helped to create a sensitivity to the need for defining territorial borders. Urbanization, communication, the development of vernacular languages replacing Latin, print, capitalism, mass literacy, and industrialization all contributed to bringing disparate, localized peoples and cultures together and allowed them to develop a sense of a national "us" that required legal and political demarcation from others (cf., Motyl, 1999: 100). Whether ideas preceded technology is not a problem we can unravel here, but it is important to emphasize that by the late nineteenth century, broad classes of people throughout Europe had substantially changed their perspectives on territoriality.

Modern territorial practices

The organic link between a "people" and their territory that developed in nineteenth-century Europe led to a whole new set of practices in international relations. These included passports (not widespread until the Great War [Salter, 2003]), border controls, plebiscites for validating territorial changes, a precipitous decline in the incidence of military conquest of territory, and as the next section suggests, vigorous opposition by the international community to any territorial changes except through consent.

States that incorporated a "people" had to distinguish themselves from others. As a security entity, moreover, states needed to control ingress and, frequently, egress. Various devices served these purposes. During the French Revolution, the concept of "citizen" was resurrected from Roman practice and replaced the idea of the royal subject. A citizen, as the Declaration of the Rights of Man and of the Citizen made clear, enjoyed certain rights and liberties that, for example, Prussian subjects of the Hohenzollerns did not possess. One was not a citizen of a region, continent, or the world, but of a distinct nation-state, that is, of a political community imbued with moral worth. Citizenship provided rights and liberties only within the territorial bounds of the state, defined as possessing a distinct political (not ethnic or religious) nationality. Passports created the symbol of a distinct legal status. They verified and validated the nationality of the bearer (as opposed to her or his religion, race, or other attribute) and simultaneously allowed a foreign state to exclude that person if it wished. Whereas in the seventeenth century people in Europe (with means, of course) could wander about the continent and sojourn in places as long as they liked, by the early twentieth century their travels were always with the implicit or explicit consent of the host country. And when abroad, those travelers did not enjoy the rights such as voting or holding public office accorded to local citizens.

As the basis for an organized, nation-wide political community and, often, of a distinct culture, territory gained value far beyond its population, resources, or strategic worth. Because it was the physical embodiment of the nation, it could no longer be bartered, exchanged, or annexed with impunity. The French humiliation in the Frankfurt Treaty of 1871 demonstrated that future territorial revisions would need a new basis of legitimacy. The older practices of territorial change, including conquest, inheritance, marriages, exchanges, and sales – except in the colonial areas – were no longer acceptable in Europe. The big test of how to effect territorial revision occurred at the end of World War I with the collapse of the Austro-Hungarian, Ottoman, Russian, and German empires. On what bases would territorial revisions be made so that they could reflect the new conception of territory and hence enjoy some minimal degree of legitimacy? The doctrine of national self-determination served as the legitimizing principle. But it was much easier to enunciate as a general aspiration than as a practical guide to the actual demarcation of new boundaries.

The complex territorial revisions that accompanied the end of World War I revealed the difficulties involved. Armed with the doctrine of national self-determination, the peacemakers in Paris redefined the basis of nationhood from historic titles to popular demand. Obviously territorial borders could not easily coincide with population distributions, for while states are relatively permanent entities, populations and, in particular, identities are constantly changing. Hence, to make nations roughly coincide with permanent territorial vessels required a good deal of compromise. Strategic and economic factors necessarily had to be taken into account in the creation of Europe's successor states, but population characteristics were the main criteria. The Finns, subject to later negotiations with the Soviet Republic, defined themselves and their eastern border primarily in terms of ethnicity and language. So did the Balts, but there was the intractable problem between Poland and Lithuania over the possession of Vilna, a city with both Lithuanian and Polish characteristics and populations. A number of formerly internal or provincial borders or administrative units of the Austro-Hungarian Empire helped define Hungary and Czechoslovakia. Yugoslavia was configured in terms of a mythical south Slav "people" whose true character has come to be defined only in the recent past. But here, too, many of the traditional (e.g., provincial) territorial borders rather than population distributions were used. Where historic or ethnographic bases for borders were weak or contested, plebiscites were used to settle the issue. Bismarck's annexation of Schleswig-Holstein in 1864 and 1866, for example, was finally validated in 1919 by this means. Territorial questions relating to the Saar and Silesia were similarly resolved by plebiscites. The main point is that all the territorial revisions attending the end of World War I needed some form of popular validation. This was in contrast to Vienna in 1815, where territorial revisions reflected eighteenth-century practices. Historic, strategic, economic, and dynastic claims were not sufficient bases for territorial revision.

Not unexpectedly, older provincial lines and plebiscites did not solve all the problems. State boundaries could not be drawn around ever-shifting or small populations. It was not always obvious who a "people" were, and many "peoples" were entirely mixed up with other "peoples" within the same space. To resolve the dilemmas, the decision-makers in Paris in 1919 had basically three choices: to move borders, to move populations, or to create "minorities." Only in a few instances did they dare create entirely new borders because to do so would have raised a whole new series of issues. They did not yet imagine moving entire populations, since "ethnic cleansing" in a systematic manner was not a socially accepted practice (only the Greeks and Turks did this in 1922).

So they chose mostly the third option: creating the idea of "minorities." The great powers after 1919 insisted that the new states sign treaties providing their minorities certain rights. These treaties were to be guaranteed by the great powers and monitored by the League of Nations. The system worked poorly and eventually collapsed in the 1930s. The two devices of reconfiguring borders and creating minority rights were inadequate to bring social harmony. The result was a series of ethnically based crises, armed conflicts, uprisings, rebellions, and wars between the successor states, most prominently between Finland and Sweden (the Aaland Islands), Poland and Lithuania, Yugoslavia and Hungary, and after 1937, between Germany and Czechoslovakia.

Although significantly novel, we cannot claim that 1919 represented a single "big bang" type of change in territorial practices and norms. Territorial changes in the Balkans in the late nineteenth century already applied principles of self-rule and national self-determination for legitimizing purposes. We must not forget, also, that since the outbreak of war, the great powers had made all sorts of territorial promises to Italy as a means of bribing it from neutrality. Even as late as 1918, the French were engaged in secret negotiations with the Austrians, promising them Poland and Bavaria as rewards for making a separate peace (Lynch, 2002: 431). Older practices did not die out suddenly with Woodrow Wilson's wartime proclamations. However, the propagation of the faith in the concept of national self-determination brought it a new popularity that was difficult to ignore in the peace settlement. The decisions made in Paris in 1919 revealed a new respect for territory and some of the wartime promises of territorial adjustments had to be ignored or rejected, much to the consternation of the Italians and others. Unlike after previous wars, the victors did not go on an extensive campaign of territorial revision (Germany lost its conquests of 1870–1, ceded land in the east to Poland, and lost its colonies). Great Britain took only some German colonies under the mantle of League of Nations mandates, and the United States took nothing. Most critical, the tortuous attempts to define the territorial limits of the new states displayed a recognition that territory was not just real estate. It was deeply enmeshed with questions of national identity and self-determination, the bases of political legitimacy.

The era of systematic territorial predation in the 1930s and during World War II justifies the view that, in this era, practice was a form of reversion to seventeenth- and eighteenth-century patterns. The Japanese, Germans, Italians, and Soviets went on a rampage of territorial revision, annexing, partitioning, exchanging and redesigning states, usually through the threat or commission of force. Japan annexed Manchuria and occupied large swathes of China and Southeast Asia. Italy invaded Ethiopia, Albania, and Greece. Nazi Germany annexed Austria, turned Poland and Czechoslovakia into slave labor camps and satrapies, re-configured Yugoslavia, and occupied France, Denmark, Norway, and the Low Countries. It also exchanged territories with the Soviet Union, at the expense of the Poles. The Soviet Union forcibly annexed the Baltic states in 1940–1. It also took major slices of territory from Finland, Poland, Romania, and Japan. But this reversion to old practices seems to have strengthened the norm of territorial integrity in the post-war world. Unlike in earlier centuries, the international community legit-imized none of the 1930s and World War II territorial changes, with the exception of those of the Soviet Union. The insistence on undo-ing territorial conquests demonstrated a new respect for the norms of self-determination.

Territorial practices since 1945: transforming an international institution

Since 1945 there has been a decline in the number of territorial disputes leading to armed conflict even though there has been a dramatic rise in the number of states (Holsti, 1991: 307–11). Mark Zacher (2001: 223–34) chronicles some forty "territorial aggressions" between 1946 and 2000. However, some were more in the form of border disputes and mi-nor incursions rather than all-out wars. Many disputes were relatively unimportant because they involved only the exact location of borders. Others were more significant because they concerned competing claims of ownership over a single territory. But what is remarkable in terms of territorial practices is the decline in the use of armed force to re-solve these issues. Between 1648 and 1945, approximately 80 percent of the wars that had a territorial issue in contention led to territorial changes after the peace. In contrast, since 1945 this number has fallen to 30 percent. Controlling for the number of states in the central system, the number of territorial redistributions per country per year was 0.0033 for the nineteenth century, rose to 0.0073 between 1901 and 1950, and then declined significantly to 0.0015 between 1951 and 1997 (Zacher, 2001: 223). No successful cases of territorial aggrandizement have occurred since 1976 and in the Yugoslav wars of dismantlement every attempt to raise territorial adjustment as a component of a peace settlement was vigorously opposed by the United States and the European countries (Fabry, 2002).

We can barely keep up with the changing territorial map of Europe in the seventeenth and eighteenth centuries. Almost every year, states revised boundaries somewhere on the continent. In contrast, since 1945 territorial changes, particularly through successful armed conquest, stand out for their rarity.[4] They include the Pakistani invasion of Kashmir on behalf of the anti-Indian secessionists in 1947–8; the China–India war of 1962 over Ladakh; the Chinese occupation of the Paracel Islands in 1974; the Indian conquest of Goa in 1961; the Indonesian takeovers of West Irian (1963) and East Timor (1975); Morocco's occupation of parts of Spanish Sahara (1975); and the Israeli conquest of the Sinai, Golan Heights, and East Jerusalem in 1967. There have been numerous other territorial disputes in Africa, Asia, and South America, but the international community has adamantly opposed territorial revision as a formula for their settlement. While the absolute number of territorial issues on the international agenda is large, given the greater number of states in the international system compared with the seventeenth and eighteenth centuries, the proportionate number of territorial conflicts and revisions is significantly diminished compared with previous eras.

Territorial practices refer not only to revision, but also to administration of borders. With the clear delimitation of state boundaries, the (re)invention of the citizen concept, and the validation of citizenship through passports, the state became by the late nineteenth century an entity that was not only juridically distinct from its neighbors, but also physically separated by walls, customs and immigration points, and military deployments. Now states – unlike their pre-modern predecessors – had the technical means of monitoring, controlling, and even preventing the ingress and egress of people, goods, and money.

The actual practices of monitoring and controlling have varied substantially, particularly in the period since 1945. In the case of the communist countries, they controlled their borders with a tightness seldom if ever witnessed before. The "iron curtain" was in fact a series of walls, mined fields, watchtowers, barbed-wire fences, shooting platforms, and armed patrols. The citizens of these countries traveled abroad only with the written consent of the state authorities. Any deviation from strict

---

[4] By Zacher's count (2001:225–8) since 1945 there have been fourteen conflicts involving "major change" and five involving minor change. However, some of the conflicts (e.g., North Vietnam and South Vietnam) were not primarily about territory.

requirements was labeled treason, subject to the death penalty. Travelers wishing to visit these countries invariably had to obtain visas that allowed access only for very limited periods. And within those periods, secret police or other agents constantly monitored visitors.

Such practices have not entirely disappeared with the end of the Cold War. Access to countries such as North Korea, Burma, or Bhutan is extremely difficult even today. Many visitors to the United States have to stand in line for hours and days in order to obtain entry visas. Not infrequently, they also have to fill in long questionnaires regarding their life histories, their health, and their political activities.

At the other end of the border control spectrum are countries that do not require visas and that normally grant visitors extended periods of time for travel, business, research, or other activities. British subjects normally enter Canada with simple answers to a couple of questions. Likewise for Norwegian travelers to Sweden. The most dramatic alteration of border practices has been through the Schengen Agreement (1995) between some of the European Union members in which border controls have been eliminated. Dutch travelers can now enter Belgium or Germany without even stopping, as can Danes into Sweden or Spaniards into Portugal. There is no more hindrance to travel in parts of Europe than there is between states in the United States or provinces in Canada. The Schengen Agreement is, in a sense, a return to pre-nineteenth-century European practices.

Although border practices vary considerably around the world, they share one feature: state consent. States *agree* to allow ingress and egress. An essential element of sovereignty is the *right* to control access to a state, its society, and territory. No one contests that right today, nor do they deny that governments can withhold consent at any time, for any types of people or goods.[5] Investment flows, currency exchange, trade, and the communication of ideas have grown vastly over the past three or four centuries, and in a few cases there is little governments can do to control them effectively. But they have not given up the *right* to control them. Nor have governments ceded control over permanent population movements. In the nineteenth century, millions of immigrants came to Canada and the United States. Few of them had passports or other forms of legal identification. Yet they were welcomed. In contrast, most governments today have very strict rules

---

[5] For example, no one since September 11, 2001 has challenged the right of American authorities to monitor, search, and prohibit entrance to any visitors to the United States.

governing population movements, aside from casual tourism. We call these immigration policies, and borders are an integral part of them. There is a substantial and growing amount of illegal immigration, but it is centered in only a few countries and the successful border hoppers tend to live a very uneasy life as non-citizens. Taken together, the number of people who are living permanently in countries other than those of their birth or initial citizenship has not grown significantly over the past century. It is a fraction of the total world population, about 2 percent. This figure is probably lower than the number of "foreigners" who lived permanently in the countries other than their own in Europe three centuries ago.[6] In short, borders have a great deal more significance today than the term "borderless world" implies and they certainly have more import than they did in the early modern period of European history.

Border functions

Borders have several important functions. They define the territorial limits of a state's legal jurisdiction, something we take for granted but which is actually an artifact of the idea of sovereignty and thus a human invention. They demarcate the extremity of a country's laws and legitimate enforcement. The few remaining practices of extraterritoriality underline the generality.

Borders also define the defensive wall or zone against all sorts of threats and predators, whether hostile armies, terrorists, drug runners, white-slave traffickers, or commerce in endangered species. States maintain armies of customs officials, police, border guards, surveillance mechanisms, monitoring facilities, and passport controls to reduce or manage real or perceived threats. Technological innovations to manage these problems are profuse, and include platoons of olfactory-advantaged canines. Some countries also maintain large military formations along their frontiers and regularly patrol their entire length. Israel is one example.

Borders are also the lines that help identify and demarcate a political and cultural community that is in many ways distinct from all other communities. For some states, those lines coincide with important social and cultural distinctions such as language, religion, and history. Where official borders do not coincide clearly with these distinctions, we are likely to see conflict, including irredentist and secessionist movements,

---

[6] This figure comes from a presentation by Demetrios G. Papademetriou (2000).

formal territorial claims, and border incidents. The uneasy fit between states and nations has been a constant source of international conflict for the past 150 years.[7] When governments conclude that two or more communities cannot live in peace within a single state, they even prefer moving the communities to moving the borders. This was the case in Turkey and Greece in 1922, in Germany and Czechoslovakia after World War II, and more recently in Bosnia, Kosovo, Cyprus, and several areas in Africa. Territoriality defined in terms of lines of separation trumps community.

Borders also have the function of monitoring and screening the massive exchange of goods between countries. Among other things, they allow governments to keep statistics on trade, to collect tariffs, and to prevent the ingress of certain types of goods. Frequently security concerns underlie these restrictions and inspections. They may involve great inefficiencies and constitute a hidden barrier to trade. The creation of the European Common Market and the Schengen Agreement settled in favor of efficiency, but it has not become a model for other countries. Most of them continue to place a higher priority on security, broadly defined.

In the formative years of border controls in the eighteenth century, checkpoints and ports were used to control ingress, to collect taxes and tariffs, and to allow government surveillance over some of the traffic crossing borders. In the twentieth century, borders for some states have also served as means of *preventing* egress, the exit of nationals. The iron curtain was the most famous or infamous corral around the socialist societies. Egress from the various workers' paradises of the socialist bloc was carefully and successfully controlled until the heady days of 1990 when the massive exodus of East Germans into neighboring countries provoked the collapse of the socialist regime. The containing devices of the socialist states have largely disappeared, but most countries continue to use border surveillance techniques to prevent criminals or those charged with crimes from fleeing a legal jurisdiction.

Finally, borders help provide efficiency *within* political communities. Few today would be content with the floating frontier zones typical of the great historical empires. Nor would we in an age of frenetic mobility wish to return to the myriad complexity of medieval localisms, where laws, currencies, customs, and habits changed every few kilometers. National borders convey a meaning of legal consistency within

---

[7] For full elaboration of this problem, see Holsti (1996).

relatively large territorial domains. We already have achieved a great deal of efficiency by having national currencies, national laws, national standards on a wide range of transactions, and national economic regulations. The long and tortuous process of national centralization that began in the sixteenth century made possible the creation of a global economy. But a global economy, as mentioned, supplements and does not supplant national, regional, and local economies.

Norms and rules

International norms and rules relating to territorial practices have grown in tandem with the capacity of states to monitor and control their territories and with the close identification of a "people" and their territory. The Covenant of the League of Nations prohibited states from threatening or using force to change international boundaries. The main function of the organization was to protect the independence and territorial integrity of its members, and forceful attempts to alter territorial boundaries constituted a violation of the norm of national self-determination. The Kellogg–Briand Pact of 1928 committed the signatories to respect international boundaries and outlawed all acts of war to alter them. In 1931, the American secretary of state, Henry Stimson, announced that the United States would not recognize as legal any alterations of territorial boundaries resulting from Japan's invasion of Manchuria. The League of Nations subsequently adopted his position as an international norm. "The intended effects of these pronouncements," claim Jackson and Zacher (1997: 5) were "to freeze the political map of the world in its existing pattern of state jurisdiction."

These norms did not of course accord with subsequent practices in the 1930s and during World War II. The military conquests of this era were obviously incompatible with them, but in the sense that World War II was a contest to preserve the Westphalian territorial states system against those who wanted to build regional or universal empires based on racial or Confucian principles, the norms prevailed. After 1945, most of the states of Europe retained or regained their pre-war frontiers. The Soviet Union was the major exception. Through peace treaties and other arrangements, it retained its territorial conquests from Finland, Poland, Germany, Romania, and Japan. However, the major Western powers did not recognize as legal the Soviet annexation of the Baltic states. The 1930s and 1940s thus present many instances of throwbacks to earlier territorial practices, where norms were weaker or non-existent.

Numerous multilateral agreements and resolutions since 1945 have clearly specified that territorial revision without consent has no international legitimacy. The United Nations Charter explicitly links territory to people and declares that non-consensual territorial revision violates the principle of self-determination. It also declares that the threat or use of force to change the territorial *status quo* is a "threat to international peace and security," thus justifying international sanctions, including armed force. Regional collective defense arrangements allowed under Article 51 are also premised on the idea that parties can legitimately use armed force against any attack on their territorial integrity.

When the Charter was drafted and negotiated in 1945, the participants had Europe primarily in view. The purpose of the new post-war organization was explicitly to provide protection for the smaller states that might face threats of the kind posed by Hitler and the other aggressors of the 1930s. But what of the host of new states that were being born in the prolonged process of de-colonization? Here, the norms first enunciated in 1919 were now universalized. The colonies were to be given independence with their existing borders (the principle of *uti posseditis*). Those borders raised serious problems because often they did not coincide with ethnic, religious, language, or other cultural attributes of the colonial "people." Who in fact were the "people" of India, Burma, Indonesia, Nigeria, and dozens of other colonies? The answer, claimed various United Nations resolutions, was that the "people" were the jumble of ethnic, religious, language groups that inhabited the European-created, socially artificial, and territorially mixed entities called colonies. Their nationality was thus defined in civic rather than cultural or ethnic terms. Most of the new states encompassed numerous distinct population groups and in many cases the colonial boundaries cut through entire communities. Recognizing the potential for state disintegration along cultural or other attribute lines, in 1960 the United Nations drafted its "Declaration on Granting Independence to Colonial Territories and Countries." It stated boldly that "any attempt at the partial or total disruption of the national unity or *territorial integrity* of a country [e.g., colony] is incompatible with the purposes and principles of the United Nations Charter" (Resolution 1514) (my italics). The international community sought to establish the colonial *status quo* as the basis for the territorial definition of the new states. And it sanctified the concept of the civic, territorial state rather than the more nineteenth-century idea that linked territory to a people defined in terms of language, religion, or ethnicity.

Since 1960, the legal principle of *uti posseditis*, which originally arose in the context of the independence of the former Spanish colonies in South America, has become universal. It was enshrined in Article 3 of the Charter of the Organization of African Unity in 1963 and has served as the basis for all attempts to mediate or resolve African territorial disputes. The 1964 Declaration of the African Heads of State and Government reiterated the principle. The 1961 Vienna Convention on Treaties specified that the principle of *rebus sic stantibus* no longer applies to internationally recognized borders. That is, states can no longer argue that changing circumstances or conditions justify claims to change borders. The Helsinki Final Act (1975) of the Conference on Security and Cooperation in Europe reiterated the older norms associated with notions of self-determination and declared that "frontiers can [only] be changed . . . by peaceful means and by agreement," that is, by consent. The Charter of Paris (1990), a document that established the principles upon which the post-Cold War territorial order in Europe would be based, reiterated the principle of consent and negotiation and ruled out the threat or use of force as a means of promoting or accomplishing territorial change. In the 1990s, both the European Union and NATO insisted that any new states seeking membership in those organizations must first negotiate and agree upon all outstanding territorial issues with their neighbors.

In the contemporary state system, then, we have what Jackson and Zacher (1997: 10) refer to as a "territorial covenant." It is a set of carefully articulated norms that have the effect of raising established international boundaries to a value as great as peace. The norms include the following principles:

1 only existing territorial boundaries are legal and legitimate;
2 no territorial change effected through the threat or use of force is legitimate;
3 any territorial revision must be achieved through negotiation;
4 any territorial revision must be consistent with the principle of national self-determination;
5 any territorial revision must have the consent of those affected by it;
6 the affected parties include both "peoples" and states;
7 secession or any threat to the "integrity" of the state will not receive international support unless achieved through negotiations and consent;

8 if such consent is forthcoming, the territorial limits of the seceding
state should approximate the former administrative boundaries (e.g.,
provinces, states, regions, and the like).

Most contemporary territorial changes or challenges to existing territorial boundaries have been consistent with these norms, suggesting
that they have earned substantial legitimacy and international consensus. The international community has refused to accept practices that
deviate from these norms and has been unwilling to accept what amount
to *de facto* coercive territorial revisions. As an example, Cyprus has been
effectively bifurcated by the "Green Line" separating its Greek and
Turkish communities since 1964. There is little commerce or communication across this line and no indication that the two communities
are prepared to reintegrate into a single state. Yet, the line has no legal
status and is not officially a border. The armistice line between the two
Koreas has also served as a *de facto* border but continues to be treated
as a military rather than political border recognized by other countries.
And in the case of Bosnia, the 1995 Dayton Accords insisted that the
traditional province/federal boundaries of Yugoslavia must serve as its
new international boundaries.

Perhaps most telling, the hundreds of claims of minority groups and
secessionist movements for the right to create their own states under
the norm of self-determination have fallen mostly on deaf ears in the
international community. While there are plenty of people who commit
their loyalties fundamentally to "ethnoscapes" rather than to traditional
territories, the territorial conception of the state has trumped the ethnic conception, except in cases where secession has been negotiated by
peaceful means. There have been several successful violent secessions
(e.g., Bangladesh, Croatia, and Turkish Cyprus), but the international
community did not recognize the results until after they were accomplished, and in the case of Cyprus, it has not recognized the seceding
entity. And in no case did it accept any revision of former domestic divisions. The seceding entities, in other words, had to accept their previous
provincial boundaries as their new international frontiers. In almost all
of the many dozens of armed conflicts based on attempts at ethnic secession since 1945, most states have adopted a neutral attitude or have
come to the support of the traditional territorial state (cf., Heraclides,
1990). We have seen a great deal of "ethnic politics" in the world in
the past two hundred years, but in the vast majority of cases where
ethnicity and traditional state territoriality clashed, the latter prevailed

largely thanks to the policies of the international community. Territory and statehood are inextricably linked in the contemporary political mind.

The territorial institution is an example of *transformation*. In Time One – roughly from the late seventeenth to the late eighteenth century – patterned *practices* featured constant territorial revision and conquest, *ideas* of territory as a commodity and personal-patrimonial possession, and weak *norms*. Contemporary practices, in contrast, are largely consistent with the permanency of territorial demarcations, conceptions and ideas of territoriality having almost sacral status, and strong norms that discourage or prevent territorial changes effected through coercion or armed conflict.

Today, the territorial map of the world has the quality of being "frozen," norms have effective application, and boundaries have taken on social values that far exceed those found in traditional polities or among earlier European states. On matters of territoriality, states for the most part pursue policies and practices of "appropriateness." They follow the norms and rules of territoriality rather than of opportunity. This significant example of institutional transformation is symbolized by an expert's statement published in 1937: "The peaceful surrender of a portion of territory by one sovereign state to another is so normal and common a procedure as to need little explanation" (Crutwell, 1937: 51). Could that statement be made today? That it would not attests to a significant change in the ideas and practices of territoriality.

Explaining the "territorial compact"

The ideas and norms of self-government and self-determination of peoples were already in play in some of the territorial arrangements in the Balkans in the late nineteenth century. They became major criteria for arranging the territorial limits of the states that succeeded the breakup of the German, Austro-Hungarian, Russian, and Ottoman empires in 1919. Woodrow Wilson was the main champion of the idea of national self-determination and exploited the prestige of the American participation in the latter stages of the Great War to persuade his Allied colleagues to abandon territorial claims made through secret treaties prior to and during the war. More than a decade later, the United States again took the road of principle in refusing to recognize Japan's territorial revisions in the conquest of Manchuria. This position was adopted as a new norm by most of the members of the League of Nations in 1931. Territorial revision now had to be effected with the consent of the populations concerned, and territorial gains made through aggression would have no legal standing.

All but the Soviet territorial conquests of the 1940s were undone in the various peace treaties that terminated World War II. Italy, Japan, and Germany had to cede all of their conquests to their previous owners, and in the case of Japan's conquests in the Pacific, they were turned into United Nations Trust territories under American administration. The international community insisted in 1960 that the principle of *uti posseditis* must be applied to the territories emerging from colonialism and that any attempts to change territorial dispositions would be regarded by members of the United Nations as a threat to international peace and security. A universal consensus on the "sacred" status of traditional territorial divisions was thus well on the way to being formed. Most of the de-colonization process was consistent with it, although disagreements on the location of lines, irredentist pressures, and claims for territorial change were certainly part of the diplomatic agenda of the 1960s and 1970s. In brief, the norms and ideas underlying the "territorial compact" were well in place by the 1960s, but practices were not always consistent with them. The great powers in particular were not consistent supporters and enforcers of the main norms and rules. For example, the major powers acquiesced in (and the Soviet Union and China championed) the Indian conquest of Goa in 1961. They played only a limited role in the brief war between China and India over the Ladakh area in 1962. They looked the other way or provided support when Indonesian troops marched into East Timor and annexed it to Indonesia in 1975. The United States generally supported Morocco in its annexation of Western Sahara territory, fearing that the opposition Polisario Liberation Front was under communist influence. In several other cases – particularly regarding Israel – one or more of the major powers provided aid and diplomatic support for governments that made revisionist territorial claims or used military force to effect them.

We can use 1975 as the marker of significant change. Approximately at that time, the major norms of the "territorial compact" were spelled out in detail in major diplomatic documents such as the Helsinki Final Act. After this date, the major powers and others began to act with a consistency that suggests a high degree of institutionalization. Behavior and norms increasingly coincided. The major powers began to use their power and influence to ensure that territorial change could not be effected through military means. We saw this in the breakup of the former socialist states. The United States, in particular, insisted that if the Yugoslav federation could not be held together, the seceding states had to accept the internal federal state frontiers as their new international boundaries. Along with the members of the European Union, they refused to accept any claims for territorial revision and made acceptance of the territorial *status quo* a condition for recognition. The United States also warned the Greek government not to initiate territorial claims against Albania, claims that could be justified on grounds that a significant proportion of the population in southern Albania was in fact Greek. The breakup of the Soviet Union raised a large number of territorial issues, but largely through Russian insistence, the former Soviet republics more or less accepted their traditional frontiers. A number of claims for territorial revision remain in play, but it is increasingly unlikely that they will be resolved through the use of force. The major powers, finally, have refused to accept the division of Cyprus as constituting two sovereign states and have actively sought to restore the territorial integration of the island. In the case of East Timor, they reversed their earlier indifference to, or support of, the Indonesian conquest of 1975.

In this case of institutional transformation, ideas and norms appear to have preceded the application of national power. First, haltingly, in the late nineteenth century the major powers accepted national self-determination as a major (but by no means the sole) criterion for arranging territorial changes in the Balkans. They did so again in 1919, thanks largely to the insistence of the United States. For the first time in history, at the end of World War II, the major powers, with the exception of the Soviet Union, abstained from making any territorial claims and ignored the traditional argument that spilling blood and spending wealth justified some territorial rewards after military victory. This type of territorial magnanimity is without precedent and reveals an entirely new approach to one of the major sources of international conflict of the previous centuries. That approach recognizes that any territorial change, even as a reward for national sacrifices, must be consistent with the principles of self-rule and national self-determination. The major powers after 1945 did not consistently follow this path, but by 1975 national power increasingly supported the norms and ideas. As we write, most states most of the time support the norms and rules of the "territorial compact."

The case for obsolescence

A day hardly goes by without some analyst's reference to the declining significance of territory in international politics. These claim, for example, that territoriality is becoming "unbundled" (Ruggie, 1993), more permeable, a heavy tax on commercial transactions, and superseded by "region states" (Ohmae, 1995) or other associations that transcend national frontiers. Others speak of "communities of fate" replacing or challenging traditional communities based on kinship, territory, and nationality (Held and McGrew, 1998). When still others address the decline of the nation-state, they frequently refer not only to the state's loss of influence in the face of globalization processes, but also to the increasing irrelevance of territory as a basis of political authority, identity, and emotional attachment (cf., Strange, 1996: 189; Badie and Smouts, 1999: ch. 1). These claims suggest a trend toward obsolescence as implied in the popular term "borderless world." In either case, the physical basis of the state – its geographical location and attributes – no longer holds the significance of previous times.

There are at least two types of arguments supporting these claims. The first emphasizes the increasing *transparency* of states, as technology such as the world wide web has created the means both to bypass borders and to take the lid off territory by satellites and other technical devices. It has become increasingly difficult for states to conceal themselves and to prevent their citizens from communicating with the outside world. It is not impossible, of course, as North Korea, Bhutan, and Albania (before 1991) have demonstrated. But for most countries, the costs of attempting to maintain *exclusive* influence, and of preventing outside surveillance and communication penetration, far outweigh the advantages.[8] The technology-causes-obsolescence analyses can also be applied to economic transactions. Kenichi Ohmae (1995), for example, has argued that traditional concepts of state territoriality are an encumbrance to rational economic activity. He observes the declining significance of borders and a concomitant rise of the "region state," areas of high-density economic transactions that take place both within states (e.g., the Boston–Washington corridor, the Hong Kong–Guangzhou area in China) and between states (Cascadia area in the United States–Canadian northwest, the San Diego–Tijuana complex between the United States and Mexico,

---

[8] No state in history, to my knowledge, has attempted to maintain exclusive *influence*. Authority is another matter; statements today that imply that external authorities are invading the state demonstrate a poor understanding of that concept.

and the like). He predicts that in the contest between economic rationality and state authority, the latter will eventually give way. For economic transactions, borders as barriers to trade will ultimately disappear, as they are doing in the European Union.

The second type of argument emphasizes the influence of "borderless world" transactions on the emotional identification of people and on their attachment to traditional concepts and practices of territoriality. Not only are states becoming more transparent and borders more porous, but people are also changing the ways they relate psychologically to territory. James Rosenau (1997: 4–5), for example, has noted that "landscapes are giving way to ethnoscapes, mediascapes, ideoscapes, technoscapes, and financescapes . . ." He underlines the growing incapacity of governments effectively to monitor and control unwanted intrusions, but his real emphasis is on the person–territory nexus. He argues that territoriality is for many people a declining intellectual and emotional reference point. So many activities and identities carry individuals beyond their territorial confines that emotional loyalties to territorial spaces are being replaced or uprooted by occupational, ethnic, religious, and other forms of emotional anchoring. "It seems clear," he argues, "that people have begun to accept a widening of [their] political space . . ." (p. 127). Today individuals may look beyond territorial boundaries for identities and emotional attachments.

Critique

There is little question that the number of transactions across international borders has grown at an amazing pace over the past half-century. No matter what statistics we choose – the numbers of transnational organizations and associations, tourism, trade, investment, or drug trafficking, for example – the figures are at historic highs and growing exponentially.[9] The costs of trying to exclude the outside world grow as technologies for circumventing boundaries proliferate. Many claim that

---

[9] However, such figures are often absolute rather than relative, thus providing a perhaps unwarranted impression of change. In the area of trade, often used as an indicator of globalization or increased interdependence, ratios of trade to Gross Domestic Product (GDP) suggest quite a different conclusion. For France, the Netherlands, and Japan, for example, the ratio actually declined between 1913 and 1996. For the United Kingdom and Germany, the ratio increased by less than 10 percent. Only in the case of the United States, among the world's great trading nations, did trade as a proportion of GDP increase dramatically, in this case by 63 percent over the twentieth century.

the state is now more permeable (and perhaps vulnerable) than at any other time.

But if this is indeed the case, why is it that territory has reached such absolute status in international norms? Why have not states sold off unproductive provinces or regions to private entrepreneurs? Why do states no longer exchange or sell territories, even when it might be socially and economically profitable to do so? Why do peacemaking arrangements move populations rather than borders? This is surely a much more costly and ethically ambiguous solution. Why do states continue to use military force, thus expending scarce resources and lives, to defend or occupy small tracts of useless land in remote corners of their peripheries (e.g., Eritrea and Ethiopia)? Why do governments typically claim that they will spare no cost to prevent the loss of even a few meters of territory? And why will the vast majority of a people come to the support of their government when their territories are thus challenged?

One reason such questions are seldom raised, much less answered, is that many of the proponents of the view that the significance of territory is declining incorrectly assume that identities are singular, that they are *either* global or national, national or local, ethnic or religious, occupational or territorial. This is a false assumption. Social scientists for years have known that identities change and that loyalties are multiple (Guetzkow, 1955; cf., Sørensen, 2001: 138)). There is no reason to believe that because, for example, there are growing academic networks that transcend state boundaries, professors enjoy research and sabbatical sojourns in other countries, or more students spend one year studying abroad, they thereby become more "international" and less "national." To become "international" does not in any way necessitate loss of a national identity, loyalty, or psychological affiliation. And it does not change one's citizenship.

Since at least the mid-nineteenth century, territory has not been conceived as merely a piece of real estate. It is, rather, the basis of a political community and helps define that community. It is a moral good, part of an overall package of identity, political rights, culture, and the good life.[10] It has permanence that even physical occupation or separation over decades cannot obliterate (witness the re-emergence of the Baltic states after seventy years of being part of the Soviet Union, or the continued problems associated with the division of China and Korea). If there is such erosion of the emotional bases of territoriality, the urges to

---

[10] This is not the case, of course, in many weak states, as described in the previous chapter.

reunify Vietnam, Germany, China, and Korea would have been abandoned years ago and the effects of eighty years of trying to build the Czechoslovakian and Yugoslav states would probably have succeeded.

A hard case of this generalization comes from the European experience during the past half-century approximately. The meaning of territory in Europe has undergone significant change as a result of the development of the common market and the dismantling of border points resulting from the Schengen Agreement. Flows of Europeans from one country within the zone to others have grown dramatically over the past decades.[11] There is something akin to a unified labor market in Europe, with millions of people working in European countries other than those of their nationality. Within the Schengen Agreement countries, border crossing no longer involves formalities. Trade, investment, tourism, communication, and other forms of transactions have all grown apace. It is within the European Union that the most dramatic changes in the ideas and practices of territoriality and sovereignty could be expected. Despite all these immense changes, however, William Wallace (1999: 99), a noted authority on European integration, concludes:

> The central paradox of the European political system . . . is that governance is becoming increasingly a multi-level, intricately institutionalized activity, while representation, loyalty, and identity remain stubbornly rooted in the traditional institutions of the nation state. Much of the substance of European state sovereignty has now fallen away; the symbols, the sense of national solidarity, the focus for political representation and accountability nevertheless remain.

This generalization is sustained by empirical research based on the World Value Surveys. Tanja Ellingsen (2000: 15–16) has demonstrated that identities in European Union countries are overwhelmingly *both* national and European, but with the national significantly predominant. Only small fractions (on average, 4.4 percent) identify themselves first as Europeans. "The vast majority identify most with the town they live in, followed by the district and country, and finally the continent and the world as a whole" (p. 13). The strength of national identity changed only slightly between 1984 and 1996, a time of massive increases in travel, population movement, and economic transactions in Europe. This is strong evidence that sheds doubt on the assertion or assumption that

---

[11] For example, arrivals of nationals from European countries into Great Britain increased from 1.8 million in 1960 to 27.5 million in 1997. Even greater figures are probable for border crossings between the "core" states of Europe – France, Germany, and the Benelux – and between all Europeans and Spain and Italy. Figures cited in Wallace (1999: 89, fn. 30).

increased transaction flows have proportionate impact on identities. Ellingsen's empirical work confirms that the zero-sum assumption of identity change in much of the globalization literature is incorrect: new identities do not necessarily replace old ones.

> What [the notion of a "global village"] fails to take into account is the fact that in Sweden a person from Norway might feel as being a Norwegian, but in Europe the same person might feel as being a Scandinavian, in North America as being a European, while in Africa and Asia as being a "Westerner." Thus, identities vary with distance from home. In principle, then, people can identify with, and express loyalty to, a region and its organizations – in addition to keeping their national identities intact. (Ellingsen, 2000: 13)

The situation in Europe is not entirely different from many other areas of the world, either today or in the past: identities are multiple and malleable. They may change, but they may also proliferate so those old ones coexist with new ones. One scholar of Palestinian identity (Khalidi, 1997: 19) notes for example that in the late nineteenth and early twentieth century Palestinian intellectuals and politicians identified with the Ottoman Empire, the Muslim religion, Arabism, their Palestine homeland, their city or region, and their family. They did not rank order them or notice contradictions between them.

A major problem with the argument that territoriality is declining or becoming obsolete under the onslaught of technology is that it fails to provide any benchmarks against which we can measure increases or decreases in the strength of international institutions. Without iron curtains, the world today may seem more "borderless" than it was during the Cold War. But certainly the technical capacity of governments to control ingress to their territories is much greater than in previous eras. Israeli armed forces patrol the entire length of that country's borders daily. Thanks to modern communications technology, in December 2000, Czech border police, armed with descriptions and photos of violent protesters made available through the internet and e-mail, prevented almost 600 people from entering the Czech Republic to protest meetings of the International Monetary Fund in Prague. No eighteenth-century monarch or nineteenth-century government could have done this. Most governments allow ingress of goods, services, and people by explicit or implicit consent. All retain the right to restrict access, and most have the means to make such restrictions reasonably effective.

Prior to passports and accompanying control of entry points, governments could not monitor and control population movements to the extent that they can today. As for commodities and currency flows, there is much more widespread freedom of access and exchange, but always as the result of treaties and other agreements negotiated by governments. In fact, a large majority of governments still maintain various types of controls and regulations on such economic transactions. These include prohibitions against sale of land to foreigners, foreign investment in key industrial, communications, and defense sectors, and innumerable banking regulations. In the supposed "borderless" world of trade and finance, all sorts of controls over transactions remain.

Territoriality matters most in terms of population movements. The world is a long way from having a free labor market. People cannot just go to where the jobs and opportunities are. There is a certain amount of – and probably growing – illegal immigration, but is it proportionately higher than it was when there were no controls over entry points? Many more people – about 100 million – migrated around the world (with a majority moving to North America) in the nineteenth century than in the period since 1945 (Wolf, 2001). Population movements are closely controlled by national immigration policies and by requirements for visas and other instruments of state consent to (limited time) foreign visitors.

Conclusions

New technologies have indeterminate consequences for both individuals and societies. When it comes to territory, we must not fall into the determinist trap. While some technologies may make borders more permeable or more difficult to monitor and control, others in fact vastly enhance the capacity of the state to survey its territorial limits. Thanks to icebreaker and satellite technologies, for example, Canada is able to maintain surveillance over its Arctic archipelagos in a manner that was not possible only one generation ago. Compared with two hundred years ago, state authorities today know exactly where limits of jurisdiction exist. They have a much greater capacity to keep out unwanted visitors and thanks to the concept of citizenship they also have a legal, not just physical, means to include or exclude. They have the surveillance mechanisms to chart or monitor movements of goods and people that would have been unthinkable even at the turn of the last century. It is certainly a myth that borders today are more "permeable" *than ever*.

They were far more permeable in eighteenth-century Europe than they are today in most of the world. The obvious exceptions to these generalizations refer to some forms of criminal activity (the drug trade) and to the flow of information, both of which are very difficult to control effectively. But in other domains, where flows take place through government consent, increases cannot indicate "erosion" of territoriality. Borders, the physical representation of territoriality, continue to have major functions as spaces in which societies and individuals are both brought together and separated. Ours is becoming not a "borderless" world, but one in which some fences are being rendered more porous while others are being strengthened (cf., Newman, 2001: 138, 142).

But these are essentially physical questions. Social consequences are even more problematic. Here I detect a certain amount of wishful thinking in academic and popular discourses on the "shrinking planet," "global village," or "borderless world." This is the idea that in order to develop a truly global society (modeled on which societies: American or Mongolian?), national loyalties based on concepts of territoriality *should* erode, diminish, or disappear. There is a long history of communitarian thought that attributes to national identities and statehood major sources of the world's troubles. Many want to see the demise of territoriality because, they believe, it has served as the source of too many brutal wars, revolutions, and genocides. Presumably the eradication of loyalties to states and their territories would diminish these social evils. An examination of non-territorial and non-state polities (e.g., Somalia) might change those opinions.

But the evidence that this is a trend does not bear much authority. Outside of certain processes in the European Union, there are in fact very few signs of boundary erosion, loss of the emotional connection between physical geography and national sentiments, or depreciation of the overall value of territory. The growing strength of territorial norms can be demonstrated empirically, as can the declining practice of treating territory as a possession or commodity. We still have some paradoxes – for example, increased transparency coexisting with enhanced control and monitoring technologies – but an examination of the ideas, norms, and practices of territoriality leads to the conclusion that territoriality is a young but critical foundational institution of international relations. The relative strength of the territorial institution provides another line of defense for state sovereignty and the self-determination of peoples. The significant decline in the incidence of interstate war in the past half-century or so can be explained at least in part by the effectiveness of the "territorial compact," and by the willingness of major states to enforce it. The claim of sovereignty over identifiable territory remained only a claim as long as most states continued to regard territory as a commodity or real estate that could be conquered, partitioned, exchanged, and sold. With the solid entrenchment of anti-territorial revision norms, sovereignty claims may be easier to transform into realities.

4 Sovereignty

In what ways is sovereignty an international institution? Many would argue that it is such a nebulous and contested concept that it has no fixed or essential meaning or application in international life. But if we think of sovereignty as a set of practices, ideas, beliefs, and norms, its significance as a foundational international institution becomes clearer. Without it, the life of political communities, even if organized into states, would be vitally different. Consider some of the common individual and state practices that we take for granted, yet are the consequences of sovereignty. At the individual level, when a traveler commits a crime in a foreign country, he or she is immediately subject to the host's laws. He or she cannot appeal to some other authority for protection or release. That same traveler does not stop to ponder why a passport is necessary to enter another country. It is just done, and that is the way things are. But passports are a creation of the twentieth century (although they existed shortly during the French Revolution as well). They are an expression of sovereignty in the sense that they identify the citizenship of the bearer, which means that he or she has differential rights based on location. The passport does not confer anyone's *right* to enter a country. The host can exclude anyone it wants. So we travel abroad because governments agree to let us enter. Consent is a critical fact of sovereignty. We also take for granted that states have the right to exclude or to screen the importation of certain types of commodities such as drugs, endangered species, tainted foodstuffs, and the like. Every time we show our passport to gain entry into a foreign country, exchange currency, purchase postage stamps, or accept the laws of a foreign jurisdiction, we are recognizing and practicing sovereignty.

At the level of states, we also take it for granted that diplomats have access to the officials of the governments to which they are accredited,

that only states shall be members of the United Nations, and that summit meetings will be attended only by heads of state or government. We
would think it strange if the CEO of, let us say, Yahoo Inc. demanded
and expected to attend such a meeting, or if Greenpeace applied for
membership to the United Nations, or if the Mafia claimed that its envoys around the world should enjoy standard diplomatic immunities.
What often seems ordinary and routine in international life is really a
result of long-established rules, norms, ideas, and customary practices
deriving from sovereignty.

We can divide the sovereignty concept into two components: those
rules and norms that constitute states (defining the players of the game),
and those that regulate how states relate to each other (rules of the game)
(cf., Fabry, 1998: 39). This chapter deals with the constitutive rules of
sovereignty. Subsequent chapters will deal with some of its procedural
aspects.

The constitutive rules and functions of sovereignty

Sovereignty is a foundational institution of international relations because it is the critical component of the *birth*, *maintenance*, and *death* of
states. Sovereignty helps create states; it helps maintain their integrity
when under threat from within or without; and it helps guarantee their
continuation and prevents their death.

Although tomes have been written about the idea of sovereignty and
it remains one of the notable contested concepts in social science, its
meaning for international relations is reasonably clear. It refers, internally, to a supreme authority within a defined territorial realm. It is the
ultimate source of law (social regulation) and it transcends any particular ruler or ruling group (government). Sovereignty defines the limits
of a legal realm. Jurisdiction exists only within a specified territory and
extends no further. This means, for example, that criminal acts committed within a state's jurisdiction must be tried and punished within that
jurisdiction. No state has a right to extend its laws into the territorial
domain of another state.

The external aspect of sovereignty is that the state has constitutional
independence. It is not legally subject to any external authority. In
Waltz's terms (1979: 96), the state "decides for itself how it will cope
with its internal and external problems, including whether or not to
seek assistance from others . . . States develop their own strategies, chart

their own courses, make their own decisions about how to meet whatever needs they experience and whatever desires they develop." If a state declares this as a right, it implies that it must recognize as legally equal those who claim similar rights. I cannot claim a right to exist as a sovereign person unless I am willing to concede the same right to my neighbors and associates.

Sovereignty is a *constitutive* rule of statehood because it defines and helps create legitimate actors, those who have a unique juridical personality. It provides the criteria for recognition of statehood (entrance into the society of states), for rules of succession, and the extinguishment of the special status. In common parlance, it answers questions of creation ("how do we get to be?"), identity ("who are we?"), continuity ("what happens if the government changes?"), and extinction ("how can we prolong life?").

At this point we must re-emphasize our discussion about the distinction between authority and influence in chapter 2. Sovereignty is a distinct legal or juridical status. A state either is sovereign or it is not. It cannot be partly sovereign or have "eroded" sovereignty no matter how weak or ineffective it may be, just as one cannot be simultaneously 75 percent a Norwegian citizen and 25 percent an Australian citizen, or 60 percent pregnant and 40 percent not pregnant (cf., Sørensen, 2001: 147). It is an absolute category and not a variable. Interpretations of the term, as well as sovereignty practices, change with time, but its foundational principles have remained essentially intact – with one important exception – since the late seventeenth century.

This is not to deny all sorts of anomalies, of which there are quite a few, but not enough to constitute a pattern or regular practice. For example, Article 1 of the Covenant of the League of Nations stipulated that any self-governing state, dominion, or *colony* could apply for membership in the organization. Hence, India was a founding member of the League of Nations long before it became independent. Hong Kong, legally a part of China today, has separate membership in the World Trade Organization. These all represent deviations from standard practice, but no more. They are anomalies. There is a standard practice, and that is that a polity cannot participate in the great games of international politics unless it is sovereign.

Who decides who is sovereign? Any polity can claim sovereignty, but aside from internal governance the claim establishes no rights in relation to other states (cf., Philpott, 2001: 15–16). It is the other states that validate the claim through the act of diplomatic recognition. They determine who will join the club. The act of recognizing a state in effect creates its special legal status. This is by no means an automatic decision. Many polities today that have some or even most of the traditional requisites for membership – a defined territory, control over it, effective administration, and the capacity to enter into and meet treaty obligations – have not been recognized as sovereign states and thus have no legal standing abroad. Somaliland, the Turkish Republic of Northern Cyprus, and Taiwan are examples. Contrariwise, some polities that cannot meet the traditional minimum qualifications are nevertheless sovereign states. Somalia between the early 1990s and today has no central government that effectively controls a defined territory, yet it continues to be a member of the United Nations and to participate in a limited fashion in a variety of regional and international organizations. Anomalies are by no means scarce. But the crucial distinction is not facts, but status. And it is the other states that determine that status.

C. A. W. Manning's (1975: 102ff) metaphor of a club best illustrates the constitutive aspect of sovereignty. The club was founded in the seventeenth century, and since then the members decide among themselves who are to be asked to join. The criteria they use to determine qualification change over time, and sometimes for reasons of expediency, friendship, previous commitments, and strategic opportunity, they will waive or bend those criteria to suit their purposes. In the nineteenth century, despite repeated requests, the great powers denied admission to the club to Hesse and several other German states, all of which technically met the entrance requirements of territorial limits, capacity to make and meet treaty commitments, and effective governance within the realm. But their rulers did not, in the estimation of the rest, meet the appropriate qualifications of royal lineage (also an eminently flexible criterion). Yet they allowed Bavaria to retain membership in the club until 1914, even though it had been legally a part of the German Empire since 1871. After 1945, the club allowed more than 150 new applicants to enter, even though several of them could not meet the most elementary traditional criteria. Merely having been a colony was a sufficient qualification.

Without the grant of recognition – entrance into the club – a polity cannot play the games of international relations. It cannot exchange diplomats, it cannot join international organizations, it cannot appeal for funding from the World Bank, it cannot enter into treaty relations with other states, and in many other ways it remains isolated. It can use subterfuges such as sending "representatives" rather than ambassadors abroad, hiding a virtual embassy under the name of some sort of institute or trade office, or asking for the opportunity to address the General Assembly of the United Nations. But without the full recognition of sovereignty it operates under very severe constraints. Most basically, it cannot claim a right to political independence and territorial integrity, as can sovereign states. In brief, sovereignty defines the essential actors of international politics and endows them with a unique legal status.

Second, sovereignty defines the essential characteristics of those actors. They have ultimate legal jurisdiction over a specified territory, which means in the negative sense that they do not have jurisdiction over other territories.[1]

Third, sovereignty defines the essential characteristics of the relations between the actors, namely that no actor has a *right* to command others, and that none has the *obligation* to obey. In a technical sense, we call this anarchy (no government). It means that all agreements and rules between states have to be based on *consent*.

Why sovereignty? The answer is that it provides essential advantages to a polity and to the relations between all polities. These include:

Protection. Sovereignty provides an essential ingredient for the security of any political community. The status of sovereignty includes a presumption toward continued independence and some sympathy from other states in the event that more powerful states seek to conquer the weak. It is difficult to conceive of a massive international response to Iraq's conquest of Kuwait in 1990 had not Iraq violated one of the most fundamental norms of sovereignty, the independence and territorial integrity of a state. Sovereign status has been used repeatedly in recent years, as in the past, to protect the weak against the strong, to establish rights over control of a society's economic and natural resources, and to rally international support when threatened (cf., Bull, 1977: 292). It has also been used to protect governments against outside meddling, or as Naeem Inayatullah (1996: 50) suggests, it "shields states' internal deficiencies and failings against external pressures and actions." Sovereignty is a sort of "no trespassing" sign that has exactly the same

---

[1] Ultimate authority is not the same as exclusive authority. Many analysts mistakenly claim that sovereign status is exclusive (it cannot be shared). But sovereign authority may be divided, as in federations and in colonial systems of constitutional rule (Keene, 2002: ch. 3), and even shared over the same territory, as in some policy areas in the European Union. In federations, typically the federal constitution is the ultimate source of authority so that provincial or state laws cannot supersede it.

consequences: it provides a measure of security and a legal basis for claiming compensation or redress should a violation occur (cf., Vincent, 1974: 331). It indicates that entry is possible only with the consent of the owner.

Continuity. In early discussions about sovereignty, the claim of independence from superior authority was made on behalf of particular kings, princes, or estates. Sovereignty resided in the figure of the dynast. By the mid-seventeenth century, analysts and policy-makers increasingly referred to sovereignty as an attribute of the *state* and not of its rulers. It thus provided the political community with a legal status and continuity regardless of the fate of individual rulers. The distinction between the status of governments and that of states continues in recognition policy. Some states refuse to recognize a particular government, but continue to recognize the state. Even states that have been conquered may obtain some prospect of future resurrection, thanks to this distinction. For example, many governments refused to recognize as legal the formal Soviet annexation of Lithuania, Latvia, and Estonia in 1940–1 and continued to treat those territories as sovereign states, even though they had no governments. Technically, their sovereignty was not restored in 1991, because most of the great powers never acknowledged that it had been lost a half-century earlier. Here we have another example of the distinction between a legal status and political facts, a problem that has encouraged many to declare mistakenly that sovereignty is no longer important. In F. H. Hinsley's (1967: 252) words, "we can believe that sovereignty will continue to be a viable concept without denying that it will continue to fail to fit all the facts."

Club membership. Sovereignty establishes the minimum requirements for entry into the club of states. Those requirements change over time and with circumstances, but no state gains recognition of sovereignty merely by making the claim. The international society of states ultimately decides who is to become a state. State recognition is therefore a constitutive and fundamental practice in international politics (cf., Fabry, forthcoming: 8).

Constraints on behavior. The norms associated with sovereignty proscribe certain forms of behavior such as interference in the internal affairs of states. Sovereignty rules are thus rules of conduct of club members among themselves.

Establishing right. Sovereignty rules also create rights, as in the right to send ambassadors and to establish embassies abroad, the right to enter into treaty relations, and into various international organizations.

The Grundnorm of the system of states. Sovereignty rules buttress political particularism – the system of independent states – and thus help protect against potential hegemons. Those who have sought to create international systems on bases other than the sovereign state – such as Napoleon, Stalin, and Hitler – have had their enterprises de-legitimized by the other sovereign states. None of these empire-builders generated much international support precisely because they wanted to destroy the Westphalian states system and replace it with structures that denied the principle of sovereignty.

A source of international order. Sovereignty has the function of providing order for the system. It defines the legitimate actors, makes possible a system of laws between legal equals, sanctifies the principle of independence, self-rule, and territorial integrity, and establishes norms and rules that bring predictability, transparency, and a modicum of security. It is precisely this order-creating function that helps explain why for many in the fifteenth and sixteenth centuries a system of independent polities was preferable to the medieval hierarchy which was an order of superiors and subordinates, command and obedience. In a sense, the dynasts of early modern Europe preferred the risks associated with anarchy – and they were many – compared with the certainties of obedience. Freedom was more important than subservience, despite the insecurity it created.

How did all of this come about? Why did the European states of the seventeenth century concoct the idea of sovereignty?

The problem of authority in the medieval era

In the early medieval period up to the thirteenth century, both practices among the polities and ideas emphasized the unity of Christendom under God. The church served as his religious authority on earth (*sacerdotium*) while political authority, though not entirely distinct from the religious, was vested in the Holy Roman emperor (*regnum*) who was also the ruler of the Habsburg dynasty seated in Vienna.[2] The cosmology was one of hierarchy, organic unity, and relations between superiors and subordinates, all bundled together in the great *respublica Christiana*.

---

[2] The lengthy history of quarrels between the Holy Roman Emperor and medieval popes relates to issues of ultimate authority, and their outcomes had system-transforming consequences. Here, we pick up the story only when other princes began to question the authority of the Holy Roman emperor over them. For details of the earlier quarrels, see Fabry (1998: ch. 3).

The hotchpotch of local authorities, ranging from earls, barons, dukes, through city-states, and kings or queens were all part of this larger Christian community under the reign of God. In the twelfth century, any declaration of independence by a local authority was considered a crime against God's law (cf., Jackson, 2000: 157). By the thirteenth century, however, serious conflicts over the limits of jurisdiction and authority arose between the empire and the church on the one hand, and between both of them and the growing ambitions of the kings and other rulers who were developing their realms, on the other. Emperor Henry VII was among the many rulers of the Holy Roman Empire who claimed to be the supreme and lawful overlord of all Europe, a claim buttressed by charges of heresy against any who might dispute it. But many did, led by French kings who as early as 1302 proclaimed that *"qui est imperator in regno suo"* (Ullman, 1949: 15). By the late fourteenth century, secular rulers might concede that on religious matters the pope "ruled," but in the secular realm the emperor increasingly challenged them. The fact of independence had created arguments that kings had an exclusive right to rule. The first effective challenge to the emperor's claims to universal authority came from King Robert of Naples who defied imperial edicts and, armed with legal reasoning developed by the Neapolitan school of lawyers, claimed that he was "emperor in his own domain," and could thus legislate on all matters and even pass laws that contradicted universal imperial law. This was not a question of fact, he claimed, but a right. When imperial authority was based on force and coercion rather than on consent, it did not have legitimacy within the realm of the king. The matter came to a showdown in 1312 when the emperor charged Robert with *crimen laesae majestatis*. Robert ignored a summons to the emperor and was found guilty of high treason. Pope Clement IV intervened on the side of Robert and in the bull "Pastoralis Cura" denied imperial authority over the king. The pope further claimed that he had superiority over the emperor. Thus Henry's verdict over Robert was null and void: the emperor has no authority over the king, and the pope has superiority over the emperor. The papal bull effectively put an end to imperial claims of *dominus mundi* and thus to the idea of an organic, single Christian polity (Ullman, 1949). Equally significant, Clement IV's pronouncement also brought forth the idea that sovereignty has a limited territorial dimension; its exercise by a king is confined to specific spatial limitations (Bartelson, 1995: 99). This idea became a key component of later eighteenth-century concepts of sovereignty, in which the legal jurisdiction of the royal figure finally had prevailed over the laws of subordinate units such as free cities and duchies. It also implied that the laws of one realm cannot be extended to another.

Since the pope claimed both ecclesiastical and secular authority or superiority, the issue of particularism versus universalism was not settled. That contest played out over the next three centuries, with both kings and legal scholars increasingly challenging church authority over secular matters within kingdoms. Two of the most influential jurists of the sixteenth century, Vitoria and Suarez, both argued that the pope cannot overrule the civil laws of Castile, and that he has direct temporal authority only over his own realm (later known as the Papal States). The pope rightfully has authority over spiritual matters, except in the case where a secular ruler becomes an apostate and is excommunicated by the church. As for the Holy Roman emperor, he cannot make civil laws outside of his own realm. He is more than just another king, for he has special "honor and dignity" as the protector and defender of the church and papal office, but his authority is only moral not legal (Hamilton, 1963: 88–95).

Royal claims for *final* authority within realms escalated in the sixteenth century. In 1516, the Concordat of Bologna gave Francis I of France the authority to appoint bishops and abbots and their means of livelihood. This amounted to a nationalization of the clergy and church properties, implicitly limiting papal authority in these realms (cf., Kegley and Raymond, 2002: 28). Henry VIII of England reiterated the earlier French claim that "in my realm I am emperor," when in 1533 he divorced Catherine of Aragon without papal permission and married Anne Boleyn. Many issues relating to sovereignty were not yet fully spelled out in the various actions, ideas, and decisions of the sixteenth century, but the trend was clear: Europe was heading toward an order of political particularism. Except for lingering ideas about the *respublica Christiana* and the myth of a universal Christian (European) community, the power and increasingly the authority of the secular princes was undermining traditional imperial and papal prerogatives. Reflecting the facts on the ground, Vitoria could write that Castile was a "complete community and not part of another community. It possesses its own laws and its own courts and its own magistrates" (quoted in Brown, 1934: 205). And in a famous end run around the pope, he held that "nothing is further from my mind than to suppose that princes are . . . vicars of the Church, or of the Popes; on the contrary, I believe that they have received judicial power from God, even as the Popes themselves have received such power, and that spiritual power cannot interfere with the exercise of this temporal power . . . " (quoted in Brown, 1934: 250). Vitoria asserted that the prince's right to rule came directly from God and not through the intermediary of the pope. This implied that the church had no right to oversee, much less overrule, questions of civil authority and legislation.

The Protestant Reformation critically eroded papal and imperial authority (cf., Philpott, 2001: esp. ch. 7). Here was the first great organized heresy, for Luther's theology sanctioned secular rulers to assert their independence from the church in both religious and political issues. This was in conformity with the aspirations of those rulers, who used Luther as further justification for their claims to absolute and exclusive authority (cf., Jackson, 2000: 61). The Peace of Augsburg (1555) as we have seen transferred from papal claims the right of princes to choose the religion of their subjects.

These debates between the fourteenth and seventeenth centuries contained arguments and claims about authority, superiority, subordination, and obligation. Crucial elements of sovereignty, such as its direct connection to territory or its characterization as an aspect of statehood rather than a relationship between individuals, remained to be worked out. These were to come in the seventeenth century.

The critical seventeenth century: Westphalia

Ideas about sovereignty developed rapidly in the seventeenth century. Hugo Grotius, Thomas Hobbes, and many others, following the lead of Jean Bodin, Vitoria, and Suarez in the previous century, made signal contributions. Grotius, for example, established that sovereignty is a legal status and not just a question of influence and power: "that power is called sovereign whose actions are not subject to the legal control of another" (quoted in Suganami, 1990: 230). Hobbes attacked the medieval idea that all authority is exercised within the constraints of God's laws, and those of the church, and insisted that sovereign authority is unrestricted. Bodin had already established that sovereignty attaches to the polity, and not to an individual, or as C. A. W. Manning (1975: 101) so nicely put it in his metaphor, "the club carries on as a club, not for kings, but for kingdoms." Thus sovereignty is continuous and permanent regardless of the fate of particular princes. This idea gave the state a measure of security and longevity that was unusual in a world in which claimants to sovereignty regularly swallowed up their neighbors, conquered their territories, or dismembered them. Yet, the idea of sovereignty as an attribute of the royal figure did not die out with Bodin. As the quotes on p. 118 indicate, the royal figures constructed sovereignty as one of their personal attributes. *They* were sovereign, and their lands were personal possessions. The idea of the state as embodying a sovereign popular community did not emerge until late in the eighteenth century (cf., Hall, 1999: ch. 4).

A second set of ideas in the seventeenth century reflected the growing recognition that sovereignty is not only a legal status for a polity, but also an equal legal status. If one prince can claim sovereign status as a measure for protection, security, and continuity for his state, it had logically to consent to similar claims by others. This gives rise to the idea of legal equality. States may vary along many dimensions, but their rights *vis-à-vis* each other are equal.

The Thirty Years War (1618–48) was a major catastrophe for Europe. It involved more players and more destruction, and took place in more territories than any previous armed conflict going back to the Roman era. Vast swathes of central Europe were de-populated, towns and cities burned, and massive (for the day) armed marauding armies and their camp followers marched back and forth living off the land, looting, pillaging, and raping their way around the center part of the continent. Peace negotiations began in 1644 but did not lead to any conclusion until four years later with the treaties of Osnabrück (mostly for the Protestant combatants) and of Münster (for the Catholic participants). This was the first pan-European peace conference.

The two treaties run to several hundred pages, recording territorial exchanges, indemnities, compensation for war damage and requisitions, territorial partitions, the secularization of cities and towns, the fate of castles, free cities, and enclaves. The word sovereignty as a generic concept does not appear in the document, but many of the ideas deriving from publicists' and kings' claims over the past three centuries were now recorded in a multilateral treaty, thereby becoming part of the "law of Europe."

The delegates to the conferences were hardly innovators. They were not attempting to create a new order. On the contrary, much of the negotiation revolved around restoring the "ancient liberties" of the princes and estates of the Holy Roman Empire which, according to the French and Swedes, had been increasingly usurped by imperial authority (cf., Osiander, 1994: 73). But those "ancient liberties" had revolutionary implications for the idea of a hierarchical European order, for they underlined the importance of the freedom of princes and estates rather than their obligations to the pope, emperor, or anyone else.

Among the most important principles found in the treaties are:

1 Denial of the right of the church to interfere in civil and secular matters of the various princes.
2 Prohibition against the estates and princes trying to convert one another's subjects, or taking up their cause against their rulers – a particular instance of an injunction against interference in other states' internal affairs (Osiander, 1994: 40). The treaty (Article 64) contains a general prohibition against both the estates and princes on the one hand, and the imperial authority, on the other, "molesting" (e.g., interfering) in the religious, tax, and governmental affairs of other members of the empire.
3 The restoration of the right of the members of the empire to enter into treaty and alliance relations with other states, so long as those treaties did not harm the emperor (Article 65). This later came to be regarded as an exclusive authority of sovereign states to enter into treaty relations, implying a prohibition against such a right for non-sovereign entities within a realm (e.g., dukes, free cities, and the like).
4 Elaboration of the principle that these rights, and some corresponding duties, apply equally to sovereign states regardless of their size, military power, or the religion of their inhabitants.

The Peace of Westphalia helped establish the foundational principles of a society of states by defining more clearly the agents that had a right to international representation (including the estates of the Holy Roman Empire), by prohibiting interference in their internal affairs by the church or the emperor, by providing states with a monopoly of the right to make treaties, by confirming the principle of legal equality, and by establishing the principle of consent as a necessary basis for all agreements and treaties. All of these constituted the norms of the system and they are to be found today in the constitutions of numerous international organizations, in common practice, and in the corpus of international law.[3]

---

[3] After decades of neglect in the study of international relations, scholars have recently rediscovered Westphalia and its significance for diplomacy. Particularly notable recent contributions include Krasner (1999), Philpott (2001), Kegley and Raymond (2002), and a dissenting view about the significance of the treaties, in Osiander (2001).

The Peace of Westphalia: practical consequences

International practice following the Peace of Westphalia was not always consistent with the norms that were implicit or explicit in the two great treaties. However, those practices did change notably after 1648. For example, most states most of the time ceased to meddle in many of the succession quarrels that beset all monarchical systems (Louis XIV was an important exception; he was constantly involved in British succession conflicts). Contrary to the common belief that Europe of the early modern era was politically homogeneous, dominated by hereditary monarchies, in fact it was heterogeneous. The royal absolutism of Louis XIV coexisted with republics in Venice and Genoa, elected monarchs in Denmark (until 1660), Poland, Hungary, and Sweden, a semi-republic in Holland and (briefly) in England, and ecclesiastic city-states throughout the empire. Westphalia helped to create tolerance for these different political forms.

The Westphalia settlement effectively terminated the great religious sources of international conflict typical of the sixteenth and seventeenth centuries. For the most part the post-Westphalia sovereigns respected the domestic arrangements of their colleagues. They dabbled in foreign court intrigues and occasionally took sides in succession quarrels, but there were no significant armed interventions to change governments or the religious preferences of their societies between the end of the War of the Spanish Succession and 1787, when Prussia intervened to topple the republican government in Holland.[4] The pattern of war and intervention in the sixteenth century as compared with the post-Westphalia era is substantially different. The earlier period was characterized by deep religious quarrels, frequent armed forays to assist religious brethren or to massacre religious enemies, and the obliteration and annexation of principalities, duchies, and aspiring monarchs. The latter period had frequent wars and numerous territorial exchanges or gains and losses, but a new type of moderation developed between the new sovereigns. They basically learned to live with each other, to respect their diverse domestic arrangements, and to buttress each other's sovereignty. No longer could any spokespersons, whether Catholic, Lutheran, Calvinist, or Orthodox, "sustain a claim to a political order of a uniform faith" (Philpott, 2001: 89).

---

[4] Of the fifty-eight European interstate wars between 1648 and 1815, the protection of religious confreres was one of the issues that generated conflict in seven wars. Since the wars would have taken place without this issue, they cannot be considered as armed interventions. For figures and discussion, see Holsti (1991: chs. 3–5).

Diplomatic practice moved in the direction of a monopoly for sovereigns. The settlement catalogued the roster of sovereign polities, a total of 343 in Germany alone, of which 158 were secular estates, principalities, and electorates, 123 were religious principalities, and 62 imperial cities (Kegley and Raymond, 2002: 116). Over the next 150 years this membership in the "club of sovereigns" declined steadily until the Congress of Vienna 1815, when there was a major culling of entities that claimed sovereign status. Lesser entities eventually stopped sending envoys abroad and many proto-sovereigns that sought formal recognition as states in the broader European system (as opposed to members of the empire) failed to gain that status.

The church continued to involve itself in spiritual and ecclesiastical matters but it dropped its claim to have a right to levy taxes without sovereign consent. States increasingly behaved as sovereigns. This meant they had freedom from any higher authority, but also new legal obligations toward each other. Most fundamentally, they had to acknowledge that externally if they claimed sovereign status from others, they had a reciprocal obligation to respect the political independence of the other princes and states. These rules within the empire made it an oasis of peace within central Europe almost until its formal abolition in 1806. According to Anders Osiander (1994: 73),

> it is clear that, small as almost all of them were, they [the German states] could not have survived unless they jointly respected and upheld the Empire and its constitution. This is entirely typical of what a stable international system involves – some realization that individual objectives (in this case, the very fundamental one of self-preservation) are more easily attained in a stable environment, so that maintaining such an environment becomes a collective goal.

The Peace of Westphalia: ideational and normative consequences

What of an overall sense of obligation to respect the sovereign status of neighbors, allies, and competitors? Seventeenth-century thought on this problem was split. On the one hand, legal positivists emphasized the freedom side of sovereignty: sovereigns could be constrained solely by treaties to which they had given consent. Otherwise they were free to conduct their relations with other states as they wished. This included an unfettered right to wage war and to engage in foreign conquests. Hugo Grotius and his successors, on the other hand, emphasized the continuing relevance of an international community. By the late eighteenth century, the idea of a European society of states became increasingly accepted. Sovereignty, Emerich Vattel and his supporters suggested, is not a license for aggrandizement, war, and plunder. It is not absolute freedom. There is, rather, a natural, if secular, international community to which the sovereigns belong. Contiguity and historical development had created a unity of sorts, and that unity must be governed by legal arrangements. Earlier theorists such as Grotius had attempted to develop laws relating to the conduct of war. Vattel, in contrast, developed ideas about the role of legal norms in times of peace. Vattel, in short, sought to develop the legal modalities for a system of peaceful coexistence between sovereigns who theoretically had complete freedom of action. These ideas had a powerful impact on the rulers of the day and increasingly affected the policies and practices of the sovereigns (cf., Hinsley, 1967).

The connection between ideas and sovereignty practices were notable in this era. Monarchs used the arguments, vocabulary, and concepts of the publicists and scholars to buttress their claims to a monopoly of legitimate authority at home, and to disarm and subjugate lesser authorities within their realms, including free cities, duchies, and the like. They eagerly embraced the idea that sovereignty was complete and indivisible and used it to de-legitimize the constant rebellions, attempts at secession, and civil wars that raged throughout Europe in the early seventeenth century. In the Catholic countries, as we have seen, the rulers used the idea to contain and resist the authority claimed by the pope (Oresco, et al. 1997: 2). They also copied each other, repeating the claims of sovereignty, but amplifying them with each expression. Peter the Great declared in 1716, virtually copying a similar statement issued by the Swedish *riksdag* in 1693: "His Majesty is a Sovereign monarch, who is responsible to no one for his actions, but has the power to rule his state and his lands as a Christian lord according to his will and good understanding." In 1755, Louis XV, outdoing even the tsar, declared: "C'est en ma personne seule que reside l'autorité souveraine don't le caractère propre est l'ésprit de conseil, de justice et de raison. C'est à moi seul qu'appartient le pouvoir législatif sans dependence et sans partage. L'ordre public tout entier émane de moi" (quoted in Orseco et al. 1997, 2, 3).

These claims were only partly descriptive and largely rhetorical, but they demonstrated the extent to which the rulers of the era defined their authority in terms of ideas enunciated during the previous three centuries by jurists, publicists, and scholars. By the end of the eighteenth century, analysts had constructed long lists of sovereign rights and powers, including making war and peace, conducting foreign relations, appointing ambassadors, striking money, granting pardons and making final judgments, legitimizing bastards, naturalizing foreigners, and making laws. Those rulers who exercised few of those rights were then not truly sovereign.

By the late seventeenth and early eighteenth centuries, ideas about legal equality – a critical corollary of sovereignty – also began to infuse diplomatic practice and discourse. The distinction between a legal status and actual influence is nicely summarized in a French note in 1644 conceding that "although the crowns, in regard to their sovereignty and independence, are equal, there is always pre-eminence, and, of necessity, one [status] must give way to the other" (quoted in Osiander, 1994: 83). The negotiations leading to the Peace of Westphalia emphasized the autonomy of the various actors, but as Osiander (1994: 87–8) notes,

> Equality was the unavoidable corollary of autonomy. The more the was of the one, the more there had to be of the other. In the German subsystem [the empire], where autonomy of the estates fell short of complete independence, a hierarchical order was still practicable to some extent. In the European system at large, rejection of the universal authority formerly vested in emperor and pope logically implied complete equality for all the actors that recognized each other. In a system where the autonomy principle was accepted fully, the question could no longer be that of where in the system actors ranked, but merely whether or not they legitimately . . . belonged to the system.

By the time the negotiations to end the War of the Spanish Succession (1701–13) took place in Utrecht, the legal equality of members of the European society of states was firmly established through standardized practice. The position of the Holy Roman Empire at Münster had been unique, and some elements of hierarchical practices – particularly in the elaborate arrangements and arguments about precedence and protocol – remained. But at Utrecht, the status of the emperor was no longer an issue. He was the equal of the other European crowns. The peacemakers at Utrecht dispensed with the troublesome questions of rank and precedence that rankled the negotiations in Osnabrück and Münster, and in championing the principle of autonomy, they in effect institutionalized the idea or norm of legal equality. What had been perhaps more of an aspiration than fact in 1644–8 had become reality by 1713 (cf., Osiander, 1994: 120–1).

The idea of an interdependent European society of states with a common fate was also firmly established in the thinking of princes and diplomats of the time. Lord Bolingbroke, the main English architect of the Utrecht settlement, constantly referred to a "system for a future settlement of Europe," or to the "general system of power in Europe," or even to the "constitution of Europe." Indeed, the diplomats made a distinction between the private interests of individual princes and the general welfare of Europe. They used the latter concept (the "repose" of Europe) as a vague notion to judge the legitimacy of the actions of the kings and queens of the era. Private aspirations were only legitimate if they were compatible with the notion of Europe's "repose" (Osiander, 1994: 110–11). The various treaties that make up the Utrecht settlement contain numerous references to the "repose," "equilibrium," and the "public good of the peace." Increasingly, diplomatic practices were becoming consistent with some of the main components of the concept of sovereignty. Only in the area of territorial partition and the trading of crowns, principalities, and cities (e.g., the transfer of Spain's "holdings" and crowns in Italy – Sicily, Milan, and Naples as the most important – to the empire and to Savoy) was there a continuation of pre-seventeenth-century practices and systematic violation of the principle of sovereign independence and territorial integrity.

Sovereignty and the birth of states

Sovereignty practices did not suddenly shift with the settlements at Westphalia, but the treaties of Osnabrück and Münster established new yardsticks for identifying rules or customs for recognizing states, that is, the entrance criteria for club membership. In the eighteenth century, many of the smaller members of the Holy Roman Empire, free cities, and princes of dubious lineage and estates that had not gained formal international recognition were denied the right to establish official embassies abroad. Next came a wholesale relative downgrading of polities at the Congress of Vienna in 1815. Many sought to upgrade their rulers to princes and kings, but the great powers denied their requests. The Final Act of the Congress listed thirty-nine states as comprising the European diplomatic system. This figure was much lower than the number of polities that claimed to be sovereign. If there was any doubt about the issue in the eighteenth century, the Congress of Vienna firmly established that polities would not enjoy the rights of sovereignty until recognized by other powers, meaning primarily the great powers of the day. While France, Prussia, Sweden, Venice, Spain and others may have been sovereigns by historical longevity, new claimants to this status had to be *recognized* to gain entrance to the club. A state could exist in fact, but until it had received diplomatic recognition it had none of the rights associated with sovereignty. Recognition, then, is crucial to the *creation* of states.

Recognition practices in the Europeans' relations with the rest of the world were paradoxical. On the one hand, in the seventeenth century, European envoys, missionaries, commercial agents, and the great English and Dutch charter companies dealt with Asian potentates as if they were sovereigns. They negotiated treaties with them, made alliances, and fought wars, frequently adhering to the protocols found within Europe itself. On the other hand, they did not urge or allow their Asian counterparts to join the European club of states. They exchanged ambassadors with Turkey already in the seventeenth century, but Turkey did not obtain general European diplomatic recognition until 1856. China, Japan, Siam, Persia, and a few other non-European states did not receive general recognition until the late nineteenth century. In addition to the standard requirements for recognition (defined territories, administrative capacity and effective rule, and ability to enter into treaty relations), the European states established an added "standard of civilization," an eminently flexible set of racial and legal criteria that "pagans" and "barbarians" had to meet before permanent embassies could be established. As for the "savage" societies, there was absolutely no question that they could become members of the club; their role was to act as good colonies, as experimental stations for the imperialists' grand design of civilizing them.[5] In between the colonies and the Turks, the Europeans established a variety of statuses for their clients: protectorates, spheres of influence, buffer zones, and the like. None had the status of states.

After World War I, recognition criteria changed again. In order to be recognized, the successor states of the Russian, German, Austrian, and Ottoman empires had to meet the new criteria of, first, democratic constitutions, and, second, guarantees for the rights of their minorities. Running from Finland in the north to the kingdom of the Serbs and Slovenes (later Yugoslavia) in the south, none of the new states received

---

[5] European cultural analysts, buttressed by ethnographers, created a strict racial hierarchy that guided social policy, diplomacy, and the arts. The pagans were at the top, followed by barbarians, with savages at the bottom. For an examination of the influence of the hierarchy in various realms in Europe, see Wan (1992).

recognition until they had met these criteria. The entire discourse of state creation at the Paris Peace Conference was founded on ideas of constitutionalism, democracy, and minority rights. According to Daniel Philpott (2001: 37–8), these minority treaties were among the first major limitations on major sovereignty norms. In today's parlance, they represented an investiture of "conditional sovereignty," that is, the withholding of recognition subject to certain limitations on sovereign authority *within* states.

After World War II, recognition practices changed again. The colonial powers and other states extended recognition to the former colonies without requiring any tests, whether related to domestic political institutions or to the traditional criteria of effective control over a defined territory and population. An eminent international lawyer outlined in 1955 what he considered to be the traditional and essential minimum requirements for gaining membership into the club of states. Those included clearly established boundaries and reasonable prospects of maintaining them; an administration with *de facto* capacity to govern the area; laws and institutions capable of giving reasonable protection to aliens and minorities; maintaining reasonable standards of justice among all inhabitants; and a public opinion, and institutions for manifesting it, which gives reasonable indication of a desire for independence and a reasonable assurance of the permanence of the two preceding conditions (Wright, 1955: 185). In fact, as the record of war, secession, and state collapse since the 1950s indicates, many of the colonies at the time of independence could not meet these criteria. Nevertheless, they gained recognition and entered as full-fledged members of the United Nations. The bar to recognition had been lowered almost to invisibility. Colonial status was sufficient in itself to gain admission to the club.

In the 1990s, in contrast, many governments insisted that they would recognize the former constituent units of the Soviet Union and Yugoslavia only on condition that they commit themselves to democratic political institutions, guaranteed rights for minorities, and free market economies. Recognition practices were reverting back to the principles of 1919, except that free market economic institutions were added to the list of conditions.[6]

---

[6] Statement of conditions was one thing; actual recognition policy was another. The United States had insisted on the conditions as a requirement for recognizing, among others, Uzbekistan. James Baker, the American secretary of state, went there in 1992 to review the conditions. He was met at the airport by the Uzbekistan president, who waved a copy of the constitution at Baker to prove that the country was now democratic and adhering to free market principles. This was sufficient to persuade Baker to grant recognition.

Sovereignty and the maintenance of states

Sovereignty is no less critical for the *maintenance* of states. The international community generally addresses the question of states under threat of dissolution with a strong bias in favor of territorial "integrity" and continuation of the state. This is seen for example in the lack of support for secessionist movements. Generally, states have withheld recognition from secessionist movements unless or until they have succeeded in creating new states. Only four African states recognized the Biafra secessionist movement in the 1960s, but three of them did so only toward the end of the war for humanitarian reasons. Only India recognized the forcible secession of Bangladesh from Pakistan before it was an established fact. No one recognized the Tamil Tigers as representatives of a sovereign state. On the contrary, even India, which might be expected to support its Tamil ethnic kin in a neighboring country, intervened on behalf of the government of Sri Lanka, that is, in support of the integrity of the state. Cyprus remains divided. Only Turkey has recognized the government of the Turkish Republic of North Cyprus, while UN the Security Council has passed Resolution 550 (1984) stating that the TRNC's declaration of independence is null and void. No one has recognized the *de facto* secession of Somaliland from Somalia, and most states do not maintain formal diplomatic relations with Taiwan. Perhaps most problematic, the major NATO states and Russia that dealt with the Kosovo crisis in 1999–2000 refused to sanction the formal secession of the province from Yugoslavia. The Rambouillet Accords (1999), which the allies used as a justification for the bombing campaign to stop the ethnic cleansing of the Kosovars by the Serbs, provided substantial autonomy for the province of Kosovo, but maintained that the ultimate purpose of the accords was to maintain the sovereignty and territorial integrity of the Yugoslav federation. All of these secessionist movements led to the creation of *de facto* states – they meet the traditional criteria for statehood – but they have failed to obtain entry into the club because most members of the United Nations are mutually protective of their sovereignty and territorial integrity (Pegg, 1998). In general, despite the frequent violations of the non-interference norm, states today take very seriously any policies or actions that might permanently change the territorial map of the world, and the roster of states which make up that world. While on the one hand the international community relaxed the criteria for recognition for post-colonial states, once states have been admitted to the club, would-be states within them have almost no chance of separating from them and subsequently gaining membership. The one obvious exception is where the secession has been peaceful, and usually validated through a plebiscite or some other mechanism demonstrating public support. This was the case of the ex-Soviet republics and of the split up of Czechoslovakia in 1993 (the "velvet divorce").

Sovereignty and the death of states: the problem of conquest

The constitutive aspects of sovereignty deal primarily with legal equality, state creation, and recognition. But if states are sovereign and if one of the rights adhering to sovereignty is the use of force, then what happens to states or other types of polities that are the objects of conquest? In this area we see an example of obsolescence, where an old right has been abolished. Of all of the rules and norms associated with sovereignty, this is the one that most clearly distinguishes a society of states from a mere collection of polities that regularly interact. In no other historical system of states was there ever a formal renunciation of a right of conquest. Conquest, on the contrary, was a normal part of the lives of most polities.

In the fifteenth and sixteenth centuries the Europeans developed the idea of conquest as a *right*, and not merely a standard practice. Jurists and church authorities outlined a set of rules that legitimized Spanish and Portuguese conquests in the Western Hemisphere. Certain rituals and procedures had to be followed in order to establish as legitimate the formal annexation of territories secured in the name of the Spanish or Portuguese kings and queens of the era. The European states subsequently transformed these rules and regulations into a general right of conquest that entitled conquerors to annex territory, to establish new government structures in the conquered areas, and to attach legal title to new acquisitions. This amounted to a legal charter for predation. It was justified as a logical corollary of sovereignty.

In the great debates about Spanish conquests in the New World, the standard view was that these were justified on a number of grounds, not the least of which was the "barbaric" practices of the indigenous populations. Vitoria and some others argued to the contrary: since the natives had their own forms of governance, social institutions, and use of land, conquest was legitimate only in certain cases, for example, where the natives prohibited peaceful commerce and missionary activities or where they violated natural law, as in the case of human sacrifice. Conquest of uninhabited lands (*terra nullius*) was permissible if various institutions of control (e.g., settlements, forts, and the like) were put in place. As for conquests within Europe, they had to be based on some sort of legal claim (e.g., rights of inheritance or succession). If those were "just," then the use of force to advance or protect those claims was legitimate. As we have already noted, the political map of Europe in this era changed almost on an annual basis as territories were sold, bartered, exchanged, partitioned, and conquered. Wars involving territorial issues predominated over those involving other types of issues during this period and until the end of the Napoleonic wars (Holsti, 1991: chs. 3, 5).

Eighteenth-century philosophers such as Jean Jacques Rousseau and Immanuel Kant based part of their criticism of despotic governments on the grounds that they indulged in foreign conquests, often for the sake of royal prestige, but with disastrous consequences for those who paid the taxes to support foreign adventures. Under the legal doctrines of the day, conquest was still a corollary of sovereignty, but increasingly the attentive public condemned the practice. Hence, the French revolutionaries, in proclaiming a "new world" in which the corrupt repertoire of royal practices would be abolished, publicly renounced foreign conquest in 1790. They formalized the declaration in the 1791 constitution that proclaims that "the French nation renounces undertaking any war with a view of making conquests . . ." (Fabry, forthcoming: ch. 1). Napoleon nevertheless quickly renounced such self-abnegation by organizing unprecedented conquests and territorial revisions throughout Europe.

The negotiators at the Congress of Vienna (1815) recognized that Napoleon, in practicing unlimited conquests throughout the continent, had fundamentally unsettled the order of Europe. He had annexed territories to France, carved up others and attached them to his satellite states. He also created a number of fictitious states such as the Rauracian, Batavian, Anconitan, Ligurian, and Cisalpine republics and extinguished a number of old states by partitioning them among his friends and allies, or simply swallowed them into the French empire.

To prevent new depredations, the delegates in the Vienna Final Act declared that sovereignty could no longer be acquired merely by conquest, nor could it be transferred to the conqueror without the consent of the vanquished. While the delegates made numerous territorial changes in 1815, significantly none of the parties pressed their claim on the basis of a *right* of conquest. The Congress of Vienna thus effectively began to undermine the old right of conquest.[7] Future transfers of sovereignty could take place but they would have no legal status unless other states recognized them. Just as states would require recognition to establish their sovereignty, so the "club" of states would have to validate any alterations in the legal status of territorial or other changes relating to sovereignty. Here again we see the idea of a society of states legitimizing its members' actions; without its approval, changes to the roster of states and to their territorial configuration would have no legal standing. Limiting the right of conquest was a major change in sovereignty norms. It provided a strong foundation for the claim that one of the essential functions of sovereignty is protection of the state and its territory. And it established firmly that sovereignty is not a license for total freedom of action in the external realm. Coupled with the changing norms regarding the use of force in international politics (see chapter 9), serious qualification of the right of conquest became a major constraint on freedom of action.

Ideas about conquest also changed substantially with the development of nationalism and its corollary, the doctrine of national self-determination. If a defined territory incorporated a historical and cultural "people," then military conquest by foreigners – at least in Europe – contradicts the norm of self-government, a norm that had become widely accepted and applied, particularly in the Balkans, by the late nineteenth century (cf., Fabry, 2002). By the twentieth century, conquest became de-legitimized. The League of Nations Covenant specified that the highest purpose of the organization was to protect the sovereignty, independence, and territorial integrity of its members. The Stimson Doctrine (1931) declared that the United States would not recognize as legal any territorial changes brought about through the use of armed force. The League of Nations subsequently adopted this position as a new rule of international relations. The United Nations Charter (esp. Article 2(4)) effectively terminated any remaining vestiges of the old legitimacy accorded to conquest. This means that today there is no legitimate means of bringing about the death of states. Any forcible action that extinguishes sovereignty is the most fundamental "crime" of contemporary international politics. Sovereignty is thus a guarantee against the death of states.

---

[7] This act challenges the popular view that the Congress of Vienna sought only to restore the pre-revolutionary world. Limiting the right of conquest was a revolutionary change.

The case for transformation of sovereignty

The contemporary theoretical literature on international relations is replete with statements to the effect that sovereignty is "perforated, defiled, cornered, eroded, extinct, anachronistic, and even interrogated" (Fowler and Bunck, 1995: 2). Others have suggested that it has become "unbundled," "fragmented," "transcended," "subverted," "shared," "reduced," "shifted," "pooled," and "surrendered." (cf., Fabry, 1998: 29, fn. 9). Hardly a day goes by that some or other analyst proclaims that a particular treaty, agreement, or proposal for economic integration involves the "surrender" of sovereignty. Most importantly, the processes of globalization are rendering the whole idea of sovereignty an anachronism. The type of change is toward obsolescence. To take one typical example, Jan Scholte (1997: 21, 29) argues that globalization "has rendered the old core principle of sovereignty unworkable . . . both judicially and practically. State regulatory capacities have ceased to meet the criteria of sovereignty." He arrives at this conclusion because he incorrectly defines sovereignty as "comprehensive, supreme, unqualified, and exclusive *power*" (Scholte, 1997: 26; my italics). Richard Falk, an international lawyer by training and profession, insists that "the globalized 'presence' of Madonna, McDonald's and Mickey Mouse make a mockery of sovereignty as exclusive territorial control" (Falk, 1993: 853). Similar statements dot the literature.

Probably in no other area of the field of International Relations is there such misunderstanding of an important concept and institution. In the chapter on the state we already noted the common error of confusing authority with power or influence. This same error is commonly reproduced in many contributions to contemporary discourse on sovereignty. What is the basis for the numerous claims about the "erosion" or "loss" of sovereignty in the contemporary world? Most analysts point to a variety of trends, including the increasing inability of governments to regulate and control flows of capital, ideas, fads, drugs, diseases, and other transactions in a "borderless" world. Governments, moreover, no longer have the capacity to develop their own priorities to meet social needs, but must adopt policies that are friendly to foreign investors, including the famed "electronic herd" of computer investors who can invest and divest billions of dollars in an economy in a matter of moments (cf., Friedman, 2000: esp. ch. 7). They are vulnerable to a host of external actions that bring about all sorts of negative consequences that they cannot fend off. Sovereignty has thus been lost or at least badly compromised. Or they point to changing identities with the argument that people no longer give their loyalty and allegiance to their national governments in an unqualified fashion, but prefer to identify themselves according to subgroups and fragmenting ideas such as religion, race, ethnicity, language, or sexual orientation. We have already considered this argument in the previous chapter. Finally, others claim that states give up their sovereignty when they join regional trading groups, or even when they sign treaties that constrain their domestic policy choices (e.g., human rights accords, prohibitions against trade in endangered species, commitments to reduce pollution, and the like).

These diagnoses focus on transactions, power, and influence, but not on authority. They refer to sociological phenomena, not to a legal status. They also confuse and conflate the constitutive aspect of sovereignty with sovereignty rules. If we were to accept Scholte's definition of sovereignty – comprehensive, supreme, unqualified, and exclusive *power* – no state has ever been sovereign. None has ever achieved complete freedom of action and invulnerability to outside influences, and none ever will. Sovereignty is an institutionalized legal or juridical status, not a variable or sociological condition. That status is conferred on polities by other states, not by private groups, including the electronic herd. Some states may indeed be increasingly vulnerable to transactions such as the drug trade, or they may have difficulty controlling what their populations read, consume, or believe. While a host of sociological trends indicate that many states face increasing external constraints in their decision-making on domestic priorities (their autonomy is increasingly constrained), this is not the same as losing sovereignty. If millions of investors remove their funds from Malaysia, as they did in the summer of 1997, does this nullify Malaysia's standing as a sovereign state? Does it mean that Malaysia loses its membership in the United Nations and dozens of other international organizations? Does it mean that Malaysia no longer has the right to enter into treaty relations with other states? Or that it loses its votes in the International Monetary Fund? Or that Malaysians cease to be citizens of a legal entity called Malaysia? Or that in the event of a complicated case involving international law, Malaysia may not take the case to the International Court of Justice?

To illuminate the distinction between legal or juridical status, and autonomy, power, or influence, let us use an analogy of an individual who seeks a bank loan. She signs a contract that in exchange for the receipt of a loan of $10,000, she agrees to pay a certain sum monthly until the full sum plus interest has been paid off. She is now obligated to pay. In a world where money can be spent on millions of commodities and services, her freedom of choice has been reduced to the extent that instead of spending a sum to purchase expensive clothes, holidays, or works of art, she must now use those sums or at least part of them to repay the bank. She is increasingly constrained. But has she lost her sovereignty? Is she now a slave who must follow the commands of a superior without her consent? Has she ceased to be a citizen, with no legal standing in her community? Has she given up her rights to free speech and association? Obviously not. She has limited her complete freedom to spend, via a contract based on consent, but she has not compromised her sovereignty as a free person who enjoys all the rights and duties of citizenship in a community or state.

Governments signing treaties that impose obligations on them may limit their autonomy, but by doing so they are in fact confirming not undermining their sovereignty. They confirm their sovereignty because they sign a treaty by consent. In hierarchical systems such as empires, superiors order and coerce, and subordinates obey. The question of consent does not arise. As in the medieval system, lower actors are obligated to obey a higher authority. The assault on this obligation starting in the fourteenth century, as we have seen, eventually gave rise to the idea of sovereignty. In anarchical systems, in contrast, all collective actions or agreements are based on consent.[8] Notice, moreover, that all treaties contain a specific term, say five years, for the legal obligations to be binding, as well as modalities for withdrawal from the treaty or organization. No treaty based on consent removes sovereignty. The only way sovereignty can be lost today is either by formal conquest and annexation or by the voluntary amalgamation of a polity into a larger political unit. Since 1945, only one independent and commonly recognized state – South Vietnam – has lost its sovereignty. After its conquest by North Vietnam (recognized as a sovereign state only by fellow communist countries) in 1975–6, it ceased to exist. An integrated Vietnam replaced it.

---

[8] There are a few instances where consent is not required. For example, under Chapter VII of the United Nations Charter, states may be obliged to contribute troops to help repel an act of aggression or a breach of the peace. In fact, the Security Council has never taken a decision of this sort. In the two instances (Korea and Kuwait) where collective armed force was chosen, member states were asked to contribute troops. No one was compelled to do so. The only other case is where the World Trade Organization makes a decision on a trade issue or dispute. Its final decisions are binding and thus do not require consent in the formal sense.

What about the countries of the European Union? Members of the European Union retain their sovereignty, but in select issue areas such as a common currency or human rights, they have delegated authority to European bodies. The decisions of the European Court of Human Rights, for example, take precedence over national or local laws and regulations. Decisions of the European Commission have similar status. As Philpott (2001: 39) summarizes the status of sovereignty in the European Community:

> For the first time since the demise of the Holy Roman Empire, a significant political authority other than the state, one with formal sovereign prerogatives, became legitimate within the boundaries of the Westphalian system . . . The European Union does not replace states, but rather "pools" their sovereignty into a common "supranational" institution in which they no longer make decisions independently.

But note that even in such a context, members of the Community have the right to withdraw and they cannot be compelled to participate in certain policy initiatives without their consent. The government of Great Britain, for example, has not joined the common currency, but it remains a member of the Community.

All of this is to point out that sovereignty is not the same as autonomy, influence, constraints, or even power. States can be inefficient, vulnerable, poorly governed, or highly constrained in their domestic policy choices. Or they may be powerful, highly organized, efficient, and enjoy both popularity and loyalty. State capacity in the contemporary world varies greatly from the very weak to the very strong. But that does not make them less or more sovereign. As long as the international community confers sovereign status on a state, it is sovereign, and it enjoys all the rights and must meet all the obligations of sovereignty.

Even in fairly extreme cases, sovereignty is not extinguished by external intervention. During the early years of the Cold War, the political systems of the so-called East European satellites were highly penetrated by Soviet intrusion. In some cases, Soviet citizens actually occupied cabinet positions in East European governments, and the security services in those states were under the effective control of the Soviet KGB. The Soviet Union blatantly interfered in the internal affairs of those countries, as the United States has historically done in Central America. However, the international community continued to regard those states as sovereign. They made treaties with them, exchanged ambassadors, and encouraged them to join the wide variety of international organizations. Some participated in the proceedings of the International Court of Justice. All had their own armed forces, flags, and other symbols of sovereignty. All were highly constrained in their domestic policy choices, but in no case was the formal constitutional independence of those states abrogated or extinguished. The Soviet Union could not apply its domestic laws in, for example, Poland, any more than the United States could apply its law in Honduras or Guatemala. A citizen of the latter country who is charged with a crime is tried in a Guatemalan court, under Guatemalan law. American corporations may be powerful actors in Guatemalan domestic politics, and the United States government may frequently interfere in Guatemalan affairs, but all of this does not add up to the "loss" or "erosion" of Guatemala's status as a sovereign state. This is in contrast to the situation in medieval Europe where ecclesiastical courts could and did apply church law to individuals and corporate groups within kingdoms.

Sovereignty, then, is a matter of political authority, involving the right to rule (legitimacy) and the duty to obey. No one today within Canada has a duty to obey American law, any more than an American, in the United States, has a duty to obey Mexican law. So long as this situation prevails, states are sovereign. It is not only a quality of single states, but the fundamental feature of the international system. It is thus an international institution that describes the external limits on the authority of any one estate in relation to other states (Hurd, 1999: 393–9). It establishes authority (the right to rule) and the duty to obey within a specified territory, but by definition, then, it also limits authority to that domain. No state has the "right to rule" in another state. This is sovereignty. It has nothing to do with the ability to control the drug trade, or vulnerability to financial flows, or to the popularity of Madonna or Mickey Mouse within a society. The preposterousness of the latter claim is revealed if we simply switch the symbols. Would anyone argue that because North Americans like to eat sushi (Japan) and pizza (Italy), to drink Scotch (Scotland), to dance the samba (Brazil), and to take saunas (Finland) the sovereignty of Canada and the United States is "eroding"?

There are many types of dramatic sociological and technological changes taking place in the world today, as they have been for several centuries. It does not follow that they have transforming effects on international institutions as we have defined them, and particularly not on the constitutive rules of the system. After all, the constitutive concept of sovereignty did not change in its fundamentals because of the scientific revolution of the seventeenth century, the Enlightenment of the eighteenth century, or the nationalist and industrial revolutions of the nineteenth century. Those revolutions were no less dramatic (even if somewhat slower paced) in their social and political consequences than the technological revolution today. Sovereignty as a set of ideas, norms, and practices, though changing over time, survived those revolutions, so there is no automatic reason to believe that it must tend toward obsolescence today (cf., Jackson, 2000: 41). The case for transformation (erosion, unbundling, or generally in the direction of obsolescence) is based on a fundamental category error. It confuses influence with a legal status. The first refers to quantities; the second to a quality. The argument confuses autonomy with authority. The first refers to freedom; the second to a right (the "right to rule").

We must acknowledge, finally, that sovereignty as a constitutive rule and legal or juridical status also reflects an ideal. Political reality has never been completely consistent with it. Because of some inconsistencies and anomalies, some analysts claim that sovereignty is tending toward obsolescence, or that it was never more than a figleaf that the strong use to coerce and dominate the weak. But inconsistencies and anomalies do not prove obsolescence, irrelevance, or transformation. Historically there have always been anomalies. For example, although the Westphalia settlement restored freedom to the principalities and other independent units of the Holy Roman Empire, those same principalities continued to be subject to certain imperial legal provisions and court jurisdictions. These did not end formally until 1806, but it would be foolish to argue that Saxony and Prussia were not full sovereign states throughout the eighteenth century. Likewise, even today India recognizes the queen of England as the head of the Commonwealth, and until 1982 ultimate constitutional authority with regard to Canada lay with the Judicial Committee of the British Privy Council. Symbolically, therefore, Canada was not a sovereign state until it repatriated its constitution in 1982. Yet, the international community recognized it as a sovereign state as early as 1919. Canada was a founding member of the League of Nations. There are other contemporary anomalies and bizarre cases such as official labor union representation in the International Labor Organization, or Monaco's membership in the United Nations. None is sovereign, yet all have some form or other of membership in the club, and they participate in some (usually only a few) of its activities. But because they are anomalies and are commonly regarded as such, they constitute more the exceptions that prove the rule than serious contenders to suggest that sovereignty is a hopelessly outmoded concept. We will probably never have a perfect fit between the ideal of sovereignty and the facts on the ground. But the rough edges do not provide adequate or convincing evidence that sovereignty has lost its meaning or significance in international relations.

What has changed?

So far, we have dealt only with the constitutive rules or norms of sovereignty. In subsequent chapters we will assess some critical changes in the procedural aspects of sovereignty such as the use of force, the question of intervention, and the rule of non-interference. But the core ideas of the constitutive aspects of sovereignty, including constitutional independence, exclusive legal jurisdiction within a defined territory, and legal equality, have remained essentially the same throughout the ages since sovereignty became the *Grundnorm* of the society of states in the seventeenth century. They have been interpreted differently in varying political contexts, but they have not been transformed into competing principles or made obsolete. The rules of sovereignty constitute, in Philpott's view (1999: 145–7), the "constitution" of the society of states. It is no less so today than it was by the late seventeenth century. The only critical change – and it has fundamental consequences for the texture of international politics – is the obsolescence of the right of conquest, once considered an essential attribute of sovereignty. The main point to be made from its obsolescence is that it has helped solidify the other aspects of constitutive sovereignty and some of the procedural ones as well. In our categories of change, then, sovereignty can be classified as an institution of increased complexity, but with the important exception that the old derivative right of conquest has become obsolete.

As a foundational institution of international relations, sovereignty remains at the core of all relations between states. Its main functions – protection, identification of the legal actors, recognition, state continuity, and equalizing the legal relations between strong and weak – have not fundamentally changed. They have been made more complex perhaps and occasionally reinterpreted – as in the case of recognition practices – but they continue to stand as the ideational and legal foundation of a society of states. Millions of people, hundreds of thousands of officials, and hundreds of top-level decision-makers in almost two hundred states practice sovereignty daily, usually without thinking about it. The great diplomatic documents of our era such as the Charter of the United Nations and the Charter of Paris do not just contain rules about how states should act, but in effect summarize how most states do act most of the time. That there are anomalies in and violations of the rules cannot lead to the conclusion that the rules do not exist. The main ideas, the subject of debate, struggle, and sometimes armed conflict for almost one-half of a millennium (between the twelfth and seventeenth-centuries), while the subject of constant analysis, reinterpretation, and advocacy today, continue in their essential seventeenth-century forms. Thus, as an authoritative analysis of the status of sovereignty claims (Danish Institute of International Affairs, 1999: 27),

> State sovereignty is still a cornerstone of the international legal and political order, but to a growing degree the classical perception of sovereignty is challenged by the norm that the legitimacy of the exercise of the rights of sovereignty is dependent on respect for human rights . . . This is not an abrupt change from sovereignty to something else. The principle of sovereignty has throughout its 3–400 years history been continuously re-defined and modified. Although the form has been constant, the content has changed.

Without sovereignty we would not have international law; without international law we would not have a society of states; and without a society of states we would have little order, stability, and predictability. The history of states systems that did not incorporate a sovereignty-like principle is one that most would not wish to duplicate today. It may not have been a war of all against all, all of the time, but as the historians have chronicled, the rulers of the Chinese "warring states," the Greek city-states, Rome, and the Renaissance Italian city-states were preoccupied more with the preparation and launching of wars than with the bases of peace and order. So they were in seventeenth-century Europe, but the gap between sovereignty norms and standard practices narrowed slowly in the eighteenth century, and then became deeply inscribed in the mental repertoires of nineteenth-century statesmen following the demise of Napoleon.

5   International law

Politically distinct groups, whether tribes, city-states, kingdoms, or other types of polities, have been in various kinds of contact with each other for more than 7,000 years. For some, connections were thin and intermittent. An example would be the irregular and limited trade that took place between the Chinese Empire after 220 BC and its Roman counterpart. At the other end of the spectrum would be the regular and patterned transactions between many of the Chinese states of the "Spring and Autumn" and "Warring States" periods (771–220 BC) or the relations between the city-states of Greece between the seventh and third centuries BC.

Although considerable variation existed in the nature of these relationships, many were conducted within the context of certain rules and norms indicating proper behavior. We find that even in relations between groups from different cultures, certain norms typically helped regulate relations. Among these would be the norm that treaties or other forms of contracts are binding, or that messengers or other forms of diplomatic representation should enjoy certain immunities. Even in warfare, polities often observed certain rules or limits. These rules were usually culture-specific. In warfare between polities of different cultures, the lack of restraint was typical. The Romans defeated Carthage twice and in the final Punic war, they razed the city, slaughtered all its inhabitants, and sowed the ground with salt. The military relations between Christians and Muslims during the era of the crusades were similarly brutal. More recently, the Spanish conquest of the Aztecs and Incas featured unrestrained slaughter of resisters. British colonial forces likened their military campaigns in Africa to a safari, killing all natives indiscriminately. American armed forces, vigilante groups, and militias practiced virtual genocide and massive ethnic cleansing of native Indians from the seventeenth century into the late nineteenth century.

The record of establishing and observing rules and norms to guide and restrain relations between independent polities throughout history is thus checkered. We find both primitive prototypes of modern international law, as well as unrestrained and barbaric behavior. While there have been many pre-modern systems of states, few of them could be termed, in the sense that Hedley Bull (1977) implied, a *society of states* whose members shared a common interest in maintenance of the system and who mutually recognized their sovereign equality (Stivachtis, 1998: 189). More common were suzerain systems in which laws, norms, and convention prescribed distinct but unequal roles, practices, and functions between superiors and inferiors. In contrast, the international law that developed in Europe since the seventeenth century is a corpus of regulations, duties, obligations, and rights pertaining to legal equals, in this case sovereign states. Before reviewing briefly the institutionalization and globalization of that law, we should recapitulate the earlier discussion of institutions and their component ideas, practices, and norms.

Norms, rules, and law

Rules, norms, and etiquette guide international relationships, as in all social relations. This is not to say that without them, such relationships would necessarily resemble a perpetual war of all against all. A voluminous literature demonstrates that self-interested actors that come into contact with each other, without a previous history of a relationship, can nevertheless develop rules and norms that lead to a semblance of peaceful coexistence. These guides to interaction can be formal, as in codes and treaties, or informal, as in "rules of the game" or "politeness." If they successfully guide behavior, if they are taken into consideration in decision-making, and if they persist over time and eventually become custom or convention, then whether or not they are formally codified makes little difference. No one legislated that gentlemen should open doors for ladies, but for many generations most gentlemen most of the time practiced this behavior that had become customary.

We can say that international law has become institutionalized when, first, practice by most states most of the time is consistent with its rules and norms; second, there is a reasonable consensus on the interpretation of norms, rules, and rights; and, third, when the law has some authority independent of the particular interests of particular states at a given time. Further evidence of institutionalization appears when the rules, norms, and rights are translated into binding obligations formalized in treaties and conventions, and when they are interpreted though court-like organizations and procedures. Consistency of practice further validates the law. In other cases, practices may come first. They then lead to a customary obligation, which only later – if at all – becomes inscribed into formal legal language. As an illustration, the custom of vessels passing on the left started as a coordinating practice to reduce collisions. Later the practice became a convention of the "rules of the road," and ultimately was inscribed into international treaties and other forms of international legislation.

International law, as we shall discuss it, refers to those duties (obligations) and rights of states and individuals that have become generalized across the international system or society of states. We will not refer to the millions of specific obligations and contracts contained in tens of thousands of bilateral and multilateral treaties; but we should acknowledge that most of them are consistent with general principles of international law. Because they contain general principles (e.g., applicable to all states equally), they chronicle the contemporary rules of the game in the mutual relations of states. International law, as reflected in this great body of treaties, prescribes what its subjects can do (permissive), what they cannot do, and what they must do in certain circumstances. Dorothy Jones (1990: 124) likens it to a code of professional ethics, as among lawyers, teachers, doctors, and dentists. The major principles have been developed and interpreted over several centuries. Most are consented to implicitly by the act of becoming a state. Others are accepted as customary law, to which consent is automatically granted upon joining the society of states. Formal treaty obligations must gain explicit consent to conform to the permissive and constraining rules and norms. There is common understanding that to violate them will incur costs, including expulsion from the society of states. Today we use the term "rogue state" to describe those polities that regularly violate the rules of coexistence.

In addition to the more than 40,000 United Nations registered bilateral and multilateral treaties, there is also a vast body of rules and rights spelled out in major international conventions. These include, among others, the Charter of the United Nations, the Helsinki Final Act (1975), the Charter of Paris (1990), the Universal Declaration of Human Rights and subsequent multilateral treaties, the charters of regional organizations such as the Organization of African Unity (now the African Union), the Organization of American States, and the Association of Southeast Asian Nations, and the decisions of international courts and legal scholars. Many of them affirm and reaffirm the basic principles of relations between states, such as sovereignty and territorial integrity. The fact that these principles are duplicated in a variety of cultural and diplomatic contexts is further evidence of the institutionalization of contemporary international law. It is a legal system in part because its principles are universal and apply equally to all states regardless of their political, social, economic, or cultural characteristics.

We need not delve into the particularities of norms, rules, and etiquette and the distinctions between them (cf., Kratochwil, 1989). We can use the commonsense notions of obligations (to do or not to do certain things), rights (designating permissive behavior or entitlements), and exchanges (I will give you this if you give me that) for our analysis. Here it is sufficient to point out that in Europe since the seventeenth century, and increasingly around the entire world during the past century, governments have developed a global consensus on the fundamental rules according to which they will conduct their mutual relations. Whether ideas (including ethical norms) or practices came first is less important than whether they are consistent in the relations between states most of the time. Violation of the rules does not render them less law-like, unless violation becomes common practice. Indeed, the common outcry against violations proves the vitality of the law. In a curious way, practices that violate legal obligations may actually strengthen them because publicity of legal norms helps to refresh their legitimacy and authority (Malmvig, 2001).

Early ideas about international obligations

Europe in the sixteenth century had no public international law as we know it today.[1] There were no codes or organizational charters that defined the fundamental principles. But there were vigorous legal debates surrounding a host of issues that dominated the European agenda of that era, and there were arguments about the sources and types of law. What were these issues?

As we have already seen in chapter 3, the greatest debates concerned the nature of political community in Europe. In the sixteenth century, the

---

[1] There was, however, a corpus of private law that regulated economic transactions between societies. It was known as the Law Merchant (*lex mercatoria*), and exists today.

most common conception was of a Christian community – the *respublica Christiana* – under the authority of the pope and the Holy Roman Emperor. This community was threatened by an external enemy, the Turks, upon whom it was entitled and even obliged to make war. The wars between Christian princes were regarded in effect as civil wars, not wars between states as we would understand them today (Tuck, 1999: 29). Following this representation of the political community, relations with *all* infidels were of a different order and kind to relations among Christians. The pope legitimated the foreign conquests of the Spaniards and Portuguese in the early part of the century and indeed even claimed the authority to allocate unexplored lands to their conquerors. The formal justification was that force and conquest were necessary to protect missionaries and to stamp out the sins of Indians against natural law in matters of sexual morality (Tuck, 1999: 62). Papal jurisdiction even extended to the seas. The pope could and did allocate "ownership" of sections of the seas, a practice that was undermined only in the seventeenth century.

Others had a very different conception of Europe. They were the champions of the growing power of secular princes, and of the various notions of sovereignty that were used to challenge papal and imperial claims to "universal" authority. The Spanish conquests in the New World were made in the name of the Spanish king, and not the pope. But aside from some presumed right of conquest, analysts of the period could not agree upon the rules that would regulate contacts with the natives. Some argued that the barbarian practices of the natives, particularly as relating to sex and human sacrifice, justified forceful conversion, virtual slavery, and appropriation of all lands. Others, such as the Spanish lawyer and theologian Francisco Vitoria, argued otherwise. In their view, natural law is common to all men because it derives from the faculty of reason. Natural law is thus universal. There is no natural hierarchy among humans, and thus no inherent right of conquest and appropriation. Vitoria generally questioned the legitimacy of Spanish claims to rule and outlined general principles of peaceful coexistence between "nations" and peoples. Conquest and the use of force were legitimate only in highly specific circumstances.

Other subjects that constituted the discourses of seventeenth-century figures such as Grotius, Wolff, and Pufendorf included freedom of the seas, the inviolability of ambassadors, enslavement of prisoners of war, the status of treaties made with infidels, the freedom to travel, and that issue that continues to generate debate today, under what circumstances, if any, it is legitimate for one political community to intervene militarily in another. Here are two quotations on the issue. The language is archaic, but the reader will immediately notice that the opinions expressed are contemporary. In his famous *De Jure Belli ac Pacis* (1625) Hugo Grotius wrote:

> War may be justly undertaken against those who are inhuman to their Parents . . . [against those who kill Strangers that come to dwell amongst them] and against those who eat human Flesh . . . and against those who practice Piracy . . . War is lawful against those who offend against Nature; which is contrary to the Opinion of Victoria . . . and others, who seem to require, towards making a war just, that he who undertakes it be injured in himself, or in his State, or that he has some Jurisdiction over the Person against whom the War is made. (quoted in Tuck, 1999: 103)

In contrast, Pufendorf insisted that:

> it is . . . contrary to the natural *Equality* of Mankind, for a Man to force himself upon the World for a *Judge*, and *Decider of Controversies*. Not to say what dangerous Abuses this Liberty might be perverted to, and that any Man might make War upon any Man upon such a Pretens. (quoted in Tuck, 1999: 160–1)

Such debates preoccupied analysts in the seventeenth century. They had not run their course even a century later. Emerich Vattel, the greatest analyst of international law in the eighteenth century, argued that armed intervention is legitimate "if a prince, by violating the fundamental laws, gives his subjects a lawful cause for resisting him . . . any foreign power may rightfully give assistance to an oppressed people who ask for its aid" (quoted in Tuck, 1999: 194).

All these issues constituted the stuff of academic debates about the nature of law, and derivative rights, duties, and principles. Some became inscribed in treaties and thus created particular obligations. A few major ideas, such as those enunciated by Grotius regarding the freedom of the seas, became general principles that effectively guided behavior.

What of natural law doctrines, those ideas that had pervaded legal discourse in the sixteenth century? Those ideas had emphasized the unity of mankind and did not distinguish between individual and state obligations (notice the reference to Man rather than a state in Pufendorf's quotations above). Natural law did not establish particular rights and obligations – law narrowly defined – but provided the theoretical principles from which the rights and duties of states and their rulers could be derived (Hurrell, 1996: 234). As Grotius put it, natural law is the "dictate of right reason which points out that a given act, because of its opposition to or conformity with man's rational nature, is either morally wrong or morally necessary, and accordingly forbidden or commanded by God, the author of nature" (quoted in Fenwick, 1965: 59). Natural law was a body of thought that outlined what sovereigns or states *ought* to do. It could guide policy, therefore, only to the extent that the princes of the era felt morally compelled to follow its dictates. When there were incompatibilities between state interests and the moral precepts of natural law, the latter usually gave way to the former. Consequently, jurists and philosophers increasingly began to look at the actual practices of states when analyzing the "law of nations" rather than to earlier debates about moral precepts. By the late eighteenth century, natural law was in retreat and was increasingly displaced by "positive" law, or the basic principles of coexistence that had developed through practice, as well as treaties and the principles they embodied.

This had major consequences for the theory or main ideas underlying the development of international law. First, it ended the burden of trying to decide what God's will is on matters of human conduct, and refocused on what types of commitments states were actually making toward each other. Second, the nature of obligations under natural law did not distinguish between individuals and states. The way around this problem, as Vattel pointed out, was to render humans into the representatives of states. Since it is humans who make policy in the name of the state, the state is no less compelled to follow the obligations of natural law than are humans (Butler, 1978: 59–60). By this sleight of hand, Vattel was able to underline that it is essentially states that carry rights and obligations under international law (not individuals as in the sixteenth century), and that state morality is not fundamentally different from individual morality. Yet, by the early nineteenth century, the individual had been relegated to an object of law. Positivism raised the state to a position of exclusivity within the society of states. And finally, positivism destroyed the universalism of natural law. Analysts increasingly regarded international law as a set of principles, norms, and rules that derived from the common Christian cultural tradition of Europe, and hence was not applicable to humans and their varied polities in the "non-civilized" (e.g., non-Christian) world. As in so many other respects, Vattel was a captive of past intellectual constructs – natural law – but also a harbinger of the newer positivist ideas. The conception of Europe as a single cultural and religious entity was still reflected in his writings, but he also saw that the great problems of his era derived from the behavior of the great powers. Vattel, notes Hurrell (1996: 247), struggled "with the need to combine a universal foundation of law and morality with the increasingly divisive and conflictual political realities of his time. In this he reflected the tension between identity and difference, between pluralism and unity . . ."

The main ideas underlying the law of nations thus underwent considerable transformation between the sixteenth and nineteenth centuries. Notions of hierarchical order, of law inferred through reason and reflecting divine priorities, and the clear melding of legal with moral obligations increasingly gave way to the idea of law as a creation of equal sovereigns, binding through their consent, and carrying rights and duties only to them and their states. Law was to be inferred and located from practice, not from moral principles. The evidence of law came from what states did, not from what man reasoned or inferred from God's wishes. Yet, we must not make too much of these distinctions, for most of the norms and principles of the body of law of the two eras did not change. Some continued, but new ones like sovereignty also appeared. Let us review the main norms that underlay the law of nations in the mid-eighteenth century, about the time Vattel wrote his great work that was a synthesis of naturalist and positivist notions of law.

Norms in early modern Europe

Hedley Bull (1977: ch. 1) has claimed that the sanctity of promises and contracts – including treaties in international relations – is one of several foundations for order in any society, whether tribal, state, or international. The essential norm underlying international law is the reciprocal obligation to observe rights, duties, promises, and exchanges contained in formal agreements, including international treaties. More recently, we could add the binding quality of custom. The importance of the norm of keeping promises is illustrated in the ceremonial etiquette and invocation of divine sanction to international agreements. Until the mid-nineteenth century, the opening paragraphs of peace and other major treaties typically invoked God's will – and possibly retribution in case of violating their terms – as a reason for the treaty.

All of this does not mean that treaties were subsequently observed. Indeed, in the lexicon of diplomatic practice, the term "lasting peace" usually ends up being violated within several years or less. Yet, as Vattel observed, "the faith of treaties" is the foundation of international stability and predictability, and as signed commitments, they are "sacred between nations" (Butler, 1978: 49). Lawyers and diplomats may dispute the interpretations of treaties, they may denounce them (most treaties specify a definite time period in which the mutual obligations are operative), and they may argue that the conditions under which the treaties were initially signed have changed sufficiently to justify renegotiation or termination.[2] The doctrine of *rebus sic stantibus* is the corollary to the notion of treaty sanctity: no one could be expected to meet treaty obligations that become injurious to one of the parties.

A second critical norm implied or explicitly stated in early modern European international law was the moral worth of independent political communities. Sovereignty is one derivative of this norm: it basically holds that political independence and territorial integrity are, in the relations between states, the highest values to observe, promote, and defend. As I have argued in chapter 3, the original notion of sovereignty was essentially a protective device, a form of insurance against meddling by the church in the family and internal affairs of the sovereigns. Today it is buttressed by ideas such as self-determination. The norm, expressed through the sovereignty doctrine and other eighteenth-century documents, prohibits states from "extinguishing" each other, and grants no legitimacy to those who violate it. Although there may be numerous sources of the significant decline in the disappearance of states in the past two centuries, the norm of respect for political pluralism and the independence of distinct historical communities is certainly one of them. To repeat the opening ideas of this chapter: where such norms did not exist, the relationship between polities was typically that of insecurity and frequent warfare.

A third norm that derived from notions of natural law and the development of legal doctrines in the seventeenth and eighteenth centuries was legal equality. States and political communities may differ in many dimensions – size, population, location, type of political system, and the like – but in the society of states they have equal rights, duties, and responsibilities. This is also a corollary of the doctrine of sovereignty: one cannot claim political independence and seek recognition from other states without at least implicitly consenting to the major rules of the system. To claim superior rights – or to avoid certain common duties – is to deny sovereignty. While the principle was systematically violated in

---

[2] This was the argument used by the George W. Bush administration when it withdrew from the 1982 Anti-Ballistic Missile Treaty. Bush argued that the Cold War conditions that had spawned that treaty no longer existed.

Europe's imperial expansion, it was done without a sense of hypocrisy. Those over whom colonial power was exercised did not in the European view constitute "states" at the time of settlement or conquest, and hence did not hold a status as legal equals.

The norm of legal equality did not suddenly appear. It developed slowly in the seventeenth and eighteenth centuries (Vattel made the most famous claim in his observation that "a dwarf is as much a man as a giant; a small republic is no less a sovereign state than the most powerful kingdom" (quoted in Hurrell, 1996: 239). But today it underlies all international relationships and, as a norm, is constantly repeated. The United Nations Charter (Article 2(1)), for example, states that "The Organization is based on the principle of the sovereign equality of all its members."

If all states, regardless of their differences, have equal rights, duties, and responsibilities, and if they are sovereign, then it follows as a fourth norm, that they cannot be compelled to make agreements without their consent and that, as stated in Article 37 of the Westphalia Treaty, treaties made under duress or threats and "extorted illegally" are invalid. Moreover, treaties concluded between two or more states do not create obligations for non-signatories. The foundation of early modern European international law was based on consent, just as in domestic civil law no contract is binding without the consent of all parties to it.

A fifth norm was non-intervention. If there is moral worth in the independence of a political community, then no outside party has the *right* to interfere in its domestic affairs. The norm is buttressed by ideas such as self-determination and the doctrine of sovereignty. As in most other realms of international law, practice did not correlate perfectly with the norm – indeed in some eras it diverged significantly (see below) – but it is safe to generalize that in the relations between most states most of the time, the norm is observed with considerable regularity.

Practices

All of these norms and rules had become well established in Europe by the late eighteenth or early nineteenth century. But the question remains: were they just norms floating in space or embedded in a variety of international treaties? Was behavior generally consistent with them? Or did we have a situation of "organized hypocrisy" (Krasner, 1999), where treaties, speeches, and diplomatic notes professed respect for the norms, but where behavior diverged significantly?

We must remember that norms and laws do not only constrain behavior. They also enable. The sovereignty doctrine, for example, allowed rulers to do things they never could have imagined when the early dynasts were essentially under papal authority. Friedrich Kratochwil (1989: 61) explains the relationship between norms and law:

> Only very few rules and norms are simply constraining; many legal prescriptions are rather *enabling* rules that set actors free to pursue their own goals. Rule-following is therefore not a passive process in which the impact of rules can be ascertained analogously to Newtonian laws governing the collision of two bodies: it is, rather, intensely dynamic. Actors are not only programmed by rules and norms, but they reproduce and change by their practice the normative structures by which they are able to act, share meanings, communicate intentions, criticize claims, and justify choices.

Throughout the two early centuries of international law, many states organized their practices, either to conform to custom or to meet consensual treaty obligations. The scope of legally consistent behavior also expanded during this era. The great debates and armed conflicts over possession of the seas in the sixteenth and seventeenth centuries had become basically settled by the early nineteenth century. States cooperated to control the scourge of their times – the counterpart to contemporary terrorism – sea piracy. They increasingly defined aspects of law of the sea, such as transit through straits, the extent of territorial jurisdiction, and abolishing letters of marque and reprisal. Common practices on the recognition of new states developed, as did the laws of war and diplomatic immunities. Most important, until Napoleon, there were no serious ideological challenges to the norms we have described above. His defeat was a victory for the sanctity of those norms and the resulting 1815 Treaty of Vienna strongly endorsed them.

Despite these advances in the development of law and in common practice, the norms embodied in treaties and practice became increasingly Eurocentric. The questions raised by Vitoria in his conceptions of *jus gentium* – what are the rights of indigenous peoples, when can force legitimately be used in conquest of non-European territories, what do we mean by natural law? – dropped from legal discourse. What mattered were the norms the Europeans found convenient to regulate the mutual transactions of the new European sovereigns (Ortega, 1996: 112). The "public law" of Europe was limited to the "civilized" and Christian people of Europe or to those of European origin (e.g., United States). Both the new republics in North America and South America, upon gaining independence, incorporated European norms and practices into their own repertoire of diplomatic action. By the early nineteenth century, the settled "law of nations" defined and regulated the basic mechanics of interstate relations. These included:

1 the limits of territorial jurisdiction
2 the definition of states and fundamental state rights and duties
3 the procedures for granting recognition and establishing and maintaining diplomatic relations
4 the forms and laws of treaties
5 the laws of war and neutrality (cf., Brownlie, 1984: 359).

Universalizing norms and practices

The expansion of the European "law of nations" is an interesting tale, full of twists, turns, and contradictions. It was not a case of a fully developed "law of nations" imposed by the Europeans on others (Stivachtis, 1998: 73). In fact, in the eighteenth century, many of the European treaties with non-Christian polities elsewhere were between nominal equals, particularly as they pertained to commercial practices. Even alliances between Christians and infidels were regarded as equal so long as they were not directed against other infidels (Stivachtis, 1998: 89). The list of Great Britain's treaty partners in the eighteenth century is impressively universal. These included pacts with Tripoli, Tunis, the Marattas, the Nizam of Hyderabad, the Mogul Empire, Mysore, the Rajah of Nepaul, the Rajah of Assam, Muscat, Kabool, Kandy, Ashantee, the King of Madagascar, Johore, the Sheiks of Bahrein, the King of Siam, Burma, the King of the Zulus, the King of Bonny, the King of Shoa, Dahomey, Borneo, and Abyssinia (Brownlie, 1984: 360).

But while the norm of keeping promises underlay all of these agreements, fundamentally they did not imply diplomatic and legal equality. Promises and exchanges could guide international relationships, but this did not signify that the non-Christian or non-European treaty partners could become members of the club of states. The Europeans, after the eighteenth century, did not regard their treaty partners as states or legal entities of the same status as their European counterparts. This was not just a question of European discrimination, but a universal characteristic of different cultures in their mutual relations. The Ottomans until the early nineteenth century refused to acknowledge any form of equality to the European "infidels," whom they regarded as inferiors. Similarly, Chinese emperors forced European interlocutors to accept symbolic and other forms of inferiority (the "kow tow" was the most common form). But for a variety of practical reasons, as the advantages of commerce and diplomacy with the Europeans became more apparent, non-Europeans began to court membership into the "club of states." In 1716, the French *Almanach royal* for the first time listed the Romanovs as one of the reigning families in Europe (Stivachtis, 1998: 78). In 1856, following the Crimean War, the Ottoman Empire was admitted to the Concert of Europe. In the latter half of the nineteenth century, the Europeans developed the "standard of civilization" as the criterion that had to be met for membership into the club. Applicants had to adopt not only European rules but also the values and ethical standards inherent in them. The criteria included:

1 constant intercourse with the members of the (European) Family of Nations and consent to be bound by the rules of European international law;
2 observation of certain European economic standards and commercial practices, particularly where they affected foreigners;
3 the protection of life, liberty, and property of those same foreigners;
4 certain minimum (e.g., "civilized") standards in governance and rule over their own populations (Gong, 1984: 14–15; Stivachtis, 1998: 90).

The parade of applicants grew rapidly. Japan was the first Asian country to gain full international status as a "civilized" state, in 1899. China, Siam, Persia, and others followed shortly after. They sent delegates to the Paris peace negotiations in 1919 and were among the charter members of the League of Nations. With the process of de-colonization (see chapter 8), international law became universal.

Continuity, complexity, and change in contemporary international law

All law changes with the times. International law is no exception. New technologies, expansion of commerce, travel, and communication, industrialization, and the application of technology to the conduct of war require new forms of regulation. But it does not follow that in every realm, new types of legal principles must be developed. As we will see, in many cases, such as in outer space, old principles are modernized and applied. This is an example of increased complexity rather than transformation. In other areas, new principles have to be developed to regulate unprecedented problems. Synthesis is another form: older principles are melded with newer inventions to create a blend, or possibly a transformation. And finally, some principles may become obsolete. We can neither review all of these possibilities nor explore the totality of the broad scope of international law. Rather, we will isolate four areas where changes in ideas and practices have played a singular role in altering older norms or initiating new norms. These are in the areas of human rights and armed intervention to protect them, war and conquest, the question of consent, and the legal standing of individuals.

Ideas and norms of human rights and armed intervention

One of the oldest topics of debate among political philosophers has been the circumstances under which subjects and citizens have a right to oppose tyrannical rule. This has been no less a matter of theoretical argument among the great figures in international legal discourse. The question is: given rules of sovereignty and its corollary of non-intervention, are there circumstances when foreign governments/peoples have a right, or even a duty, to intervene on behalf of those who are suffering from misrule? Vitoria engaged this question when the Spaniards claimed a "right to rule" the Indians because of their practices of slavery, sexual relations, and human sacrifice. He agreed that in certain circumstances such violations of natural law warranted or justified foreign occupation. Grotius, Wolff, Vattel, and many others came to similar conclusions. While the first two grounded their position in terms of natural law, Vattel – the figure who bridges the natural and positivist law traditions – came to a similar conclusion. He emphasized that sovereignty means that all nations have a right to be governed as they think proper, and that no other state has the "smallest" right to interfere in the government of another. But he also claimed that "if the prince, by violating the fundamental laws, gives his subjects a legal right to resist – if tyranny, becoming insupportable, obliges the nation to rise in their own defense – every foreign power has a right to succor an oppressed people who implore their assistance" (quoted in Hurrell, 1996: 243–4). Except for slight changes in language, this statement approximates any number of recent declarations by secretaries-general of the United Nations, heads of state, prime ministers, or foreign ministers. Few lawyers and analysts have claimed that sovereignty is absolute and that it can be used as a shield behind which to conduct systematic abuses of human rights. Even most positivists have claimed that the question of intervention is ultimately resolved on political and moral, rather than legal grounds. What they have resisted is the enunciation of a *right* or *obligation* to intervene to protect individuals from the abuses of their governments. While the classical figures all spoke of permissible justifications for intervention and in some cases spelled out in detail the criteria that would have to be fulfilled for intervention to be legal, they stood back from taking the plunge into a general right.

So, the problems of human rights, their protection, and the limits of sovereignty are not new. In the area of human rights, the form of change has been primarily added complexity. While Vitoria could condemn some of the cultural practices of the Indians of the New World, and while Vattel could speak of tyranny, the task of specifying and defining concretely the content of human rights and the limits of government actions toward their own citizens has been primarily undertaken only since the late nineteenth century. At that time, the primary concern was with the sultan's treatment of Christian minorities in his realms. Under some duress, the Porte was compelled to sign treaties guaranteeing minimum rights of worship and education for his Christian subjects, and it was commonly understood – if not stated clearly in these treaties – that the powers could intervene diplomatically and coercively to protect those subjects should the sultan's government violate those guarantees. After World War I, some of the new states of east and central Europe were required to grant constitutional guarantees of minority rights in exchange for recognition by the other European states.

The codification of human rights in a systematic manner began only after World War II. In the years since the Universal Declaration of Human Rights (1948), dozens of declarations, treaties, resolutions, and domestic laws have spelled out in detail the rights of individuals against their governments and in relation to each other. Indeed, of the fifty-three international instruments and declarations that, according to Dorothy Jones, constitute the contemporary "code of international ethics," fully 90 percent of them deal in some fashion with the rights of human beings, either as individuals or as members of groups. And these instruments are not confined to the European core of the international system. They have become universal. Hence, the final communiqué of the 1955 Bandung Conference of non-aligned states listed "respect for fundamental human rights" as one of the first duties of all states (Jones, 1990: 155). The charters of all regional organizations (e.g., the Organization of African Unity) repeat those commitments. The 1991 "Santiago Declaration" of the Organization of American States boldly established peoples' right to democratic rule and even sanctioned foreign armed intervention in the case of military or other types of *coups* against democratic regimes. This comes close to enunciating a *right* of intervention, but such statements have not been reproduced in other organizations.

On the issue of intervention to try to terminate systematic abusive rule, the Santiago statement is the most radical. It conflicts with Article 2(7) of the United Nations Charter that prohibits interference in the internal affairs of member states. But even that prohibition is not without qualification. It states that interference cannot take place on any issue that is *essentially* within a state's domestic jurisdiction, and further qualifies it by other provisions that allow the Security Council to take measures to deal with situations it deems to be a "threat" to international peace and security. And so, while there is no agreed norm that contradicts the spirit of Article 2(7), much less a universally accepted *right* of intervention, the international community has used the subterfuge of declaring massive violations of human rights, or impending or actual humanitarian emergencies, as "threats to international peace and security." Using this maneuver, the United Nations has mandated international humanitarian relief, economic sanctions, and/or military intervention against the white supremacist government of Rhodesia (1961) and South Africa, and has intervened with military or peacekeeping forces in Somalia (1994), Haiti (1996), Bosnia (1992), East Timor (1999), and several other places. In the case where United Nations action was precluded because of the threat of a veto, NATO nevertheless undertook its bombing campaign in 1999 to put an end to the massive ethnic cleansing of the Kosovar population by the Serb military and police. In 2003, again facing a veto in the Security Council, the American administration attacked Iraq, according to President Bush, to "free" the Iraqi people from Saddam Hussein's tyrannical rule ("Operation Free Iraq").

Because of the increasing number of humanitarian emergencies and instances of systematic abuse of populations by their governments, the General Assembly of the United Nations in 2000 established a commission to weigh the alternatives among the competing views about the limits of sovereignty. The International Commission on Intervention and State Sovereignty (ICISS) published its report in 2001. To summarize a lengthy document, the commission proposed that there is no *right* of intervention in cases of severe threats to or practices of abusing populations or denying human rights, but that "State sovereignty implies responsibility, and the primary responsibility for the protection of its people lies with the state itself" (ICISS, 2001: xi). This statement clearly associates the sovereignty norm with state responsibility. Indeed, the responsibility to protect a state's population is an integral part of sovereignty. Thus far, the report firmly endorses the sovereignty principle, but insists that it is not and never has been a license for governments to abuse their citizens. But what if states do not meet their responsibilities? The answer: "Where a population is suffering serious harm, as a result of internal war, insurgency, repression or state failure, and the state in question is unwilling or unable to halt or avert it, the principle of non-intervention yields to the international responsibility to protect" (ICISS, 2001: xi). Notice that this is not a statement claiming a right to intervene, but rather a responsibility to act. The report does not state who specifically has a responsibility, but notes that the United Nations Security Council should authorize any military intervention. If it fails to act, for whatever reason, the case should be taken to the General Assembly or to a regional organization, but "subject to their seeking subsequent authorization from the Security Council" (ICISS, 2001: viii). In the event that this organ cannot take a decision ("if it fails to discharge its responsibility to protect in conscience-shocking situations crying out for action") then "concerned states may not rule out other means to meet the gravity and urgency of that situation." In sum, "concerned states" may intervene if all efforts to obtain international community or regional authorization fail. The report thus emphasizes responsibilities rather than rights and states clearly that unilateral intervention can take place only when all other avenues have been exhausted. Nothing in the report proposes a change in Article 2(7), but it offers an implicit agreement: the norm of non-intervention generally applies in the relations of states, but where states refuse or are incapable of meeting their sovereign responsibilities to protect their populations, then other states may intervene subject to authorization from an international body. Since more people have been killed by their own governments than by foreign troops since 1945, this is an important step toward trying to prevent or remedy the most egregious violations of human rights by governments, or to take actions in impending humanitarian catastrophes. The problem is that a distinction between a right and a responsibility is not always clear, nor is the situation where a state might be abusing its population.

Overall, we can conclude that while ideas about human rights have been more clearly specified and codified, the status of intervention as a type of activity to terminate systematic abuses of civilian populations remains, as always, uncertain. Many have argued that the legal position is changing toward older notions embedded in natural law and that the current trend is toward the establishment of a *community right* to intervene in egregious cases of systematic government abuse of populations. This may or may not be the case, but it is highly unlikely that the member states of the United Nations will join together to change Article 2(7) which is designed to protect states against uninvited outside intervention. The ploy of declaring systematic abuses of human rights as a threat to international peace and security is probably as far as we can expect to see change. In this case, practices have become increasingly regularized. Since Resolution 688 of April 1991 (establishing the no-fly zones over Iraq to protect the Shi'ia and Kurd populations), the Security Council has acted with military force without the consent of the target government in Iraq, Somalia, Bosnia, Haiti, Rwanda, and elsewhere. If these practices continue, even though justified under the "threats to international peace and security" criterion, a *de facto* norm that trumps Article 2(7) in certain circumstances may develop (cf., Philpott, 2001: 41–3). Collective intervention undertaken by an international organ on behalf of the community of states for the enforcement of the principles and rules of international law has been recognized for a long time and certainly precedes the recent debate about intervention in human rights abuse cases (Von Glahn, 1992: 160–7). What has changed is the elaboration and codification of specific human rights. This is a case, then, of added complexity, and not a transformation. Yet the possibility remains that the non-intervention norm will become, if not obsolete, at least increasingly qualified.

However, in one area linked to human rights, there has been a true transformation. This has been in terms of the immunities of states and of the personal immunity of foreign sovereigns. Until the mid-1990s, the recognized customary rule of international law was that all heads of state and/or government enjoy immunity from suit or judicial process in the territory of another state (Von Glahn, 1992: 156–7). Recent practice has overturned that old standard. The Nuremburg tribunal that prosecuted Nazi war criminals after World War II established the principle that agents of the state, including the head of state, cannot escape individual responsibility for war crimes and crimes against humanity. The Hague War Crimes Tribunal, established by the United Nations to deal with the atrocities in the former Yugoslavia, has indicted and tried the leader of the Yugoslav government of the time, Slobodan Milošević. A British court refused to turn over the Chilean military dictator Augusto Pinochet to a Spanish court that had indicted him for crimes against humanity, but it was on the grounds of ill health. It did not deny that a court in Spain might have jurisdiction to try a former head of state. The new Permanent International Criminal Court, established by treaty in 1998, similarly lifts the immunity of heads of state or government who are charged with crimes against humanity, the laws of war, rape, genocide, and other systematic violations of human rights. It also establishes the principle of universal jurisdiction, that is, that any party or court may hear a case of suspected violations of the specified crimes. In this area related to human rights, old ideas, conventions, and laws have been overturned. This is a transformation of considerable legal and diplomatic significance.

The coexistence of states: non-intervention, ideology, and strategic interests

The non-intervention norm does not relate solely to problems arising from abuses of human rights. The Westphalian settlement was among other things a solution to the problems arising from the schism in Christianity in the sixteenth century. The Protestant–Catholic divide was the source of intense conflicts and massacres between and within states. Politics and religion in the era were not separate realms, and so the diplomacy of the period was intimately connected with religious issues. Westphalia confirmed the Peace of Augsburg's (1555) recipe for toleration of differences: the princes would determine the faith of their subjects, but those individuals who dissented or proclaimed the opposite faith would enjoy rights to practice and teach their version of Christianity and would in addition receive proper burial. After 1648, governments of the day no longer claimed a right to intervene abroad to hunt down heretics or to protect religious confreres who might be under threat. They also generally tolerated the diverse political forms that dotted the European landscape. By the eighteenth century, foreign intervention was a rare event so that Vattel and others could claim that when it did occur, it represented a deviation from the accepted norms of sovereignty. But of all the norms and principles associated with sovereignty and the requirements for tolerance of political pluralism in the world, the non-intervention norm has been the one most often violated and abused. It began with the French Revolution.

Like all revolutionaries, the French claimed that their mission to liberate others was universal. Accordingly, the wars of the French Revolution, which began as a defensive response to the threat of dynastic intervention by Prussia and Austria, soon turned to French interventions to liberate "oppressed" peoples throughout Europe. Even Napoleon's attempt to build a Paris-centered empire was justified as an act of liberation rather than imperialism. That era saw the first great tension between the norm of sovereignty and a self-proclaimed duty to liberate others.

The issue arose again with the Bolshevik Revolution, whose early leaders were dedicated to the proposition that the new Soviet workers' republic would never be secure until there was world revolution. The Soviet Union thus had a duty to promote that revolution through any means available. The response of Great Britain and the United States was to intervene on the side of the Whites in the Russian civil war, in an attempt to overthrow the Bolshevik regime.

During the Cold War, armed intervention and subversion to protect strategic interests, promote revolution, or to overthrow regimes of perceived odious complexion became standard *modus operandi* of both the Soviet Union and the United States. The former helped organize and conduct communist *coups* or revolutions in Eastern Europe and the Balkans, while the United States helped overthrow regimes, including democratically elected ones, that it disliked. The victims included Iran, Guatemala, Chile, and Peru. The United States organized an armed assault on Cuba in 1961, intervened militarily to save a constitutional order in the Dominican Republic in 1965, ousted an authoritarian government in Grenada in 1983, and repeated the exercise in Panama in 1989. It also attempted to subvert the Sandinista revolutionary government of Nicaragua through most of Ronald Reagan's term of office (1983–8). Unique among modern states, the United States also supported or directly attempted and/or carried out assassinations as a means of overthrowing governments for ideological or strategic reasons. The targets included Fidel Castro (Cuba), Patrice Lumumba (Congo), Ngo Dinh Diem (South Vietnam), Muammar Qaddafi (Libya), and Saddam Hussein (Iraq). The British and French, for their part, intervened frequently to help protect client regimes in their former African colonies.

The non-intervention norm, while recorded and underlined in dozens of international treaties, covenants, charters, and communiqués, is thus one that is perhaps most frequently violated in practice. However, no government today asserts a right to intervene unilaterally when it chooses, so we cannot say there has been a change in the norm.[3] The

---

[3] Prior to its attack in March 2003, the Bush administration in 2002 did not claim a legal right to intervene to oust the Hussein regime in Iraq, but argued that the latter's possession

norm remains essentially as it was in the eighteenth century. On questions of collective intervention to save populations at serious risk, the norm is becoming more conditional and qualified, but as a rule to guarantee political tolerance, it continues to be put to the test and violated. It is primarily in this rule of peaceful coexistence between states that we find what Stephen Krasner (1999) has termed "organized hypocrisy," the condition where norms and actions are inconsistent. But violation of the norm by a few states some of the time does not prove that it has become obsolete or is changing in other ways. Quite the contrary. The non-intervention norm has been internalized by most states to the point where it is taken for granted. Most states observe it as a matter of course most of the time. Were it not so, then the occasional violations would not receive the great attention that they do.[4]

The coexistence of state: the right of conquest *and* jus ad bello

Conquest refers to the violent wresting away of control over a territory and its population and proclaiming one's own legal jurisdiction, or the "right to rule" over the territory and its inhabitants. In traditional international law, conquest was a *right* derivative of sovereignty (cf., Korman, 1996). Conquest is usually achieved through the use of force, but it can involve subversion and other less violent techniques.

Conquest, despite the fact that it was often "unjust," created entitlements. In the older tradition of international law, no doctrine so blatantly established that right derived from might. The majority of the Western conquests in the New World from the fifteenth century on were based either on papal dispensations or on claimed rights deriving from conquest or *terra nullius*. Where the territories in question were inhabited, whatever claims the natives might have had to sovereignty over their territories were simply extinguished by the superior military might of the conquerors. In a famous American Supreme Court decision in 1823, for

(assumed, not demonstrated) of "weapons of mass destruction," and the threat to international peace and security they presented, was sufficient grounds to justify the use of force. Of the major powers, only Great Britain publicly endorsed this position.

[4] As in other realms, the practices of states within the European Union constitute important exceptions to generalizations about sovereignty and the rules of international law. The European Union has strict conditions for membership and has claimed a virtual right of (non-armed) intervention should one of its members deviate from the path of democracy, guaranteed rights for minorities, and other democratic principles. When the Austrians elected a far right-wing party with the largest number of seats in the legislature, in 1999, some European Union members imposed various sanctions on Austria.

example, the Chief Justice maintained that "discovery gave an exclusive right to extinguish the Indian title of occupancy, either by purchase or by conquest" (quoted in Korman, 1996: 45). Throughout the eighteenth and nineteenth centuries the great powers and others made territorial acquisitions through conquest and annexation. Few contested the *right* to conquest, although they might object to particular incidents. Until World War I, "territorial acquisitions obtained by force regularly gave rise to recognized changes in sovereignty" (Korman, 1996: 93).

The right of conquest, as we have seen, was renounced in the French Constitution of 1791 and collectively modified by the great powers at Vienna in 1815. But it took more than a century to generalize this act of self-abnegation into a general norm of the society of states. The period prior to and during the Great War had seen numerous secret treaties that involved annexations, partitions, and the validation of conquests. But two major events undermined the old right. First, the Bolshevik revolutionaries, upon seizing power, denounced all former tsarist treaties and announced that henceforth the new Soviet government would apply the principle of national self-determination in its relations with other peoples and would abjure all foreign conquests (Korman, 1996: 136). More significantly, Woodrow Wilson made clear the American position on the right of conquest: "no right exists anywhere to hand peoples about from sovereignty to sovereignty as if they were property" (speech of 22 January 1917). This statement was a clear break from the older conceptions of territoriality and expressed the assumption that a "people" constitute a moral community that is not a mere chattel. These ideas fundamentally altered the agenda and discourses surrounding the negotiations leading to the Treaty of Versailles. Whatever its faults, that treaty, including the Covenant of the League of Nations, effectively terminated the old right of conquest, at least as far as Europe was concerned. Article 10 of the Covenant stipulated that the members "undertake to respect and preserve as against external aggression the territorial integrity and existing political independence of all Members of the League." This was in effect a repudiation of the right of conquest. If there were some exceptions in the territorial settlements of 1919 and 1945, they were justified on strategic and economic grounds, not on a general right to territorial aggrandizement. Conquest as a right has thus been effectively de-legitimized.[5] This constitutes one of the most significant changes in

---

[5] There are arguments that Article 10 of the Covenant did not necessarily or effectively prevent *all* conquests. For details, see Korman, 1996, 182–92.

international law in the past one-half millennium. The change is a part of a more general alteration in attitudes and norms regarding the role of armed force in international relations.

One of the oldest areas of debate in international relations is the type of justifications that underlie or are required for the use of force. In the early discourses about the law of nations, approximately from the fifteenth through seventeenth centuries, analysts and jurists sought to define the criteria for undertaking "just" wars. Grotius argued that military force could be used legitimately for self-defense, to punish crimes, to enforce treaty rights, and under certain well-specified criteria, to intervene on behalf of a foreign population under tyrannical rule. He developed his doctrine of just war on the basis of old natural law doctrines embodying what was right and just in human relationships. Notice that in the natural law tradition, the emphasis is on what actors *should* do (or not do), and not on observations of actual behavior.

In contrast, the positivist tradition in international law emphasized state practice, custom, and treaty obligations as the foundation of rights, duties, and obligations. The use of force, including war for territorial conquest, was considered a prerogative of sovereign rights. *Raison d'état* was a sufficient justification for the use of force, although debates about the conditions that had to be met for armed intervention continued to rage. From the treaties of Westphalia until the late nineteenth century, approximately, there were few prevailing ideas or norms that significantly interrogated the standard doctrinal point of view: sovereignty includes the right to use of force as an adjunct to or substitute for diplomacy. The list of justifiable causes for using military force was so lengthy as to make it a virtually limitless activity (cf., Kegley and Raymond, 2002: 104).[6]

As a result of fundamental changes in thinking about the use of force in international relations, as well as the increasingly destructive consequences of the application of technology to the art of war, peace societies and other groups and individuals began to raise the issue of armed force into the domain of public debate. Peace societies proliferated after the Napoleonic wars, and socialist and liberal parties throughout Europe

---

[6] They included, among others, to obtain reparation for losses or breach of a legal pact, self-defense, maintenance of a state or dynastic right, to prevent intended or threatened injury, to punish an offense (however broadly defined), to pre-empt attack, to prevent reoccurrence of attacks, to assist allies, to assist the uprising of the "unjustly oppressed" in another state, to maintain the balance of power, and to uphold the "honor" of the state or the royal figure (Luard, 1992).

in the late nineteenth century attacked the "reason of state" justification for the use of force. The Hague Conferences of 1899 and 1907 began to draft conventions designed to surround the institution of war with legal restrictions. The Covenant of the League of Nations, drafted at a time when everyone was appalled by the carnage of the Great War, provided in its preamble an acceptance by the members of obligations not to re-sort to war and denied them the right to use force except under highly restrictive conditions. Further efforts in the 1920s (the stillborn Treaty of Mutual Assistance, 1923 and the Geneva Protocol of 1924) attempted to identify wars of aggression as an international crime. In 1928, the Pan-American Conference (forerunner to the Organization of American States) adopted a resolution asserting that a "war of aggression consti-tutes a crime against the human species . . . all aggression is illicit and as such is declared prohibited" (quoted in Von Glahn, 1992: 670–1). The signatories to the Kellogg–Briand Pact (Pact of Paris) in 1928, a hortatory set of aspirations rather than a binding treaty, solemnly "renounce[d] [war] as an instrument of national policy in their relations with one another." The United Nations Charter and numerous analogues at the regional level prohibit even the threat to use force in the members' mu-tual relations. The only exceptions are when force is authorized by the governing body, such as the Security Council, or for individual and collective self-defense.

Although these types of commitments have often been violated, the onus in the use of force falls clearly upon those who unleash it. While the Kellogg–Briand Pact may have been a statement of aspiration rather than law, it was used as a basis for the trial and conviction of Nazi and Japanese war criminals. In both cases, the leaders were found guilty of waging aggressive war. This was the first example in the history of international relations of the leaders of a sovereign power being tried for planning and waging aggressive war defined as a crime (cf., Wight, 1978: 111).

Legal opinion has reached a reasonable consensus that the prohibition against the use of armed force as an instrument of state policy, except when authorized by a legitimating body such as the United Nations, or in individual or collective self-defense, is a peremptory norm of inter-national law. This represents a total reversal of the legal status of the use of force in the eighteenth and nineteenth centuries. The "reason of state" criterion or justification has become obsolete. One of the reasons for the significant decline in the incidence of war between states since

1945 is undoubtedly the prescriptive strength of the prohibitions against the use of force found in the United Nations Charter and in numerous other international documents.

The current norm of non-violence reflects transformations in the realm of ideas about war and conquest. In the seventeenth and eighteenth centuries, people regarded war as an act of God, the normal form of contact between sovereign princes, as an opportunity for honor, glory, and valor, and as tests of sovereigns' might and prestige. In our era, in contrast, war has been characterized as a crime, a disease, a tragedy, a great mistake, or at best, an unfortunate necessity (cf., Holsti, 1991). There remains a gap between ideas and norms, and practice, but the gap has been narrowing significantly over the past century. At least until recently.

In March 2003, President George W. Bush in his declaration of war against Iraq insisted that "The United States of America has the sovereign authority to use force in assuring its own national security." He uttered this classical statement of the *raison d'état* position in the context of an earlier policy statement that justified the use of pre-emptive force against any regime or group that the United States deems to be a *possible* threat to the security of its citizens or interests. Neither imminent attack nor stated intention to do harm to American interests is a necessary condition for launching an armed attack against a hypothetical adversary. This doctrine is inconsistent with the non-use of force norm in the United Nations Charter, and is a throwback to the days of the unlimited prerogative of sovereigns to use force to pursue or defend their foreign policy interests. It remains to be seen whether other governments will claim similar prerogatives, or whether this is just another example of American "exceptionalism." Whatever the case, the American doctrinal innovation represents a serious challenge to any claim that the limitations to the *jus ad bello* have been moving in an increasingly restrictive direction.

The problem of consent

In the natural law tradition, the source of what states *ought* to do was in human reason, corresponding to the laws of nature instituted by God. In the positivist conception, the sources of law include, primarily, treaties (reflecting the norm of consent), custom, the standard practices of states, court decisions, the writings of eminent jurists, and general principles that are recognized by all states. We have already noted the hortatory character of the Kellogg–Briand Pact, but what started out as occasional multilateral references to what states *should* do and what new conditions they aspire to has turned into a veritable flood of pacts, charters, covenants, conventions, protocols, declarations, pronouncements, communiqués, and resolutions. Dorothy Jones (1990: 115) has termed them collectively a "code of ethics"; others have used the term "soft law." They cover such diverse fields as human rights, the environment, terrorism, water sharing, health standards, endangered species, and the like. But what is their status? Do they require compliance, even without the consent of states?

It is not possible to generalize. Most resolutions of the United Nations General Assembly or multilateral conference declarations do not create binding obligations. Statements of aspiration are just that. They express what the parties hope to achieve, but they do not constitute legally binding commitments. Communiqués are equally vague in their consequences. On one hand, they may create implicit obligations and serve as the basis of subsequent treaties; on the other, they may be little more than public relations exercises. Some types of resolutions of international organizations or multilateral conferences, if passed unanimously or with near unanimity, can become "instant" customary law and reflect the international community's adoption of certain principles. And if subsequent state behavior is mostly consistent with the norms, rights, and obligations of those resolutions, there is more evidence of custom. In some circumstances, the general principles enunciated in these instruments could become *jus cogens*, peremptory norms of general international law (cf., Thakur and Maley, 1999: 277). In an American interpretation of the legal effect of, for example, UN General Assembly resolutions, the position is that, in "exceptional" cases, such resolutions can create law if they gain virtually universal support, if they are intended to create law, and if the content of those resolutions is reflected in general state practices (Von Glahn, 1992: 15).

However, the principle of consent, one of the early essential norms of international law, has not been overturned in these interpretations. The fundamental rule that states are not bound by treaties to which they object remains intact. Yet, some argue today that *international consensus* provides one basis for creating new universal obligations. The general rule is that law-like resolutions or treaties of an international organization or multilateral conference, passed and ratified by a significant majority, create new obligations for all except those states that explicitly refuse to acknowledge them. Consensus thus does not replace consent, but it does create a presumptive norm. In a recent example, the 1998 Rome Treaty creating the International Criminal Court has been ratified by a majority of the states in the world, but the United States has refused to accept its provisions. Thus, American military personnel cannot be tried by the court in cases of charges of crimes against humanity, violations of the laws of war, genocide, or other criminal activities.

To the extent that "soft law" effectively regulates or influences behavior – and we must remember that for most of it to be effective, it must entail changes in domestic law as well – the role of ideas as an underpinning for international institutions is becoming ever more important. Broad generalizations such as the "common heritage of mankind," to narrower standards such as national emission levels specified in the Kyoto Protocol (1997), all flowed originally from individuals, nongovernmental organizations, scientific establishments, global, regional, and national pressure groups, universities, and other private sources. Government agencies generated many of them as well. Taken together, this great and expanding body of "soft law" is an overall expression of the priorities of our times: protection and advancement of human rights; social justice; non-use of force; gender and other forms of equality; protecting the environment and sustaining a high "quality of life"; protecting health; economic development, and the like. While some of these problems have generated new ideas, many older principles of international law have simply been modernized or extended into new domains. For example, the seventeenth-century doctrine of freedom of the seas has been extended to regulate activities in outer space. The old territorial limit of 3 miles of sea has now been extended and amended to a standard of 12 miles, along with a 200-mile economic and environmental zone. Many measures to protect the environment reflect old legal norms dealing with state responsibility.

Individuals and international law

International law developed initially as a set of rights, obligations, and commitments between sovereigns. It later became the law between sovereign states, or "the law of nations." General rights and obligations, as well as specific undertakings, are between polities that have acquired sovereign status. There remains a special domain of "private" international law that regulates transnational relationships between individuals and private organizations and associations. But no individual can, by him- or herself, press a claim against a state. Only the state can do so on behalf of the aggrieved party. This remains the situation in general, but important exceptions are appearing more frequently. For example, European citizens have the right to appeal or challenge policies and actions of their own state, or of the European Union, at the European Court of Human Rights. The court can rule against either level of government, and its decisions are binding. This is tantamount to supranational jurisdiction and is, indirectly, an area of ceded sovereignty. But the crucial point is that the citizen can appeal as an individual and does not have to obtain consent from his or her government. Finally, individuals can appeal directly to the United Nations Human Rights Committee to investigate claims of government abuse. The procedure is costly and seldom successful, but the principle of individual rights is a major innovation in international law. This constitutes a form of *novelty*.

In the institution of international law, then, we have a great deal of increased complexity, some obsolescence (conquest and the sovereign right to use force), and some novelties (an implied responsibility to intervene in the event of humanitarian emergencies, the creation of obligation without explicit consent, and rights for individuals). Because the law today covers so many realms of activity, it is impossible to generalize for the entire corpus of norms, rules, regulations, rights, duties, and obligations. But if we pare down our notion of international law to those areas that are foundational, crucial, and enduring – the rules of the game of international politics that allow other games, such as those of the environment, to be played at all – then we see more continuity and complexity than transformation or novelty.

The institutionalization of international law: codes, covenants, and courts

At the time jurists and philosophers of natural law were writing, the substance of international law was confined to a few bilateral treaties – usually peace treaties and treaties of alliance – and emerging consensus on some aspects of customary law. The Westphalia treaties were notable not only because they undermined the authority of the church in the affairs of states – implying sovereignty – but because they were the first multilateral agreements among the emerging sovereigns of Europe. To the extent that the treaties included statements about expected state behavior, they constituted the first formal code of conduct in the European states system.

By the eighteenth century, bilateral treaties had proliferated, a few courts of arbitration had been established, and the domain of customary law had expanded to include a consensus on the freedom of the seas and the limits of territorial control. On the other hand, most of the natural law-based prohibitions against the unrestrained use of force or the limitations on conquest of infidels and barbarians had lapsed.

It is in the nineteenth century in Europe that the great corpus of treaty law developed most rapidly. The number of bilateral treaties climbed dramatically, as did their multilateral counterparts. The latter regulated matters such as navigation on the Rhine and Danube rivers, prohibitions against the slave trade, postal regulations, and a whole host of issues arising from industrialization and growing commerce. The number of arbitration treaties also grew rapidly, and indeed became almost a fad in the late nineteenth century. The Hague Conference in 1899 established the first multilateral legally based conflict-resolution mechanism, the Permanent Court of Arbitration. At this time, many observers were convinced that legal remedies were the primary routes to resolving conflicts between states.

International mechanisms and the growing number of treaties were important indicators of the institutionalization of international law. Equally important was the incorporation of international legal principles into domestic law. The United States was among the first to acknowledge that not only must treaty obligations be met, but domestic legislation and social practice must be in conformity with international standards. Hence, the constitution explicitly states that international treaties constitute the "law of the land," and that in case of a conflict with domestic law, international obligations take precedence. By the late nineteenth century, many other countries had similar constitutional provisions. In practice, this also meant that governments had to revise domestic policies in order to meet international standards. Matters such as weights and measures, the standardization of time, the regulation and ultimate prohibition of phosphorous in the manufacture of matches, and numerous health measures emerged initially as components of international treaties which then had to be translated to domestic legislation. In many areas, the distinctions between international obligations and domestic law became a seamless web. Domestic practices in a variety of areas increasingly met treaty obligations. At the turn of the last century, then, all the components of institutionalization were in place: a full and rapidly expanding body of law; a legal profession with specialization in international law; incorporation of legal offices within foreign ministries; constitutional provisions that transformed international legal obligations into the law of the land; numerous arbitration treaties; and the first international courts.

The process continued rapidly after World War I. The Covenant of the League of Nations was the first statement of the essential principles of coexistence between sovereign states that was truly universal, for it was signed by states from every continent in the world. The essential rules of the society of states, including sovereignty, territorial integrity, and the peaceful resolution of international conflicts, were now equally applicable to all states regardless of size, culture, history, population, or level of development. A number of universal multilateral treaties governing a broad range of issues were signed, and the Permanent Court of International Justice was established to provide advisory opinions and judgments arising from legal issues or questions of fact and interpretation. The PCIJ in its brief twenty-three-year history issued a number of critically important advisory opinions and decided a number of cases in which some of the fundamental principles of international law had been challenged. The role of the court was symbolic of the universalization of international law, and of the importance of judicial proceedings in handling contentious issues between states.

At this point, we must also acknowledge the critical importance of customary law as a source of institutionalization. A large portion of the law is customary in the sense that it developed slowly out of the practices of states rather than through the mechanism of formal negotiations. Many of the rules surrounding transactions between states are based on custom, although often those customs are formalized into treaty terms. Today we have a law of treaties that reflects usage and custom; a law of diplomatic immunities that reflects the practices going back to the fifteenth century; a law of territorial jurisdiction that goes back to customary behavior in the fifteenth century and before. Upon gaining recognition as sovereign states, polities implicitly give their consent to this massive body of law and, in some cases, etiquette. Each time a state conducts its foreign relations in conformity with this part of the law, it strengthens its independent authority.

The process of institutionalization continued unabated for the remainder of the twentieth century. The new element is the luxurious growth of declaratory or "soft" law, that body of mostly multilateral statements of principle and aspiration that sets standards and ethical principles against which state behavior is measured, but a large part of which does not include formally binding obligations. Dorothy Jones (1990: appendix 1) lists seventy-nine major documents since 1919 that constitute a "code of ethics" in international relationships. These include, for example, a 1925 declaration on the rights of the child, the 1928 Kellogg–Briand Pact, a 1930 convention concerning forced or compulsory labor, a 1938 declaration in favor of women's rights, the 1942 Declaration of the United Nations, the 1960 Declaration on the Granting of Independence to Colonial Countries and Peoples, the 1961 European Social Charter, the 1970 Declaration on Principles of International Law Concerning Friendly Relations and Cooperation Among States, and the 1975 Final Act of the Conference on Security and Cooperation in Europe. A significant proportion of the seventy-nine deal with some aspect of human rights.

In addition to these are the dozens of charters of world and regional organizations (the obligations of which *are* binding, if not always observed), thousands of multilateral conventions dealing with a wide range of global and regional issues (e.g., whaling, trade in endangered species, prohibitions on the use of biological or chemical weapons, highjacking and terrorism, international trade, and the like), and more than 40,000 bilateral and multilateral treaties registered in the United Nations. Most international relationships and transactions today are rule-governed and there are permanent mechanisms to resolve disputes over interpretation, violation, and application of the rules. Nothing approaching the density of rules and the conflict-resolving devices that apply them can be found in earlier international systems or in early modern Europe. There are many areas where regulations are needed, to be sure, but increasingly the web of law-like obligations between states resembles law within states. While the society of states is formally an anarchy, where legal obligations between states are based on consent rather than authority, a clear distinction between domestic and international realms in terms of the presence or absence of law is no longer tenable.

The rules of the game in international relations: ethics and the sources of compliance

Whether we call it a code of ethics or the fundamental rules of coexistence between sovereign states makes little difference. What is significant is that the ideas, norms, and practices that constitute the institution of international law together embody a system that translates ethical norms into the rights and duties of states. These have been spelled out

Table 5.1 *The ethical foundations of the essential legal concepts of international relations*

Ethical principles and norms	Derivative legal norms, rules, or practices
1 Promises must be kept	*Pacta sunt servanda*
2 The right of independence for a political community	Sovereignty; territorial integrity; right of individual and collective self-defense
3 Self-rule and tolerance of political diversity	Non-interference; illegitimacy of conquest or colonialism; non-recognition of territorial changes brought through force or threat of force; no extraterritorial application of national laws
4 Equality of rights and obligations toward each other	Legal equality; consent as the basis of legal obligations; voting in international organizations
5 Right of self-defense	Article 51, United Nations Charter: this includes a right to collective self-defense
6 Reciprocity	Equal legal obligation of states
7 Non-violence (except self-defense or on behalf of international community)	Obligations to use peaceful conflict-resolution procedures; prohibition of aggression and conquest; non-recognition of conquests
8 Sanctity and worth of the individual	Human rights law; humanitarian law in armed conflicts

in numerous international documents, but some are more implicit than explicit. They are interwoven, but for analytical reasons we can separate them. Table 5.1 lists, in the first column, the relevant ethical norms or principles and, in the second, the rules that flow from them.

This list is not exhaustive. But it demonstrates the normative foundations of the ideas, norms, and rules incorporated into the main doctrines of contemporary international law. International politics is not just about power, prestige, and glory. It is also a story of rights and duties, and the permissible and impermissible things to do in a variety of circumstances. That there are frequent violations or arbitrary interpretations of rights and duties by a variety of states does not detract from the observation that the modern society of states is in part a legal realm and that it is becoming more so by the day.

While many of the major doctrines of international law reflect ethical or moral values, this is not to argue that the *system* of laws is primarily a moral domain. The essential rules of the system constitute a regime for the peaceful coexistence of states on a reasonably predictable basis. By outlining the dos and don'ts, it promotes an order in which rules rather than outcomes should – and most often do – prevail. The rules are valid regardless of whether they promote any particular state's purposes at a given time (Nardin, 1992: 19, 21). They are a foundational institution of international relations precisely for that reason: they transcend time, place, and personality, and they have some authority independent of the desires of particular states in particular circumstances. Terry Nardin (1992: 22–3) puts it clearly:

> To the extent that international law is regarded purely in instrumental terms, the international system becomes an order based on the existence of shared values, not a truly rule-governed order. International law exists as an independent institution only to the extent that its authority is acknowledged in the practice of international relations. And this means that its authority must have some other ground than its usefulness in promoting a desired international order. The authority of law . . . must not be confused with its rightness in relation to moral considerations or judgements regarding the desirability of the purposes it serves.

An international order could conceivably be based on shared interests of the major players, just as all voluntary associations such as clubs or sports teams can function in the absence of formal law. But in such a system, cooperation depends on the continuation of the shared interests. Once those disappear, so does the order. In contrast, in international relations for the past two centuries or so, for all powers (with a few exceptions such as Nazi Germany) there is an implicit *prior* recognition of the practices, procedures, and other rules of international law. When a state receives recognition from others, it implicitly accepts the broad corpus of international law as binding upon it. It cannot seek recognition, but state simultaneously that it refuses to be bound by the law of treaties, the laws surrounding diplomatic immunities, or the broad principle of freedom of the seas. The very act of becoming a state assumes at least implicitly an unconditional obligation to accept the authority of international law. Statehood itself is a status defined by international law, not independent of it (Nardin, 1992: 23).

Nardin's position on the authority of the international legal system is questioned by many who insist that states generally adhere to legal requirements only when it is in their interest to do so. Interests determine law, not the other way around. In Krasner's (1999) terms, governments act according to the logic of consequences rather than to a logic of appropriateness. But a growing literature on compliance shows that the incorporation of international legal rules and norms ("internalization") in national decision-making is complicated and variable, but generally occurs in such a manner as to change the definition of interests. States "come to *obey* through changes in their *perceived* interests over time, changes that occur due to enmeshment in a transnational process of legal production and legal interpretation" (Raustiala and Slaughter, 2002: 546). International legal norms also have authority because they are commonly perceived as legitimate (cf., Hall, 1999: 41). Legitimacy derives from the fact that most law was negotiated between legal equals or became inscribed only after a long process of customary practice by many states. Any order, including international law, depends upon this type of legitimacy. Thus, the dichotomy between a logic of consequences and a logic of appropriateness is oversimplified. Through various forms of socialization and internalization, and the prescriptive influence of legitimacy, norms and rules can change interests so that one does not have to choose between the two logics. Law and interest tend to reinforce each other (cf., Chayes and Chayes, 1993; Finnemore and Sikkink, 1998).

It is the authority (legitimacy) of international law that distinguishes the contemporary society of states from historical analogues. Neither among the Sumerian polities, Chinese warring states, nor the city-states of Greece or Renaissance Italy were relations defined primarily in legal terms, and there was no body of law, the acceptance of which preceded the existence and the right to existence of the interacting polities. The high death rate of pre-modern polities through conquest and physical annihilation stands in stark contrast to the relative (in historical terms) security of statehood in the past two centuries. The system of international law contains many ethical ideas, but the most fundamental is the ethic of tolerance of political diversity and the coexistence of states.

International law is thus a foundational institution of the current order. Most of its fundamental principles have not changed significantly except in four areas: human rights law; individuals and non-state organizations are becoming subjects of that law; international organizations may sanction collective intervention to protect populations at risk; and the right of conquest – also a corollary of sovereignty – has been abolished. In these four areas there has been significant change. In the first two, it is a reversion to older principles of natural law, or regression. In the last, the right has become obsolete or extinguished. Otherwise, sovereignty, territorial integrity, legal equality, non-interference, consent, and the binding character of treaties remain principles underlying diplomatic and other types of transactions that have not changed significantly over the past three centuries. There are many new areas of law to cope with new types of problems. In some cases older doctrines have been jettisoned or overturned in favor of newer legal formulations (and many Third World countries have contributed to new areas of law and proposed new doctrines). But the essential principles of international law listed above remain significantly unaltered. We have termed these the foundational principles. It is in the context of their lasting authority that the *processes* of international relations take place.

6   Diplomacy

The records of historical prototypes of diplomacy are rich with examples, but little systematic analysis. Examples include the delegations sent by various Chinese states to each other prior to the imperial unification of China in 221 BC, the evidence in the al-Armana tablets sent between Egyptian pharaohs (Cohen and Westbrook, 2000), the Babylonians, and other polities that occupied the Middle East in the second millennium BC, the more highly articulated diplomatic practices of the Greek city-states, and the regularized procedures for foreign contacts in the Byzantine Empire (cf., Holsti, 1967: ch. 2; Hamilton and Langhorne, 1995; Ferguson and Mansbach, 1996). The practices varied according to local customs and changed over time, but there were rough similarities across cultures. These included the sending of emissaries of high rank; considerable ceremony attending the arrival and departure of delegations; great concerns over the rank and status of sending and receiving parties; and various forms of diplomatic immunity. The last constituted a type of universal norm across cultures but in ancient polities, the norm was frequently violated. We know of numerous instances where messengers were put in captivity or executed by their ostensible hosts.

Early diplomatic prototypes lacked the essential ingredients of an international institution. There were fairly regularized practices within and between cultures and diverse polities, but they lacked a set of defining ideas that gave the practices a distinct and commonly understood meaning. Diplomatic contacts were typically intermittent, in some cases taking place only a few times in a century or more, and often only ceremonial. There was no idea that diplomacy is a continuous process between like units such as sovereign states. In contrast, it was most frequently an artifact of suzerain-type relationships where inferiors came to pay homage to their superiors. There was no sense of a diplomatic profession, a type of permanent activity that requires special skills, training, and previous experience. Most important, most ancient diplomats were only messengers. Their main task was to convey information, proposals (e.g., offers of peace), and messages of fealty, not to negotiate and bargain, as is the case today. The Greeks were somewhat different in that they often sent especially skilled orators to persuade the leaders and legislative bodies of other city-states. But once they had stated their case, they were not empowered to bargain, that is, to offer new proposals. Diplomacy was not continuous. The famous case of the Athenian delegation that went to Melos to persuade the Melians to become a military ally of Athens is probably typical. Having failed in their single mission of oratorical persuasion, the delegation returned to Athens. Athenian armed forces then besieged the small island city-state, put all the male inhabitants "to the sword," and carried off the women and children as slaves. By the end of the seventeenth century, in contrast, we see in Europe practices informed by sets of unique ideas, and by norms, rules, and etiquette that had become widely accepted by distinctly similar polities, namely sovereign states.

The birth of the diplomatic institution in the seventeenth century

Because contacts between ancient polities were intermittent and non-institutionalized we have only anecdotal evidence of their characteristics. In the case of Europe going back at least to the fourteenth century, however, there is a literature that chronicles the birth and early development of diplomacy as an international institution. It did not of course take place overnight, but it is relatively easy to identify watersheds. The first was the formation of permanent embassies among many of the Italian city-states in the late fifteenth century. The second was the norm secured by the sixteenth century that only sovereigns could send ambassadors abroad. The third was the two conferences between 1644 and 1648 that led to the Peace of Westphalia. These constituted the first pan-European peace conference and set critical parameters for the conduct of diplomacy thereafter. The final watershed was the text on diplomacy written by François de Callières in 1697. It elaborated a number of ideas that reveal the extent to which diplomacy had become an international institution as opposed to a set of intermittent activities organized on an *ad hoc* basis. Let us now turn to the ingredients of international institutions and narrate the slow birth of diplomacy in terms of their components.

Practices

At the time of the Peace of Westphalia in 1648, a network of permanent embassies linked most of the sovereigns and smaller polities to each other. The practices of maintaining permanent embassies on the soil of other sovereigns and appointing ambassadors to staff them for lengthy periods of time were uniquely European. Until the late Middle Ages, both public and private diplomacy in Europe had been conducted essentially as they were in other civilizations, that is, intermittently by amateur delegations sent for one specific task. In the late fifteenth century in Italy, the city-states of the peninsula began the practice of establishing permanent embassies. This was not someone's stroke of genius, but an institutional development borne out of the necessity of highly distrustful, but proximate polities requiring sustained sources of information about the politics, plans, and policies of their neighbors. *Ad hoc* delegations of amateurs could not perform the intelligence-gathering functions of diplomacy; a permanent ambassador could. Italian city-states created the network initially for their mutual relations, but as the politics of the rest of Europe began to impinge increasingly upon the Italian peninsula, some city-states – Milan in particular – began to establish permanent embassies in other areas of Europe, first in the court of the Holy Roman Empire, then in Spain, and ultimately in France and England (cf., Hamilton and Langhorne, 1995: 34–6). The Spaniards then picked up the practice by establishing embassies in other European royal jurisdictions, followed by the French and the English. It is notable, given the traditional hostility between Christians and Muslims of that era, that France established a permanent embassy in Constantinople as early as 1537. Within another century, most European sovereigns had permanent representatives at the Porte. We have, then, our first critical distinction between diplomacy as an institution of international relations and diplomacy as an intermittent activity confined mostly to the sending of messages. By the mid-seventeenth century the diverse polities of Europe were in constant contact with each other through the medium of officially accredited ambassadors or ministers residing in permanent embassies or legations.

However, diplomatic practices were so diverse, unpatterned, and unregulated by custom, etiquette, or formal rules that the degree of institutionalization was low. For example, the acts of representation and negotiation took many different forms. Some courts sent multiple ambassadors to a single counterpart abroad, each diplomat designated to have official contacts with another specific individual in the foreign court. The Dutch republic frequently used this method of representation until the eighteenth century, and Louis XIV accredited three ambassadors to negotiate with the English in 1665. Some sovereigns employed the "circular embassy," an officially accredited delegation that went from capital to capital performing various tasks in each, only to pack up and move on to the next court.

Security was not a hallmark of diplomacy at the time. Theft and kidnapping of couriers occurred with some frequency until the late seventeenth century.

The low degree of institutionalization is demonstrated by other diverse practices as well, particularly those related to recruitment and pay. At the time of Westphalia there were no professional diplomats, that is, a corps of people trained in special skills, knowledge of the history and laws of international relations, or mastery of languages. On the contrary, sovereigns had great difficulty finding people to staff their small embassies. Even as late as the mid-seventeenth century, many diplomats had to pay their own salaries and had no secretarial assistance provided by the crown. Not infrequently, a diplomat retiring from a stint in a foreign capital carried away with him a mountain of debts. Entertainment and ceremony were critical parts of the diplomatic function of symbolic representation, but sending governments rarely paid for all their immense costs. M. S. Anderson (1996: 85) reports that a French duke turned down an ambassadorship to the Holy See on the grounds that his father, who had held it previously, had accumulated debts of 200,000 livres. We can appreciate the amount of indebtedness when we examine the retinues that were considered necessary – reflecting upon status and prestige – for a major ambassadorship. The same French ambassador to Rome some years later had a male staff of 145, including a theologian from the Sorbonne, two French and two Italian secretaries, eleven gentlemen of the chamber, a surgeon, sixty-two valets and lackeys, four trumpeters, a French chef and his assistants, plus coachmen, postillions, and pages.

Part of the financial strain was relieved by a practice in some countries of the host paying for the main costs of foreign embassies (Anderson, 1996: 48–9). The practice died out in the major capitals by the middle of the seventeenth century, but remained in Russia and the Ottoman

Empire for considerably longer. Naturally there were major disputes over how much maintenance allowance should be, and whether some ambassadors received more than others did. Another practice that helped relieve the financial distress of envoys was the provision of valuable gifts by the host upon the ambassador's conclusion of his mission. Anderson (1996: 50) provides some interesting examples:

> The Maréchal de Cadenet, a French ambassador on a special mission who stayed in London for only a few days in 1621, was given by James I jewellery said to be worth £2,500, while the Duke of Buckingham . . . presented him with ponies and four albino falcons . . . The Maréchal de Bossompierre . . . after another brief embassy to London five years later, was given by Charles I "four diamonds set in a lozenge, and a great stone at the end": this was said to be worth £7,000 . . . Moreover, Bossompierre also received from the new French-born queen, Henrietta Maria, a "very fine diamond."

Overall, in the seventeenth century recruitment and payment of ambassadors was disorganized and arbitrary (Anderson, 1996: 33) with the result that many candidates would do anything to avoid service. For too many, diplomacy meant financial ruin. In the case of Venice, failure to accept a mission was punishable under law (Hamilton and Langhorne, 1995: 50). However, as the seventeenth century wore on, conditions for service improved and a group of experienced, almost professional diplomats carried on the businesses of their sovereigns.

The uncertainties surrounding short-lived and diverse practices were reflected in the lack of a common terminology designating the essential roles and tasks of envoys. In the Italian city-states, the term ambassador was used interchangeably with orator, *deputatus, consiliarus*, and *legatus*. In other parts of Europe there was considerable variety in designation of titles. Different courts had different customs and traditions, and naturally these implied status distinctions that were not always welcome. Since pomp and ostentation were extremely important components of diplomatic theater, reflecting upon the glory, rank, and status of the sovereign, the diverse practices of bestowing titles on envoys more often than not created serious frictions in the conduct of diplomacy.

The most difficult situation, again demonstrating how in the seventeenth century enormous problems of coordinating and standardizing diplomatic practices remained, arose over the question of precedence. The tradition, when there were relatively few permanent ambassadorial posts, was for papal representatives to precede all others, followed by those of the Holy Roman Emperor (Anderson, 1996: 17). But this was no longer acceptable by the seventeenth century, when papal and imperial authority over the new monarchs of Europe was waning. By the time of the great conferences in Osnabrück and Münster starting in 1644, the diplomatic representatives of the French and Swedish kings, among others, demanded equal status with the papal and imperial delegates. All sorts of disputes ranged around the issue, some quite ludicrous in contemporary eyes, but extremely serious at the time. Seating arrangements, the order of entry into a sovereign's meeting chambers, the visibility of the ambassador to the sovereign, the size of coaches, the numbers of servants and flunkies attending them, and such like were of the most serious consequence. One major tussle, involving more than fifty killed or wounded, between the retinues of the French and Spanish ambassadors on the occasion of the Swedish ambassador's presentation of credentials to the Court of St. James in 1661, almost caused a war between their two monarchs. Louis XIV demanded an apology from the King of Spain on pain of military measures. The situation was defused only with an extended apology. Many other examples could be provided.

Ideas

Between 1625 and 1700, 153 titles on diplomacy were published in Europe. Of these 114 were new contributions to the literature. The others were translations (Keens-Soper, 1973: 497). Some became best sellers or at least the handbooks that envoys took with them on their journeys. Immediately we see another difference from ancient diplomacy. In the European context of the seventeenth century, people were beginning to think systematically about diplomacy as a distinct field of political activity. Admittedly, most of the tracts dealt with the virtues necessary to make a successful ambassador. This predominant theme – what Maurice Keens-Soper (1973: 488) calls a fascination with "moral physiognomy" – at times reached ridiculous heights of casuistry and reveals some insecurity in the diplomatic *métier*. Diplomats did not have particularly good reputations at the time, as both courts and interested publics associated their activities with spying and with excesses of theater and show. The emphasis in this literature on reliability, trustworthiness, and honesty belied the actual state of diplomatic conduct. Its underlying subtext was that envoys can do better, and if they do so, some of the worst features of seventeenth-century international politics can be ameliorated.

François de Callières wrote *De la manière de négocier avec les souvereins* in 1697. It is important on many counts, but primarily because it was the first self-reflective treatise on a unique kind of political activity. It is a "tradition become aware of itself in thought" (Keens-Soper, 1973: 500). De Callières transformed the exhortative-legal tradition of the literature into a type of diplomatic theory and emphasized that diplomacy is a necessary activity in a field of conflict and collaboration between states. What matters are not so much the attributes of individual ambassadors, but the character of the system of European states. This was in his view a collection of sovereigns engaged in the pursuit of their self-interest. Insecurity and conflict are necessary results. The European states system is nevertheless characterized by interdependence, where the actions of one state have consequences on the interests of all others. It is also a *society* of states with certain common bonds of culture, civilization, and history, what he called "membres d'une même République." Echoing Richelieu, de Callières insisted that diplomacy must be continuous. It is not, as the ancients practiced it, an intermittent activity involved primarily in the exchange of messages or the display of ostentation. Negotiation is not a one-time affair, but a necessary ingredient for high-quality information upon which policy must be based. Intelligence (in both senses of the term) is critical, while oratory and theater reflect only prestige rather than the "real" interests of states. Diplomacy cannot by itself transform the society of states and its attending frictions, conflicts, and wars. They are not the result of misunderstandings, lack of communication, or the absence of a voice preaching concord and brotherhood. They are, rather, the inevitable consequences of a system of sovereign states. But the quality of international political relations can be modified or ameliorated by continuous and intelligent diplomacy conducted by trustworthy envoys. Thus de Callières expanded the scope and level of understanding about diplomacy as an international institution. Diplomatic practices by the end of the seventeenth century had become sufficiently standardized that one of its practitioners was able to theorize about it in a novel manner. There was now a common terminology of diplomacy, a developing consensus on the main tasks, roles, and responsibilities of envoys, an appreciation of the importance of a sovereign's interests, but in the context of a larger field of competing states, and a recognition of diplomacy as a distinct and honorable career. By the end of the seventeenth century, then, we have two ingredients of an international institution: increasingly regularized (though still somewhat disparate) practices, and a growing intersubjective consensus in the realm of ideas about diplomacy. We now turn to the final ingredient, developing norms, rules, and etiquette.

Norms

Norms surrounding the institution of diplomacy were very much tangled up with the issue of sovereignty and the status of dynasts. In the Middle Ages, all sorts of polities sent delegations to each other to exchange messages, make announcements, or attend ceremonial functions. Queens, kings, emperors, the pope, dukes, and independent cities had to communicate. Great feudatories conducted their own foreign relations and their right to do so was at least tacitly recognized by crown heads (Anderson, 1996: 4). But once the practice of permanent embassies had become established, serious questions of status arose: who could legitimately claim a right to establish a permanent mission in another polity? The lengthy quarrels between the pope, the Holy Roman Emperor, and monarchs over secular authority informed this question (see chapter 4). Henry VIII had declared final authority over both ecclesiastical and secular affairs in England during the sixteenth century, and other crowned heads joined in imitation. The corollary to the "independence" of states was that only sovereign polities could establish permanent embassies. The norm was not established suddenly but grew out of concerns of sovereigns that dukes and other feudatories nominally under their authority were engaging in their own diplomacy to subvert the interests of the crown. Hence Louis XI of France forbade any lesser units within the kingdom to send embassies abroad and by the sixteenth century most monarchs had made such orders stick. However, some, like the Duke of Burgundy, were sufficiently powerful to ignore the prohibition. Even as late as the eighteenth century the Duke of Milan was sending *ambasciari* to his ostensible ruler, the King of Spain (Anderson, 1996: 5). But in general, by the early seventeenth century most practices were consistent with the norm, which had been given perhaps the greatest weight by the Holy Roman Emperor Charles V. He decreed in the middle of the sixteenth century that the title "ambassador" could be accorded only to the representatives of crowned heads and of the Republic of Venice (Ferguson and Mansbach, 1996: 343). Most sovereigns imitated the decree. By 1648, the norm had become sufficiently well established that we could say it was a constitutive element of the diplomatic institution. The permanent embassy was now an attribute of sovereignty, a right to which only sovereign rulers were entitled. As with many of the practices mentioned above, the norm of sovereign entitlement to participate in the diplomatic institution replaced the great variety of rules and practices typical of the late Middle Ages.

A second major norm was the immunity of ambassadors and the extraterritoriality of the permanent embassy. Like other norms and practices, this was not legislated collectively on one occasion but grew up over a period of time as a matter of customary law. It was assisted greatly by publicists and lawyers such as Gentile (*De Legationibus* [1584]) and Grotius whose writings on the issue had become authoritative by the end of the seventeenth century. Consider how these norms affected practices. In 1524 the imperial resident in England was arrested and accused of slandering Henry VIII on the basis of dispatches stolen from his courier (Hamilton and Langhorne, 1995: 45). He lost his diplomatic immunity as a result. Immunity was not yet a rule, but a loose convention subject to constant political manipulation. The question of extraterritoriality arose over religious questions, namely the ambassador's chapel. Could a Protestant ambassador fulfil his religious duties in a Catholic establishment? The solution to the conundrum was to declare that an ambassador's chapel – and ultimately the embassy itself – was to be considered as a piece of the envoy's own territory, and hence immune from the jurisdiction of the receiving state. By the 1620s, Grotius was arguing that envoys could not perform ambassadorial functions without immunities, whatever else local laws might demand. Security of diplomatic communication was impossible, he suggested, unless the ambassador was accountable only to his sovereign. By the mid-seventeenth century, after two hundred years of ambiguity, incompatible rules, and serious disputes, the norms of diplomatic immunities and embassy extraterritoriality had become reasonably standard throughout Europe (Hamilton and Langhorne, 1995: 45).

This left the question of precedence as the major unresolved area of rules and etiquette. From today's vantage, it may seem an arcane problem but in an era when the sovereign's rank and status meant everything – what Rodney Hall (1999: 93) has characterized as an era of neurotic status anxiety – lack of rules on this issue had serious consequences for the tenor of relations between dynasts and their states. There were some rules and customs, of course. As laid down in the papal rankings of 1504, the Holy Roman Emperor ranked first among secular authorities. There was considerable consensus that hereditary monarchs ranked above elected ones, and that republics ranked even lower. But despite these customary rankings, all authorities attempted to claim higher status than that accorded by custom. Venice, formally a republic but generally ranked as an "honorary kingdom" because of its diplomatic importance, sent a delegation to James II in 1685 to congratulate him on his coronation and to ask for British help against the Turks. Given the importance of the occasion, the Venetians requested to be conducted by a duke rather than a mere earl to their audience with the king, and that their coaches be allowed to enter the courtyard of the royal palace. Such protocol was reserved for monarchs only, so their plea was rejected as unjustified (Anderson, 1996: 59). Louis XIV almost went to war with Spain over a question of diplomatic ceremony and precedence in London, and he actually sent a naval squadron to bombard Genoa because the Genoese had refused to offer the appropriate salutes to French vessels. These and other examples illustrate the close connection between the honor of the state and the status of their rulers. One could not slight the first without slighting the second (Hall, 1999: 93). There are numerous illustrations of irritations deriving from status considerations, and quite a few of them either sidetracked the real business of governments or actually caused serious conflicts. Only in the mid-eighteenth century did the norm of seniority as the basis of precedence become firmly established, although it was not put into treaty form until 1818.

Not all royal houses could afford to establish permanent embassies abroad, and there were a number of small states, principalities, and polities with uncertain status that were not allowed to send ambassadors. The diplomatic establishment had several main ranks – ambassador, minister (usually with the title "plenipotentiary" added), and chargé d'affaires – but customs for dealing with these different rankings varied from court to court, and there was the problem of other, more ancient, rankings. By the late seventeenth century norms and etiquette for only the three major rankings had become established. Another diplomatic irritant had been resolved by the end of the first era we have used for comparison of institutional change.

Other evidence of institutionalization

Standardized, peaceful practices, ideas and beliefs, and norms, rules, and etiquette form a major portion of an international institution. But bureaucratization and routinization are also important ingredients in some domains. This is the case where organizations, in addition to personnel with clearly defined status and legal standing, arise to fund, support, and provide logistics for a particular activity. In the case of diplomacy, embryonic foreign ministries and schools for the training of diplomats were important. In England, the secretary of state, originally an officer of the royal household who drafted the king's letters and kept his private seal, became responsible for maintaining the correspondence of the royal figure relating to a wide variety of issues, both domestic and foreign. The king made policy, with the advice of anyone whom he wished to consult, but the secretary maintained the entire diplomatic network. Similar organizations developed in Russia (the *posolskii prikaz*, or department of embassies), France, and elsewhere. The Russian department of embassies was organized on geographical lines, with five departments, three of them handling relations with distinct groups of European states and the other two with Asian polities. Sweden had a similar organization. Both became prototypes for the eventual geographically based foreign ministries of the rest of Europe, and for what we still have today (Anderson, 1996: 75). By the late seventeenth century, France's secretary of state for foreign affairs had one of the greatest ministries in all Europe, although even at this late date the ministry was still responsible for a number of domestic issues and regions.

The professionalization of diplomatic personnel was underway by the late seventeenth century, but still a long way from completion. There were no standards for recruitment; no regular pay scales; no definite term of service; no standardized pensions; no handbooks or training schools; in brief none of the educational or bureaucratic paraphernalia we today associate with a career. Nobles or even upper bourgeois did not covet ambassadorships because they seldom brought more than financial headaches and great distance from the centers of power, prestige, and influence in the royal courts. As one writer put it (quoted in Anderson, 1996: 80), those offered diplomatic posts chose "rather to fix themselves near to the person of the Prince; because the recompenses for that service are much greater, and much more frequent, and because those that are absent are commonly forgotten, which makes them look upon an embassy as a sort of an honorable exile." A contemporary put it even more succinctly: "Foreign service may sometimes provide a good stirrup but never a good saddle."

Under these circumstances diplomatic appointments were made in a remarkably haphazard manner, usually based on family connections, patronage, and often by luck (Anderson, 1996: 81). The first attempt to create an institution for training diplomats (the Political Academy in France) did not occur until 1712. It failed after just nine years (Keens-Soper, 1972). But it stood as a prototype for later institutions in other countries, including in Russia, which inaugurated a college of foreign affairs in 1721 with 261 members (Hamilton and Langhorne, 1995: 74).

Reflecting the development of the French state under Louis XIV, the administration of foreign affairs through bureaucratic innovation was also a major breakthrough in institutionalization. At the beginning of Louis' reign, the minister charged with the care of foreign relations had only a few assistants. By the early eighteenth century one observer estimated that "twenty coaches would have been needed to transport [the minister], his secretaries, permanent officials, heads of bureaus, interpreters, archivists, code-breakers and all . . . " (quoted in Keens-Soper, 1973: 491). Other European courts both through need and imitation did not lag far behind. At the same time, the idea of a *corps diplomatique* was already beginning to develop. Diplomacy had become a profession with a sense of its own distinguishing characteristics, mores, and etiquette. By the end of the seventeenth century, diplomatic practices had become increasingly standardized as local customs and arrangements gave way to more international standards. The administration of foreign relations became bureaucratized. And the diplomatic career began its first steps toward professionalization. Diplomacy had become one of the major institutions of the society of states.

Explaining a new institution

Explanations for these developments are numerous. States needed some permanent network of diplomatic contacts in a region of the world in which insecurity was rife, where questions of status and rank were supremely important, and where information was crucial to survival and the protection of a sovereign's interests and prestige. De Callières' statement that when one polity in Europe moved, all the others felt its effects, was a frank recognition of the growing interdependence of the units within the continent, including the Ottoman Empire. The sovereigns of the day could not construct alliances – often essential for survival – cement royal marriages (giving form and sanctity to alliances), display their glory and prestige, and remain abreast of their rivals' plans and purposes without continuous foreign representation. In the fifteenth century, ambassadors had been viewed with considerable suspicion (often with good reason) and their qualities deprecated. By the end of the seventeenth century their services were so fundamental to a state's foreign policies that their social and political status had increased significantly.

Imitation is another explanation. In the early fifteenth century, Spain, followed quickly by others, imitated the Italian city-states in creating permanent embassies abroad. The great build-up of state and military capacity under the reign of Louis XIV was broadly imitated. For status and prestige reasons, as well as the need to learn what his foreign policy plans were, other sovereigns had to keep up with the initiatives of the Sun King. The bureaucratization and professionalization of diplomacy was one of the indicators of royal worth.

Finally, there was the need for standardization. In its early years, diplomacy was as much a source of friction and conflict as were inconsistent territorial claims, colonial competition, and the search for glory and notoriety. The number of different practices, customs, and ceremonies surrounding diplomacy in the fifteenth and sixteenth centuries hindered rather than promoted communication between courts. Over a long period punctuated by innumerable diplomatic incidents, anomalous practices, norms, and etiquette were sloughed off or went into desuetude to be replaced by the practices and innovations of the leading powers of the era. Heterogeneity of practices, norms, and etiquette eventually gave way to homogeneity. The end of the seventeenth century – our first era of comparison – marked a point when the trend toward institutional homogeneity was well under way.

Contemporary diplomacy

Practices

The numbers of permanent embassies headed by ambassadors did not grow appreciably in the nineteenth century. New establishments in Japan, China, Persia, and Latin America did not completely compensate for the closure of many embassies in minor principalities and other types of polities in Europe that disappeared with the unifications of Italy and Germany. Moreover, costs and a certain desire to remain outside the main diplomatic quarrels of the era encouraged smaller states such as Denmark to downsize their diplomatic establishments. Denmark had forty-four career diplomats in 1797, but only twenty-eight in the middle of the nineteenth century, and a mere twenty on the eve of the Great War (Anderson, 1993: 104). If diplomatic representation did not expand during the nineteenth century, however, its professionalization did. The main features were the introduction of systematic recruitment policies based on merit rather than patronage or family connections, the opening of bureaus within foreign ministries to monitor the newspapers of the world and to gauge public opinion abroad, general administrative and civil service reform, the rationalization of public finances (extended to diplomatic services as well), entrance examinations, and abandoning the old practice of hiring foreigners as diplomats. Despite these innovations, foreign ministries and embassies by today's standards were small. In 1861 the British foreign ministry (Whitehall) had only fifty-two employees (Hamilton and Langhorne, 1995: 102). The Quay d'Orsay in Paris had 115 in 1873 (Guillen, 1984: 21).

These numbers were to begin a dramatic expansion at the turn of the century and they continue to spiral upward as the number of states has mushroomed from the original handful that formed the League of Nations in 1919 to almost 200 today. The number of international organizations has also proliferated, and the size of embassies having to deal with whole new sets of problems has increased apace. The entire nineteenth century saw only a slight increase in both embassies and diplomatic personnel. The twentieth century saw a veritable explosion. One estimate is that in London today there are 17,000 foreign diplomats, their families and staff (Hamilton and Langhorne, 1995: 213). Similar figures would be found in all the world's major capitals.

The growth of diplomatic interconnectedness in the twentieth century and since has been dramatic. In 1950, the world's 81 states had an average of 26 other states with which they maintained a resident ambassador and staff. By 1991, the 167 states of the world had an average of 46 other states with which they were linked formally through the medium of a permanent ambassador and his or her staff (Held et al., 1999: 54). The number of international conferences has grown from an average of about three annually in the middle of the nineteenth century to more than 3,000 today. In addition, there are about 350 intergovernmental organizations today (compared with 123 in 1951), all of which operate as venues for national delegates having diplomatic status to bargain, negotiate, inform, learn, and exchange views (Zacher, 1993: 65).

Conferencing has become so ubiquitous in the contemporary era that most people most of the time are barely aware of most of them. There are just too many for the media to cover. When we add the numerous conferences sponsored by the United Nations and its specialized agencies, and the increasing number of "global" or "summit" conferences on specific issues (UN Conference on Environment and Development, Rio de Janeiro, 1992; the World Conferences on Human Rights, Vienna, 1993, Population and Development, Cairo, 1994, Social Development, Copenhagen, 1995; the Fourth World Conference on Women,

Beijing, 1995); the number of multilateral diplomatic events is immense. And the numbers attending them continue to grow. At the Copenhagen "Social Summit" of 1995, 187 governments sent a total of 5,741 accredited delegates. Their activities were monitored, lobbied, and criticized by 2,315 accredited representatives of non-governmental organizations (NGOs), 2,863 media personnel, 405 United Nations staff, and a parallel private NGO forum with an attendance of about 10,000 representing 2,000 activist groups (for a general discussion of conference diplomacy, see Kaufmann, 1996).

The practice of summitry, conferences between heads of state or government, has kept pace with UN-sponsored multilateral conferences. The Congress of Vienna was the first European summit involving the heads of government or state of all the great powers. Several more in the nineteenth century and the Paris Peace Conference in 1919 followed it. Prior to the Great War there were a number of bilateral summit meetings, and they generated considerable public attention. Today, the heads of state or government of the European Union meet so frequently that they are barely noticed in other parts of the world. In addition, there are the annual summits of the G-8, IMF, APEC, ARF, MERCOSUR, and several others. The stream of prime ministers and presidents to the White House or to Downing Street is steady and mostly non-notable except for the media of the country from which the visitors come. The press conferences following these meetings are more likely to focus on the domestic problems of the president or prime minister than on the substance of the summit meeting. While most summit meetings are *ad hoc*, some, like the G-8 meetings, the APEC conferences, or the gathering of EU heads of government, are regularly scheduled annual affairs.

In the seventeenth century diplomacy revolved around security issues. Diplomats negotiated alliances, marriages, peace treaties, and some issues of trade or colonialism. Today, the scope of diplomacy encompasses the whole range of issues generated by modern societies. These include the environment, trade, investment, foreign aid, cultural relations, security issues, arms control, human rights, aviation, natural resources, health, international criminal activity, illegal immigration, and many others. Trade promotion, commercial reporting, and cultural relations have become major preoccupations of embassy officials, tasks that rarely consumed the energies of diplomats prior to the late nineteenth century. For many developing countries, aid and commercial questions constitute the bulk of their diplomatic workload with major Western capitals and numerous multilateral organizations. Since the end of the Cold War, commercial and financial questions – broadly conceived – have dominated the international agenda and have become the main preoccupations of diplomatic establishments everywhere. This is one explanation for the constant expansion of embassy staff, as they now require experts on imports and exports, agriculture trade, foreign aid, science and technology, environmental issues, and the like.

Although there has been massive growth in the size and number of diplomatic establishments and in the scope and number of issues with which they deal, the traditional functions of diplomacy have remained intact. They include symbolic representation, reporting, political and other types of analysis, negotiation and persuasion, and advice to decision-makers. For some, various forms of espionage can be added to the list. But for the most part since the late nineteenth century espionage work has been allocated to specialized organizations that nevertheless may use diplomatic establishments for cover.

Looking at the practices of contemporary diplomacy we see both change and continuity. The changes have been dramatic, particularly in a quantitative sense: the growth of embassies and their staff; the increasing frequency of summit meetings; the vastly expanded scope of diplomatic activity; and the professionalization of most diplomatic services. The diplomatic "corps" of the late seventeenth century numbered in the hundreds. Today, if we include technical specialists who enjoy at least temporary diplomatic status, the number may well be over one million.

Ideas

Most contemporary ideas about diplomatic institutions and processes have antecedents in the seventeenth and eighteenth centuries. We take for granted Richelieu's idea – revolutionary at the time – that diplomacy is and should be a constant activity. We assume that diplomacy is a necessary procedure for limiting or preventing major conflicts between states. We therefore propose almost reflexively that every possible diplomatic avenue be explored before states use violence – an idea popularized by Clausewitz in the early nineteenth century. The idea is explicit in the slogan "give diplomacy a chance!" Indeed, there seems to be a contemporary norm, most explicitly stated in the League of Nations Covenant, that military force cannot be used legitimately unless all modes of diplomatic negotiation have been exhausted. War is an option of the last resort. Diplomacy is, among other characteristics, an activity that seeks to prevent situations where the last resort becomes the most feasible policy. All these ideas gained popularity in previous centuries and replaced the older ideas current in the fifteenth and sixteenth centuries that diplomacy is just another form of warfare.

In the twentieth century other concepts of diplomacy appeared but they were ultimately rejected. Compared with the legion of studies and memoirs of more conventional diplomacy, they have had little appeal, and they have not served as an intellectual foundation for the transformation of the diplomatic institution. The Bolsheviks after securing power in 1917 attempted to convert their diplomats into purveyors of revolution. They abandoned the titles and protocols of "imperialist" diplomacy and sent abroad "people's representatives," or *polpreds*. The main idea was that diplomats were to become revolutionary agents, not with the traditional tasks of smoothing frictions, negotiation, and avoiding wars, but charged with promoting, organizing, and financing revolutionary parties abroad. Treaties, like pie crusts, Lenin insisted, were made to be broken. The Bolshevik government disavowed tsarist treaty obligations (and debts) and initially refused to negotiate a peace treaty with imperial Germany while also refusing to fight ("neither peace nor war"). The Bolsheviks introduced in a radical manner what Woodrow Wilson had referred to as "open diplomacy." Diplomacy was to be taken out of the backrooms and chancelleries and conducted in full public view (see below). This implied a radical shift in diplomatic purpose: from negotiation to propaganda. Diplomats were to use public fora to make speeches for public consumption, to appeal above the heads of governments, and to raise revolutionary fervor. The main purpose of diplomacy, so Bolshevik ideas held, was not to reach agreements or to negotiate treaties but to advance the cause of revolution by casting all diplomatic situations as the forces of righteousness battling the reactionary bourgeoisie and their imperial holdings.

Similar ideas gained some currency in Nazi Germany and Fascist Italy, where the traditionally clear lines between diplomacy, espionage, subversion, and war became increasingly blurred. For Hitler, diplomacy was to be used to gain time in order to further war preparations, and to create crises that could be used as pretexts to launch the Wehrmacht. He had a general contempt for conventional diplomatic ideas and practices, denouncing their ethos of bargaining, horse-trading, compromise, and war-avoidance. He regarded diplomacy as a sign of weakness in a world where might must triumph. In Mussolini he found an eager imitator and although his hatred of Soviet communism was on public record, he himself imitated many of the ideas on diplomacy propounded by Lenin and Trotsky before and after 1917.

Stalin employed a variety of diplomatic forms according to his purposes and his interlocutors. During World War II he bargained with Roosevelt and Churchill, as might any wartime leader. But after the war, the public diplomacy of his foreign minister, Vyatcheslav Molotov, or the Soviet ambassador to the United Nations, Andre Vishinsky ("Mr. *Nyet*"), demonstrated that the old Bolshevik ideas about diplomacy were still in play. But with the Soviet Union an ostensible great power and principal rival of the United States, diplomacy of the more conventional variety was also necessary. In the later years of the Soviet regime, ideas about revolutionary-style diplomacy waned to the point where it became difficult to see clear distinctions between Soviet behavior in international fora and in arms control negotiations and what we might expect of any great power. Nevertheless the Bolshevik tradition has survived in a few corners of the world. Libya under Muammar Qaddafi abandoned traditional diplomatic titles for its envoys abroad, and renamed them "people's representatives." They included in their tasks spreading Qaddafi's ideas about his "Green Revolution" and in a few instances organizing assassinations of Libyan dissidents living abroad. During Mao Tse-tung's Great Proletarian Cultural Revolution in 1966–8, ultra-leftists took over the Chinese foreign ministry and ordered home more than forty ambassadors who, they claimed, had succumbed to "Western decadence." They denounced the "bourgeois" norm of diplomatic immunities and then set about organizing Red Guards to humiliate and assault foreign diplomats. These challenges to traditional diplomatic practices, ideas, and norms did not last long, however. Regimes ultimately find that if they want to live in and do business with the vast majority of the states and societies in the world, they need to adopt or adhere to the major norms and ideas that help promote confidence, stability, predictability, and the trust that are foundations of all treaties and agreements. The ideas of Grotius, de Callières, and many subsequent commentators on diplomacy continue to underlie the network that binds states – even hostile ones – into a vast diplomatic system. Those that have fundamentally challenged the main ideas have ultimately had to accept them, even if grudgingly (cf., Armstrong, 1993).

Norms, rules, and etiquette

The early Bolshevik onslaught against "bourgeois" diplomatic practices and norms did include one idea that has stuck: public diplomacy.

The Great War was never supposed to have happened. By 1914, many thought that Europeans had reached a level of "civilization," learning, and progress that was rendering armed conflict between states (or at least between European states) unimaginable. With the spread of republicanism, democracy, literacy, education, and general standards of living, the old militaristic habits of the past were supposed to have waned. In the disillusionment that followed the Great War, analysts began searching for the causes of that great catastrophe. Among them was secret diplomacy, the set of nineteenth-century practices in which foreign policy decisions were made by cabinets with as few details revealed to the press as possible, with numerous secret treaties and less formal, but unpublicized undertakings, and with all negotiations carried out safely distant from public scrutiny. The post-war critics were particularly shocked by the revelation of secret treaties that the British, French, Russians, and Italians had made prior to and during the war.

The Bolshevik response was to publish major tsarist treaties and to insist that in all future negotiations the Russians would invite representatives of the press to observe and monitor the proceedings. These ideas caused much consternation in more traditional diplomatic circles, but once Woodrow Wilson had articulated them as one of his famous Fourteen Points ("Open covenants openly arrived at") they gained substantial public support. Wilson went to Paris in 1919 bent on revising those old diplomatic practices, including secret agreements, alliances, and the balance of power, that in his view had caused innumerable international conflicts and wars in the past. Although in Paris he negotiated with his allied counterparts in a manner not so dissimilar to his predecessors at Vienna a century earlier – that is, in secret – he insisted that all decisions arrived at would be made public. He and his colleagues offered numerous press conferences and interviews to bring the public up to date on major decisions. As the cornerstone of the new norm of open diplomacy, Wilson insisted in his draft of the Covenant of the League of Nations that debates in the Assembly would be open to the press and that members of the organization would be required to make public their treaties and register them with the League.

The norm of diplomatic openness is now fully entrenched. Most do not interpret this to mean, as the Bolsheviks insisted, that actual negotiations and bargaining must be fully exposed to public scrutiny, but there is a broad consensus that on those issues which carry inherent public interest the results of negotiations must be publicized. The great debates in the Security Council and General Assembly remain for the most part open, although many would add that the actual deals preliminary to any public decisions are always made backstage. In any event, the norm of open diplomacy, considered a radical innovation when first enunciated by the Bolsheviks and Woodrow Wilson, has become standard and guides most contemporary diplomatic practices.

Norms governing matters such as rank, diplomatic immunities, precedence, and the inviolability of embassy precincts derived from treaties dating back to 1818 and from custom. But by the early twentieth century some of these were not defined adequately to meet modern needs. In the 1920s several Latin American governments promoted the idea of inscribing in a multilateral convention all the norms and rules governing the establishment and sustenance of the complex network of diplomatic relations that allows the international system and its manifold transactions to be conducted in reasonable safety. Further pressures came from the practices common to Cold War rivalry – particularly espionage – that were placing substantial strains on many diplomatic conventions. The Vienna Convention of 1961 fully outlined the obligations, responsibilities, and rights governing diplomatic relations. These included the inviolability and protection of mission premises, communications facilities, and diplomatic immunities and privileges. Further conventions dealt with consular representation, special missions, and representation in international organizations (cf., Hamilton and Langhorne, 1995: 214).

In the realm of etiquette the generalization is that over time it has become less important and less formal. Many elements of protocol survive earlier eras – the Red Carpet Treatment being one of them – and important visits by heads of state or government remain major theatrical events (cf., Cohen, 1987). They are carefully scripted to provide photo opportunities and to allow the actors to appeal to both domestic and foreign publics. Yet many of the etiquette routines of previous centuries (such as leaving calling cards) have withered away. Matters of dress, however, may even be more important than they were in former times, when costumes were fairly standard across Europe. Many contemporary leaders don clothes that are supposed to send diverse messages to a variety of audiences. Despite his age, President Castro usually wears guerrilla fatigues to cast the image of the old revolutionary warrior. When the pope visited Havana in 1997, however, the president donned a formal blue suit for his audiences with the pontiff. Colonel Qaddafi is given to wearing brash military uniforms on visits abroad, but when receiving visitors he wears the apparel of a humble Bedouin. Depending on the audience, Chinese leaders wear either Mao-style revolutionary

gear or Western-style business suits. On major national holidays cele-
brated in embassies around the world, ambassadors often wear their
national costumes.

Overall, formal protocol and etiquette have become more relaxed, but
remain nevertheless. For example, questions of precedence, rank, and
status that were so fundamentally important in our first era of comparison persist. The president of the United States and the prime minister of
the United Kingdom have never been in the back row of a group photo
following a multilateral conference! The reasons for this are the same as
they were three hundred years ago.

Accounting for changes

The sources of the major changes in diplomatic practices and norms are
not difficult to locate. They include the vast increase in the number of
states and the expanding scope of contacts between societies to include
trade, environmental, immigration, science and technology, agriculture,
cultural, and many other dimensions. Development of the means of
rapid communication has made summit and multilateral conferences
relatively easy to arrange. The gutting of embassies, kidnapping or assassination of diplomatic personnel, and numerous incidents of the use
of diplomatic personnel for espionage purposes during the Cold War
prompted the formalization and careful delineation of all customary
rules governing diplomatic immunities and embassy inviolability in the
1961 Vienna Convention. In light of so many dramatic social, economic,
and technological changes in the past few decades, is there a case to
be made for the transformation of diplomacy? Are the media and direct communications between heads of state replacing the institution of
diplomacy? Or is it becoming obsolete?

The case for obsolescence

The argument that the institution of diplomacy is transforming is based
on a number of recent trends and developments that go beyond mere
quantitative increases in things such as the numbers of diplomatic personnel, multilateral conferences, or summit meetings. One view is that
new practices such as contracting out governmental tasks to specialists from academia, business, the media, and politics, the breakup of
foreign ministries' monopoly over relations between governments, and
the declining role of ambassadors as the main conduit of communication

between governments (replaced by direct contacts between ministries), constitute a trend toward obsolescence (cf., Riordan, 2003). A second suggests that the diplomatic institution is under physical threat and that may lead to the invention of other institutional forms as a replacement. Another insists that diplomacy is in the process of becoming obsolete because of new inventions in communications and the media. A final argument is that the luxurious growth of transnational relations has transformed diplomacy by, first, the use of diplomatic methods by a host of non-governmental organizations and private individuals, and, second, the incorporation into official delegations of the representatives of citizen activists. This "democratization" of diplomacy will eventually render older forms of representation and negotiation obsolete.

The first argument singles out such developments as the increasing use of non-diplomatic personnel for diplomatic missions. Some claim that technical specialists are marginalizing career professionals and that direct contacts between ministries of governments render most ambassadorial functions obsolete. The practice of appointing or using politicians, retired military officials, or businesspeople for diplomatic missions is indeed ubiquitous and may be increasing. In 1994 a former president of the United States, Jimmy Carter, in his role as a private citizen, negotiated an important agreement with the North Korean regime even though he was not an official of the American government. A former prime minister of Sweden represented the European Community in the post-conflict civil regime constructed for Bosnia. In 1999 the Russian government employed a former prime minister to help negotiate an end to the war in Kosovo. Many delegations to important international conferences include scientific, academic, and business people who have no background or training in diplomacy. They are mobilized for specific negotiations and then returned to their regular employment. Diplomatic posts around the world and in numerous international organizations are staffed by political exiles, "agents" of dubious backgrounds, and former politicians or military personnel looking for alternative jobs. No one knows for certain how many amateurs retain (or enjoy) official diplomatic positions, but, the argument goes, the number is now so high that to speak of diplomacy as a profession or institution no longer describes its essential features.

The second argument is that the norms surrounding the institution are being violated so systematically that governments will have to invent new ways of conducting their mutual affairs. The abuse of diplomatic establishments and regulations through espionage, bribery, kidnapping, and coercion has if anything increased, not decreased, with the end of the Cold War. During the Cold War all the major and some smaller powers abused diplomatic privileges to engage in espionage. This resulted in tit-for-tat expulsions and severe curtailment of the rights of diplomats to travel freely in the country to which they were accredited. Today, ambassadors or their assistants face increasing threats of assassination and kidnapping. Mobs in Beijing, Tehran, and elsewhere have trashed embassies, assaulted their staffs, or used them as hostages. In just a dozen years in the 1960s and 1970s, the toll of British diplomats and establishments was two ambassadors murdered and three embassies burnt down. In August 1998 terrorists targeted the American embassies in Nairobi – located in a heavily populated office building – and in Dar es Salaam, killing more than 200 people and wounding about 4,000. The record of such incidents in the past several decades suggests an upward curve that will render the traditional diplomatic formats too risky to sustain. Other forms of representation and communication will need to be developed.

The third argument claims that with new communications technologies allowing instantaneous contact between government officials, and with television and press organizations available to be sent immediately to trouble spots, the role of the ambassador and his staff in providing information and analysis for policy-makers in the world's capitals is seriously compromised. Because of bureaucratic delays and other organizational factors, government leaders can obtain the latest information on a difficult situation more rapidly from public sources than from ambassadorial reports. Are, then, the high costs of maintaining diplomatic establishments abroad worthwhile when less costly alternatives for obtaining information are readily available? The answer is no, some suggest, with the result that the ambassadorial role will diminish and perhaps become obsolete. Adherents of this position claim that now is the time to examine the entire institution of diplomacy and to come up with faster, less costly, and more reliable alternatives (Riordan, 2003). One of these alternatives is to expand direct communications between government leaders, thus bypassing normal diplomatic channels. A good deal of bilateral work is already done through direct telephone communications. Televised conference calls and computer networking should be able to take care of the growing demand for multilateral consultations and negotiations. As for the rest, a retired American professional diplomat has claimed that any reliable international tourist agency could, at great savings in costs and better services for clients, take care of most of the routine chores of embassies (cited in Hamilton and Langhorne, 1995: 231).[1]

The last argument is that the rapid growth of transnational relations in the post-World War II era has effectively democratized or fragmented diplomacy to such an extent that the old institutions have become almost unrecognizable. Consider the matter of political fragmentation, as an increasing number of sub-state or regional organizations have become involved in activities that bear a striking resemblance to diplomacy. There are regional organizations such as the transalpine councils that bring together business and local government representatives from Switzerland, France, and Italy. Throughout Europe organizations of transborder regional areas flourish, bringing their officials together to engage in bargaining and lobbying, a type of "paradiplomacy" (Aldecoa and Keating, 1999). Canadian provinces maintain offices – mini-embassies or consulates – in London, Paris, Tokyo, Washington, and other cities. They deal with regional, state, and city officials in the countries in which they are located. Quebec, a province within Canada, sends a separate delegation to biennial summit meetings of *la francophonie*. It has its own flag and otherwise acts as an equal to the presidents and prime ministers of French-speaking states. American states have approximately 187 offices abroad (Kincaid, 1999). Inter-regional and city-to-city links throughout Europe undermine traditional embassies' monopoly or hegemony over bilateral relations between governments. "As regional governments [e.g., Catalonia in Spain] develop distinct relations with each other, whole areas of developed governmental business are carried on outside the control, and often without the knowledge of, bilateral embassies" (Riordan, 2003: 77). Leaders of secessionist groups, "liberation movements," and other units of fragmentation establish virtual foreign ministries and send their representatives to the capitals of the world and to the United Nations to seek support and international recognition. The Palestine Liberation Organization achieved observer status in the General Assembly of the United Nations in the 1980s, and its leader, Yasser Arafat, addressed the Assembly several times. The PLO also joined several international organizations (e.g., the World Health Organization) while it remained a liberation organization rather than a state. The examples could be multiplied many times but

[1] There are always many appeals to reduce bureaucratic impediments to diplomacy or to reform diplomatic services. These proposals are not considered here because they are concerned primarily with reforms within present institutions, not with alterations of the institution itself.

they all make the same point: there are lots of political organizations that are not sovereign states engaging in diplomatic activities. While traditional diplomacy may carry on, it is being supplemented or, as some suggest, superseded by "people's" diplomacy and by direct links between subnational jurisdictions.

The indirect and direct participation of ordinary citizens in official diplomatic meetings is further evidence of the transformation thesis. Many non-governmental organizations regularly interact with government officials, particularly in the preparation and negotiation of documents at world summit conferences on environmental, social, and humanitarian issues. This follows a United Nations General Assembly directive to national governments to include NGOs in preparatory planning for these conferences. Thus in Rio de Janeiro, Vienna, Copenhagen, and Beijing NGOs helped governments define their positions on the major issues under debate. In addition, they lobbied delegations during the actual bargaining. In other conferences they have had observer status and in a few they were granted the right to distribute proposals or even to speak at conference sessions (Clark et al., 1998: 13). Finally, private citizens actually have been incorporated into official delegations in certain conferences. Even when not in such close proximity to the actual bargaining in these conferences, NGOs observe, monitor, and report to their networks as much information as they can obtain about the proceedings. Where the course of diplomatic bargaining is not consistent with NGO positions, their representatives lobby official delegates. In one of the more dramatic cases of the fusion between official and "people's" diplomacy, the Women's Environment and Development Organization (WEDO) sponsored a large NGO preparatory conference for a UN meeting, with fifteen hundred in attendance. The conference produced the Women's Action Agenda 21 based on the official UN conference draft documents. A Women's Caucus channeled the Agenda 21 set of demands to the conference. Women also participated in the national preparatory meetings for the UN World Conference on Women (Beijing, 1995) and negotiated with official delegations. NGOs attended most of the meetings of the governmental working groups that debated the official texts, lobbied delegates, and maintained strong contacts with the few who were included in official delegations (Clark et al., 1998: 17–21). The relationship between private citizen activists and official delegations has become so close, indeed, that some governments actually help finance the "diplomatic" work of NGOs. At the 1997 APEC meeting in Vancouver, the Canadian government not only helped organize a side-conference of NGO representatives, but also helped to fund the travel expenses of participants from countries such as Malaysia, Indonesia, and the Philippines. This type of symbiotic relationship also works to the advantage of governments. One of the unofficial bargains in these world or regional conferences is that upon completion the NGOs must help publicize in their home countries the results of the meetings. They take on an educating role that governments cannot perform entirely by themselves.

One particularly telling example of the "democratization" of diplomacy and of the increasingly close relationship between officials and private citizens was the drafting of the Anti-Personnel Land Mines Treaty (1997). What has come to be known as the "Ottawa Process" is important because it demonstrates how the "democratization" of diplomacy may become a model for diplomacy in general, in which case arguments about institutional transformation, novelty, or obsolescence would be strengthened considerably. The story of the origins of the treaty is interesting for a variety of reasons, not the least of which is that in this case public mobilization and the networking of NGOs prompted governments to accept the ban on the sale and deployment of anti-personnel land mines long before they would have done so through conventional diplomatic negotiations.[2]

At the end of the Cold War a number of on-going conflicts ended, while a host of internal wars erupted. International peacekeeping forces found the landscapes of these war zones to be infested with anti-personnel land mines that were killing and maiming thousands of people annually. Many of the victims were children. Humanitarian relief organizations and other NGOs took up the cause of seeking to ban the further use of these weapons and formed the International Campaign to Ban Land Mines (ICBL). This organization led a world-wide educational campaign that framed the issue in terms of the human costs of the continued use of the weapons. They mobilized public personalities to speak out against the mines. American congressmen joined the cause by sponsoring a one-year moratorium on the export of mines. France announced its own moratorium and decided to place the issue on the agenda of the United Nations Conference on Certain Weapons. By 1995, twenty-five countries had announced moratoria. Belgium implemented a complete ban on anti-personnel mine use, production, procurement, sale, or transfer of the weapons and

---

[2] The discussion that follows is based on Max Cameron's (1998) valuable study.

promised to destroy its arsenal. Meanwhile coalitions of national ban activists lobbied their governments and began to demand that action of the Belgian variety become their official policy. In some cases they succeeded. Norway, Austria, and Canada followed the Belgian lead by 1996.

In the official Conference on Conventional Weapons (CCW) in Geneva, government delegations from Sweden, Australia, and Canada included citizen activists and NGO representatives among their members. They enjoyed equal status with the professional diplomats and security experts who were negotiating texts. This meant, among other things, that these delegates had full access to government position papers and to the top-level decision-makers who supervised the strategies and tactics of their negotiators in Geneva. In the case of Canada, the NGO representative was a full part of the negotiating process, attending all meetings and consulted before decisions were made for the delegation. She then relayed full information to the network of NGO representatives in Canada who in turn instructed her on the positions she should adopt within the official Canadian delegation. When the CCW failed to move adequately on the land mines issue, the Canadian delegation proposed hosting a meeting of like-minded states to outline a strategy for circumventing the roadblocks in the CCW. A meeting of seventy-four governments in 1996 in Ottawa, where officials shared the stage with parliamentarians, NGO representatives, and mine victims, resulted in what came to be known as the "Ottawa process." It included a commitment by the participants to conclude a multilateral treaty banning anti-personnel land mines by the end of 1997. The representatives agreed to a two-track process, the first involving only government officials, the second involving meetings attended jointly by NGO representatives and the diplomats. The first set of meetings was not, however, an exclusively official terrain: roughly fifteen countries included NGO representatives as part of their official delegations.

The negotiations took place in Oslo during the autumn of 1997. The partnership of officials and NGO representatives was remarkable for its symbiotic characteristics. Serious American objections to the negotiating text raised fears among most NGO representatives and many government officials that "higher ups" would fashion some sort of compromise to allow states with particular defense problems to maintain anti-personnel mines for a specified period. The concern was that loopholes of this sort would be exploited by numerous states, thus diluting the entire effort. Thanks in part to the strong position of the NGOs, the official delegations did not accept the American reservations. In December 1997, 157 countries and numerous NGO representatives gathered in Ottawa for a series of workshops and discussions on the ban. At the end, 122 countries signed the treaty (the United States, China, and Russia did not) as 400 representatives of NGOs and international organizations looked on. In a follow-up survey of delegations, a research organization found that the participation of ICBL and other groups in the negotiating process was crucial to the outcome. Their influence was substantial because if government officials adopted retrograde positions, the public would soon know about it. According to the research, the movement to ban anti-personnel land mines was successful largely "because NGOs and government were working together; they were not opposing each other" (Cameron, 1998: 160). A Norwegian official explained that the NGOs provided pressure and support: "To the surprise of governments, they turned out to be reasonable people who understood international diplomacy. Without this partnership, there would have been no Ottawa process" (p. 160). Such praise was not universal, however. Apparently relations between NGO representatives and British and French officials could not be characterized in terms of "partnership." Whatever the case, the leading activists who initially mobilized the ICBL and kept the process on track received the Nobel Peace Prize the following year.

This is a remarkable story and a prime if not typical example of the "democratization" of diplomacy. It would have been unthinkable even two or three decades ago that official diplomatic delegations would include among their members the representatives of civilian activist groups. The practice in the case of the Ottawa process went far beyond anything envisaged by the Bolsheviks or Wilson under the rubric of "open diplomacy." It raises serious issues about a profession of diplomacy, about the propriety of giving official status to people who have no public mandate, and about the theory of representative government where officials are supposed to be ultimately responsible to elected legislatures, not to pressure groups. There are other important issues about democratic procedures, but our concern is with the implications of the practice for the institution of diplomacy. Does the "democratization" of diplomacy or the growth of "paradiplomacy" constitute compelling evidence of transformation, novelty, or obsolescence in the diplomatic institution?

The case for complexity

Let us review the main arguments supporting obsolescence or transformation theses. The first issue concerns the increased use of technical experts in diplomatic roles and the dramatic growth of direct ministerial contacts bypassing the embassy as the main conduit of government-to-government communication. Governments have for centuries bypassed official diplomatic channels when dealing with rivals, adversaries, and friends. This is not a new development. Woodrow Wilson had his Colonel House, Franklin Roosevelt had his Harry Hopkins, and numerous governments have sent special envoys, often diplomatic novices, on sensitive missions. Absent quantitative data that such practices are replacing rather than supplementing normal diplomatic channels, however, the argument does not support a claim of obsolescence. *Ad hoc* diplomacy by contracted technical experts and amateurs, and direct contacts between government ministries are no doubt increasing, but they supplement not supplant. It is also a trend primarily among the industrial countries and has not yet become universal. It has not yet had a notable impact on the other components of an institution such as rules, norms, and ideas.

The second argument – declining safety of ambassadors and their premises – is based on a perceived need, not on observation of practices. The embassies of great powers and their staffs may hold higher risk than others, but the response has been not to scuttle diplomatic establishments but rather to expand their security and to pursue vigilantly those responsible for attacks. Most embassies and their staffs most of the time are as free of risk as any other profession, perhaps even more so. No one has seriously entertained alternatives because of attacks on diplomatic establishments.

The third argument shows how technological developments can affect the ways governments operate. The mere fact that the argument is made suggests that things in the diplomatic world are changing and that technical innovations can alter if not eliminate traditional ideas and practices. While it is the case that governments today have more sources of information about the outside world than at any previous time, it does not follow that diplomatic reporting is any less important. The superficiality of media representations of major world events is notorious. Any government that relied exclusively on brief television reports and 10-second sound bites would be abdicating its responsibilities. Public media, particularly when dealing with crisis situations, frame issues to create maximum emotional impact, quite frequently reducing adversaries to good guys and bad guys. Their primary function is to create and sustain interest, not to offer political analysis. They are not equipped to do the latter. For example, they typically parachute reporters into a crisis situation, even though those reporters have little historical background, knowledge of the local languages, or adequate sources of information on current crisis arenas. The questions they ask in interviews are often ill informed and vapid if not stupid. Reporters emphasize drama; their role is not to provide sophisticated political analysis. In short, the public media are no substitute for professional analysis that must be the basis for government policy. Moreover, frequently it is the diplomats themselves who provide briefings for the media and who turn out to be the famous "anonymous sources" without whom the media could not operate. An extensive survey of the nexus between the media and governments reveals that it is governments and diplomats who use the media to get their message across to publics. The media become messengers for government announcements and policy preferences. This has nothing to do with reporters replacing diplomats as sources of information (Gilboa, 2000). Communications technologies may make diplomacy more complex but there is no evidence that governments are abandoning embassies and reducing staff because they can get free information from television and radio.

There is, however, one important qualification to this generalization. Many of the governments of poorer countries do not have extensive diplomatic networks. Some of them may have an ambassador to the United Nations and several important specialized agencies, along with embassies in the major capitals of the world. But beyond these, they must often rely on the public media for their major sources of information about other areas. On the other hand, their interests in many of these areas are peripheral at most, so lack of information is not costly to their interests. As a hypothetical example, the distressing situation in Sierra Leone in the 1990s would not be a major concern to the policymakers of Bhutan or Paraguay and since neither of the two has an embassy in Freetown, their governments must obtain information about conditions in the African country through other sources, including the media.

As for teleconferencing and other means of direct communication between governments, these undoubtedly speed up exchanges of views between political leaders and thus bypass ambassadors. Governments can and do communicate with each other without having to resort to formal diplomatic notes, as would have been the case in the eighteenth and nineteenth centuries. Embassies, for many governments, are no longer the main channel of communication: officials of various ministries communicate directly with their counterparts abroad. The diminished role of diplomats in such situations does not mean, however, that other diplomatic functions and tasks such as symbolic representation, trade promotion, political analysis, and negotiation are similarly reduced. Casual consultations between government leaders suggest greater complexity or addition to, not obsolescence of an institution. There is more to diplomacy than the exchange of views.

The "democratization" of diplomacy represents the most serious basis for the view that diplomacy is undergoing a transformation, either of novelty or of obsolescence. In particular, the practice of adding citizens to official delegations is a radical departure from past practices. If the Ottawa process is any indication of future developments, this innovation makes a difference to government policy. NGOs can not only help establish the international agenda by raising to public prominence issues that might otherwise be dealt with only by experts, but they can lead governments to adopt positions in negotiations that under other circumstances they would avoid or ignore. If the practice becomes widespread there would be significant changes in how governments make decisions, how they negotiate, and how they make up delegations to conferences. This practice, even if it becomes a trend, however, adds complexity to diplomacy. It does not transform it. It adds personnel to delegations, it expands the consultative processes that may precede actual negotiations, and it gives activists a direct view of how negotiations are carried out. But it does not end negotiations, it does not substitute new roles and tasks for old ones, and it does not dilute governmental *authority*. That is the critical catch.

The careful study by Clark, Friedman, and Hochstetler (1998) implies that governments sanction the increasingly complicated network, or even partnership, between NGOs and government delegations. They do this as a matter of choice, not necessity. The practice of consulting NGOs in preparatory meetings and of incorporating some of their members into official delegations has not yet been turned into a standard practice or a *right*. It has been granted more as a courtesy, and also for the reason that governments can themselves use the NGOs to popularize their own positions on global issues. Most governments have not adopted these new practices, and those that have – on a very narrow and selective basis – have made it clear that they have final authority to sign treaties and to commit themselves to future obligations. To quote, on the basis of Clark et al.'s (1998) examination of three UN-sponsored "mega-conferences," "states only provisionally accept NGOs' contributions to UN conference processes. Governments are standing firm in their claims to ultimate sovereignty over the issues that seem to most affect their ability to control the distribution of power and resources, whether at home or abroad" (p. 34). The incorporation of NGO and activist representatives into the diplomacy of multilateral conferences is a novel development and may ultimately have important consequences for how governments negotiate. But to date only a few governments have promoted this development, and only in very particular cases. It would be premature to claim that this has become a trend or pattern in diplomatic practice, that it is becoming widespread, or that it has altered the fundamental rules, protocol, norms, and etiquette of the diplomatic institution. The vast majority of governments in the world have not made it a practice and although it has helped to achieve some outstanding successes such as the land mines treaty, there is no general movement to alter the diplomatic institution to accommodate it. The "democratization" of diplomacy may move ahead, but at this stage it is a development that warrants the term complexity or addition to rather than replacement of or obsolescence.

What of the growing network of regional organizations and the "paradiplomacy" that goes on within them? This phenomenon is notable, but it is confined primarily to Europe and does not appear yet as a universal trend. This is another area of an addition to, rather than replacement of old forms with new ones. The growing network of European regional agencies for purposes of economic collaboration, transportation, environmental regulation and control, and many other issues is a significant trend, though not entirely new (the Danube Commission dates back to 1815). These agencies deal with a range of functional and regional issues, a large proportion of which include attracting investment, trade, and tourism (Hocking, 1999: 22). These are not exactly issues of "high" politics. But whatever the agencies, they act through the authority of their governments. Their delegates cannot make binding commitments that involve national resources, or require national legislation, or take treaty form, without the authorization of sovereign states. Some of the practices of the European Union may challenge this assertion, but those are the exceptions rather than the rule. As with "democratic" diplomacy, we have added complexity rather than replacement or transformation.

Overall, despite significant innovation in some diplomatic practices the diplomatic institution is robust but becoming increasingly complex. It is based on sets of ideas that find repeated expression and acknowledgment, practices that have been become routine over centuries, and norms and rules whose pedigrees go back at least two hundred years. Recent changes include open diplomacy, the professionalization of recruitment, training, and pay, the increasing number of women in important diplomatic roles, the appearance of "paradiplomacy" between subnational political entities, and at least the early stages of the "democratization" of diplomatic practices. These are all notable developments and they may even contain in them the germs of future transformations. But the evidence does not suggest that diplomacy is yet being replaced by other forms of representation and communication, that it has a new set of functions, or that it is on the verge of obsolescence.

7   International trade

A general portrait of trade in Europe and the rest of the world in the seventeenth and eighteenth centuries combines the largely local and regional, land-based economies of continental Europe with a rapidly growing, conflict-ridden and competitive sea trade that centered on the Baltic, the Mediterranean, the Atlantic, and the seas of the East Indies. Most economic activity in Europe circulated around towns and villages, where production and exchange were largely local. The average person was hardly touched by economic activities that had a longer reach, for this was mostly trade in luxuries and only on occasion in staples such as wheat or hides. However, with improvements in shipping technology and the great explorations of the fifteenth and sixteenth centuries, long-distance seaborne trade grew rapidly. By the seventeenth century, trade routes around the world were well established and many of the developing monarchical states had become involved in the game of establishing settler colonies in the New World and trade outposts (factories) on the shores of Africa, India, and the East Indies.

While the volume of trade increased rapidly in the seventeenth and eighteenth centuries, it still remained a small fraction of any polity's total economic activity. One estimate is that it comprised only 1–2 percent of world GDP (Held et al., 1999: 154). There is thus a paradox: while international trade, though rapidly expanding, constituted only a small portion of a state's economic activity, it was a major source of conflict, competition, and war. Indeed, if we were to summarize the essential characteristics of international trade practices in the seventeenth and eighteenth centuries, Hobbes' portrait of the state of nature as a war of all against all is not far off the mark. Trade relations between the emerging states of Europe were unencumbered by rules, norms, or other forms of constraint. Trade was integrally related to the more general foreign policy purposes of the dynastic states, which included building up naval and military power, making alliances, establishing colonies abroad, and conducting war.

The most concentrated trade route was in the Baltic, as it was the main thoroughfare for the shipment of timber (necessary for shipbuilding) and wheat from Eastern Europe and Scandinavia to England, France, Holland, and elsewhere in Western Europe. Amsterdam by this time had become the world's single most important commodity exchange and entrepôt (cf., Glamann, 1977). The United Provinces (Holland) held a virtual monopoly over shipping in this key route, while Sweden and Denmark were either at war or preparing for one in attempts to control tolls through the Baltic straits. The other main routes included the shipping lanes from Europe to the West Indies and the American colonies, from western Africa to Brazil, the West Indies, and the American colonies – mostly the slave trade – and around the Cape from Europe to India and the East Indies. The slave trade, involving the purchase and shipment of persons, many of whom were already held in servitude within African communities, was marked by intense rivalry and became a major source of competition. The *asiento* was in fact a monopoly, an exclusive right to supply labor to the Spanish colonies in South America and the West Indies. It began as a Portuguese monopoly, which was later grabbed by the French, and finally ceded to the English through the Treaty of Utrecht (1713). This extended pattern of transatlantic trade grew rapidly and ultimately supplanted the coastal trade so typical of Europe prior to the seventeenth century. By the time of Westphalia, there was a regular flow of traffic through an extended network of trade routes that were linked together to form a European system of redistribution centered in Amsterdam, Antwerp, London, and Hamburg (Glamann, 1977: 451). It was an exchange system in conception, but it was in fact also a conflict system in which practices were for the most part unregulated between the main players.

Practices

One main characteristic of trade was the attempt to establish monopolies. We use the term trade today as signifying an arena of open competition taking place within certain rules of the game. This was not the case in the seventeenth and eighteenth centuries. The purposes of state-sponsored (see below) trade were to establish exclusive control over access to commodities such as spices, over the slave trade, and over

markets for European manufactured goods. The reasons were both intellectual – the ideas underlying mercantilist practices – and more immediate. European demand for many of these commodities was limited.
The average Saxon peasant could not afford Moluccan nutmeg or tea
from India. A little competition either at the source of supply or at the
point of consumption could ruin the entire business. The spice trade,
according to J. H. Parry (1971: 73), "was the subject not of commercial
competition in the ordinary sense, but of ruthless fighting and intrigue
between rival monopolies, each of which endeavored to eliminate its
competition."

We must remember that much of the transoceanic trade was organized by groups of merchants chartered by the royal house or other
government agencies. They were granted exclusive monopolies and the
right to make treaties with those who controlled the sources of supply
(African slave traders, local potentates in India and the islands of Southeast Asia, and the like). They were also armed. Far from central control,
they became quasi-states in their own right and conducted their affairs
with scant interest in their nominal overseers. The Dutch East India
Company became the model for counterparts in Great Britain, France,
Denmark, and elsewhere. In other cases, trade was conducted directly
through government offices such as the Casa da India in Lisbon or the
Casa de Contratacion in Seville (Glamann, 1977: 515).

Initially these companies or government agents established forts, factories, and outposts on the shores of their trading partners. As trade
expanded in the eighteenth century, many of them became *conquistadors*
and effectively conquered and colonized great swathes of territory, ultimately with the blessings or military intervention of their home governments. Since in the seventeenth century, few of the governments had extensive navies, dockyards, or supplies adequate for long-distance naval
warfare or protection of shipping, they used privateers, buccaneers, mercenaries, and pirates to carry out raids and attempts to capture each
others' plantations, factories, and forts (Parry, 1971: 12). These activities
were not limited to the distant outposts in the East and West Indies. In
the late seventeenth century, the British complained that Flemish pirates
were attacking their merchantmen from bases in Holland. For their part,
the Dutch replied that the British had encouraged privateering against
Dutch trade, and had seized Dutch ships. The British were also aware
that the Dutch had tried to encourage the Danes to cut off the Baltic
straits to all British vessels (Wilson, 1957: 104). Lacking an established
law of the sea, the British railed against Dutch herring fisheries in the

waters off England. All of these and other issues led to three naval wars between the United Provinces and Britain in the second half of the seventeenth century.

Piracy was just one of the costs of trading. In the seventeenth century it flourished in the West Indies – often with implicit government support. In the Eastern Hemisphere the Indians, Chinese, Malays, and other locals copied European predation. Attempts to create monopolies also led to widespread smuggling. Trade between the American colonies and their French and Spanish counterparts in the West Indies was robust, despite Britain's navigation laws that prohibited such transactions. Major practices of the era also included privateering. After formal diplomatic protests usually failed to bring satisfaction for the seizure of ships and their cargoes in the open seas or in port, the crowns issued letters of reprisal authorizing merchants to outfit private vessels to recover property from the responsible country up to the value of the lost property plus costs. This type of action was symptomatic of the "war of all against all" character of trade in the seventeenth and eighteenth centuries.

The extreme insecurity of trade in this era had several major consequences. First, it led to the arming of merchant vessels, which in turn led to the privatization of armed conflict. Second, it inspired the royal governments to build long-distance fleets that could offer protection to trade convoys. This in turn led to the use of large navies as an adjunct to the land warfare that was so prominent in seventeenth- and eighteenth-century Europe. By the late seventeenth century, wars were no longer fought solely on the continent, but involved major naval engagements and attacks on colonies. The Seven Years War (1756–63) was in this respect the first truly world war, for its battles were fought in all of the oceans of the world. Third, trade insecurity prompted European governments to establish colonies and their attending monopolies to provide safe sources of supply and markets for manufactured goods. As the kingdoms of Europe became increasingly involved in trade, they also became more vulnerable to its interruption in times of both peace and war. The British, for example, could easily have their sources of timber and tar for shipbuilding cut off in case of war against the Dutch, Swedes, or Russians. But these relatively benign and protective purposes of colonial expansion were supplemented by more predatory aims: colonies could serve as strategic bases for attacking the colonies and trade of rivals (Knorr, 1944: 57, 64, 84, 101). Finally, colonies served as a guaranteed market for manufactured goods – or so it was hoped. The colonial powers could establish export monopolies and thus not have to worry about being undersold by other traders. In brief, the typical trade and predatory practices of the seventeenth and eighteenth centuries help to account for the establishment and maintenance of the European colonial empires of the era.

Given the competitive, often predatory trade and shipping practices of the era, it is not surprising that they were frequently a source of armed conflict and war. The three wars between the Dutch and British in the second half of the seventeenth century revolved around trade competition, the Dutch monopoly of shipping through the Baltic Sea, and the consequent British attempt, through various Navigation Acts, to break that monopoly. Disputes about the freedom of the seas and the extent of territorial jurisdiction and privateering added to the portfolio of war-causing issues. The War of the Spanish Succession (1702–13) involved numerous issues relating to shipping, the slave trade, and colonial conquests. Of the fifty wars in Europe between 1648 and the Napoleonic wars, 46 percent had as a source one or more issues relating to trade and competitive colonialism. After territorial conquest, trade issues constituted the second most important source of wars in the era of mercantilism (Holsti, 1991: chs. 3, 5). This does not include the hundreds of battles, forcible seizures, and local armed uprisings that surrounded colonial and trade activities. The peace treaties of the era are filled with the legitimization of conquests, cession of colonies and trade outposts, transfers of the *asiento* trade, and exchanges of trade concessions.

War itself was often an adjunct to trade competition: it allowed the adversaries to cripple each other's commodity production. For example, in the eighteenth century Britain was able through the course of several wars to destroy a large portion of the lower-cost French sugar production in the West Indies. War offered opportunities to destroy and depopulate the adversary's colonies, to burn the cane, to wreck the machinery, and, above all, to carry off the slaves. Failing the destruction of France's West Indian colonies, the next best option was to cut off their trade, starve them of provisions and slaves, and prevent them from selling and shipping their sugar (Parry, 1971: 112).

Trade as war and war as another form of trade competition continued to be the predominant characteristic of commercial relations between the European powers throughout the seventeenth and eighteenth centuries. Trade, fishing, and colonization were dangerous activities. While many profited and trade greatly expanded the coffers of the royal houses and treasuries, those activities were conducted in an ambience of insecurity, potential catastrophic losses, and armed rivalries. The ideas and discourses that surrounded these activities reflected the enmities and insecurity generated by trade, and to a great extent justified mutually predatory policies.

Ideas and beliefs

The set of ideas, perceptions, and calculations that underlay the competitive and often predatory trade and shipping practices of the era go under the name of mercantilism. This was not so much a coherent doctrine – many of its tenets were confused and inconsistent – as a set of ideas, assumptions, and prejudices that were employed in support of this or that policy. Mercantilism began with certain key assumptions about action, politics, and the state. Unlike medieval notions of the organic growth of states and the ubiquitous "plan of God" in explaining successes and reversals of political fortune, the mercantilists and the policy-makers they sought to influence were action-oriented. They had that peculiarly modern outlook on political life, the idea that problems besetting authority can be diagnosed and subject to logical analysis, and that solutions involving public authority can be found. Policy is goal-oriented and must in some cases involve a form of social engineering. The belief that the achievement of known objectives depended upon policy planning, the examination of options, and the analysis of problems employing logic and empirical evidence reflected Renaissance intellectual innovations.

The mercantilists directly linked private gains to state interests. In the case of France, the private realm was to be clearly subordinated to the state (cf., Knorr, 1944: 24). Particularly in France and England, mercantilism was not just a set of ideas, but a rough policy map indicating the steps that would have to be taken in order to save the state from the intolerable supremacy of Dutch or Spanish trade and monopoly (cf., Wilson, 1957: 24). In Holland, in contrast, the main idea was to avoid conflict in order to sustain Dutch commercial supremacy. This could be done through the development of international law, scrupulous avoidance of war, and enforcing the laws of neutrality that would sustain Dutch markets in times of war.

The development of mercantilist policies differed from realm to realm. In Spain, policy was imposed top-down, designed to advance dynastic interests and fiscal returns. In France, Louis XIV's main financial advisor, Controller-General Colbert, developed elaborate schemes of subsidies to private interests, and tariffs and boycotts against foreign products, all to strengthen the French state. In England, in contrast, policy evolved through the laborious negotiations involving private interests, the chartered companies, the crown, Parliament, and any number of government officials. It was in the course of these lengthy debates that the tenets of mercantilism were elaborated (Wilson, 1957: 153).

The first great issue in mercantilist thought was whether power and wealth – the two goals of state policy – could be achieved through peaceful exchange, or whether they required dominion. Many, including governments and trading companies, argued the former, but found themselves in a structural system in which trade could not be conducted peacefully without the agreement of all. And that consent was not forthcoming. Hence the persuasiveness of those who argued that without dominion satisfactory trade is not possible (Parry, 1971: 9). Why was this so? Because, the theorists assumed, trade is a zero-sum game. The world's resources are fixed. Those who exploit them first preclude others from gain. In such a system, monopoly becomes mandatory. Any increase in one country's share of exports is possible only at the expense of the volume of exports enjoyed by others (Knorr, 1944: 20). Hence, a private commercial advantage is also an advantage to the state, and in order to prevail in the competition, the state has to maintain a favorable balance of trade. These ideas or beliefs led to high tariffs, to the subsidization of exports and the creation of colonies, as well as to the development of naval forces to protect shipping against theft, piracy, and privateering. Indeed, the belief in the favorable consequences of trade to national power was so great that many advocated virtual trade wars to wars fought by armed force. As one British publicist observed, "beat them [the Dutch] without fighting; that being the best and justest way to subdue our Enemies" (quoted in Knorr, 1944: 21).

In such thought, wealth and power become hopelessly intermingled. At that time, wealth did not mean higher standards of living for the masses, but the elements which brought power to the state: population, trade surpluses, gold, silver, and the wherewithal to create naval and land forces. Wealth created power, and power was used to create wealth in a closed circle of economics and politics. The two were inseparable, and so any loss of trading monopolies, restrictions on freedom of navigation, or increase in imports was seen as a direct threat to the power of the state. The idea that trade might be peaceful was acknowledged, but that it might bring mutual benefits was beyond the mercantilist imagination.

The ideas and practices of trade in the seventeenth and eighteenth centuries emphasized unencumbered competition, conquest, predation, and colonization. This was not a domain of law, norms, or etiquette. True, there were major debates about freedom of the seas and the rights of neutrals, but one does not gain the impression that they figured as more than doctrines or ideas to be trotted out to justify predatory behavior or to protect advantageous positions such as monopolies. The domain of trade in this era was predominantly one in which power, strength, monopoly, guile, and wits ruled. It was not a domain of *society*. None of the requirements of an *institution* was there: rules, norms, etiquette, transparency, peaceful standardized practices, or predictability. This stands in marked contrast to the situation today.

The power of ideas: the transition to institutionalized trade

The portrait of commercial life in the seventeenth and eighteenth centuries could not be more distinct from contemporary trade practices. Certainly traces of mercantilist theory and practice remain, but for the most part trade between countries today is predictable, relatively free, and suffused with rules and regulations. How do we account for the vast changes from the bellicose, aggressive, and monopolistic practices preceding the nineteenth century? Changing domestic and national interests and national power are part of the story. But among all the institutions of international politics, ideas and academic theories have influenced none more. The story of the transformation of mercantilism into a universal trade regime effectively regulated by rules and norms is largely, though not exclusively, a tale of ideas and discourse, and their triumph over older conceptions of appropriate commercial behavior. It is also a story where the great tragedies of humankind, in particular the Great Depression and World War II, were great learning experiences that unmasked the great harm that could result from short-sighted and extreme mercantilist practices.

Critiques of mercantilist doctrines and practices had appeared in England already during the time of the Civil War (the 1640s), thanks to the proselytizing of John Lilburne. But his appeal for free trade had no impact on those who fashioned policy. In France during the eighteenth century, the Physiocrats proposed a variety of ideas that challenged mercantilist thought. Two British political economists – Adam Smith and David Ricardo – fundamentally undermined the intellectual props of mercantilism. Others, like Jeremy Bentham, James

Mill, Richard Cobden, John Bright, and members of the Manchester School in the mid-nineteenth century, added their own ideas and arguments.

Adam Smith's *An Inquiry into the Nature and Causes of the Wealth of Nations* (1776), though not entirely original, made two great contributions that ultimately led to the incorporation of free trade ideas into the foreign policies of most states. First, it systematically uncovered some of the fallacies in mercantilist doctrine, and second, it established economics as a *science* that was objectively "true" regardless of history, culture, religion, social mores, or politics (cf., Knorr, 1944: 185). In the first area, Smith was able to demonstrate that, thanks to the division of labor, free trade increases wealth for all those involved in exchange. Mercantilists had held that the main source of wealth was the God-given distribution of natural resources between different territories. If one wanted access to timber, the most efficient means of securing it was through conquest, dominion, and/or a monopoly of shipping. In contrast, Smith held that wealth derives from production and exchange.

Since this is not a text on economics, we need not delve into the finer points of these ideas. But their implications were immense. If wealth comes from exchange and the efficiencies achieved through a division of labor – rather than through territory and its resources – then conquest and dominion are no longer necessary either for wealth or for power. Moreover, the mercantilist belief that foreign trade is a fixed sum, some winning always at the expense of others, was demonstrably false. Exchange increases wealth for all (although not necessarily in equal degree), so there was no necessity to fear that trade could unduly upset the balance of power. Quite the contrary: foreign markets offered lucrative opportunities for one's own manufacturers. In Smith's words (quoted in Walter, 1996: 152):

> nations have been taught that their interest consisted in beggaring all their neighbours. Each nation has been made to look with an invidious eye upon the prosperity of all the nations with which it trades, and to consider their gains as its own loss . . . (The wealth of neigbours ought to be a matter for) national emulation, not of national prejudice or envy . . .

Smith argued that in his calculations, colonies and trade monopolies, while increasing the wealth of some private interests, were in fact a negative burden on the wealth of the nation as a whole. Monopolies and subsidies actually reduced national advantage, while the Navigation Acts, which conferred a monopoly on British vessels carrying goods to and from the colonies, inflicted serious penalties on Britain's national wealth.

The second major implication of *The Wealth of Nations* was that economics is a *science*. Its essential principles are not questions of protecting interests or of beliefs, but of truth. Mercantilists, whose ideas were often contradictory and made on baseless assumptions, could rail against the "ivory tower" aspects of scientific economics, but as the nineteenth century progressed, the empirical evidence supporting the free trade and comparative advantage ideas grew rapidly. The proponents of economic science did not have to invoke a deity, special interests, or nationalism to make their points. The proponents of mercantilism had little else upon which to make their case. They could and did argue that maintaining colonial monopolies was essential for national defense and grandeur; or that shipping monopolies were necessary aids to British naval supremacy throughout the world. But they could not meet the essential point of economic analysis, which is that free trade (1) maximizes national wealth and (2) reduces international frictions and war.

David Ricardo published his major text, *The Principles of Political Economy and Taxation*, in 1817. He provided further support, indeed a "scientific" verification, that international trade is not a zero-sum game and that it brings mutual, if not necessarily equal, benefits to those who exchange. He elaborated on Smith's ideas and produced the principle of comparative advantage that became the foundation of liberal economic theory for the next 150 years. The principle, rather stark in its enunciation but huge in its economic and political implications, states that the flow of trade among countries is determined by the relative costs of the goods produced. Ricardo's analysis demonstrated that countries tend to specialize in those commodities whose costs of production are comparatively lower. The famous example he provided to support his case was trade between Portugal and Britain. The former had a distinct advantage in producing wine (especially port), while the latter had an advantage in producing cloth. It would make no sense for the British to try to produce port, or for the Portuguese to make woolens. In more contemporary terms, Iceland has no comparative advantage in producing pineapples, but it can sell its fish in order to buy the fruit from Mauritius, which produces them in abundance. Both parties are better off by exchanging than by attempting to achieve self-sufficiency.

The ideas of Smith and Ricardo did not overwhelm mercantilist thought and practice initially. Smith himself was not optimistic about the possibilities that British policy-makers would adjust policies to the findings of the new science (cf., Knorr, 1944: 190–1). But the ideas did enter into the public agenda and became increasingly persuasive. The great public debates and discourses in England surrounding trade and colonialism following the Napoleonic wars hinged on the issues and perspectives initiated by Smith, Ricardo, and others. They helped set in train increasingly popular free trade and anti-colonial movements. These remained minority views, but they were articulate and forceful (Knorr, 1944: 241, 248). The debates culminated in the 1846 repeal of the Corn Laws (which placed tariffs on imported grain) and three years later, the repeal of the Navigation Acts. Equally significant, the British and French signed a trade treaty in 1860, the first major tariff-reduction program since the seventeenth century. This treaty served as a model for numerous bilateral trade treaties in Europe that followed over the next decade. They incorporated the most favored nation (MFN) principle that today underlies all international commerce. Other notable achievements of this era undermined mercantilist practices and heralded new, freer trade. These included the enactment of laws from the 1820s in Great Britain and the United States declaring that the slave trade is a form of piracy punishable by death, promoting the suppression of piracy, outlawing privateering (1856), and a whole raft of new regulations on neutral shipping and seizure of cargoes. Many of these steps were the result of agitation and lobbying by private groups that had become devotees of free trade doctrines. While the story of the end of mercantilism as official policy is not complete without reference to specific interests, changing class alignments in England, France, and the United States, and greater public participation in policy debates, a significant part of it lies in the realm of ideas. Although less so on the continent, by the mid-nineteenth century, the ideas of Smith and Ricardo had become part of the conventional wisdom and an essential part of the liberal creed. The followers of Colbert and his English counterparts of the seventeenth century were soon to become anachronisms, although the use of tariffs to protect domestic industries and to increase national power made a comeback in the era of economic stagnation in the late 1870s and 1880s (Lipson, 1982: 242). The movement toward freer trade did not move in a straight trajectory. But our question is not whether trade is more or less free, but whether its practices are rule-bound.

The institutionalization of trade

There was no straight line between the introduction of Smith's and Ricardo's ideas and the institutionalization of trade, that is, the development of relatively effective rules governing commercial exchange, finance, shipping, and the like, and the patterned behavior that is mostly consistent with the rules, norms, and regulations. Tariffs remained high in most of the world until the mid-twentieth century, colonial monopolies, re-christened Imperial Preferences, continued until the same time, and the arguments of mercantilists, renamed economic nationalists, were effective in promoting government policies (particularly in Germany) that emphasized the protection of "infant" industries, state subsidies, and generally high tariffs. Although many bilateral trade treaties reduced tariffs to some extent and introduced the MFN principle, the world in 1919 had not progressed very far beyond proscribing piracy, letters of marque and reprisal, and some of the more odious seafaring practices of eighteenth-century mercantilism. The Great Depression and World War II provided the essential impetus for a thorough transformation of the world trade system into a domain of rule-based activity. Both these great events constituted major learning experiences.

The sources of the depression included a number of factors, including German war reparations and hyperinflation, over-production in the United States, massive stock market speculation, the inability of the British to provide leadership in the areas of trade, finance, and money, and rising tariffs. Nazi Germany attempted to create a hermetically sealed trade bloc of which it was the master – attempting autarky for strategic reasons. Many other countries competitively raised tariffs, symbolized perhaps by the Smoot–Hawley Act of 1932 that raised tariffs across the board to their highest level in the twentieth century. All of these actions, combined with competitive devaluation of currencies, resulted in significant decline in world production and trade. International cooperation in this destructively competitive milieu was impossible. The policy preferences of all the major powers increasingly diverged, symbolized most blatantly by Nazi coercive trade policies, Japanese and Italian imperialism, and high tariffs in the United States (cf., Gilpin, 1987: 80, 130). The United States sought to promote freer trade through the Reciprocal Trade Act of 1934 – a major policy change under the new Roosevelt administration – but others did not imitate this move. By the time war broke out in 1939, trade volumes in the world were seriously diminished, trade patterns regionalized, and unemployment figures excessively high.

Serious thinking about the creation of a post-war trade order based on economic liberalism took place in Washington during the war. Among others, Cordell Hull, the American Secretary of State, promoted the view that economic nationalism, high tariffs, trade blocs, and competitive devaluations had been a major cause of World War II.

> To me, unhampered trade dovetailed with peace; high tariffs, trade barriers, and unfair economic competition, with war. Though realizing that many other factors were involved, I reasoned that, if we could get a freer flow of trade ... so that one country would not be deadly jealous of another and the living standards of all countries might rise, thereby eliminating the economic dissatisfaction that breeds war, we might have a reasonable chance for lasting peace. (Hull, 1948: I: 81)

Hull's views were roughly similar to those of President Roosevelt and many officials in the American State and Commerce Departments (cf., Lipson, 1982: 256). One sees in this quotation a summary of many of the arguments made by the successors of Adam Smith and David Ricardo in mid-nineteenth-century England. The purpose of free trade is not only to maximize wealth, but also to promote peace.

Armed with these ideas, the United States took leadership in the creation of international organizations that would develop and sustain a multilateral rule-based trading regime. This was a question not of charity, but of enlightened self-interest. The United States, the only major country to have emerged from World War II with an economy stronger than in 1939, had a clear interest in gaining market access to Europe, Asia, and the remaining colonies. In addition, it had ideological and strategic concerns, particularly after the Cold War began around 1948: it had a strong stake in binding allies to it, in promoting its values abroad, and in building up foreign economies so that they could withstand the blandishments of communism. As a hegemon, it also offered significant market opportunities for the post-war reconstruction of war-torn economies. A liberal, rule-based multilateral trade order thus coincided with the economic aspirations of most of the industrial countries. We must emphasize that the United States did not bully others into fashioning the regime. Indeed, in order to persuade others to come on board, it had to make numerous concessions, including temporary acceptance of British and other colonial powers' preferential trade arrangements. The communist governments, on the other hand, would have no part of it, portraying institutions such as the International Monetary Fund and the General Agreement on Tariffs and Trade (GATT) as instruments of American imperialism.

The Bretton Woods arrangements (1944) created a system of fixed exchange rates designed to prevent the competitive devaluations of the 1930s. Its organizational consequence was the International Monetary Fund, the main purpose of which was to provide loans and other types of assistance to countries suffering from serious trade imbalances and consequent balance of payments difficulties. The GATT (1948) provided the institutional basis for trade negotiations and set out the fundamental rules of a multilateral trade order to achieve "freer and fairer" trade through reduction of tariffs and the elimination of other trade barriers (Gilpin, 1987: 190–1).

The GATT regime was far from perfect. It did help to promote multilateral trade negotiations and tariff reductions in eight rounds of discussions (e.g., the Tokyo and Uruguay rounds), and defined an increasingly wide scope of economic transactions that should be conducted under the major norms and rules of a liberal trade regime. However, the GATT rules provided a number of escape mechanisms that allowed governments to protect or buffer domestic social and economic priorities threatened by falling trade barriers. As John Ruggie (1982: 212–15) has argued, the GATT was fundamentally a compromise between free trade principles and the domestic imperatives of economic growth and full employment (cf., Lipson, 1982: 242). The GATT arrangements perhaps are better termed an arrangement for fair trade rather than free trade. Nevertheless, under GATT auspices the average tariffs among the developed countries declined to 3.8 percent from an average of more than 20 percent in the early 1950s (Milner, 2002: 449). Trade was by no means "free," but the barriers to freer exchange were diminishing.

But it was not a ride without serious deviations, ups, and downs. During the 1970s and 1980s, under intense competitive pressures, some governments expanded non-tariff barriers as a way to protect their domestic industries and social policies. These included health requirements, quotas, various forms of "voluntary export restraints" (VERs, mainly practiced against the Japanese), barter arrangements, claimed exemptions for cultural reasons, and the profuse flourishing of the bureaucrats' joy, red tape. By one estimate, the ratio of managed to total trade increased from 40 percent in 1974 to 48 percent in 1980 (Gilpin, 1987: 195). For the developing countries, almost 20 percent of all categories of imports remained subject to various forms of non-tariff barriers (figures in Milner, 2002: 449). Some of these ploys were unmasked and declared contrary to the interests of free trade in a number of "codes of good behavior" regarding non-tariff barriers negotiated at the Tokyo Round (1973–79). The purpose of these codes was to make non-tariff barriers more visible, to decrease the uncertainties generated by government interventions into the market, and in general to slow down the increasing trend toward mercantilist practices, or what many (e.g., Gilpin, 1987: 204–15) called the "new protectionism." In addition to a variety of non-tariff barriers and government subsidies (e.g., procurement policies), the new protectionism included and continues to include the increasing regionalization of trade. The European Union has become a single trade bloc, with a common set of tariffs and non-tariff barriers, as well as special preferences for former colonies. It has used a variety of subsidies, quotas, and other restrictive devices to protect its agriculture sector and to provide similar support against Japanese competition in industrial products. Analogous, although in many ways different, arrangements have appeared in the North American Free Trade Agreement, MERCOSUR, and Caribbean initiative, and other regional trade regimes. Overall, Robert Gilpin (1987: 220) concludes that in the 1980s

> Changes in US and other national trade policies [caused] a metamorphosis of the global trading regime. The shift is clearly in the direction of negotiated market shares, bilateral bargaining, and the conditional Most-Favored Nation principle (i.e., the granting of a trade concession only if one is granted in return). The more nationalistic approaches to international trade are displacing to a considerable degree the basic GATT principles of non-discrimination, multilateralism, and the unconditional MFN principle as the governing features of the international political economy.

Gilpin's conclusion may be overstated, as some of the practices he analyzed actually declined in the 1990s, thanks in part to the Uruguay Round which, for example, phased out the Multi-fibre Agreement that limited textile trade. Various studies have also indicated that the actual impact of non-tariff barriers within OECD countries is small (Held et al., 1999: 165). It may be larger for developing countries, whose emphasis on textiles, agriculture, and some industrial sectors faces particular problems.

Many of these problems have been addressed by the successor of the GATT, the World Trade Organization (WTO) (1995). It is a more powerful organization than its predecessor. Indeed, it is the only international organization whose decisions are formally binding.[1] That is, members of the organization have agreed to withhold a fundamental tenet of sovereignty, the requirement of consent to all decisions made by bodies outside of the state. Any member may submit a case to a WTO panel to determine whether there has been a violation of trade law and, if so, what remedies can be used in response. Most critical, once the jurisdiction of the WTO has been established in a case, all parties must participate. Dispute settlement, in other words, is obligatory and does not rely on formal consent of any of the parties. Moreover, the rulings of WTO panels are, pending appeals, formally binding on states.[2] Today, more than two-thirds of the states of the world belong to the organization.

Although some aspects of the "new protectionism" remain in place, various rounds under the auspices of the GATT and WTO have resulted in a significant continuation of tariff reductions, the proscription of many non-tariff barriers to trade, and the extension of trade rules to new areas of commerce. One study (cited in Held et al., 1999: 165) estimates that at the end of the last millennium, two-thirds of the world's economies (measured by GDP) were operating broadly open trade policies. That figure continues to rise as major economies such as that of China join the WTO.

Under the auspices of the WTO, and propelled by the internationalization of production, interest has shifted to the examination of domestic regulations and laws governing competition in different countries. The thrust is toward the harmonization of regulatory structures to preclude artificial competitive advantages (e.g., taxation policy). The WTO, in short, has, in addition to its traditional function of helping to reduce tariffs, the major task of developing common rules for conducting business, even *within* its members. The importance of this work increases dramatically because of the slow but steady growth of trade as a percentage of the GDP of most countries.[3]

---

[1] Under Chapter VII of the United Nations Charter, decisions by the Security Council made after determination of a threat to the peace or an act of aggression are technically binding. In several instances, most recently against Iraq, the Security Council imposed sanctions that must be observed by all members of the organization.
[2] Compliance with WTO rulings is, however, problematic, although it is significantly less so than was the case for GATT, where non-compliance with GATT panel rulings approached 30 percent (Busch, 2000).
[3] Some sample figures: exports as a percent of GDP (constant prices) increased between 1950 and 1997 as follows: from 5.6 to 20.1 percent for France, from 4.4 to 23.7 percent for Germany, from 2 to 11 percent for Japan, from 12.2 to 28 percent for Sweden, from 9.5 to 21 percent for Britain, and from 3.3 to 11.4 percent for the United States (from Held et al., 1999: Table 3.11, p. 180).

The areas for further work do not end with these new developments. Numerous trade barriers and subsidies remain in the agriculture sector. Agricultural tariffs across most of the world remain at 40 to 50 percent, while those for manufactured goods have fallen below 10 percent (The Economist, 2001: 83). In total, the wealthy countries of the world spend more than $300 billion annually or almost $1 billion daily in subsidies and other trade-restrictive policies to protect their national markets (Pettigrew, 2001: 3) and this sum will rise significantly as the United States implements further agricultural subsidies to the tune of $180 billion until 2012. The sums are immense and constitute a major depressant on the agricultural exports of developing countries, for their production is undermined by the cheap food dumped into their markets by the protecting and subsidizing states. One estimate is that cows in European Union countries receive more in support through subsidies and tariffs than one-half of the world's population has to live on (The Economist, 2002: 109). Domestic American protectionist groups have prevailed on the US government to use countervailing measures against allegedly unfair trade practices in a manner that is often predatory and inconsistent with international trade rules. The main concerns of the developing countries, including unfettered access to the OECD markets, agricultural subsidies in the United States and the European Union, the declining terms of trade (cf., Finlayson and Zacher, 1988), and the highly skewed rewards resulting from globalization, remain to be negotiated. Indeed, the whole set of procedures associated with WTO decisions needs to be opened up and made more transparent in the light of violent protests in Seattle, Quebec City, Genoa, and elsewhere. For many, the WTO, the World Bank, and the International Monetary Fund loom as major forces for undermining democratic control over national economic policies, for promoting the interests of multinational corporations against the cultural and economic priorities of weak economies and societies, and for guaranteeing unfettered and unregulated predatory practices by international capital. For many, the development of a rules-based international trade and monetary system has led to major maldistribution of social and economic rewards and to the greatest political potency capital has ever enjoyed.

The evidence suggests that today there is a medium to high degree of institutionalization in international trade. Starting from a level of almost zero in the mid-nineteenth century, the contemporary trade system is characterized by a high degree of international regulation of economic transactions between societies. Consider the scope of regulation.

Starting with GATT negotiations in the early 1950s, the areas of regulation covered primarily tariffs in industrial trade between developed countries. In the various "rounds" of GATT-sponsored negotiations from the 1960s to the early 1990s, the scope of regulations expanded to include the trade of many developing countries, non-tariff barriers, trade in services and agriculture, issues of tariff transparency, and numerous areas of domestic legislation bearing upon trade. Many areas remain to be negotiated (e.g., intellectual property rights), but the movement is clearly in the direction of comprehensive rule establishment in all facets of international trade. To date, the crowning achievement of institutionalization has been the creation of the WTO, with its compulsory jurisdiction and decision-making authority. Although areas of contention and predatory practices remain, compared with the seventeenth century, trade practices have become for the most part peacefully patterned, and effectively regulated through a dense network of rules and norms.

The norms of international trade

The GATT system and its successor, the World Trade Organization, have overseen the development of several essential norms surrounding trade activities. In the late nineteenth century, trading nations had already developed one of the most robust rules, *non-discrimination*. The most favored nation principle became established in many bilateral trade treaties, thus extending negotiated tariff reductions by one pair of states to others. The principle is simple: trade with all other partners will take place on the same level of tariffs as with the most favored nation. For example, if Norway applies a tariff of 7 percent on rubber tires it imports from Malaysia, it cannot charge 15 percent on tires it imports from Korea or from anyone else.

The norm of non-discrimination, or "unconditional most favored nation," formed the first article of the GATT treaty and thus symbolizes its importance. However, other arrangements in GATT and the WTO allow customs unions and free trade areas in which tariffs *are* differentiated between the member countries on the one hand and non-member countries on the other (cf., Finlayson and Zacher, 1982: 278–80). Moreover, the European Union has special trade arrangements with former colonies, again in contradiction of the non-discrimination norm. The norm was permanently amended in the Tokyo Round of negotiations to include the General System of Preferences (GSP) (1971) for developing countries. In effect, this formed a subsidiary norm: the rule of non-discrimination should be waived in the case of developing countries that have a moral and economic claim to special treatment by virtue of their poor economies.

The second norm is *reciprocity*, which is the mutual lowering (or raising) of tariff and other barriers to trade. The actual levels are usually negotiated bilaterally and multilaterally (e.g., the Uruguay Round, ending in 1993); they do not mean that the rewards of increased trade are necessarily equal. Although the GSP and other special exemptions contained in GATT rules contradict the reciprocity norm, Jock Finlayson and Mark Zacher (1982: 286–7) conclude that the reciprocity norm, despite its ambiguities, "has had a profound impact on almost all agreements in the GATT." Most important, perhaps, it has allowed governments to justify their own concessions on the grounds that others were reciprocating them. This is an important argument against mercantilists who tend to see trade agreements as giveaways. In brief, the reciprocity norm helps to make agreements possible.

Transparency has been sought through various negotiations. The norm is that all barriers or restraints to trade should be clearly stated and visible. One of the WTO's main tasks has been to identify varieties of domestic regulation that constitute effective barriers to trade or that help provide "unfair" advantages to particular countries.

The underlying or foundational norm of all of these principles is a rough notion of *fairness*. Trade is roughly analogous to organized team sports. Most of the rules are clearly stated and their underlying ethos is that no one team should enjoy advantages unavailable to the other. The playing field should be level. But this does not preclude teams from developing tactics and moves that do provide an advantage, particularly if they are unobserved. So it is with trade: governments have a host of domestic programs that effectively subsidize their own producers or that discriminate against imports. When are health regulations only concerned with protecting a domestic population from disease, as opposed (at least in part) to being a device to exclude certain products from other countries? The dividing line is never clear, but that such regulations exist is well documented. One study estimated that non-trade barriers (cited in Held et al., 1999: 165) affected approximately 18 percent of the world's exports in 1992. Policies that in effect undermine the fairness norm remain high on the agenda of the WTO and constitute one of the main sources of cases taken to WTO panels for decisions.

Finally, the *liberalization* norm carries through the promise of neoclassical economics, that free trade benefits all. The preamble of the GATT held that the reduction of trade barriers is one important means to achieve economic growth, full employment, and increasing incomes. But trade liberalization, as suggested, was a norm or goal that was not to threaten various national economic and social policies. Hence, the GATT treaty and the WTO provide for a variety of loopholes and exemptions for industries facing severe adjustment problems. Article XII of the GATT, for example, acknowledged that domestic stabilization and full employment took precedence over trade liberalization (Finlayson and Zacher, 1982: 282).

In addition to these general norms, the WTO and various regional trade arrangements contain thousands of more specific rules that cover numerous aspects of commercial transactions between societies and economies. The list is so comprehensive and constantly growing that we could not cover even a fraction of it in this discussion. The point is that this immense corpus of rules stands in stark contrast to the rule-free environment of trade in the seventeenth and eighteenth centuries.

The scope of application of these norms and rules is high, but not complete. They refer primarily to trade in manufactured goods, to some services (e.g., insurance, banking), and to communications. But agricultural products remain largely outside the domain of regulation, and trade in cultural "products" remains an item of strong debate. In other words, the norms, while regulating an increasing portion of the total economic transactions between societies, do not cover all of them. But the norms are clear and for the most part clearly understood. For most commercial entities involved in trade with societies outside of their own, their transactions are regulated, safe, secure, and predictable. Few face the perils of eighteenth-century trade, transactions that were often monopolistic, predatory, and subject to the uncertainties of widespread piracy, illegal seizures of vessels, and currency manipulations that could cause the difference between profits and losses.

Accounting for institutionalization

Materialists would account for the notable changes in trade patterns and practices from the mercantilist era to today by emphasizing innovations in technology and altered state interests. Technological innovations in transportation and communication have made international commerce much cheaper, safer, and faster, but also more voluminous. One large freighter today can carry loads that would have required several hundred galleons, schooners, and Dutch "swifts" three centuries ago. That freighter can transfer its load from North America to Europe in about one week. By air, it requires about six hours. In the mercantilist era, it would have required more than one month. The argument would be that with such breakthroughs in transportation technology, rules and norms would have to develop just to keep the traffic from resulting in frequent accidents and general chaos.

An interest-based account would suggest that as producers and traders became increasingly distanced from royal patrons and regulation, they sought private gain rather than state security, national "wealth," or power. After all, long-distance traders in medieval and Renaissance times had developed their own rules and regulations (the *lex mercatorio*). The mercantilist era, they might argue, was a deviation from previous patterns in the sense that it substituted national priorities for considerations of private gain. Had governments in the seventeenth and eighteenth centuries left trade essentially as a private activity, the main agents would have developed rules and norms to ensure security of transactions and to minimize transaction costs. In this view, the creation of a liberal post-war trade regime after 1945 symbolized the recapturing of trade regulation by private interests. Governments negotiated only what their trade clients would have brought about in the absence of formal state regulation. The penchant for freer trade and the concomitant attack on mercantilist thought reflected the growing political influence of the middle classes, first in England, later throughout Europe, and ultimately in the United States.

Interests are related to power. Many have argued that the slow development of trade norms such as liberalization and non-discrimination served the national interests of England in the nineteenth century and of the United States since 1945. Governments with the necessary resources led the way. It would be difficult to reconstruct the history of trade negotiations in the 1944–7 period, producing the same outcomes without American leadership (power). As Charles Lipson has argued (1982: 257), the original GATT coalition's congruent purposes "can hardly be disentangled from America's decisive military victory or America's crucial role in rebuilding war-shattered economies and polities." American leadership was the crucial variable in explaining the institutionalization of trade rules favoring liberalization. Moreover, as the hegemonic position of the United States declined in the 1970s and 1980s, some authors also noted a concomitant growth of trade practices that were inconsistent with GATT norms and rules. In other words, mercantilist practices gained strength and trade institutionalization weakened with American power decline. A significant debate about this question – the "hegemonic stability theory" – engaged American scholars in that era, but with inconclusive results. The fact was that even if there was a temporary decline of American economic hegemony (defined in part as the American proportion of the world's total economic product, or as the American proportion of total world trade) in the 1970s and 1980s, and even if the practices of the "new protectionism" were rampant, the movement toward freer trade via the multilateral reduction of tariffs and other trade barriers did not come to an end. Indeed, it picked up momentum in the Tokyo and Uruguay rounds. As Lipson (1982: 268–9) notes, the logic of creating international regimes may differ from regime maintenance. For a variety of organizational, burden-sharing, and cost reasons, regimes, including their norms and rules, can flourish in the absence of a hegemon that must expend its superior resources to keep it afloat.

These arguments have merit and explain at least in part the institutionalization of trade that began slowly in the mid-nineteenth century and culminated in the post-war liberal trade regime. But a satisfactory explanation must also include the revolution in ideas that took place in the late eighteenth and early nineteenth century. The ideas of Smith and Ricardo were not entirely original but they were the first to be based on the presumption of scientific truth rather than policy or personal preference. It was that much more difficult therefore to refute them except on the grounds of preference rather than evidence. The ideas of free trade increasingly commanded the public discourses in Great Britain, France, and elsewhere in Europe, and in the United States during the nineteenth century. They were the stuff of parliamentary debates, thousands of pamphlets, hundreds of books, and innumerable speeches, colloquia, and seminars.

By the 1830s, the idea of free trade had become a creed, promoted with great passion by its advocates. It was not just another set of justifications for particular interests, or even a class outlook, but an expression of the emerging belief in humankind's secular salvation through a self-regulating market (Polanyi, 1944: 133–7, 152). Hundreds of prominent public figures, including Tories who had earlier championed various mercantilist measures, "converted" to free trade as they would to a religion. Charles Kindleberger (1975: 36) in a comprehensive examination of the rise of free trade thought and policies in Europe argues that

> [v]ested interests competing for rents in a representative democracy, thrusting manufacturers seeking to expand markets, or faltering innovators, trying as a last resort to force exports on shrinking markets . . . none of these explanations seems free of difficulties as compared with an ideological explanation based on the intellectual triumph of the political economists, their doctrines modified to incorporate consistency.

Much of Europe by mid-century shared a conviction that the teachings of the political economists, including free traders, were scientifically precise, universally valid, and the intellectual foundation for greater profits, increasing real wages, productivity, and efficiency, and as a bonus, a source of peace between nations (cf., Kindleberger, 1975: 50).

These ideas and their entrepreneurs could not be ignored. Nationalists, as in Germany after the Bismarck tariff of 1879, had to respond to those ideas, but they could do so only on political grounds: the state must protect infant industries in order to build up its own strength. Protection was a *national*, not a business, priority. These types of arguments continue today in the context of preventing foreign ownership of strategic and other national priority industries, the necessity to subsidize research and development, government contracting in defense industries, and the like. But in all these areas, the arguments make the claim that for reasons of national security there must be exceptions to the norm, which is to promote free trade within the context of a multidimensional set of rules. They cannot argue that everyone in the world will be better off through restrictions to free trade.

Although numerous amendments to the original ideas of Smith and Ricardo have appeared over the years, the intellectual foundations of the free trade argument have remained essentially in place (cf., Gilpin, 1987: 175–80). The basic norms and many rules of institutionalized trade thus derive from intellectual constructs and theories that have scientific as opposed to policy preference status. These sets of ideas have not been successfully challenged by competitors. The arguments surrounding trade today have to do with conceptions of fairness, justifications for exceptions and exemptions, the trade consequences of domestic legislation on health, environmental, and labor policies, the protection of national cultures, and other matters. There are no serious schools of economic thought that have successfully challenged Smith, Ricardo, and their Manchester School descendants. Thus, of all the international institutions surveyed in this study, trade is the area where ideas-based explanations for change are the most robust and compelling.

The critical role of ideas is underlined again in the significant changes to state economic policies among developing countries in the 1980s. Recall that this was a time of resurgent protectionism via non-tariff barriers among many developed economies, the relative economic decline of the United States, and the strong impact of socialist thought and dependency theory on the economic and trade policies of many developing countries. Strong state management and ownership, import substitution, self-reliance, nationalization of foreign firms, and high tariffs were the orthodoxies of economic practices in the Third World during the 1960s and 1970s. All of this changed in the 1980s. The same governments that had championed self-sufficiency, state-led industrialization, protectionism, and strict limits on foreign investment suddenly changed course almost 180 degrees. Historic bastions of economic nationalism and protectionism such as India, Nigeria, and Brazil liberalized foreign investment, opened up their markets, joined the GATT, lowered tariffs, privatized state-owned enterprises, and abandoned the main ideological props – varieties of socialism – of their former economic nationalism. Indeed, by the mid-1990s, it was the governments of developing countries that most strongly embraced the liberal trade and investment creed. They vigorously promoted a stronger rules-based system to replace the power politics and exemptions of the GATT (Ford, 2002: 130–1). The new orthodoxy represented the intellectual victory of neo-classical economics.

In a comprehensive exploration of the possible explanations for these significant changes in economic thought and policy, Thomas Biersteker (1992) argues that domestic interest groups in the relevant countries, while they may have promoted reforms, did not demand the kinds of policy changes that emerged. Indeed, many of the "reforms" were contrary to the interests of entrenched elites, whether commercial or bureaucratic. In Biersteker's judgment (1992: 115) "[i]nterest explanations appear more suited to explain the potential bases of opposition to economic reforms than account for the origins of support for them." Other forms of explanation do not fare much better. Biersteker concludes that the changes in the developing countries were primarily, though not exclusively, the results of imitation of the main economic ideas and policies of Margaret Thatcher, Ronald Reagan, and Helmut Kohl, all economic conservatives who strongly believed in the "magic of the market."

234

Neo-classical economic ideas had been around for a long time, but they clearly gained new force, visibility, and legitimacy in the 1970s and early 1980s through a series of international reports and changes in British, American, and German policies (Biersteker, 1992: 119). Also important were the economic achievements of the new industrializing countries (NICs) of Asia, most of which had jettisoned their state-led and autarkic policies and had achieved significant economic gains through integration into the international economy.

Ideas come to play a significant role in promoting change through a variety of mechanisms, including policy imitation, the publications and discourses of prominent intellectuals, the publicity and policy promotion of international institutions such as the World Bank, and "epistemic communities" comprising bureaucrats of leading countries, academic experts, and international civil servants. Ideas, however, may not sell themselves solely on their merits. There has to be an environment that is conducive to their reception. In the case of the 1980s, according to Biersteker (1992: 120–2), it was the recession of the early part of the decade in the developed world that cascaded into a full-blown depression in many developing countries, including the famous debt crisis of that era. This emergency "provoked a rethinking of the basis of economic policy throughout the developing world." Just as the depression of the 1930s in the developed countries was the crisis that helped launch the post-war international trade order, so the counterpart in the developing world in the 1980s brought about a fundamental change in policy. The orthodox ideas of economic nationalism and socialism that had prevailed in the 1960s and 1970s provided no exit from the ravages of depression in the early 1980s. The environment at that time proved receptive to new ideas, ideas that had been popularized in the policies of some leading industrial countries. Ideas, buttressed by a permissive environment, provide a better avenue for explaining institutional change than do power or interest-based explanations.

The change from trade as an alternative to, or form of, warfare, to trade as a regulated, peaceful patterned activity that brings benefits to all (or at least to many) is an example of *novelty* in our categories of change. One might also make a case for *transformation* because vestiges of mercantilist ideas and practices remain. Most governments, responding to the blandishments of particular industries or economic sectors, or those concerned with issues of national security, continue to use a variety of protective devices and subsidies as methods of increasing strategic trade advantages or state strength. Modern versions of the *lex mercatorio* – private trade law – also remain, though a good deal of this was "nationalized" by the governments of the major powers during the eighteenth and nineteenth centuries (Cutler, 1999: 305). In general, however, the scope, intensity, and volume of trade, and the norms that underlie them, reflect ideas that were introduced in the late eighteenth century, and developed since. The *novelty* is change from an essentially lawless and violent state of affairs in the seventeenth and eighteenth centuries, to a situation where norms, rules, and actions largely coincide for most states most of the time. The case for novelty is thus more compelling. We must also acknowledge that the institutionalization of trade has not been confined to commercial matters. There were also crucial changes in international law, particularly in maritime law, that helped to foster the dramatic increases in trade that have taken place during the past two centuries. And finally, any explanation must leave room for imitation and major events such as the Great Depression, World War II, and the depression in the developing countries in the early 1980s. Those events helped undermine most of the ideological props of mercantilism and autarky as avenues for economic growth and employment, and demonstrated the need for international monetary regimes and freer trade. Other avenues for explanation are available, but offer much less compelling stories.[4]

The stability of institutionalized trade

If we view trade from the long-term perspective, there seems to be a fairly clear trend away from mercantilism and toward institutionalized and freer trade. Between the British repeal of the Corn Laws and Navigation Acts in the mid-nineteenth century and the creation of the World Trade Organization in 1995, the number of bilateral and multilateral treaties that incorporate the norms and rules of free trade has grown at a rapid pace. Whereas GATT began in 1947 with only 23 members participating in the first round of tariff reduction negotiations, by the early years of the new millennium, the WTO had 144 members, including all of the world's largest economies. The norms and principles of free trade have also been incorporated into regional trade groups around the world. Institutionalized trade has not only become nearly universal; it has all the accoutrements of *conventional wisdom*. It is, in a sense, taken for granted as the normal state of affairs.

---

[4] For a review of various theories of economic policy change, see Milner (2002).

Hedley Bull (1977) reminds us, however, that the elements of power politics and international collaboration are variables that sometimes co-exist and sometimes predominate in various historical periods. The 1930s were a Hobbesian world of aggression, conquest, territorial change, and beggar-thy-neighbor commercial policies. The commercial world since 1945, in comparison, appears overall as one of collaboration, rule-making, and dramatic decreases in tariffs and other trade-inhibiting practices. This is largely the case, but we must recall that this period, outside of the communist bloc, was also one of overall economic growth and stability. The economic background of the institutionalization of trade is one of relative plenty, rapid post-war reconstruction, and economic development in many of the former colonial areas. In the late 1940s, Japan, Korea, Singapore, Trinidad, and many other countries were desperately poor. At the time of writing, many of them have per capita incomes higher than those of the older "developed" countries. But not all the news is welcome. Not only do many countries, particularly in Africa, remain poor, but some have actually become poorer in the absolute sense. International disparities are increasing, not decreasing. The consequences of these trends for overall economic well-being are not yet apparent. Some countries (e.g., Jamaica) have suffered dramatic sectoral downturns as a result of freer trade and investment. There is, indeed, a growing consensus that the hopes of across-the-board economic improvements resulting from freer trade are not taking place in many countries. The result is erosion of the strength of free trade ideas in some quarters.

Most important, while there have been economic downturns and recessions in the long post-war period, there has not been a depression of the magnitude of the 1930s. In a cautionary way, part of the explanation for the seemingly direct line toward the institutionalization of trade may lie in the general era of prosperity that has characterized large portions of the world during the past six decades. In other words, one can argue that the institutionalization of trade took place because governments could afford to opt for the route of collaboration and mutual tariff reduction in a general environment of economic growth.

What would happen in the event of a new global depression? Since national economies are more closely linked to each other than ever before – trade as a proportion of total economic activity is at an all-time high – then it is quite easy to predict that a serious economic downturn in one area will have severe contagion consequences. The Asian economic crisis of 1997–8 occurred when the North American economies were booming. Those economies retained high demand for Asian exports. Had the United States, Canada, and Europe been in recession, the crisis in Asia not only would have been prolonged, but could have spread rapidly to other areas of the world. It is not difficult to imagine scenarios of global economic crisis. Were one to occur, would the institutions of trade hold up? In brief, if the institutionalization of trade is in part a product of economic good times, would bad times reverse the situation and would we see a renewal of mercantilist ideas and practices? Most of the other institutions analyzed in this volume did not disappear in times of international crisis. Sovereignty, territoriality, the state, and many aspects of international law survived the two great world wars of the twentieth century. While we have noted changes in most of them, they are primarily in the form of growing complexity rather than transformation or obsolescence. In contrast, the changes toward the institutionalization of trade and monetary relations that occurred in the second half of the nineteenth and in the early twentieth century for the most part did not survive World War I; the Great Depression destroyed what was left after 1919. We do not know whether institutionalized trade can withstand future crises of the same magnitude. Global depression could produce one major challenge. We must recall that obsolescence is also a type of institutional change. Colonialism provides one important example. Under certain extreme circumstances, institutionalized trade might be another.

8   Colonialism

In the chronicle of relations between distinct groups and polities, conquest and empire-building figure prominently. History is in significant part a story of the rule of one "people" over others. Empires, not nation-states, have been the predominant forms of political organization throughout recorded history. Some empires, as typified in the Mongol sweep into Eastern Europe and the fertile crescent areas in the twelfth to fourteenth century, were based on systematic violence, plunder, destruction, and depredation. Such polities seldom endured beyond the lives of the great conquerors (e.g., Tamerlane, Ghengis Khan). Others, like the Roman Empire, while created primarily by force and subjugation, eventually developed legal systems that gave them a modicum of longevity and legitimacy. The colonization of the "New World" starting in the early sixteenth century resembled – at least for those who were conquered – more the Mongolian pattern. The early European colonial ventures in the New World amounted to a system of massacres, ethnic cleansing, forced labor, and coerced religious conversion. Though it had some legal underpinnings, it was more a process of conquest than of institution-building. Our concern is not with this early stage of European expansion, but with the creation of the modern empires that began in the early 1880s. This phase had all of the characteristics of international institutions as we have defined them.

Modern colonialism as an international institution

Here was a form of expansion in many ways distinct from its fifteenth- to eighteenth-century European predecessors and scarcely resembling most historical conquests. Unlike the ancient empires, or the vast expansion of Genghis Khan's realms all the way to Europe, it was not primarily a process of military conquest, of massacring, looting, marauding, and pillaging (although all of these were occasionally practiced). It was a set of practices aimed at political control, but practices corseted in a highly developed discourse on law, ethics, and ideas (Jackson, 1993). The practices were also regularized in such a manner as to minimize violence between competing imperial ambitions, and they were imbued with norms and frequently with certain etiquette. In this way modern colonialism was an international institution. We need to describe its main features and to explain why within a matter of several decades it became obsolete.

At the middle of the nineteenth century, there were few non-settler colonies. The British crown took formal authority over India from the East India Company in 1858, and possessed a number of small strategic areas, such as Gibraltar, Mauritius, and Hong Kong. France conquered Algeria in 1830. Starting with the establishment of a French protectorate over Tunisia in 1881, however, a massive expansion of formal colonization took place. At that time, there were only a few European enclaves on the coasts of Africa, while most of the Middle East was ruled as part of the Ottoman Empire. Russia had deeply penetrated the Caucasus somewhat earlier, but others joined the massive scramble for overseas territories only in the last two decades of the century. Japan (Korea) and Italy (Libya) established the last two formal colonies in 1911. There was then a hiatus until 1935 when Italy invaded Ethiopia and 1938 when Nazi Germany created virtual colonies (Austria and Czechoslovakia) in central Europe. On the eve of World War II, of all the territories of Africa, the Middle East, and Asia, only Siam, Persia, and Afghanistan were not formally a part of some empire. Forty years later, most had become independent, sovereign states.

Colonial practices

The establishment of colonies was not a major preoccupation of European governments in the 1870s. Indeed, no government of the era sought to emulate Great Britain, Spain, or the Netherlands, the major countries with overseas possessions. However, there was a great deal of private activity in areas remote from the major capitals of the world. Explorers, missionaries, traders – whose ranks include Stanley, Brazza, and Rhodes – were conducting a variety of activities in previously unknown (to Europeans) territories throughout Africa. Most of these were

unrelated to government policy. Gann and Duignan (1967: 32) characterize the cast of characters:

> The personal motives of empires . . . almost beggar description of their
> variety . . . Some, like Sir Alfred Sharpe . . . first went to Africa as big-
> game hunters. Cecil Rhodes and others suffered from a weakness of
> the lungs and sailed for the Cape in search of a better climate . . . An un-
> happy love affair drove Frederick Lugard to seek oblivion in the African
> bush. Doctors went abroad to study new medical problems . . . There
> were bankrupt swindlers. There were refugees from tsarist oppression
> and from Continental conscription laws. English gentlemen's sons who
> could not get through Sandhurst or failed to pass the difficult Indian
> civil-service examination might turn to Africa for an administrative
> career.

Much of the actual expansion of these activities was not reported to
governments. For example, a governor appointed in Paris organized
the small French community at the mouth of the Senegal River. On his
own authority, he began a military conquest of the river valley, annexing some territory while establishing protectorates over others. He built
ports and aqueducts to aid economic activity. None of this was under
the control or authorization of Paris (Power, 1966: 78). Neither European
governments nor publics were partners in these activities, and many
were not even aware of them taking place. While governments ultimately came to establish formal authority over the areas carved out
by private and semi-private activities, fully 20 percent of all the new
colonies established in the nineteenth century were organized by chartered companies or private persons (cf., Strang, 1996: 35). The British, in
particular, granted charters to private firms to conduct business in Africa
and elsewhere. Many of them failed as enterprises and were formally
taken over as colonies by the crown. The most famous of all private
firms was King Leopold of Belgium's "International Congo Association." He frankly explained its essential features: "The Congo state is
by no means a colonizing state, it is not a state at all; it is a financial enterprise" (quoted in Ansprenger, 1989: 14). The colony was run neither
in the interests of the natives nor in the economic interests of Belgium.
It was intended to bring Leopold the maximum in personal income.
This constituted the content of the work of "government." In all these
activities, the natives were primarily nuisances and sometimes sources
of labor. But the colonizers' purpose was to build great economic enterprises, railroads, and settler communities, and to control strategic

locations against competitors. There was no intent to create political systems, states, or nations.

How was this expansion accomplished? In some instances, government-sponsored military campaigns were used to pacify resisting "natives," both in the processes of expansion and in maintaining order once a colony had been established. Wesseling (1997: 14–19) counts at least seventeen major wars waged by colonial authorities in the period 1873 to 1905. In the period 1888 to 1902, there had also been eighty-four military operations which "were serious enough to be defined as 'battles' according to German military law" (p.15). In the case of Kenya, in the twenty-year period 1894 to 1914, there were fifty incidents, which, according to the British authorities, were so serious that it was necessary to resort to force. Similar statistics can be found for Dutch activities in Java, and French colonial administration throughout its far-flung empire.

Unlike Spanish and Portuguese conquests of the fifteenth and sixteenth centuries, where claims to territory were made on the grounds of *terra nullius* (no human occupation, hence no previous ownership) or the un-Christian habits of indigenous peoples, late nineteenth-century imperialists recognized the existence of local communities with rights of both local political authority and ownership of land. Where these were compromised, it was often done with consent, usually in the form of treaties. It is worthwhile to quote Hedley Bull (1984: 111–12; cf., Korman, 1996: 65) on the question of the legal foundations of colonial occupation:

> There is no *a priori* reason to doubt the genuineness of treaties concluded between European states and African political communities... [T]he principle of the sanctity of agreements was no less well understood by African than by European societies. Problems of definition and interpretation are not insurmountable, even in the absence of a common language or culture, and African rulers were not ignorant of diplomacy or unskilled in its arts. The uncertain claims of some of the African parties to these treaties... do not appear to have been an obstacle to the conclusion of these agreements, any more than they were in the case of the many treaties concluded in modern times between European powers and the Muslim powers of north Africa, at a time when they were not sovereign states but vassals of the Ottoman Sultan. Treaties facilitating trade, conceding trade monopolies, or ceding territory for trading posts were not necessarily the result of coercion, which Europeans were often in a position to apply, nor did they necessarily confer unequal or disproportionate benefits on the parties.

Bull also points out that African rulers were often eager to enter into treaties. They gained prestige, protection against domestic or external enemies, access to superior technology, and other benefits. In some instances, the initiative to cede territories or trading monopolies came from local rulers themselves. Fraud, coercion, and violence were not unknown – Neta Crawford (2002: 215, 222–4) cites a number of treaties that were imposed by force or fraud – but more often colonial status was initially based on negotiations and their resulting agreements – usually in treaty form. Yet, with the systematic partition of Africa and Southeast Asia in the late nineteenth century, legal niceties were often ignored or overlooked. Territories were exchanged, partitioned, and purchased, all without the consent of the local parties. The extended negotiations between European powers that resulted in "spheres of influence" never included local political groups or leaders. Some territories were subdued purely by military conquest (e.g., Algeria in 1830, Madagascar in 1895), and others were taken as booty from victorious wars against European colonial powers (the American takeover of the Philippines after the Spanish-American war of 1898).

As we might expect, the modern colonialists brought with them the traditional diplomatic practices, prejudices, and assumptions of international politics, as they knew them. The most important assumption was that of exclusive territorial jurisdiction. Although there were a few areas designated for free trade, most colonies and protectorates were designed for the exclusive exploitation of both private and government officials. Officials in foreign and colonial offices drew lines on maps, surveyors located them on the ground, and military officials built fortresses to monitor and control the exclusive space. Where competing interests were not reconcilable through armed force or diplomacy, government officials might create neutral zones (as between the British and French competing over the Mekong River in the 1880s; cf., Guillen, 1984: 364–8) or the ever-nebulous but still often respected "spheres of influence." Territorial delimitation was not an exact science but it was the standard practice of all colonial governments and of many of the private interests that preceded formal colonial authority. Western conceptions of territoriality were foreign to many indigenous groups, but sometimes they helped provide them with security that they lacked in pre-colonial times.

Unlike ancient conquests, European colonial authorities and their imitators in the United States, Russia, and Japan founded their authority on legal bases. We use the term colonialism to denote an ostensibly legal arrangement formalized through treaties and constitutional law. The practices on these matters varied considerably from government to government, but there was typically some formal foundation established through legal instruments. In some cases, territories were formally annexed to the "mother" country and became an integral part of it. This was the constitutional status of Algeria. It was just another *département* within France. Other jurisdictions were formal colonies. They remained distinct entities, separate from the "mother" country, but attached to it through various legal devices. In the case of Great Britain, most were designated as crown colonies. They were ruled according to the terms of the Foreign Jurisdiction Act that set down precise rules for the occupation and administration of the colony (Jackson, 1993: 115). Less formal arrangements were established in the case of protectorates. In these, local rulers were guaranteed full autonomy and self-government, but defense and foreign affairs jurisdiction accrued to the metropole. In practice, many protectorates also granted the metropole the right to advise on matters of finances and administration. Spheres of influence were less formal arrangements, but their scope was usually defined through international treaties.

The practices of governance in colonies and other types of jurisdictions varied considerably, but there was also a great deal of international copying. We must keep in mind that the colonial enterprise was always a sideshow of European politics and never commanded the administrative or military resources employed in the homeland. In the Sudan, for example, the British had only about one thousand administrators overseeing a population of about 9 million inhabiting more than 2 million square kilometers. In the 1930s, the British governed the Gold Coast (present Ghana), with a population of about 4 million, with ninety-one administrative personnel and a hundred military and police officers (Gann and Duignan, 1967: 212). One authority concluded: "[Seldom in human history] were so many people governed by so few with so little fuss as during the heyday of African colonialism" (Kimble, 1960: 306).

Colonial authorities established a number of institutions of governance, ranging from virtual one-man shows run by pro-consuls such as Lyautey in Algeria, to limited parliamentary systems that included significant representation of native peoples. As in the processes of establishing colonies, the metropolitan governments copied each other's governing styles overseas. After annexing Ethiopia in 1936, for example,

Italy's King Alphonso III assumed the title "Emperor of Ethiopia," copying Queen Victoria's title in India. Dutch colonial policies in Java and the Spice Islands were considered to be progressive and effective and were broadly copied by the Belgians in the Congo and even by the British in some of their territories.

Within the variety of colonial institutions, two models of governance became predominant. The Dutch had ruled Java and the Spice Islands for several centuries employing native elites to carry the brunt of administration. The British, copied by the Belgians in the Congo after 1908, employed a strategy of indirect rule that was originally nothing more than the necessary practice of colonial authorities almost everywhere (Smith, 1982: 164). Given limited administrative capacities, colonial authorities had to rely upon traditional indigenous ruling modes. Tribal chiefs were left in place and granted their traditional roles and authority structures. It was generally easier to buy off indigenous elites with a share of power than to repress them. Frederick Lugard, British high commissioner of northern Nigeria between 1900 and 1907, raised this form of rule to a high art and later converted it into a doctrine of governance. In its simple aspiration, it called for "a single Government in which the Native Chiefs have clearly defined duties and an acknowledged status, equally with the British officials" (quoted in Betts, 1985: 67). Over the years, however, the chiefs tended to become mere administrative personnel, with little latitude of choice. Western rationalist bureaucratic models eventually replaced a system that had significantly devolved authority to local levels (Betts, 1985: 69).

The British also introduced parliamentary institutions into some of their areas of governance. In 1920 the Legislative Council of Ceylon (present Sri Lanka) obtained a majority of "non-official" members, that is, partially appointed and partially elected representatives of the enfranchised population. In 1931 the British extended the franchise to 50 percent of the population and made native ministers responsible to the legislative body (Ansprenger, 1989: 66–7). Throughout the remaining period of British colonial rule, parliamentary bodies became increasingly common and, ultimately, the foundation for most administrative authority.

The French model, our second example of rule, originated in a decree of Napoleon III that stated "The colonies [with some exceptions] will be ruled by the Emperor by means of decrees" (Ansprenger, 1989: 77). This translated in practice to direct rule by a French governor-general.

In 1917, the governor-general of the French territories in West Africa issued the command to all his authorities that

> [Native chiefs] have no authority of their own of any kind, since in the [intermediate administrative unit of the colonies] there are not two authorities – the French and the native authority – but only one! The [French] commander commands alone. He alone is responsible. The native chief is only a tool, an assistant...the native chief...never speaks or acts in his own name, but always in the name of the Commandant... (quoted in Ansprenger, 1989: 78–9)

French policy was clear-cut, authoritarian, and hierarchical. It was based on assumptions of the absolute supremacy of French concepts of order and governance, and required the dissolution of all native authority structures into the single schema of French top-down authority. Unlike the British and Dutch, whose notions of indirect rule implied ideas of cultural relativism and the worth of local and indigenous forms of authority, the French philosophy was one of assimilation: colonial peoples were to become French and to the extent that they succeeded in this transformation, they could participate in French mainland political institutions rather than develop their own local but modernized forms of rule.

Other colonial powers developed some unique forms of rule, but most of them approximated the British or French models. The Americans, for example, developed legislative institutions in the Philippines. The Italians, Japanese, and Portuguese favored the more authoritarian French model. Some of their colonial governors were virtual dictators under only limited supervision from central authorities.

Norms, rules, and etiquette

Late nineteenth-century imperialism involved rules, norms, and legal documents to establish some legitimacy for rule over colonial lands, but also norms and etiquette between the imperial powers themselves. They cloaked their activities in a regime of rules and courtesies that they observed toward each other in their mutual relations on the continent. There were a few crises (e.g., Fashoda in 1898) and minor wars over colonial issues and rivalry, but for the most part, the imperial "game" in the nineteenth century was conducted in the context of standard diplomatic formulae and etiquette found in the Concert of Europe (cf., Holsti, 1992). There were both formal agreements and informal "rules of the game" that imbued the diplomacy of imperialism. The Berlin General Act of 1885 was a major piece of rule-creation to guide colonial policy. Many of its major provisions were systematically violated in subsequent years, but others provided the foundations for the peaceful settlement of colonial disputes. Although the General Act was not a complete recipe for the partition of Africa (Wesseling, 1997: 93–7), it did lead to numerous bilateral treaties establishing boundaries between colonies. Its signatories were required to inform each other of "effective occupation" (after, not before the fact, however), there were certain rules about the extent of jurisdiction available from coastal colonies, and most important, it contained an implicit notion that any bilateral deals made between colonial powers needed wider endorsement by all the great powers (Bull, 1984: 110). The Act was also the first statement involving obligations to act as trustees for the welfare of dependent peoples; this idea emerged later in the Mandates system of the League of Nations and in United Nations provisions for Trusteeships. The so-called "scramble" for Africa was thus in fact a process of European expansion undertaken within the context of rules, regulations, and guidelines that minimized friction between the competitors. It is perhaps astonishing that a major arena of colonial power competition eventuated in only a single all-out war between imperial rivals, in this case between the United States and Spain.

In addition to the norms and regulations of the Berlin General Act, the colonial powers regulated territorial issues in the context of older European traditions. These included compensation, partition, exchange, and spheres of influence. They were major mechanisms for neutralizing conflicts and for maintaining some sense of balance among the competitors. In 1890, for example, the British and Germans made a major exchange of territories nominally under their control, involving Zanzibar and land tracts in east, south and central Africa (Robinson and Gallagher, 1965: 293). The French and British were involved in lengthy negotiations to determine their respective zones in Southeast Asia (Guillen, 1984: 360–7), and the British and Russians negotiated important spheres of influence agreements in Persia. Unlike the treaties with African rulers, which were often tossed aside or ignored in the numerous exchanges and partitions, treaties with other colonial powers had the status of international law and thus became major "lines in the sand" that helped prevent armed conflicts. Our claim that colonialism was an institution of international relations is strongly supported by the evidence of norms, rules of the game, and etiquette.

Ideologies and belief system foundations of colonialism

Late nineteenth-century colonial expansion was largely a game of international politics, prestige, and military security (see below).[1] It was not dissimilar to the general tenor of diplomacy, conflict, and war on the continent or to the norms and customs embodied in the Concert of Europe. We can account for the dramatic expansion of territorial control largely in terms of traditional power politics. But the fact that colonialism was also a normative enterprise indicates that expansion was carried on within the context of a complex set of ideas that both justified rule over others and guided policy to a certain extent. Competitive territorial expansion had a distinctly strategic dynamic (if A gains something abroad, B must gain something as well), but in an era when politics were leaking out from cabinets and courts into the domain of public and legislative discussion, ideas also played a role. Power politics needed validation and that validation needed moral and ethical dimensions. The policy-makers who ratified treaties, directed military campaigns, and negotiated with other imperial powers were products of their class and nation, but they also operated within complex sets of belief about what was right, proper, and justifiable.

There were many streams of thought that whirled around the imperial enterprise. Often they were mixed and jumbled, but they all contained normative content that established some sense of a "right to rule" others or that validated *our* claims compared with those of others. We must not forget either, that in all the major colonial powers, there were many critics of expansion, and that in general the mass population was not much concerned with colonial issues. When we speak of pubic opinion in the late nineteenth century we refer primarily to the views of specific organized interest groups such as the church, anti-slavery societies, some businesses with colonial investments, certain elements of the armed forces, and legislators. The typical individual in the pub was seldom interested in colonial debates, although by the end of the century colonialism had become coupled to nationalism and patriotism. Thanks

---

[1] Debates about the sources of late nineteenth-century imperialism continue. Marxist and Leninist explanations are well known, but easily challenged using empirical materials. Geo-strategic explanations, which I emphasize here, are also significant in the literature (cf., Doyle, 1986). Rodney Bruce Hall (1999: ch. 8) sees this stage of imperialism as primarily a form of "cultural aggression" expressive of the bourgeois domination of politics in the imperial countries of the era. The task of evaluating the persuasiveness of competing explanations is beyond the scope of this chapter.

to world fairs and numerous publications, the successes of colonialism became a matter of national pride.

Liberalism

Liberalism was one of the early intellectual foundations of external expansion. The general idea was that free economic activity is a foundation for learning, mutual empathy, economic progress, and ultimately, peace. Economic activity would ultimately lift the less developed peoples of the world into an era of progress. Not the least of the considerations was also the quest to put an end to slavery wherever it was practiced (cf., Robinson and Gallagher, 1965: 1–3). Part of the nineteenth-century liberal view also held that human progress depends upon the development of the institutions of self-government. The conventional European and American opinion in the mid- to late nineteenth century was of progress as depending upon both political and economic institutions. The traditional despotic institutions (which everyone in these two areas thought were the only form of government in Asia, Africa, and the Middle East) presented great barriers to progress. Liberals thus had a duty to instruct backward societies in the ways of representative government. One of the great apostles of British colonialism, Arthur Balfour, summed up the liberal view of things in a statement in Parliament in 1910:

> Western nations as soon as they emerge into history show the beginnings of those capacities for self-government . . . Nations of the West have shown those virtues from the beginning, from the very tribal origins of which we have first knowledge. You may look through the whole history of the Orientals in what is called, broadly speaking, the East, and you never find traces of self-government. All their great centuries – and they have been very great – have been passed under despotisms, under absolute government. Conqueror has succeeded conqueror; one domination has followed another; but never in all the revolutions of fate and fortune have you seen one of those nations of its own motion establish what we . . . call self-government. This is a fact. It is not a question of superiority or inferiority (quoted in Thornton, 1959: appendix, 357).

Paternalism

Liberal theories justifying colonialism were closely related to theories of *paternalism*. This was the view that Westerners had a moral duty to provide order, law, and good government to subject peoples. In the absence of colonial authority, despotism, cruelty, corruption, and incompetence would prevail. The memoirs of former colonial civil servants, whether Dutch, British, or French, have a common thread that unites them: they have been called to serve "backward" peoples. They are responsible for providing education, economic opportunity, "lifting up" (a common term of the era), and peace and security. Today we combine these notions under the rubric of "development," but the ideas are similar (cf., Wesseling, 1997: 30). While not denying self-interest, colonial authorities commonly described their activities in terms of duties, moral obligations, and responsibilities. Among the missionaries, the duty to save souls, to convert, and to terminate "barbaric" practices such as slavery, polygamy, and female circumcision, was also prominent in a paternalistic sense. For many, then, colonialism was a form of rescue service (cf., Thornton, 1959: 69), to which opponents of colonialism made the point that whenever the colonial powers went in to prevent anarchy, they actually created it (p. 72).

Colonial authorities thus travailed under an ethos of a sacred obligation to serve the interests of dependent peoples, to lift them from a state of barbarism to a higher level of civilization (e.g., like "us"). To the French statesman Jules Ferry, "the superior races have a right as regards inferior races. They have a right because they have a duty. They have a duty of civilizing the inferior races." According to Kaiser Wilhelm, "God has created us to civilize the world"; to Cecil Rhodes, "I contend that we are the first race in the world, and the more of the world we inhabit the better it is for the human race" (quoted in Klein, 1974: 51). And Albert Schweitzer reminded his African faithful, "I am your brother, but your older brother" (quoted in Ansprenger, 1989: 4). The overall image was that the more the subject peoples become like "us," the better off we would all be.[2]

The various threads of paternalistic thinking went under the rubrics of "civilizing missions," "white man's burden," and "sacred trusts." The last term, coined initially by the British, became enshrined in the League of Nations Mandate system, specifically under Article 22 of the Covenant which specified that "there should be applied to principle that the well-being and development of [dependent] peoples form a sacred trust of civilization and that securities for the performance of this trust should be embodied in the Covenant." The notion of trusteeship dominated much of the colonial discourse in the 1930s. Colonialism was

---

[2] This idea survives in the present. It is seen in numerous declarations regarding economic development, the pressure to adopt "free markets," and in the massive advertising campaigns of Western-based companies in the developing world.

thus a "required" activity that would only pass when the subject peoples were fit to assume political and economic responsibilities themselves. That state of affairs, virtually every non-communist politician averred, had not been achieved by the outbreak of World War II (cf., Betts, 1985: 58–9).

Economic development

Strategic and prestige considerations were the initial impetus for colonial expansion starting in the 1870s. But by the time the colonies had been secured and their legal foundations enunciated, ideas of development helped sustain the vast governmental efforts required to make some economic sense of the conquests, peaceful acquisitions, exchanges, partitions, and spheres of influence. The British Colonial Secretary, Joseph Chamberlain, often used developmental arguments to make the case for colonial consolidation. In addition to security reasons, he argued in an 1895 cabinet memorandum, it was now time to have the state lead in the process of economic development. Private initiative was insufficient. The imperial treasury should provide loans to make roads, railways, and harbors, "the lack of which had turned away the private merchant and investor" (quoted in Robinson and Gallagher, 1965: 397). The benefits of development would accrue equally to British investors and the Africans, although their roles would differ. The Africans would provide labor and taxes; the British would supply capital and rational administration. In an appeal to the British public, Chamberlain, who had already popularized the terms "development" and "welfare," made the analogy between colonies and private estates:

> I regard many of our Colonies as being in the condition of undeveloped estates, and estates which can never be developed without Imperial assistance . . . If the people of this country are not willing to invest some of their superfluous wealth in the development of this great estate, then I see no future for these countries, and it would have been better never to have gone there. (quoted in Robinson and Gallagher, 1965: 398)

Ideas of development played little role in the original European expansion, but by the turn of the century they had become a major theme of colonial discourse. In many instances, it was the prosperity and profitability of the Dutch in Java that stood as a model of economic progress (Wesseling, 1997: 32). By the 1930s, development had become virtually the only rationale for maintaining colonies; the heroic phase of colonialism was a thing of the past. Economics had replaced strategy, civilizing missions, and prestige as the moral foundations of foreign rule:

> The *porte-plume* had replaced the bandolier; the report in triplicate supplanted the retort to artillery. District officers in the field and colonial administrations with obligations to the League of Nations amassed statistics and undertook surveys that appeared in voluminous reports, all of which were designed to make colonialization a scientific and rational undertaking, one no longer performed idiosyncratically by strong or unusual personalities who roamed worlds they did not understand. (Betts, 1985: 4)

The first British Colonial Development and Welfare Act of 1940 formalized what had been policy for some time in most colonies: the state should subsidize economic development in the colonies not just for economic betterment, but also to prepare the indigenous population for self-government.

Racism

In the late nineteenth century, strains of racist theories also pervaded colonial debates. This was the era when social Darwinism was popular, when notions of *inherent* (not cultural) superiority and inferiority found receptive audiences. In much of the discussion about moral duties to "lift" backward peoples, the intellectual constructs had been primarily cultural. The very notion of "lifting" suggests that lower and higher stages of civilization are primarily the result of cultural, religious, and political habits. People and societies are malleable, and with proper training and education they can reach a higher stage of civilization. But a variety of people challenged this cultural relativism and optimism by arguing that the differences between races are biological. The "natural" order of humanity is one of different levels of civilization. Some anthropologists of the era provided "scientific" evidence of the inherent and unchangeable distinctions between savages, barbarians, and pagans; others established hierarchies based on skin color, with the blacks at the bottom, the yellow as intermediate, and the whites at the top (cf., Vincent, 1984: 240–1). The world fairs of Paris in 1889 and St. Louis in 1904 produced exhibits that tended to verify such distinctions. The Chinese and Japanese pavilions emphasized the high cultural and artistic levels achieved (and greatly admired by most Europeans) in those "pagan" societies, while the displays of Africans and Polynesians demonstrated degrees of primitiveness not seen in Europe even in the

Dark Ages. There was suggestion in the displays that the vast differences in levels of civilization could not be eradicated by government
programs; rather, these were innate and biological and therefore unchangeable (Wan, 1992). Other racist arguments focused on the problem
of the "yellow peril," that nascent threat that grudgingly admitted that
the Chinese and Japanese were in some senses the equals of Europeans.
In the late nineteenth century, quite forgetting that only one century earlier they had vastly admired the achievements of Chinese civilization,
many Europeans now saw Orientals as a potential threat. The French
premier, Leon Gambetta, wrote that one day, "European civilization will
have to struggle against the subversion of the Chinese race . . . France
must retain its role as the soldier of civilization" (quoted in Guillen, 1984:
180; my translation). While many supporters of imperialism played the
race card in Europe and the United States, the Japanese – targets of that
racism – developed their own notions of racial hierarchies and biological
superiority and used them to justify military expansion and domination
of areas on the Asian mainland (cf., Hall 1999: 226). By the turn of the
century, colonies had become not only a major status symbol of Western
cultural superiority, but also a major basis of entitlement to rule others
because of their biological inferiority.

Humanitarianism

A final late nineteenth-century train of thought we can label humanitarian. It focused on the problem of the slave trade in Africa, notably
the traffic in humans that took place between Arabs – particularly in
Zanzibar – and Africans. The issue of slavery found a receptive audience in several colonial countries and became at least one factor in official
decision-making regarding British policy in east Africa in the 1880s. The
drive to create colonies, based mostly on strategic considerations, was
easy to sell among those audiences who had made anti-slavery one of
the most popular causes of the nineteenth century.

From humanitarianism and paternalism to strategic necessity

By the 1940s, many of these themes in the colonial discourse had become
obsolete or even embarrassing. With the onset of the Cold War, the case
for maintaining colonies became couched primarily in terms of economic and political development, and military strategy. The British and
French governments, in particular, used the argument of maintaining
colonial responsibilities as a contribution to the struggle against communism. Their military bases, for example in Cyprus, played a major role

in the communications networks of NATO allies. The Suez Canal was vital to the economic survival of Great Britain and had to remain under effective British control. There was also the fear that the national liberation movements, once in power, would ally with China or the Soviet Union. In the case of Indochina, that movement was formally linked to Moscow and Beijing, and thus a matter of concern in Washington as well as Paris. These kinds of strategic-diplomatic arguments were couched in terms of on-going responsibilities for the safety of the "Free World." They were joined to the numerous threads of development discourse that became fashionable in all major capitals as well as in the halls of the United Nations. Following earlier concepts of "trust," the major ideas now were explicitly economic. The West, roughly, had an obligation to promote the economic development of colonies as a precondition for their eventual turn to self-rule, and possibly independence, and to avoid "falling to communism." The view of the "natives" was no longer one of being backward, but of suffering from poverty and potential totalitarian rule. The imperative of making "them" like "us" nevertheless remained – as it does to this day.

The game of imperialism

In the official memoranda and diplomatic communications during the era of modern colonialism, one searches in vain for major arguments couched in the belief systems of humanitarianism, liberalism, paternalism, racism, and the rest. Much of the discussion and analysis was conducted in terms of interests, prestige, security fears, and control of strategic assets. It was a game of international politics, an offshoot of the rivalries and competitions among the great powers in Europe. On the one hand, the policy-makers were dealing with great unknowns; they had virtually no knowledge of the peoples and cultures that were to become their wards. Few had ever traveled outside Europe, Russia, or the United States so their understanding of problems in the field came only through written reports from self-serving adventurers, missionaries, businesspeople, and colonial administrators. On the other, they had had long experience with European diplomacy, often knew personally their foreign interlocutors, and learned through schooling and government work of the interests and conflicts that animated European diplomacy in the mid-nineteenth century. The public discussions about civilizing missions were familiar to the policy-makers, but this corset of liberal, paternal, racist, and humanitarian thought was not commanding or even influential until long after the colonial project had begun. Ideas and beliefs sustained imperial expansion and colonialism as an institution, but they did not create it. In fact, none of the strategists of colonial expansion – Jules Ferry, Benjamin Disraeli, Otto von Bismarck, or William McKinley – could be called an "imperialist." None assumed office on the basis of an imperial platform. None knew much or cared about colonies (India excepted), and certainly the great public debates of the early 1880s did not include the promotion of expansion abroad. All the commanders of imperialism became advocates only while in office, and often only after having held leadership positions for some time. Why did they ultimately champion causes that initially had little popular support or sympathy?

The answers are complex and often analyzed. We need not review them here. From our perspective the interesting question is the connection between old-fashioned European diplomatic rivalry and the institutionalization of colonialism. The competitive carving up of Africa, the Middle East, and the Far East into colonies, protectorates, spheres of influence, and "open doors" could have taken place for purely diplomatic-strategic reasons. That this unprecedented expansion became imbued with legalism and justified in terms of elaborate liberal, paternal, racist, and humanitarian arguments shows in part how colonialism became an international institution as distinct from mere conquest. By the end of the century, the successors of Ferry and the others were fully imbued with the imperial ethos and came to understand the value of colonialism in a manner only glimpsed by the leaders of the early 1880s.

Early European expansionists, including traders, missionaries, and adventurers, thought little of national grandeur or great power competition. They lobbied for official sanction and protection of their activities, but over the years these private actors became more the tools of government policies than their originators. Expansion was a multi-pronged phenomenon, not just a diplomatic game, but the various layers of unofficial activity inevitably became linked to the purposes of government. Take one example: one might think that missionary activity was essentially a private church affair. But not untypically the French foreign minister circulated a memorandum in 1880 explaining that "in their evangelical works [French missionaries] represent the name and influence of France" (quoted in Guillen, 1984: 38; my translation). The French minister in Beijing (then Peking) was encouraged by Paris not only to promote religious activities, but also "to use to the profit of France the connections and progress accomplished by [French] missionaries among the Chinese population" (Guillen, 1984: 38; my translation). By the end of the century tens of thousands of French missionaries worked in the various colonies and protectorates, and they received large government subsidies to carry on not only religious, but also French cultural activities. Similar patterns were found in Great Britain, Germany, the United States, Belgium (after 1908), Holland, and Russia. Reversing the Leninist thesis that large enterprises served as the bridgehead of imperialism and that governments served primarily their interests, the evidence is overwhelmingly the reverse. Two of the main experts in the field summarize the argument as follows:

> The British colonies and protectorates in tropical Africa had not been claimed originally because they were needed as colonial estates. Rather, they had been claimed for strategic reasons, and they had to be developed as colonial estates to pay the costs of their administration. Their economic development was more a consequence than a motive of the "Scramble." As an explanation of European rule . . . the theory of economic imperialism puts the trade before the flag, the capital before the conquest, the cart before the horse. (Robinson and Gallagher, 1965: 409)

This statement as an explanation of British policy in Africa could be applied with considerable accuracy to French, American, and Russian expansion as well. The evidence is that while policy-makers dutifully listened to the importunings of traders, investors, anti-slavery and missionary societies, and other humanitarian groups, their decisions ultimately reflected calculations of national interest, security, and prestige. In other instances, governments moved only because others moved earlier. As H. L. Wesseling (1997: 83) explains, "Dutch imperialism was not a matter of action but of reaction. It was . . . almost exclusively a function of international politics. In short, the only reason for Dutch imperialism was the imperialism of others."

What were these international politics? Why imitation? In what sense did the game of imperial expansion feed upon itself? Two of many examples illustrate Wesseling's point: the French establishment of a protectorate over Tunisia in 1881, and the British occupation of Egypt one year later. Both help explain the predominance of security concerns, the dynamics of imitation, and how one imperial possession required new conquests or claims to make it secure.

In the case of Tunis, an Italian operator successfully purchased a railway in Tunis for about four times its actual value. The French learned that the Italian government actually funded the purchase and guaranteed earnings that were unrealistic. Officials in Paris interpreted this action as the crowning evidence of Italian plans to take over the public utilities of Tunis, then an autonomous region within the Ottoman Empire. The French considered Tunis to be within their sphere of influence because, having occupied Algeria in 1830, they needed a friendly government to the east to protect their new conquest. The French premier wrote that he had told the Italian ambassador that

> The great interests created by us in Algeria do not permit us to allow another power to establish its influence in opposition to ours in a territory like Tunisia, which is the natural annex and the military key to our African holdings . . . In the domain of private interest there is absolute freedom of competition between French and Italians . . . But when it is a question of a state enterprise [the railroad], of the political direction of the regency, we cannot admit this division, which would be a constant threat for us and an inevitable source of conflict. (quoted in Power, 1966: 41)

Further incidents of this sort soured Italian–French relations during the following months. Wishing to deflate French boasts of revenge over the loss of Alsace-Lorraine in the war with Prussia in 1870–1, Bismarck supported the French. Finally, tribal groups in Tunisia were conducting raids into Algeria and the Bey of Tunisia was unable or unwilling to control them. Ultimately France coerced him to sign a protectorate treaty, which allowed him to reign in theory only. Tunisia became thereafter the second French acquisition in North Africa.

One year later British troops occupied Egypt and annexed it as a colony. A British governor-general took over formal authority, although the Khedive was left as the ostensible ruler. A crisis between the Khedive and nationalist groups in Egypt had led to the collapse of authority and to a major financial crisis. European bondholders faced immense losses and, hence, the story that the British took over to save their interests. This appears as a classic case of financial imperialism. But strategic concerns were the compelling considerations. The British annexation caused a major diplomatic crisis with France, which also had numerous interests in Egypt. For decades the British and French had pursued their interests in the area through diplomacy and sometimes through coercion. The direct British concern was to prevent the French from establishing themselves across the Suez route to India. But Egypt was part of a much larger British strategic problem. The Russians during the 1870s had been pressing closer upon the Ottoman Empire and were in the throes of extending their influence into the Mediterranean. The Russians had already defeated the Turks in 1876 and had made substantial territorial gains in the Balkans through the Treaty of San Stefano. In the British prime minister's mind, the crux of the British position in the Mediterranean, and hence throughout the world, was being threatened from the east. Secure control of Egypt became essential for the entire British position in the world. The plight of European bondholders was at best a minor and marginal consideration in British decision-making.

As the policy-makers of the era saw them, events in Africa were not unrelated to this larger strategic problem. The British move into Sudan, and the ultimate annexation of Uganda and other parts of east Africa were designed to pre-empt French, German, and Belgian moves into those areas. Control of them by Britain's rivals would have constituted a major threat to the British position in Egypt. Like the French in Tunisia, the British expanded into large areas of the Nile basin and Africa to protect their main strategic asset, Egypt, which in turn was the key to maintaining British power in India, the "jewel" of the empire. It was clear that the main purpose of British policy in Uganda and the Sudan was neither to "protect missions nor to peg out claims for posterity, but to defend the British occupation of Egypt" (Robinson and Gallagher, 1965: 326). These two students of British imperial policy conclude (1965: 464) in their detailed study of the era that

> If the [policy] papers are to be believed, [the British] moved into Africa, not to build a new African empire, but to protect the old empire in India. What decided when and where they would go forward was their traditional conception of world strategy ... Much of [the statesmen's] experience confirmed that Britain's strength depended upon the possession of India and preponderance in the East, almost as much as it did upon the British Isles. Therefore, her position in the world hung above all upon safe communications between the two.

The story of Britain's expansion into Africa is thus primarily a tale of strategic concerns. British ministers listened to the importunings of missionaries, traders, philanthropists and investors, but lobbying by these groups was seldom decisive in the policy-makers' considerations. More traditional concerns over control of vital communications routes, the rising influence of Russia in the Balkans and the Ottoman Empire, and general considerations of the balance of power in Europe were critical. Slogans from colonial discourse, questions of putting an end to the slave trade, and the ideologies of expansion, Robinson and Gallagher suggest, were more public justifications than the actual reasons for policy choices (1965: 308, 463).

But what may have been of strategic concern to the British was viewed differently in Europe's capitals. A conquest by one great power created pressures for others to emulate. Describing the tenor of the times in Paris after Britain's conquest of Egypt in 1882, the Belgian king wrote: "They are furious in Paris. Now there must be two revenges, against the Germans [for the loss of Alsace-Lorraine] and the British in Egypt. They want to expand in all directions. Tunisia no longer suffices. The French must take the Niger, the Congo in Africa, Tonkin in Asia and all the available islands in the Pacific Ocean" (Guillen, 1984: 177; my translation). In Asia, the main French argument for establishing authority over Cochinchina (Tonkin) was the growing influence of Great Britain in Burma and the "crushing preponderance" of Britain in the Far East (Guillen, 1984: 179). By the late 1880s, imperial expansion had become a highly competitive activity, with the increasing sense of a zero-sum game, where the parties perceived gains by others as involving losses for themselves. There were thus intense pressures to match forward moves, to claim compensation, and to justify conquests and annexations as necessary to maintain the security of previous acquisitions, and to sustain in general parity, prestige, and one's "world position." As the British colonial secretary put it in responding to German moves into east Africa,

> I agree ... that there is something absurd in the scramble for colonies, and I am as little disposed to join in it as you can be; but there is a difference between wanting new acquisitions and keeping what we have: both Natal and the Cape Colony would be endangered ... if any foreign Power [Germany] chose to claim possession of the coast lying between the two. (quoted in Robinson and Gallagher, 1965: 208)

And those that made successful moves were quite convinced that they added to the prestige and grandeur of the state in European circles and diplomacy. Colonies thus became in themselves foundations of national power and prestige for the conduct of diplomacy on the continent. Colonialism was thus largely an extension of the European diplomatic game. Concerns of diplomatic weight, position in Europe, and the balance of power (and for the French, compensation for the loss of Alsace-Lorraine) – not investment or philanthropic concerns – were the fuel of foreign expansion.

But positions cannot be held, influence cannot be wielded, and annexations cannot be considered without the necessary means. These included both the "hard" elements of power – military capabilities – and the general concern with questions of prestige, the "soft" basis of influence in diplomacy. All the major colonial powers of the era expanded their military forces in order to protect lines of communication, conduct conquests, and fight wars against native resisters. But equally important was the necessity of keeping up with the imperial Joneses, the idea that international respect was to be gained primarily by visual displays of military might. Despite economic depression in the mid-1880s and 1890s, national parliaments regularly voted to increase military budgets. Politicians and other public figures of the expansionist community constantly sang the praises of the military as among the major sources of international prestige and respect. Not unexpectedly, admirals and generals and their staff sustained their requests for more funding in terms of concepts like prestige, national honor, and maintaining world standing.

But what of the Leninist-inspired argument that imperialism was a necessary stage in the development of capitalism? Some of the public debate surrounding colonial activities injected economic considerations, and a few commercial groups sought government protection or the imposition of "law and order" among restive native populations so that they could conduct their business unhindered. But there was no commercial groundswell for official colonialism; indeed, in many cases business interests argued *against* the imposition of formal colonial authority. The major studies of colonialism of the last two decades of the nineteenth century concur that the economic aspects of expansion played a minor role in policy-making. The economic stake in the colonies was minute. Figures on foreign investment demonstrate that flows from Europe went primarily into other parts of Europe, into portions of the Middle East (particularly Egypt), into the Ottoman Empire, and into the Western Hemisphere. In 1902, for example, only 3.5 percent of French foreign investment went into the North African colonies, only 6 percent into the rest of Africa, and less than 2.5 percent into Asia and Oceania (Guillen, 1984: 57). The figures for the period when foreign expansion became competitive – after establishing a protectorate over Tunisia – are even smaller.

In the establishment of the early colonies, there was little of economic worth to protect. Even after the colonies began to be developed, the economic stakes for most metropolitan economies were limited. On the eve of World War I, of France's total foreign investments, only 9 percent were located in the colonies. The corresponding figure for Germany was 2 percent. Britain had a much larger stake, but most of it was invested in the old "white" dominions (Betts, 1985: 21). Certain sectors or niche productive areas were critical, of course (tin, rubber, gold, and the like), but their profits or tax revenues were never substantial enough even to pay the full costs of administering the colonies from which they came. If there were significant economic gains to be made from colonialism, they help more to explain the course of decolonization than the origins or sustenance of expansion in the 1880s and 1890s.

Finally, colonial expansion or the imperial "game" has to be linked to domestic politics in the participating countries. There were colonial factions within parties, supported and boosted by relevant interest groups such as churches, colonial societies, and philanthropic organizations. Ferry, Disraeli, and Bismarck, among others, converted to imperialism in large part for domestic political reasons. In the case of the British prime minister, earlier attempts to build cross-class coalitions and to mend extreme political fragmentation in England through social legislation and democratization had not entirely succeeded. As Woodruff Smith explains (1982: 96–7),

> On the surface, an ideology and policy of imperialism seemed the ideal way to link together disparate interests and social groups and to create broad public support...A highly emotional imperialist ideology could perhaps overcome seemingly irreconcilable class and interest differences by emphasizing shared images of national greatness and shared fears of danger to that greatness...Disraeli's turn to imperialism, like those of other imperialists in both major parties, was thus in large part motivated by [domestic] political considerations.

Roughly similar considerations underlay Bismarck's adoption of imperialism after 1882.

The story of the imperial game is thus largely one of traditional European international politics, the extension of those politics to the Middle East, Africa, and the Far East, pre-emptive moves to secure early colonial possessions, concerns for international status and prestige, and domestic politics. Initially, the expansion was not of a form that we could call an institution. There were some early rules of the game and "gentlemen's agreements" that helped keep rivalries in the domain of competition rather than armed conflict, but the development of the main ingredients of institutionalization – regularized practices, commanding ideas and a public ethos of imperial grandeur or philanthropic service to lower peoples, and formal rules of competition and colonial administration – did not develop until the late 1880s and toward the turn of the century. On the eve of World War I, colonialism throughout areas of the world that were barely known a century earlier was well established and gave every evidence of becoming a permanent part of the arrangements of the society of states. Both great and lesser powers strengthened their unique identities through their overseas possessions, and the extent of those possessions was a clear indicator of the status, power, and prestige of the metropolitan state. There were numerous political parties and humanitarian organizations who opposed colonialism, but in 1914 very few people would have predicted that colonialism was in fact only a temporary institution of the society of states and that its ideological and normative underpinnings contained a fatal contradiction: the ultimate goal of liberalism, paternalism, and humanitarianism is freedom, not subjugation. World War I was the first major step towards de-colonization and the end of colonialism as an international institution.

Toward obsolescence

We tend to think of de-colonization as primarily a post-World War II phenomenon. Quantitatively, this was indeed the case, but the early foundations for de-colonization appeared already in the late eighteenth century. The thirteen American colonies were the first to secede from the mother country. The Spanish possessions in Latin America followed three decades later, also through armed rebellion. In the mid-nineteenth century, the British government began the long and peaceful process of turning the "white" colonies of Australia, New Zealand, Canada, and Ireland into dominions ultimately enjoying all but the symbolic trappings of full sovereignty. In 1922, Great Britain granted independence to Egypt, but in fact maintained a military force in the country and colonial officials to advise the government on finances and administration. Egyptian foreign and defense policy remained under British control. Iraq achieved a similar status in 1927.

The greatest wave of de-colonization began with India's independence in 1947, followed rapidly by Burma (1948), Indonesia (1949), and the first spate of independence in Africa. The last phase of de-colonization was pretty well completed in 1975 with the withdrawal of Portugal from Angola and Mozambique. Between 1945, when the

United Nations was founded, and 1975 more than one hundred independent states were born. The vast majority had been colonies.

The processes of de-colonization varied. Most colonies achieved independence through negotiations and what could be termed constitutional procedures. Independence was *granted* and in some senses earned. Nineteen gained independent statehood only after protracted wars of national liberation involving vast human destruction. These included Indonesia (against the Dutch), Indochina and Algeria (against the French), Cyprus (against the British), and Angola and Mozambique (against the Portuguese). In Rhodesia, the white settlers organized a *coup d'état* against the British authorities and set up their short-lived independent state which, however, received no international recognition. However accomplished, no one in 1945 would have predicted this massive devolution of Western authority in other areas of the world. Even though most colonial authorities had committed themselves to various notions and institutions of self-government, none thought that the emerging indigenous political forms would be capable of running a modern state at least for decades or perhaps even centuries. General Charles de Gaulle made it clear in 1944 that the French colonies in Africa would never become independent. At the Brazzaville Conference of that same year, French negotiators balanced all African statements about "rights" with a reaffirmation of the French assimilationist philosophy and statements that independence for colonies was "neither a necessary nor a desirable destination" (Holland, 1985: 155). In a truly Napoleonic statement at the conference, the French declared that "the goals of the task of civilization accomplished by France in her colonies rule out any idea of autonomy, and possibility of evolution outside the French bloc of empire; the eventual creation, even in the distant future, of self-government for the colonies is to be set aside" (quoted in Betts, 1985: 190). In the 1930s, the Dutch, too, had claimed that independence for the Javanese and other dependent peoples under the Netherlands authority was to be considered in centuries, not decades. As late as 1960, British colonial officials declared that Kenyan independence was not to be contemplated in the foreseeable future (Wesseling, 1997: 118–19).

Explaining obsolescence

What happened in the very brief interval between these assertions and the achievement of independence? As in any explanation of a major social change, the demise of colonialism cannot be understood as the outcome of a single process or event. Part of the story emanates from the changing ideas, beliefs, and actions of leaders within the colonies, the individuals and their movements who negotiated, bargained, and sometimes fought to expel the colonial administrations. This type of explanation emphasizes local resistance to domination and the determination of indigenous leaders, armed with Western liberal ideas and the norm of self-governement, to achieve liberation. But their actions were set within a historical context, in particular the legacies of two world wars and the Boer War. More immediately, changes in colonial practices were moving inexorably (but not in all colonies) toward self-government, one obvious implication of which was ultimate independence. These changes took place within a more general, system-wide alteration of norms about colonial governance. This in turn was fed by, reinforced, and initiated by alterations in the realm of ideas and beliefs. Finally, the economic weakness of the major colonial powers at the end of World War II was an important mitigating factor. It is not possible to weigh the relative importance of these various sources of institutional obsolescence. We consider them briefly in turn, without ascribing to any one particular or decisive explanatory power. All the sources were combined in complicated ways and were not always of equal relevance to each individual case of de-colonization.[3]

Indigenous political activity and resistance

Resistance by indigenous elites and organizations took many forms. In some areas, there were mass movements inspired by Christianity and combinations of local religions. The Maji-Maji rebellion against Germany in east Africa in 1905, the Boxer rebellion in China during the same period, and the Mau Mau uprising in Kenya during the 1950s are illustrations. All failed to expel the foreigners. In others, charismatic leaders like the Mahdi in Sudan during the 1880s led armed groups against colonial armies and settlers. In all, colonial authorities waged at least twenty full-fledged wars in efforts to pacify territories they had come to control (Wesseling, 1997: 14–15). The resisters included Javanese against the Dutch (Aceh War, 1873–8), the Ashanti against the British (1873), the Afghans against the British (1878–80), the Zulus against the British (1879), the Turkmen against the Russians (1879–81),

---

[3] Daniel Philpott (2001: Part III) offers a detailed examination of the development of anti-colonial ideas in Great Britain and France, and the role of various "couriers" to agitate on their behalf. He also considers alternative explanations for de-colonization, concluding that none has the purchase of an ideas-based analysis.

the Indochinese against the French (1882–4), the Burmese against the British (1885), the Cubans against the Spaniards (1895–8), the Ethiopians against the Italians (1895–6), the Arabs against the Belgians (1892–4), and east Africans against Germany (1905). A guerrilla war against American authority in the Philippines (1900–3) was put down with typical brutality leading to the deaths of more than 100,000 people, a majority of whom were women and children. Armed resistance was more prominent in the early years of colonial authority, or when that authority was being established, than later.

All the armed resistance in the early stages of colonialism failed. The colonial authorities had superior military capabilities, among which the machine gun was most important. But although there were many casualties in these wars,[4] the colonial edifice was not highly militarized. Colonial authority was to a large extent based on indifference or passive consent. The vast British colony in India was sustained by fewer than 80,000 British troops, supplemented by 200,000 natives. The French colonial expanse contained only 20,000 French troops, supported by 50,000 natives. At the turn of the century, the Dutch maintained only 9,000 troops in Java and the Spice Islands, supplemented by 16,000 natives (figures from Wesseling, 1997: 18). Compared with the metropoles, which had become involved in a massive arms race, the colonial system was sustained primarily by non-violent means until World War I.

Armed resistance continued after that war, with major uprisings among the Druse in Syria (against the French), and the Rif wars against Spain and France in North Africa. But it was this period that saw the beginnings of what might be called nationalism and the organization of political groups on Western models. These groups were influenced by the tenets of liberalism, and in some cases (e.g., Indochina) of Marxism-Leninism. Most were led by Western-educated elites who created the myths and motives for broad popular support. To these must be added as well colonial producers, unions (where allowed), farmers' associations, as well as adaptations of religious organizations (Smith, 1982: 228–9). These were the bases of the nationalist movements that came to

---

[4] Accurate figures were difficult to obtain, as they either were not kept, or when attempted, were inflated or deflated according to political purposes. In the Maji-Maji rebellion against Germany, the official report given to the Reichstag lists a total of 75,000 African dead; other estimates raise the total to double that figure. In the Zulu war against Great Britain, about 8,000 warriors died, compared with 1,430 on the British side. In the Aceh war in Indonesia, 60,000 to 70,000 was the estimate for native deaths, compared with 2,000 Dutch soldiers. Another 25,000 Indonesians died from forced labor and disease in captivity. All figures from Wesseling (1997: 19).

dominate the politics of de-colonization in the 1940s and 1950s. Armed resistance had largely failed prior to 1914, but the development of mass political organization in the 1930s significantly changed the terms of negotiation between colonial and native leaders.

The consequences of European wars

The shift in the balance of power between rulers and ruled in the colonies is in part accounted for by the great wars of the era. The Boer War (1899–1902) was at least a symbolic British defeat. Opinion within Britain became highly fractured over the war, despite all the propaganda. The consequences of World War I were even more profound. As a result of the 8 million casualties in a four-year carnage, Europeans lost their bellicose and jingoistic attitudes that had been so prominent prior to 1914. More important, perhaps, a large number of African and Indian troops fought in that war, providing for them substantial evidence that the white men were neither gods nor immune to fear, cowardice, and stupidity. The war contributed significantly to the moral and political downgrading of Westerners in the eyes of many colonial subjects.

World War II was even more effective in undermining the legitimacy of colonial regimes. The Japanese defeat of the British and Dutch in Southeast Asia again demonstrated the military weakness of the colonial edifice, and Japanese grants of independence (albeit more a form of protectorate than true independence) to Burma and the Philippines, and a promise of independence to the Indonesians demonstrated that the former colonial powers would have to restore their authority over peoples that had at least nominally achieved independence.

The war in Europe also seriously undermined Western claims of moral or civilizational superiority. Nazi extermination policies on the eastern front and the genocide against European Jews and Gypsies demolished the old nineteenth-century discourse about civilization and barbarism. The Europeans, the war demonstrated, were capable of levels of barbarism that no colonized peoples had ever practiced before or during the colonial era (cf., Salter, 2002). In addition, the United States made it clear throughout the war that it would not expend American lives to save the British and French empires. As a major Western participant in the war, its policies, including the pledge to grant independence to the Philippines in 1946, played the major role in establishing the post-war international agenda. The re-establishment of colonialism was not high on that agenda, and the colonial powers began their restoration projects very much on the defensive. The anti-colonial stance of the United States was joined by that of the Soviet Union, which loudly took on the role of the headquarters of the anti-imperialist struggle. It was relatively easy for the Soviets to join the classic capitalist versus proletarian conflict to an imperialist state versus colonially oppressed peoples dichotomy. Once the Cold War was underway, the Soviet Union became the major champion of armed revolution, "peoples' wars," and de-colonization. In some instances it provided arms, funds, and training to demonstrate its commitment to the liberation of colonial peoples. There were other international factors that helped undermine the colonial position, but the wars and their outcomes were very important. They all had major consequences on colonial practices, ideas, and norms, to which we now turn.

Changes in colonial practices

In hindsight, it might appear that de-colonization was a steady, smooth, and even inevitable process. Numerous comments by colonial authorities to the effect that full independence was out of the question, or that it was sometime in the distant future, suggest otherwise. Even as late as 1943, a British Colonial Office memorandum claimed that "A good many years (perhaps a good many generations though it would be impolitic to say so openly) must elapse" before the transition to African self-government could go beyond the local level (quoted in Jackson, 1993: 123). Such thoughts were typical in the era. Nevertheless, there were some significant changes in the practices of colonial governance during the 1930s and 1940s. They were most notable in the case of the United States and Great Britain, although barely noticeable for the other colonial powers where, as Betts (1985: 61) notes, "few colonial officials were genuinely interested in substantially modifying their patterns of activities, except when forced to do so. Throughout most of Asia and Africa, empire remained, nearly to the end, based on a paternalistic attitude; colonial change was more rhetorical than factual." In the case of the United States, it developed the "Good Neighbor" policy for Latin America, pledging to avoid the interventionist and quasi-colonial activities for which it was noted at the turn of the century and during the 1920s. In 1934 it gave Commonwealth status to the Philippines and pledged to grant it independence in 1946. A secessionist rebellion in Ireland earned it independence in 1921. Egypt was granted nominal independence in 1922. Iraq, a British mandate under the League of Nations system, achieved sovereign status in 1927, although its defense and foreign policies remained under British control. In India, there was steady movement toward self-government and the achievement of dominion status in the 1930s, on a par with the formal constitutional positions of Australia, New Zealand, and Canada. In Ceylon, as noted above, responsible parliamentary government was achieved in the 1930s. There was of course no discussion of full independence, but the next obvious question was "if we are capable of governing ourselves successfully along British models, why should we remain dependencies?"

British practices of promoting self-government in some of the colonies found counterparts in the American administration of the Philippines, the Dutch authority in Indonesia, and in a few other places. These practices reflected early nineteenth-century and Wilsonian liberal thought that designated self-government as a major hallmark of civilization. Such innovations were not, however, widely copied in other imperial domains. The French maintained their strictly hierarchical notions of authority. The Italian colonies were run as the personal fiefdoms of their governors. The Soviet Union, through the centralized Communist Party, ran its vast domains in central Asia as mere reflections of Stalin's will, and the Japanese maintained highly authoritarian and central control over Korea. Thus, change in colonial practices tells us more about the timing and character of de-colonization in particular locales than about the obsolescence of the international institution.

Changes in systemic norms

The question of colonial authority arose explicitly at the Paris Peace Conference in 1919. The innovation designed to deal with the colonies of the defeated powers was the Mandates system. Most authorities agree that the Mandates system was just a rhetorical means of awarding traditional spoils of war to the victors. Britain, France, Italy, Japan, and Belgium carved up Germany's African and Pacific holdings, while the British and French took over the Ottoman territories in the Middle East. Subsequent French and British policies in these transferred territories provide much support for the view that the Mandates system was a trope for more traditional policies. This puts it too simply, however. As with a good deal of the Paris negotiations, the Mandates system was a compromise between Wilsonian aspirations and principles deriving from self-determination and the American experience of self-government on the one hand, and traditional European practices of power politics, colonial administration, and concern with prestige on the other. Wilson had originally proposed that the German colonies should become the common property of the League of Nations and that they should be administered by small powers – thus excluding traditional spoils of war (Thornton, 1959: 173). The British and French would have none of this and held out for formal transfers of authority. However, they accepted the compromises that authority would be exercised under the nominal supervision of the League of Nations and its Mandates Commission. There was never much supervision and without funds or capabilities for conducting on-site investigations within the colonies, the commission was mostly powerless. However, the language of the Covenant relating to the Mandates is significant because it was the first explicit statement that political independence – full sovereignty – should be the ultimate goal of colonial policy. Embedded in Article 22 of the Covenant, among all the paternalistic phrases about trusts and tutelage, is the comment with reference to the "A"mandates that "certain [Arab] communities formerly belonging to the Turkish Empire have reached a stage of development where their existence as independent nations can be provisionally recognized subject to the rendering of administrative advice and assistance by a Mandatory until such time as they are able to stand alone." The precedent was now set and the terms of the debate had to change as a result. The question was no longer whether colonies should remain as an essential component of great power identity and of the society of states, but when independence should be granted.

While the individual mandates suffered or prospered pretty much according to the priorities of their colonial administrators, the actual operation of the system (the reports and discourses surrounding the administrations) helped undermine the intellectual and practical foundations of institutionalized colonialism. Neta Crawford (2002: 288), who made a systematic analysis of the Mandates system, concluded that:

> In one of the great reversals of international politics, the leaders of the same powers that practiced colonialism on a scale never before seen in the world, would construct with the League of Nations Mandates system, an institutional mechanism that would gradually deconstruct colonialism. This was an outcome the architects of the Mandates system never intended, nor apparently even foresaw, yet it was a consequence of their ethical and practical arguments. Colonialism was thus denormalized, delegitimized, and an alternative reformist conception was put on the table and gradually institutionalized.

The types of practices required in the Mandates system were strengthened in the Trusteeship arrangements in the United Nations Charter. Annual reports, appeals to the Trusteeship Council, and a primitive form of investigative authority were incorporated into the United Nations. However, Chapter XI of the UN Charter entitled "Declaration Regarding the Non-Self Governing Territories" spoke only of "self-government" and avoided the term independence – on the insistence, of course, of the British and French governments. Yet, colonial practices had changed sufficiently during the war that independence became an increasingly likely event. Most of the colonial services during the war had become increasingly indigenized, and in the Japanese-occupied European colonies, they were largely eliminated, to be replaced by locals under Japanese tutelage. In India, the colonial service by 1940 was almost evenly divided between British and Indian officials (Betts, 1985: 193). Only in the French and Portuguese colonies did practices remain basically unchanged after the war. The colonies of the defeated Italians and Japanese either became independent (Korea, although divided), Trusteeship territories of the United States (former Japanese possessions in the Pacific), or virtual wards of the United Nations (Somaliland, Libya, and Eritrea).

The growing consensus on self-determination within countries such as the United States and Great Britain was matched by the coordination of many governments that were beginning to champion the anti-colonial cause. These included the members of the Soviet bloc, a good portion of Latin America, and former colonial countries such as Iraq, India, and Egypt that had gained membership in the United Nations. They sponsored a series of resolutions in the United Nations that progressively undermined arguments in favor of the retention of colonies put forth by the French, Portuguese, Belgians, and Dutch. Resolution 421 (1950) called for a study of the ways and means "which would ensure the right of peoples and nations to self-determination." General Assembly Resolution 637 two years later stipulated that the right of self-determination "is a prerequisite to the full enjoyment of all fundamental human rights" (notice the direct coupling of colonial and human rights agendas). Resolution 1188 (1957) stated that self-determination is a right deserving due respect from all member states (Jackson, 1993: 124). The anti-colonial coalition was scoring more and more points as the 1950s progressed.

Three years later a United Nations resolution that passed by a vote of 89 to 0 officially undermined the last intellectual props of colonialism. The Declaration on the Granting of Independence to Colonial Countries and Peoples (Resolution 1514) stated that "all peoples have the right to self-determination," and that "inadequacy of political, economic, social and educational preparedness should never serve as a pretext for delaying independence." The norm of self-government was now officially declared an unconditional *right*. Eleven years later, General Assembly Resolution 2869 expressly eliminated size, limited resources, or geographic isolation as valid objections to attaining sovereignty. Thus 1960 serves as the watershed year. Resolution 1514 effectively eliminated all the major components of the imperial ethos. Liberalism, paternalism, and humanitarianism (e.g., anti-slavery) could no longer justify, explain, or support the rule and authority of one people over another. However, the large anti-colonial coalition that sponsored these revolutionary resolutions insisted that they applied only to *overseas* colonies. Hence, the components of the Soviet empire were exempted from the right to self-determination.

Ideas and beliefs

The obsolescence of colonialism was not a "big bang" event, but a lengthy process founded on the residues of world war and changing capabilities, and most of all, on intellectual change involving reconstruction and deconstruction of ideas and beliefs, the unveiling of inherent ideational contradictions, and the undermining of the myths and stories upon which colonial authority had been founded and legitimized.

The whole edifice of nineteenth-century liberal, paternalistic, racist, and humanitarian ideas justifying colonialism underwent intense scrutiny and serious challenge as a result of native resistance and world war. The Great War was largely responsible for the shift in mood. Prior to that war, colonial empire and the "small" wars in exotic places had once seemed glamorous. The vast carnage in France and on the eastern front turned large swathes of European opinion in the direction of pacifism. And now militarism and imperialism became strongly connected, and the heroic military figures of colonial expansion became icons of farce. As A. P. Thornton (1959: 303) noted,

> In the 1880s the 'modern major-general,' personified by Sir Garnet Wolseley, had had his many admirers, even among Radicals; but in the 1920s and 1930s the modern major-general had been demoted in rank and degraded in name, now appearing in David Low's cartoons as the figure of Colonel Blimp – a brick-red countenance calling hoarsely for its tiffin when not voicing some fatuous admiration of Mussolini.

All sorts of anti-imperialist ideas circulated, particularly in Great Britain and the United States. Some were based on the view that colonialism was a drain on national budgets rather than a source of strength;

others – particularly in France – adopted Leninist interpretations of imperialism; and, finally, the Wilsonian concept of self-determination that was used to justify the creation of independent states out of the ruins of the Russian, German, and Austro-Hungarian empires could not be limited solely to "white" peoples. Unless one was a racist, the principle of self-determination had to be universal and could not be squared with most colonial practices. As in that key statement in the Covenant regarding mandates, by the time World War II ended, the question was no longer whether colonial peoples should ultimately become independent, but when. Of course, indigenous colonial elites and advocates of "liberation" immediately grabbed on to the concept of self-determination and used it to justify their claims for ultimate independence. The Europeans used it to foment resistance against Nazi occupation. The Atlantic Charter endorsed the right of all peoples "to choose the form of government under which they will live." The word was everywhere and leaders like Franklin Roosevelt (much to Churchill's displeasure) insisted it was universal. The British Left adopted it as a major source of their attack on imperial policy during and after the war. As a headline of the *Daily Herald* observed after an interview with Clement Atlee, the leader of the Labour Party: *"The Atlantic Charter*: IT MEANS DARK RACES AS WELL" (quoted in Louis, 1984: 205).

Developments in scholarly work and movements for civil rights undermined "scientific" racist doctrines that had significant popularity in the late nineteenth century. In addition to the obvious contradiction between the liberal claim of civil rights and the right of self-determination as *human* rights, and their differential application in the colonies, there were also the visibly horrendous consequences of racist policies taken to their extreme: the vast exterminations of Hitler's regime prior to and during World War II. The Nazi leader's racial policies effectively destroyed social Darwinism and a whole school of anthropological thought that had claimed that racial differences justify the rule of superiors over inferiors (cf., Crawford, 2002: 306–9).

Economic and financial constraints

World War II devastated the economies of the major colonial countries. At the same time that they faced immense reconstruction costs, public demands for extending welfare state provisions and full employment were escalating. The Cold War was underway by 1948 and those same governments also confronted increasing needs for defense spending. Armed rebellions and nascent wars of "national liberation" began in Indochina and Algeria, adding to the economic burdens of colonial governments. In such circumstances, the costs of maintaining overseas holdings began to outweigh any benefits, including those of status and prestige. By the late 1950s only Portugal held out in insisting that it would maintain the integrity of its colonial empire at any cost. The British had opted for independence on a case-by-case basis (starting with India in 1947), followed by the Dutch who, under immense international pressure, gave way in Indonesia. Military defeat in Indochina (1954) compelled the French to abandon their holdings in Southeast Asia, and the protracted war in Algeria that cost more than a million lives and billions of French francs helped persuade Charles de Gaulle to grant independence to a territory that had been considered an integral part of France. The financial burdens of colonialism had proved too great for many, and could not be carried while other priorities increasingly took precedence. The inability of the Western powers to prevail militarily in wars of "national liberation" symbolized the lack of will to hang on to colonial holdings at an acceptable cost.

De-colonization was thus a complicated process involving a mixture of colonial demands and rebellions, and strategic and domestic political changes, all in the context of World War II and its aftermath. The revolutionary changes in ideas provide an important part of the story. They outline the ways that notions of legitimate rule changed in less than seventy years: how paternalism changed from the notion of a "sacred trust" to civilize the barbarians to one where economic development and the eradication of poverty took precedence; how the notions of self-government and self-determination became universalized and how they came to be seen as rights coupled to human rights; and how after 1945 the right to sovereign statehood trumped the old liberal notions of *learning* the arts of democratic self-government and the rule of law through colonial tutelage. These changes in the normative elements of the colonial institution are largely accounted for by the results of the great wars of the twentieth century, by the increasing influence of the United States and the Soviet Union over the colonial agenda, by the appropriation of liberal discourses on self-government and self-determination by indigenous elites, by armed resistance in some cases, and by the financial constraints facing colonial governments after World War II. All of these elements reinforced each other and built momentum in the late 1940s. The result was the greatest explosion of state creation in world history. Within two decades, between 1955 and 1975, more than one hundred former colonies and dependencies became sovereign states. This was the major legacy of the obsolescence of the colonial institution.

By the late 1880s, colonialism had become one of the important institutions of the European-centered states system. It had all the hallmarks of an international institution: patterned practices, various norms (including legal norms and constitutions) that helped regulate behavior and provide predictability, and a broad set of ideas and beliefs about the bases of relations between superiors and inferiors and the various duties "civilized" states had to reduce the gap between them. But unlike sovereignty, territoriality, or diplomacy, colonialism has become obsolete. Immense power and economic differences remain between many former colonies and the main industrial countries, but there is no remaining *legal* system of domination of one over the other. The former colonies have attained sovereignty, which means legal equality. No industrial country has the *right* to command, and no former colony has the *duty* to obey. Whatever the power differences between former colonies and the metropoles, they are worked out by negotiations and bargaining, through regular diplomatic channels, and by agents who are responsible solely to their own citizens. Colonialism is our single example of institutional obsolescence. It ranks as one of the most important processes in international politics during the twentieth century, with consequences that are in many ways more significant than those of globalization or the declining significance of territoriality. Among those consequences is the pattern of war since 1945.

9   War

War has been a common form of interaction between independent polities since they first arose in the mists of history. There is evidence of organized warfare more than 10,000 years ago in the ruins of Jericho. The recorded history of the great early empires, including Assyria, Egypt, Chou China, Mongolia, and Persia is in large part a chronicle of organized violence. As Quincy Wright (1965) notes, the polities of the Mediterranean basin and Europe between 700 BC and the mid-seventeenth century AD sustained themselves in large part through subduing neighbors, defending themselves against "barbarians," and protecting their trade routes through armed conquests and more defensive measures. Where they failed in these tasks, they often collapsed or were conquered by their competitors. The polities of China during the "Warring States" period (403–221 BC) were similarly "fighting states" constantly faced with security dilemmas and the backdrop of war in their daily lives. As one illustration, Duke Huan of the state of Ch'in went to war twenty-eight times in a reign lasting forty-three years (Li, 1965: 50). Although punctuated by short periods of peace, the Chinese polities during the "Warring States" period and the Greek city-states between 492 and 404 BC were in almost constant multilateral wars. Bilateral armed contests of some kind were taking place within these domains on an annual basis. The pattern appears again during the Roman conquests, the great armed battles between the Europeans and Saracens for control of the northern Mediterranean littoral, and the Mongol conquests of the twelfth to fourteenth century.

In the Mongol invasions of central Asia, Persia, and Eastern Europe in the twelfth to fourteenth century, many of the Roman campaigns, the actions of the Spanish conquistadors in Mexico and Peru, American wars against the Pequots and Seminoles in the seventeenth to nineteenth century, and some of the European colonial wars, unrestricted mass killing was the order of the day. The victims were commonly portrayed as "beyond the pale," and treated as sub-humans. War was not an armed contest between organized polities searching for a way to reconcile their conflicting interests, each granting the other legitimacy and legal equality, but campaigns of conquest, genocide, and theft between the "chosen" people and inferiors. War was not an institution including elements of restraint and discipline, but a death machine designed to eradicate inferiors and to grab their possessions, including land, women, slaves, and treasures.

Yet in many societies there were elements of institutionalization long before the Treaty of Westphalia. In some areas and eras, we note the development of articulated theories or ideas of warfare, regularized procedures for engaging in it, a great deal of "international" imitation, and norms, rules, and etiquette to constrain it. Several examples illustrate the point.

In the case of the Chinese polities prior to the "Warring States" period (when all constraints collapsed), wars were suffused with ceremony, rank distinctions, rules regulating the treatment of prisoners, and normative symbolism associated with the termination of hostilities. The Greeks also developed rules of warfare and often gave sacramental qualities to peace treaties. They copied each other's forms of military organization, strategies, and tactics and developed some primitive norms similar to later European notions of *jus ad bello*. They eventually came to see war as an enterprise requiring some form of normative justification.

The Thirty Years War (1618–48) shared few of these characteristics. It was fought throughout central Europe with a ferocity and destructiveness not to be seen again in Europe until World War II. According to some estimates, the population of the Germanys (as it was then called) declined from 13 million to 4 million as a result of the fighting, pillage, marauding, raping, and looting, and the diseases that were their residues. Of some 35,000 villages in Bohemia, only 6,000 were left standing by 1648. Michael Howard (1976: 37) describes the essential characteristics of the soldier's lot:

> A soldier . . . was well described as a man who had to die so as to have something to live on. His condition was no better than that of the peasants he tormented. Armies were in a continued state of deliquescence, melting way from death, wounds, sickness, straggling, and

desertion, their movements governed not by strategic calculation but by the search for unplundered territory . . . [War] degenerated . . . into universal, anarchic, and self-perpetuating violence.

The dilemmas of governments of the time were less cruel perhaps, but also more challenging from a collective point of view. Some of the generals became "loose cannons," who developed their own private purposes and escaped government control. The French had to disengage from the German theater because the costs of the war outstripped government revenues. The only way to continue combat was to increase the plunder of the peasantry for taxes, but this tactic led to frequent peasant rebellions. In brief, the Thirty Years War challenged the authority of the state. The assaults came both from the field and on the home front. The Thirty Years War was thus a powerful learning experience for the monarchs of the day whose main task was to close the gap between their protestations of sovereignty and the actual flimsy controls they had in their territories. While it has become fashionable to accept the quip (Tilly, 1990: 32) that "states make war and wars make states," in fact the Thirty Years War was a major threat to the continued existence of the state. It is no accident that a highly organized and effective rebellion against the rule of Louis XIV and his centralization of the French state (the *fronde*) took place just a few years after the end of that war.

Institutionalizing war in eighteenth-century Europe

The organization of military strength in the aspiring monarchies after the end of the Thirty Years War reflected the lessons learned from that great tragedy. Led by Louis XIV, Charles XII in Sweden, and the Great Elector Frederick William in Prussia, the monarchs set about centralizing and gaining full political control over their military forces. Their main idea was to create a full-time, professional, well-trained armed force that would do the king's bidding to serve state interests.

Ideas

Karl von Clausewitz, an important figure in the service of the Prussian king during the Napoleonic wars, produced in systematic form the main ideas that had underlain the conduct of war in the eighteenth and early nineteenth centuries. In some ways he was an intellectual innovator, but in others he reflected the common assumptions and military practices of the day. He had a very concise and clear image of war – an ideal vision of what war should be – as well as a keen appreciation for the difficulties of reconciling actual combat conditions with that image. His discussion of war during the Napoleonic era highlighted the increasing ferocity and destructiveness of war in that period compared with the typical wars of mid-eighteenth-century Europe. Michael Howard (1979: 3) offers a concise definition of the typical eighteenth-century image of war:

> The prime characteristic of the military is not that they use violence, or even that they use violence legitimized by virtue of their function as instruments of the state. It is that they use that violence with great *deliberation*. Such violence, purposeful, deliberate, and legitimized is normally known as *force*, and the use of *force* between states is what we mean by war. War consists of such deliberate, controlled, and purposeful acts of force combined and harmonized to attain what are ultimately political objectives.

In Clausewitz's famous dictum, "war is the continuation of politics by other means." Force is *an instrument of statecraft*. It is to be used primarily in conjunction with diplomacy and other instruments, and usually only as a last resort when other techniques fail. *Politics,* sometimes called diplomacy, is the normal relationship between states that are legal equals. But sometimes politics fail or are inadequate, in which case force may have to be used. It is thus a continuation of politics, not a substitute for it. Diplomacy continues during war, and force or its threats may have to be used in diplomacy. Diplomacy and force are thus not opposites but mutually reinforcing techniques of influence to be used by states for political purposes. Politics drives the use of force, whereas during the Thirty Years War, the equation was often reversed, with disastrous consequences for all parties.

This Clausewitzian definition of eighteenth-century war remains very much in the popular imagination although it is more than two hundred years old. Our image of war still features highly trained armed forces under the control of governments, arrayed in campaigns against each other, terminating with cease-fires and peace treaties that ultimately lead to new relationships devoid of violence. This image is largely inconsistent with the facts on the ground in many contemporary wars (see below), but continues to underlie military planning and the allocation of resources for armed forces in many parts of the world.

This conception of war spread throughout Europe in the late seventeenth and early eighteenth century and became the intellectual foundation for all aspects of military life: recruitment, training, funding, strategy, tactics, political control, weapons development, the conduct of campaigns, peace treaties, and etiquette. It bore the stamp of Enlightenment thought about the need for balance, proportion, and rational control in social relations and politics. It was an inherently conservative view of war because it assumed the legitimacy of states, their legal equality, their right to exist, and the unofficial code of honor that existed within and between Europe's nobles.[1] In the eighteenth-century idea of war, military instruction trains soldiers to kill, but it also teaches restraint and discipline (Ignatieff, 1998: 117, 157). It instructs the rulers to keep their political aims limited, an injunction that to Clausewitz's critical mind, Napoleon did not observe.

Patterned practices

It does not matter which of the fifty-eight intra-European wars between 1648 and 1791 we examine, but they share many common characteristics. In this sense, war was a patterned activity. This should not be surprising because the European monarchs shamelessly copied each other's military innovations, strategies, tactics, and weaponry. Perhaps the most important indicator of institutionalization was the development of the military academy, schools of instruction in the arts and science of warfare. First in Peter the Great's Russia, but soon copied throughout the continent, these organizations reflected the Clausewitzian idea of war and its associated ethos of professionalism and restraint. The military was now a full-time career requiring long hours of study and repeated practice and preparation. During the Thirty Years War, many of the commanders were low nobles who had no specific military training but led by virtue of their social position. Others were military entrepreneurs whose commands were virtual fiefs. Senior generals considered themselves as partners of the state in joint enterprises, not as subordinates to the state. These military entrepreneurs frequently had their own agendas and effectively resisted state authority (Duffy, 1987: 15). In the professional army of the eighteenth century, in contrast, command was based

---

[1] As they did in many other cultures. The notion of "warrior's honor" is seen throughout history in diverse locations. In Japan, for example, it was the "boshido," both a code of conduct and an ethic of responsibility.

on merit irrespective of birth, and the generals and marshals were clearly designated as servants of the state, commanding a rigid hierarchy under the clear political control of the monarch.

Throughout Europe, military thought and strategic planning also were seen as a *science*, that is, as an intellectual discipline that could be learned through rigorous analysis and mastering principles of physics and engineering. The rise of military academies and military journals accentuated the importance of theory and helped standardize strategy, tactics, and weaponry throughout the continent. Mimicry and copying assured patterned behavior both on the field of battle and in the barracks. In the latter, a large part of military life was concerned with the creation and maintenance of the distinct identity of soldiers through uniforms, ranks, insignias, and even personal appearance. Duffy (1987: 48) describes that life as conducted – and copied throughout Europe – by the Prussian cadet school: "[T]he first waking hour of every day was spent in fastening back and plastering down the hair with wax and talc; the next half hour was devoted to buttoning up the gaiters with a special hook, after which attention turned back to the hair, which was dusted heavily with powder."

The conduct of war was also highly patterned. It typically began with matched mobilizations, a formal declaration of war, seasonal campaigns, and battles. The battles were orchestrated with a standard repertoire of actions and little room for individual initiative among the front-line troops. Envelopment, guile in the distribution and location of forces, and quick wheeling movements were as important as firepower. The purpose of combat was to force the opponent to surrender. That could be achieved by entrapment or even superior tactical position; it did not require the physical annihilation of the enemy. Victory came from maneuver, not from maximizing body counts.[2] Battles and sieges were followed by formal surrenders, after which the parties returned to the negotiating tables to work out a peace treaty. It is important to emphasize that in the eighteenth and nineteenth centuries, all of the parties to the armed conflict negotiated its end, thereby reinforcing the notion of legal equality and the doctrine of sovereignty. This common practice stands in stark contrast to the usual fate of defeated polities in the pre-industrial era, where cities were commonly sacked, their inhabitants killed, their treasures stolen, and the public buildings and private habitations razed to the ground.

---

[2] In colonial-type wars, matters were different.

Norms, rules, and etiquette

The strongest evidence of institutionalization comes from the norms, rules, and etiquette that were associated with eighteenth- and nineteenth-century wars in Europe. The main norms derived from fundamental intellectual distinctions that underlay the ideas of war and the strategies and tactics that were employed to prosecute them. The first was the distinction between combatants and civilians. In the Clausewitzian concept of war, force is an activity between designated combatants who are identified by distinctive uniforms and professional standing. War is an affair between warriors. Civilians are outside its ambit. According to Frederick the Great, the ideal war is one in which ordinary citizens are not even aware of its existence. The subjects of the crown must of course pay for the wars, but otherwise they should conduct their lives according to the normal routines which means that trade, commerce, and travel involving the subjects of warring princes should continue as usual. Most importantly, civilians are not to be targets of military action.

The second distinction was between combatants and neutrals. The laws of war as they developed in the eighteenth century clearly specified the rights and duties of those parties who had not declared war. They could trade with all belligerents, but not in *matériel*. They could continue to have diplomatic relations with both sides, but they could not allow their territory to be used for military purposes by one side or the other.

The third distinction was between the government and the military. The state commands, the military obey. This way, the political/diplomatic purposes of the state predominate and the military commanders cannot develop their own political agendas.

Finally there was the distinction between peace and war. The declaration of war launches a new *legal* domain in which rules peculiar to warfare supplement or in some cases supplant the laws of civil society as they exist in a state of peace. This means new or different rights and responsibilities for combatants, their governments, and civilians.

All of these distinctions incorporated norms about the limits of human behavior in war. They assigned specific roles, responsibilities, status, and rights to the main actors involved in war. They defined both the permissible and at least implicitly, the impermissible. War is then no longer a random, anarchic activity, but a highly regulated domain with a normative core.

The rules of warfare developed in the eighteenth century and elaborated in much greater detail in the second half of the nineteenth century dealt with matters such as the treatment of prisoners, the circumstances under which a commanding officer in a besieged town or city could surrender with honor, the numerous rules of the road and signaling devices of naval squadrons, the prohibition against shooting messengers, bearing arms secretly, and sacking towns (unless commanding officers refused to surrender). By the late nineteenth century, the laws and regulations of war in most countries filled several volumes. Indeed, it was one of the most fully elaborated areas of international law.

Etiquette was not so precise, but it gave a certain aura to warfare that anyone today would envy. For example, captured officers were generally treated with respect and courtesy and could be ransomed to return to their homes. Not infrequently, officers of the opposing armies would gather together for social occasions both before and after battle. Sometimes front-line troops did the same. Fraternizing between enemies reflected the ethos that war was a business between states – a professional job – and not between peoples. Surrender ceremonies were lavish and filled with the symbolism of equality, respect, and honor. The purpose of victory was achieving a known political goal, not punishment or humiliation. After these ceremonies, with the troops and their commanders disarmed, the defeated side could go home. They did not face incarceration, torture, slavery, or liquidation.

The etiquette of eighteenth-century war reflected the older "cult of honor" that imbued the military profession and the code of chivalry of the nobility. That cult was an important constraint on the ferocity of war, because it justified resistance against brutal actions, even when ordered by superiors. The constraint is nicely summarized in the 1753 *Dienst-Regelment* of the Saxon military: "The point of honor commands us to prefer duty to life, and honor to duty. The point of honor forbids kinds of behavior which are permitted or even encouraged by the law, just as it allows certain conduct which is legally forbidden" (quoted in Duffy, 1987: 79). Honor precedes all other justifications for actions, including patriotism, ideology, and religion. Honorable officers do not massacre civilians, torture prisoners, rape women, or indulge in ethnic cleansing . . . all hallmarks of many contemporary wars.

Were actions and practices mostly consistent with this characterization of the institution of war in the eighteenth and nineteenth centuries, and particularly with the norms, rules, and etiquette described above? No systematic studies have posed this particular question, but the historical narratives and analyses of war available suggest that there was a reasonable fit between practices, and norms and etiquette. Certainly there were numerous instances of pillage, burning, and destruction of property – particularly in towns or cities that refused to surrender when besieged. Because of poorly developed logistics, armies often had to live off the land on which they camped. They extracted their food from the local peasantry and refusal to cooperate could lead to executions and forced extractions. Plundering was not a rare event, particularly when leadership was weak. However, self-interest dictated prudence, for if the soldiers plundered too much or ruined the peasants' fields, they could not rely on provisions in later campaigns (Duffy, 1987: 13). In any event, compared with the atrocities of the Thirty Years War and with many wars of the twentieth and twenty-first centuries, the typical war of the eighteenth century was a model of decorum, self-restraint, and rule-observance. Etiquette and the cult of honor were not just romantic fictions, but effective constraints on actions.

Overall, we can conclude that war achieved a high degree of institutionalization in this era. It was an activity based on clear ideas about the appropriate role – and limits – of force in diplomatic relations. Numerous practices, organizational characteristics, training, and strategy became standardized across Europe, and hence patterned. The norms and rules of warfare were clearly specified in treaties, codes, war manuals, training routines, and public expectations. Napoleon's wars, in which systematic plunder, annihilation of adversary armies, and organized brutalities (particularly in the Spanish campaign) took place, provided a hint of what was to come in the twentieth century. As that century progressed, war became increasingly de-institutionalized.

The de-institutionalization of war

If one studied war solely from the documents that addressed this as an issue of international relations, one might gain the impression that there has been a steady progression toward more humane conduct of war. For during the twentieth century both aspects of war – *jus ad bello* and *jus in bello* – have undergone significant changes. In the first instance, as we discussed in chapter 4, war has been de-legitimized as an instrument of policy except in the case of self-defense or in fulfillment of Security Council obligations. War is no longer a sovereign prerogative in theory, but must find some justification either from the necessities of self-defense or from a warrant of the international community as expressed in Security Council resolutions. In terms of the laws of war (the conduct of war), the volume of regulations on the use of force has grown exponentially. Some of the eighteenth-century rules regarding neutrality still obtain. Major signposts since then include the 1863 United States General Order No. 100 (the Lieber Code), the 1864 Geneva Convention for the protection of the sick and wounded, the 1868 St. Petersburg Convention prohibiting the use of certain kinds of missiles (and also reiterating the Clausewitzian notion that the "only legitimate object which States should endeavor to accomplish during war is to weaken the military forces of the enemy"), the 1899 and 1907 Hague Conventions, the 1922 Hague Aerial Bombardment Rules, and the 1949 and 1977 Geneva Protocols. Humanitarian law has also developed to prohibit a wide range of practices such as rape and pillage.

In the twentieth century's great wars there was almost a perfect inverse correlation between the volume and scope of the *jus in bello* and the actual conduct of operations. The greater the degree of legal institutionalization, the greater the violations of the norms and rules of war. The trend continues in the present century, with the evidence of de-institutionalization even more pronounced. We can examine the problem from a variety of perspectives, but let us do so by comparing typical military behavior in the twentieth century and today with the norms and rules that were implied in the Clausewitzian idea of war and as they were enunciated in the eighteenth century. The critical distinctions outlined above can serve as our point of reference. They also form the core of the contemporary laws of war and humanitarian law.

The first distinction is between combatants and civilians. Statistics tell the tale how this distinction was obliterated in military practice during the past century. In World War I, civilians suffered approximately 5 percent of the casualties. U-boats attacked neutral passenger liners. Flimsy airplanes dropped small bombs on towns. German troops, according to Allied propaganda, shot and raped innocent civilians during their march through Belgium in 1914. In World War II, the figure for civilian casualties rose to 50 percent. In the eighteenth century, the French philosopher Jean Jacques Rousseau, very much reflecting a Clausewitz-type image of war, declared that in war, "one kills in order to win; no man is so ferocious that he tries to win in order to kill." Unhappily for humanity, World War II turned Rousseau (and Clausewitz) upside down. Adolf Hitler launched the Wehrmacht against his eastern neighbors primarily so that they could prepare the ground for the ethnic cleansing, enslaving, and massacring of local populations. He created bureaucratic organizations both within and outside the armed forces whose main task was to kill Jews, Gypsies, prisoners of war (about 3 million Soviet victims), and other "undesirables," including intellectuals and church authorities. Military force for Hitler was a necessary prelude to his larger program of genocide. In actual operations, his forces deliberately targeted civilian populations as a means of terrorizing them. The Allies soon copied and unleashed great firebomb raids against Hamburg, Dresden, and Tokyo that killed far more civilians than the two atomic weapons dropped on Hiroshima and Nagasaki. All sides in the war violated regulations about dealing with sick and wounded prisoners, and in the case of the Japanese and Germans, they did so systematically.

Since 1945, the figure for civilian casualties has risen to almost 90 percent. The wars in the Sudan, Sri Lanka, Nigeria, Nagorno-Karabakh, Myanmar, Colombia, Rwanda, Sierra Leone, Liberia, Bosnia, Kosovo, and many other places have had as their most conspicuous feature the deliberate targeting of civilian populations, including women and children. The main strategic purpose in these wars is to terrify the population so it will flee to safer surroundings, thus allowing the "troops" to plunder and kill, or to destroy the legitimacy of incumbent governments that cannot offer adequate protection. In many cases, it is governments themselves that undertake wars against their own populations. The telling statistic here is that since 1945 far more people have died at the hands of their own government than at those of the armed forces of foreign enemies. In these wars, there is no distinction between civilians and warriors. In many of them "militias" that go around looting, raping, and killing are made up not of trained soldiers but of criminal elements, frequently convicts who have escaped jails.

Symbolic of the decline of institutionalization is the lack of distinctive uniforms and standard issue that historically served as the visual markers between armed forces and civilians. In World War II, armies were still visibly distinct, hierarchically organized, and centrally controlled. Today, rag-tag militias may wear something akin to "fatigues," but often they are not dressed in a manner to distinguish them from the local population. The practice of impressing children into service makes the distinction even hazier.

The second distinction between combatants and neutrals has also faded. Combatants use foreign territories and their populations for raising funds, conducting illegal trade in diamonds, timber, oil, and other valuable commodities, and safe havens. Friendly regimes likewise provide various forms of support for guerrilla and other types of armed movements in neighboring states. The laws of neutrality were frequently violated during World War II, as those who declared themselves neutrals nevertheless conducted trade in strategic goods with belligerents on one or both sides. Indeed, since almost any good can have potential military application (toothpaste aids soldier morale, for example), the old laws of neutrality have little meaning today.

The distinction between state authority and military obedience has similarly declined. Many contemporary military units – and that stretches the term – operate virtually as private enterprises under little or no central control. Or they are local warlords who may pay symbolic homage and sometimes taxes and other forms of symbolic supplication to legal authorities but who basically operate on their own. In the Bosnian conflict of the 1990s, for example, more than eighty private militias (Bojicic and Kaldor, 1997: 159) conducted armed operations, sometimes with the guidance of central authority, but often without it. These militias usually trained their guns against civilians rather than against the adversary's military forces that were in the field. Military hierarchy, discipline, and central control are increasingly diluted, to be replaced by locally organized, undisciplined groups.

These private enterprise armed units help erase the line between war and criminality. Since most do not have government funding, they engage in a variety of illegal enterprises such as drug and gun running, forced labor and prostitution, extortion, and the sale of plundered natural resources to foreign companies. Many also thieve from international relief operations. In the case of the IRA in Ireland and the various factions in Palestine, some elements direct terrorist operations on their own initiative and efforts by governments or dissident leaders to control them are mostly ineffective. Most telling of the de-institutionalization of war is the increasing use of children as soldiers. They are mobilized both voluntarily by the offer of security and loot, and by coercion through kidnapping. They undergo little training, wear no uniforms, and have no idea of political purpose. Their main source of income is through extortion and looting.

Finally, in many contemporary wars the distinction between peace and war is vague and when it does appear, it seldom holds for long. One of the characteristics of these wars is their duration. On average, wars since 1945 have lasted more than 25 years, which is a significant contrast to the average 2.5 years of European wars prior to 1945 (Holsti, 1996:

ch. 2). The parties to these military operations no longer "declare" war; they just begin with different types of incidents aimed at undermining the morale of the adversary and/or the civilian population. Sometimes these wars just peter out, or more likely, they may go underground for a while, only to reappear later. A high proportion of the cease-fires and peace treaties that terminate some of them are systematically violated within months, and about 40 percent collapse entirely within five years (Heraclides, 1997; Wallensteen and Sollenberg, 1997; Licklider, 1998).

The evidence of de-institutionalization based on the erasure of critical distinctions in Clausewitzian war is commanding. We can state this in another way, by examining the three criteria of institutions: patterned actions, ideas, and norms, rules, and etiquette.

Most wars since 1945 have displayed few characteristics associated with patterned social action. Wars have broken out almost randomly, although a high proportion have occurred in new states, all legatees of a colonial history. Their strategy and tactics follow few rules and resemble opportunism of an extreme kind. The fortunes of war ebb and flow, with armed actions sometimes disappearing for protracted periods of time, only to reappear later. Political goals may be stated by leadership, but they tend to wash away over time as the *raison d'être* of action becomes more commercial and criminal. In some cases, victory is not sought because it would mean an end to a way of life that pays psychic and economic rewards. Peace is thus elusive; the sects, factions, warlords, and militias do not see it as an appealing state of affairs compared with the advantages gained through military and terrorist actions. The goal of war is not a new political/legal/social plan for a society or community, but the status and economic gains that can be achieved through perpetual violence. In these wars violence pays compared with the alternatives. There is thus a randomness to many contemporary wars that was not characteristic of the eighteenth-century version.

Ideas play little or no role in these wars. No Clausewitz or Mao Tse-tung of "wars of national debilitation" (Gelb, 1994) has yet appeared. The communist theories of revolutionary war informed the strategy and tactics of the Viet Cong and North Vietnamese army during the Vietnam War, but have played little role in violent conflicts since the 1970s. There may be vague notions of *jihad* or holy war against poorly defined enemies, but those are used primarily to mobilize sentiments rather than to craft strategic or tactical principles. Many post-1945 armed conflicts, and most of those of the 1990s, have been hit-and-miss affairs based on opportunism and in-the-field innovation. Their historical ancestor is the Hundred Years War (1337–1453) which Fernand Braudel (1988: 159–60) has described as

> nothing like modern conflicts . . . It would be more appropriate to call it a "hundred years of hostilities." . . . The battles – sociological and anarchical as much as political – were intermittent, punctuated by truces and negotiations. On average, there was perhaps one year of actual fighting in five. But the countryside was laid waste, either by pillaging troops, who invariably lived off the land, or by scorched earth tactics.

Braudel was wrong: many modern wars resemble the Hundred Years War more than the wars of the eighteenth century.

In addition to the atrocities, lack of clear political purposes, and failure to distinguish between civilians and combatants, the resemblance of many modern wars to the Hundred Years War is seen in the reappearance of mercenaries. There have always been soldiers of fortune, and though they have been disavowed in various international treaties, they have never disappeared. In the 1960s and 1970s characters such as "Mad Mike" Hoare, Bob Denard, and "Black Jack" Schramme, followed by their troops of ex-soldiers, war junkies, and criminals, rampaged through the Congo plundering and organizing attempted *coups d'état*. But these are primarily figures of the past. Today, mercenaries are organized into modern corporations that have "more in common with a Wall Street banker than 'Mad Mike'" (Bruce, 2002). Private military companies have as their clients primarily the governments of weak states whose own military resources either are so poor as to be ineffective, or are under no effective government control. In some cases, these companies are hired precisely to prevent government troops from plundering and molesting the citizens of their own country. In other instances, they serve their clients by protecting the major sources of government revenue – oil fields, mines, and timber resources – from various predators, including armed rebels. Employees for these companies are predominantly ex-military from Great Britain, the United States, South Africa, and Israel. All are highly trained, and in addition to organizing protective services for their clients, they provide advice, training, logistical support, and de-mining tasks, and in some cases, they engage in combat operations (Cook, 2002: 2). The reappearance of mercenaries, while helping us recall the role of the *condottiere* in fifteenth-century Europe, is an important symptom of the nature of armed conflict in many regions of the world today. They are just one of several responses to the de-institutionalization of war, an attempt to provide protection where mayhem, crime, and predation are the main characteristics of armed combat.

The distinctions between Clausewitzian-type wars and many current armed conflicts in terms of tactics and strategies are also clear. In the eighteenth century military action was a highly choreographed spectacle, with rigorous rules of engagement, formation, marching, wheeling, confronting the enemy, and surrender. In contrast, terror, guile, stealth, deception, and anonymity today characterize armed operations. As the St. Petersburg Declaration of 1868 made clear, the sole legitimate purpose of armed conflict in the older wars was to weaken the military forces of the adversary. Today, the main purposes include terror against civilians, ethnic cleansing, pillage, theft, reprisals, and rape. All of them are prohibited or proscribed in the laws of war and in humanitarian law, but all such laws are systematically violated in combat and terror operations. We thus see almost perfect inconsistency between law, norms, rules, and etiquette on the one hand, and actual behavior on the other.

War and terrorism

Many of the wars of national "debilitation" have vague political purposes – mainly obtaining and sustaining power – in addition to the more crass motivations of private wealth, personal status, access to resources and women, and the like. These wars, though often verging on criminality, nevertheless have some characteristics that enable us to term them "wars." In the case of terrorism, most is without known political purposes. It is thus the antithesis of the Clausewitzian concept of war. The main purposes of terrorism seem to be to inflict maximum damage on innocent populations as an avenue for expressing revenge or hatred. The purposes of traditional wars – territory, control of governments, access to resources and strategic assets, establishing and holding on to colonies, and the like – are generally known. In the case of terrorism, there are no demands, no objectives, and nothing that can be negotiated. Violence is thus not an extension of politics, a course of action entered upon when negotiations fail, but an end in itself. In these circumstances, the traditional principles of strategy are essentially irrelevant. Doctrines of deterrence, assured mutual destruction, *blitzkreig*, or defense do not address the problems posed by terrorists. Those are better, though not exclusively handled by police and intelligence work. Military operations may be important, but incidental. Under the circumstances, the use of the word "war" is an arbitrary one. Terrorism contains few of the elements of classical war, and perhaps best symbolizes the de-institutionalized form of contemporary violence.

Explaining de-institutionalization

The usual suspects that help explain the change from Clausewitzian-type wars to the "total" wars of 1914 and 1939 are technology and ideology/nationalism. The marriage of science and technology to war not only created a vast array of new types of killing devices, but opened up two entirely new domains for operations: in the air and under the sea. Long-range artillery and air power rendered walled towns and border fortifications obsolete. Aerial bombing took the "lid" off the state and opened the entire society to destructive attacks. The increasing destructive power of munitions has grown exponentially over the past three hundred years. At the time of the Thirty Years War one cannon could potentially kill about two dozen adversary soldiers or civilians if they were concentrated. In World War II, Nazi and Allied bombing of cities typically killed between 10,000 and 80,000 civilians. Today, one thermonuclear bomb could destroy more than 10 million people in a large city.

Of course such weapons of mass destruction are not necessary to create large body counts. In the month-long genocide in Rwanda in 1994, organized gangs and larger mobs managed to kill close to 800,000 Tutsis and their friends with small arms, machetes, spears, and bludgeons. The weapons of choice for terrorists in most modern wars include small arms and the various forms of explosives that can be used to fashion bombs aimed at civilians. In brief, massive killing can be achieved without the benefits of complex technological weapons. So, technology is only part of the explanation for the de-institutionalization of war.

The second explanation emphasizes human passions. Eighteenth-century wars were fought by professional armed forces to defend or extend state or royal interests. The officers of these forces could fraternize between battles because they saw themselves as members of the same professional fraternity doing their jobs, and not as representatives of some hated nation, ideology, or ethnic group. The lack of passion as a source of war could be seen in the types of peace treaties the victors and vanquished negotiated in that era. Most involved the cession or partition of territory, the payment of indemnities, exchanges of colonial holdings, gaining control or ceding strategic territories or fortifications, and the like. The purpose of these treaties was to augment a state's power or strategic position, status, commercial opportunities, and prestige. Punishment had little to do with them. Peace treaties meant little to local inhabitants. Duffy (1987: 12) describes a typical outcome of war in the 1700s:

> The influence of the state did not usually reach far into the lives of individuals. When frontier provinces changed hands at the end of a war, the affair was normally managed with a sedulous regard for established local institutions, so that from being an "Austrian" you could find that you had become a "Sardinian" without noticing any difference in your everyday routine. We are a world removed from the twentieth century, when wars have frequently been fought with the purpose of eliminating the core area of an enemy state and imposing an alien regime and ideology.

The peace settlement of 1919, through the Versailles Treaty, changed all of this. That peace was dictated to the Germans and not negotiated as had been the European practice up to that time. The terms of the treaty were clearly punitive, based on the theory of German war guilt: Germany, it was assumed, began the war for its own aggrandizing purposes, and because of the destruction it had caused, it must pay. In the "settlement," the Allies stripped Germany of its colonies, occupied part of its territory, sank (or grabbed) its navy, reduced its army to 100,000 men, and inflicted ruinous economic reparations. The purpose of war now changed from "weakening" the enemy's forces to punishing the loser by reducing its status to that of a second-rate power.

World War II ended on even harsher terms. Under the doctrine of unconditional surrender, the winners imposed any conditions they wished. The Allies in this case considered the Nazi and Japanese wartime regimes to be "beyond the pale," and hence not worthy of negotiations to end the war. The purposes of that war were not just to weaken the adversary's military strength, but to destroy outlaw regimes representing odious ideologies, to punish the populations that had sustained them, to occupy their lands, and to reconfigure their political, economic, and social institutions in the image of the victors. Except for the Soviet plundering of the eastern part of Germany after 1945, there could be no question of reparations because the German and Japanese societies and economies were largely in ruins.

Mass hatred, then, has driven most wars during the period of de-institutionalization. Urges for destruction, revenge, the physical liquidation or ethnic cleansing of enemy populations, and retribution are all emotions underlying modern wars, whether between states or within states. These sentiments help drive actions that are inconsistent with the rules and norms of war as they have been spelled out in numerous international instruments or national codes.

But this list of passions is incomplete. Most wars since 1945 (and some in Europe before then) have in one way or another also been fought for freedom or national self-determination. The whole edifice of colonialism, as we suggested in the previous chapter, crumbled under the onslaught of liberal ideas of self-government and political independence. A large majority of post-1945 wars involved one political community seeking independence from a larger community. These have been wars of secession and attempted state creation. They started with the American war of independence in the late eighteenth century, followed by similar wars in Latin America and Greece, unsuccessful uprisings in Poland and Hungary in the mid-nineteenth century, and the birth of new nations throughout Central and Eastern Europe following the collapse of the Russian, Austro-Hungarian, and Ottoman empires in 1918–19. They continued with nineteen post-1945 wars of anti-colonial "national liberation" stretching from Algeria, through Israel, Cyprus and Kenya, to Burma and Vietnam, and subsequent secessionist wars in Nigeria, Sri Lanka, Burma, Kashmir, Palestine, Bosnia, and elsewhere. In many of these wars, those fighting for independence or national self-determination had only weak military resources and hence had to rely on improvisation, terror, and unconventional tactics and weapons. They focused on undermining public confidence in established authorities. Virtually all of these contemporary states gained independence through means that we would classify as "terrorist" today. And in a few, major revolutionary theorists such as Mao Tse-tung and Vo Nguyen Giap developed military doctrines that emphasized unconventional tactics that were largely incompatible with the rules and norms of eighteenth- and nineteenth-century warfare. In brief, in wars of independence or secession, those seeking change are weak militarily and find themselves compelled to employ "dirty" tactics and weapons and to propose normative arguments that emphasize ends justifying the means. We saw this form of reasoning in both the American war of independence (when sometimes guerrilla tactics were used to the horror of the English troops) and most recently in the Palestinians' justification for suicide bombing against Israeli targets. In these wars, the strong – the colonial powers or the recognized state – have numerous choices of weapons and strategies to "maintain order," while the weak have few options except terror and killing civilians who might support the regime in power.

Post-colonial economic and other conditions in many of the new states also help account for the de-institutionalization of war. Contemporary or recent wars in the Congo, Sierra Leone, Liberia, Sudan, Somalia, and in Angola have had little to do with national liberation, state creation, anti-colonialism, or ideology. They are primarily wars to gain control of economic resources, labor, and lucrative trade in drugs, small arms, and other prohibited goods. Only in the sense that the adversaries employ organized force can these be termed wars. Their motivations and rewards more closely resemble organized crime, and criminals have little knowledge of or interest in such niceties as the laws of war (cf., Bojicic and Kaldor, 1997; De Waal, 1997; Duyvesteyn, 2000; Mueller, 2001).

No doubt other forms of explanation for the de-institutionalization of war can be relevant. For example, we continue to live in an age of ideologies, religious and secular, in contrast to the eighteenth century. The Thirty Years War was characterized by mayhem, murder, pillage, and any number of forms of atrocity because it was in part a war between Catholic and Protestant sectarians. Religion was the most important issue that started and escalated the war. Once those issues were largely resolved in the Westphalia treaties, religion significantly declined as a source of war between states (cf., Holsti, 1991: chs. 2–4). Secular and religious ideologies underlay the brutal character of wars in Vietnam and Afghanistan in the 1970s and 1980s, and continue to plague relationships in the Middle East and elsewhere today. Wars between "true believers" of whatever kind tend to be long, nasty, and brutish. The laws of war, in contrast, reflect eras of ideological homogeneity (the eighteenth and a large part of the nineteenth century), military professionalism, and increasing humanitarian sentiment. In an era such as ours when adversaries are normally demonized by the national media, the purposes of war tend to inflate to include maximizing body counts, whether of civilians or soldiers.

Fear is also a foundation of atrocity and wars involving ethnic cleansing and extermination. In recent years a number of "failed states" have been the arena of major humanitarian catastrophes. Peace within societies is maintained by both the exercise of state authority and the legitimacy of governments. When state authority collapses, security becomes a rare commodity. The condition of mass insecurity under certain conditions, including "incidents" when civilians become victims, can spiral into intercommunal killing. If one cannot trust one's neighbor of a different ethnicity or religion, then the best tactic for assuring one's own survival may be to kill that neighbor before he or she kills you. Lack of security and collapses of state authority are powerful motives for launching atrocities (cf., Ignatieff, 1998). These conditions are prevalent in several of the newer states in the world today but they are not unique to them. The bloody war in Bosnia (1993–5) was the scene of grass-roots killing deriving from the lack of state authority, as well as from more conventional operations.

"Smart" munitions and the re-institutionalization of war?

While most armed conflicts in the world today share more similarities with medieval than with eighteenth- and nineteenth-century European wars, there is another notable trend. It goes under the name of the "revolution in military affairs," or RMA. It refers to the application of the most modern technologies, particularly information technology, nanotechnology, and precision guidance technology, to warfare. The purpose is to reduce the "fog" and "friction" of war, providing commanders with nearly perfect "situational awareness." It is also to sanitize war, that is, to direct firepower exclusively at military targets and to avoid civilians. It represents a return to eighteenth- and nineteenth-century concepts of targeting, and equally important, to a Clausewitzian notion of the use of force for known political purposes. Once those are achieved, or won, the war terminates. This was the pattern in the 1991 Gulf War, the 1999 war in Kosovo, the anti-terrorist coalition operations in Afghanistan in 2001–2, and the American-led coalition attack on Iraq in 2003. The RMA is also consistent with the classical principles of proportionality and discrimination in the laws of war, and thus suggests a return to more traditional conceptions of war. I will not go into the arcane areas of information or cyber war, terrorism, and other methods the weak can employ against the strong, but only emphasize that developing technology at least holds the potential to return war to a contest between armed forces. This is not a picture without blemishes, of course. In 1991 and 2003, some coalition missiles hit civilian concentrations in Baghdad. In the Kosovo war, bad weather hampered the use of laser-guided munitions. The most modern surveillance systems did not erase uncertainty as they failed to identify the exact locations of Serbian troops and vehicles. The Apache helicopters were vulnerable to surface-to-air missiles. Allied bombs and guided munitions killed more than 500 Yugoslav civilians and destroyed the Chinese embassy in Belgrade. In Afghanistan, approximately 3,000 civilians died from American bombing. This number is higher than the battle casualties suffered by al-Qaeda militants, but most were victims of the inevitable technological failures and human errors of any large man-made venture. It is reasonable to assume that, despite the high probability of human errors and technological failures, one would rather have been a civilian in Baghdad in 1991 or 2003, Belgrade in 1999, or Kabul in 2001 than one in Dresden or Tokyo in 1945 or the Congo, Sudan, or Chechnya today. "Smart" weapons have largely made unnecessary the massive, civilian-destroying carpet bombing of World War II, where on average it took 9,000 bombs to achieve a 90 percent probability of hitting a single target. Now it requires only a single precision-guided bomb or missile.

But low casualty figures in recent conflicts can be misleading. In American and other NATO-member military operations, legal person-nel fully conversant with the laws of war and humanitarian law often play decisive roles in the selection of bombing targets: their role is to ensure that operations are consistent with the norm against deliberately targeting civilians. However, notions of military necessity can trump the norm, and in many cases civilian assets can have military utility (the "dual-use" problem). The "Basic Rule" of Article 48 of the 1977 Geneva Protocol Additional to the Geneva Conventions insists that parties to a conflict must "distinguish between the civilian population and combat-ants and between civilian objects and military objectives and . . . direct their operations only against military objectives." However, in modern standard war the line between civilian and military targets is hardly clear cut. In the Gulf War, for example, the allies bombed water treat-ment plants, food processing plants, irrigation sites, and sewage treat-ment plants (Smith, 2002: 364), all with dire consequences for the civil-ian population. Although the war which saw more explosive ordinance dropped on Iraq than was contained within the atomic bomb dropped on Nagasaki in 1945 killed about 3,000 civilians, the post-war suffering and death caused by bombing essentially civilian targets with *possible* military applications would raise the figure much higher. Overall, the allies did a great deal to avoid or minimize collateral damage, but the selection of targets resulted in a much higher number of deaths, injuries, and long-range illness than those killed outright by explosions. Thomas Smith (2002) concludes that recent high-tech wars, while bringing victory at a much lower cost in civilian lives than in the two great world wars of the twentieth century, are only *seemingly* consistent with the laws of war and humanitarian law. In the actual campaigns the doctrine of military necessity and the concept of dual-use targets assure that there is more of an appearance of legality than is warranted by the facts. The numbers of civilians killed directly in combat operations today may be low by the standards of the twentieth century, but if we include the thousands of post-war victims of chemical poisoning, unsafe water, destroyed power facilities, and the like, the picture is not so clean. On the other hand, that most modern governments include scores of legal experts in their militaries, who inject their judgments into the decision-making processes in the conduct of war, attests to a fairly high degree of institutionalization. The laws of war are known, codified, and regularly applied – sometimes at significant cost to the belligerents – but there is some distance to go before military operations are fully "clean."

The RMA involves primarily a significant change in the accuracy of weapons, their protection, and mobility. No less important is the vastly enhanced capacity to communicate between units, and to "see" the battle environment. Technological innovations greatly enhance the integration of air, land, and naval operations, and introduce an element of stealth previously unknown (cf., Buzan and Herring, 1998: 10–11; David, 2000: 216). Unmanned drones can locate and destroy faraway targets; the accuracy of munitions enables the armed forces in some cases to "decapitate" the command and control headquarters of adversaries, thus destroying their ability to operate in a coordinated fashion . . . in short, their capacity to resist. From the point of view of the laws of war, the technological innovations allow strategy to shift from destruction to neutralization, thus avoiding most targets where civilians would be at risk (David, 2000: 220).

The consequences of the RMA are revealed not only in the relatively low civilian casualties suffered in recent wars involving Western powers, but also in their duration. The 1991 Gulf War lasted about five weeks; the time between the beginning of NATO bombing and surrender in Kosovo was about ten weeks; the war against al-Qaeda and their Taliban supporters in Afghanistan lasted about two months, although small operations in rough mountain terrain continued much longer. The major combat operations against organized Iraqi military forces lasted only three weeks in 2003 before Saddam Hussein's grip on power was eliminated.

The RMA is a matter of considerable debate: will it increase or decrease the likelihood of war? What happens when others inevitably begin to catch up with and imitate American technological innovations? What are the vulnerabilities of high-tech weapons systems, particularly through "cyber war"? Is the RMA relevant to the "wars of national debilitation" that plague Africa and other areas of the world? How can you "decapitate" or "neutralize" armed forces that are not under central command, that live off the land through extortion, pillage, and theft, and that have no distinguishing marks? What about this type of war in the case of terrorist attacks or other new types of threats in the international system (cf., Freedman, 1998–9)? This is not the place to enter the fray. Let us simply reiterate the point that the most modern technology can help to make the actual conduct of war more consistent with the laws of war. It can ameliorate the situation of organized hypocrisy, where the laws of war develop further and pile up on each other, only to be ignored and systematically violated by combatants. It may help restore the ideas and sentiments underlying Rousseau and Clausewitz, where killing has a known political purpose (presumably an ethically justifiable one), and where winning is defined as achieving that ethically justified goal.

Is war an institution?

War was throughout modern European history one of the major forms of interaction between states. It occurred 117 times among the members of the European states system between 1648 and 1941,[3] or one war every 2.5 years. Since that time, wars between recognized states in the system have declined significantly, and in the OECD area, they have disappeared entirely. If we count ex-Yugoslavia as part of this area, the perfect record would be marred by three wars (Yugoslavia–Croatia, Bosnia, and Kosovo) in the 1990s. But one may reasonably speculate that within large areas of the world, including South America, North America, and Western Europe, war is no longer an institution in the sense that members contemplate, plan, and commission acts of organized violence against each other. A Swedish–Norwegian, Spanish–Portuguese,

---

[3] The figure includes only wars between sovereign (commonly recognized) states in the system and excludes all colonial wars and wars between polities that were not members of the system (e.g., Siam and Burma in 1759).

297

Argentina–Brazil, or Canada–United States war has a probability of happening in the foreseeable future of close to zero. This large "zone of peace" or "security community" is an object of considerable theoretical and empirical inquiry and need not detain us. But it is important to point out that the pattern represents a major historical change, and if our present analysis were confined to this area, we would have to conclude that war as an institution has become obsolete. Unfortunately, the high incidence of armed interventions (e.g., United States–Iraq, 2003), intrastate wars, the collapse of states, the ever-present crisis between Israel and its neighbors, and the phenomenon of organized terrorism that requires a military response shows that it has not disappeared. Military budgets, while declining in many areas of the world after the end of the Cold War (except in the United States), are a metric of increased security of states and their populations against foreign predation. But the other metrics, including casualties, displaced persons, and refugees, do not allow such a conclusion. The use of armed force and violence remains a prominent feature of the contemporary international system.

From an institutional point of view, then, we have a schizophrenic situation. On one hand, war in certain areas of the world has virtually disappeared, and elsewhere modern militaries have developed technologies that seek to minimize "collateral damage," re-establish the old distinction between combatants and civilians, and bring the war to some sort of definitive end (e.g., Kosovo). Military forces are increasingly trained to perform a variety of non-combat roles, including peace-keeping, monitoring and implementing peace agreements, civic rebuilding, monitoring the creation of durable political institutions, and the like. All of these activities promote the re-establishment of peaceful conditions and are consistent with the laws of war and humanitarian law. The actions are becoming increasingly patterned, although not always predictable, and the conduct of armed operations seeks to minimize civilian casualties. Part of the justification for collective armed intervention is precisely that the coalition members can point to their overall observance of the laws of war and humanitarian law, in contrast to the behavior of their adversaries who systematically violate them.

On the other hand, we have a continuation of the wars of "national debilitation" in which armed units, including private militias, systematically violate the rules of war. There is little pattern to the violence, a dearth of ideas justifying it, and the almost total ineffectiveness of classical rules and norms. There is certainly no "cult of honor," much less etiquette, to act as a constraint on violence. We thus have three contradictory tendencies in the world: the obsolescence of war, the re-institutionalization of war, and its continued de-institutionalization. Admittedly, the portraits of both of the latter are in sense ideal types, but a thorough empirical study would likely find that the realities on the ground in most wars approximate them. Hence in our summary of institutional change in international politics in the concluding chapter, we will have to underline the opposing tendencies. It is not possible to make a single overall judgment on this institution.

10 International institutions: types, sources, and consequences of change

We have now examined eight international institutions. More would be possible, but they are not necessary to allow us to make some judgments about one important marker of change in international politics. This concluding chapter has five purposes:

1 to map, collectively, the pattern of institutional change in international politics over the past three centuries, approximately;
2 to evaluate the types of changes in these institutions;
3 to offer judgments about the degree of institutionalization in each domain of international politics;
4 to outline some of the sources or explanations of change; and
5 to explore the "so what" question: do institutions matter?

Table 10.1 summarizes the discussion of the foundational and process institutions.

All four foundational institutions were new in the late seventeenth and early eighteenth century. They had no precedents in European or world history. All have changed in the past three centuries, but the main type, with the exception of territoriality, has been complexity, not transformation or obsolescence. The state, for example, has taken on many new tasks and functions, developed ever-expanding sources of revenue, and instilled loyalties that were unknown or only nascent three hundred years ago. Yet, its late seventeenth-century antecedents are clearly recognizable as states. They had many of the same functions, although more limited in scope, and they had institutional continuity not typical of earlier types of polities. Similar comments could be made for sovereignty and international law. Territoriality is a case of transformation, where most old practices, norms, and ideas have undergone dramatic changes,

Table 10.1 *International institutions: types and sources of change, 1700–present*

Domain	Type of change	Degree of institutionalization	Present tendencies	Major sources of change
State Territoriality/ borders	Complexity Transformation	High High	Maintaining strength Some qualification; decline in Europe	Power centralization; nationalism Nationalism; state administrative capacity; surveillance technologies
Sovereignty	Complexity	High	Some conditionality; European dilution	State power and centralization; national legal, monetary, educational, military institutions; "national" history
International law	Complexity	Medium	Strengthening (scope, depth)	Need for regulating transnational processes; anti-war sentiments; human rights sensibilities
Diplomacy	Complexity	High	Strengthening	Professionalization of civil services; imitation by new states; need to regulate new practices
Trade	New	Medium	Strengthening; greater scope	Free trade ideas; "science" of economics; depression; US power/leadership; globalization of trade
Colonialism	Obsolescence	De-institutionalized	Appearance of UN-sponsored protectorate-type relationships (temporary only)	Self-rule ideas; legacies of World War II, economic weakness of colonial powers; anti-colonial policies of USSR, China, and partially USA
War	a Reversion to eighteenth-century practices	a Medium	a Toward more regulation	Anti-war sentiments and norms; human rights sensibilities; "smart" technology
	b Reversion to pre-Westphalia	b Low	b De-institutionalizing	Collapse of state authority; economic opportunities through violence; secessionist sentiments; severe economic deprivation; ethnic mobilization
	c Obsolescence (in OECD area only)			The "democratic peace"

but where some residues of the past such as the idea and norm of exclusive legal jurisdiction remain. Of the procedural institutions, trade is the sole new institution, colonialism is the only example of obsolescence, and in the case of war, change involves two types of reversion and in some areas of the world, obsolescence.

If we use international institutions as our marker of change in international politics, then the claim that we are living in a new era where old rules no longer apply and where discontinuities prevail over continuities seems premature. The claim might have had more resonance in the middle of the eighteenth century than today, when the change from medieval to "modern" institutions was more marked. The two instances of reversion also raise serious questions about contemporary novelties. The portrait we have drawn of the foundational institutions of international politics does not fit well with the fashionable contention that the days of the nation-state are numbered, that sovereignty is eroding or disappearing, or that we live in a de-territorialized, borderless world. Change in the institutions of international politics has been ubiquitous, but most of it has been in the form of increased complexity. The three areas of what might be termed revolutionary change include the delegitimization of conquest, the end of colonialism, and the institutionalization of trade. These are seldom singled out as the indicators of a new era or new world, yet they are the only domains that could justify such monikers. Taken together, the map of institutional change does not support the claim that we live in a post-Westphalian world. A good deal of the contemporary institutional context within which states pursue and defend their interests is recognizable in late seventeenth- and early eighteenth-century antecedents. There has been plenty of change but the main rules, norms, and ideas surrounding them were clearly visible three hundred years ago. The major exceptions to this generalization include the institutionalization of trade in the past sixty years, and the transformation of territoriality in the past one hundred and fifty years, approximately.

The third column of Table 10.1 indicates the degree to which each domain has been institutionalized. Making such judgments is hardly a precise exercise. They are based on the evidence in each of the chapters. The criteria are (1) the degree to which there is standardization of norms, rules, practices, and ideas and (2) the extent to which modal behavior of *most states most of the time* is reasonably consistent with those institutional elements. If there is a reasonable concordance, then we can claim that in a particular realm of activity, institutionalization is high.

It does not signify the absence of deviant behavior by some states some of the time, just as in the domestic realm we would not claim that a fairly standard rate of law violation constitutes the breakdown of law and order in a society. A perfect fit between norms, rules, ideas, and behavior would occur only in a utopia, but if most states most of the time conduct their mutual relations in accordance with custom and various forms of norms, then we can infer a reasonably high degree of institutionalization. If, on the contrary, deviant behavior is practiced by many states a fair amount of the time, then the judgment is that there is a medium degree of institutionalization. Frequent transgressions of trade law, the use of questionable or illegal subsidies – especially in agriculture – problems of compliance with WTO decisions, and major disputes about what is and is not allowed in trade regulations suggest that there is still a fairly great distance to be traveled until trade is conducted according to the norms and rules of the WTO and various regional organizations. Similarly, although there is a trend in modern warfare to restore the distinction between military and civilian targets, there are still many civilian casualties in the major armed conflicts. Equally important, as Kosovo and the Anglo-American attack on Iraq in 2003 suggest, the use of force is itself of questionable legality in some instances. In the case of the "wars of national debilitation," there is almost a perfect inverse correlation between the rules of war and international humanitarian law on the one hand, and the conduct of military operations on the other. Violations of the rules are systematic, persistent, and widespread, meaning that this type of war is the perfect candidate for the category of de-institutionalization. Since the assignment of categories is a fairly arbitrary exercise, there is room for argument. But the evidence in each of the chapters lends a certain degree of authority to the choices.

The main factors leading to changes in international institutions combine the ideational with more traditional sources such as alteration of power relations. There is no pattern for all institutions. Changes in the institution of diplomacy came slowly with the standardization and imitation of practices, punctuated by several key occasions (1815 and 1961) for codifying norms, rules, and etiquette. But this slow accretive change reflecting greater complexity of tasks and roles would probably not have come about without a major discourse in the seventeenth and eighteenth centuries about the proper tasks, roles, and functions of diplomats in the European states system. In the case of trade, ideas played a pivotal role in undermining the intellectual props of mercantilism and providing solid empirical foundations for free trade doctrines. But it was American power and leadership, along with the economic destruction of Europe's traditional great powers during World War II as background conditions, that led to institutional design at Bretton Woods and the establishment of GATT. Surveying technology and improvements in cartography were critical foundations for establishing the borders of European states in the seventeenth and eighteenth centuries. Technological innovations similarly help account for the de-institutionalization of war, particularly as seen in the conduct of campaigns deliberately targeting civilian populations during World War II. Yet, technology may also offer the means to re-institutionalize war. However, ideas and attitudes, expressed in codes dealing with humanitarian law and anti-war norms found in the United Nations Charter and other multilateral instruments, are also key sources of more recent attempts to restore the classical divide between combatants and civilians. While it is no doubt the case that most international institutions reflect the interests of states, and particularly those of the great powers, those interests were often shaped in critical ways by ideas and various norms and values promoted by individuals, "idea entrepreneurs," and groups outside of governments. The story of institutional change is thus complex. No single category such as power or international structure can explain the patterns of novelty, greater complexity, transformation, reversion, and obsolescence. Of the processes of change, some took place slowly, more like trends but occasionally punctuated by fits of codification (e.g., diplomacy). Others were more similar to the "big bang" marker of change, with particular events catapulting governments to make substantial changes through institutional design or codification (e.g., Bretton Woods and the creation of GATT after the failure of the International Trade Organization). Major events often have lasting consequences (although often over-predicted), but clearly they are not necessary conditions for institutional change. The history of international law is primarily one of slow, accretive change, with a great deal of debate every step of the way.

International institutions and the international system

The overall portrait of the contemporary international system is of a set of arrangements between states that for the most part allows them to coexist peacefully a good portion of the time, and to conduct their mutual relations in rule-bound environments that enhance the opportunities for communication, trade, and the flow of people and ideas between societies. This is a portrait that differs substantially from the typical Realist rendering of a world of states in which, as Hobbes and Rousseau noted, there is a constant disposition to insecurity, concern with relative gains and status, and war. At the time they wrote, years of warfare in the relatively narrow space of Europe outpaced years of peace by a ratio of almost two to one (Wright, 1964: 55–6), so we can understand why they argued that the necessary consequence of anarchy is perpetual insecurity. But in the contemporary world the years of peace – as measured by the absence of war between states – outweigh the years of war. This is the case even allowing for the much higher number of states in the present system compared with its seventeenth- and eighteenth-century predecessors. If we eliminate two areas of contemporary chronic warfare, the Middle East and South Asia, then the years of peace vastly outnumber the years of war. Similarly, if we compare the realm of trade between the two eras, then the differences are even more magnified. Hedley Bull and his colleagues were thus justified in using the concept of a "society" of states, and Wendt (1992) similarly accurate in claiming that "anarchy is what states make of it." Conflict, insecurity, and war are not inevitable consequences of anarchy. States through their policy-makers can both create institutions by design – the Bretton Woods arrangements and GATT, for example – and develop them through customary practices that over the ages take on normative characteristics. These institutions narrow the choices of policy-makers and create both opportunities and constraints on how they go about pursuing and defending their interests. In almost all cases they reduce transaction costs and risks substantially. The institutions we have examined may not always be highly visible or contested. Many in fact become part of our day-to-day intellectual constructs. That we usually take them for granted does not diminish their importance. On the contrary, because we *do* take them for granted, we can see their influence. From the mundane – accepting the use of passports – to the more political – respecting the outcome of elections in foreign countries – the ways ordinary people and governments conduct their transactions abroad is deeply conditioned by institutional arrangements. This then raises the ultimate "so what" question: do institutions make a difference?

The influence of institutions

It is important to re-emphasize the domain of inquiry. This is a study of the institutional framework of international politics, that is, of the context and arrangements in which states conduct their mutual relations. We have said little about change in the larger milieu, or what might be called "global sociology." None of the analysis denies the importance of vast areas of technological innovation, changes in ways people relate to their countries and governments, the various forms of globalization, or the general compression of time and space. But we cannot legitimately infer that changes in those domains automatically *transform* international institutions such as the state, territoriality, diplomacy, or international law. They certainly have impacts, but in many cases they lead to or account for greater complexity rather than transformation or obsolescence. The major tasks, roles, and functions of diplomats, for example, have broadened over the years, and communications developments have altered the way they go about their tasks, but their essential roles, functions, and etiquette have not changed significantly, despite great social and intellectual upheavals such as the Enlightenment, nationalism, the Industrial Revolution, the Cold War, and globalization. If we go by the evidence provided in the substantive chapters, changes in ideas, values, and norms have been more important sources of institutional alteration than technological or social "revolutions." In any event, the impact of global social and technological change remains an empirical question not answered glibly by assertions of a "new era," "borderless world," "spaceship earth," and the like.

International politics is a distinct field of activity between public authorities of separate states. It is the story of what they seek to achieve and defend – their purposes – through contacts with each other. All states have a common repertoire of purposes. They combine welfare, security, status, and the promotion of certain values, ideas, and ideologies in different proportions. Most are content to emphasize welfare, while a few take it upon themselves to try to transform the world. They are the ideological crusaders.

How they defend and pursue their purposes is tempered by international institutions that encompass ideas, norms, rules, and etiquette. When some states reject those institutional arrangements or seek to create radically different arrangements, war is a likely outcome. Napoleon sought to create a Paris-based continental empire, systematically violating the rules established at Westphalia and the balance of power system created in the Treaty of Utrecht (1713–15). Although a matter of continuing dispute, from the perspective of the participants of the day,

Germany's attempt to create hegemony over the continent in the years prior to 1914 (which included plans to invade the United States) was inconsistent with the institutions of sovereignty and territorial integrity and with the more general conception or identity of the European society of states. The Bolsheviks dreamed of smashing the European states system and its colonial appendages and replacing them with a global workers' republic. The communist utopia was based on a rejection of "bourgeois" institutions such as sovereign statehood, diplomacy, and international law. Hitler's dream of a "new order" was, as he himself admitted, designed to destroy the Westphalian order of sovereign states and to replace it with a German-centered, hierarchical system based on race.[1] Every attempt to destroy the institutional arrangements of a system of sovereign states – the society of states – has met determined opposition, which suggests that the members of the society place great value on them. Indeed, without necessarily implying a teleological "purpose" to these institutions, as an ensemble they help guarantee a reasonable amount of peaceful coexistence between states. If they have a design, it is precisely to prevent the kind of behavior typical of states in anarchical systems in general, and of the recent examples of Napoleon, Kaiser Wilhelm, Lenin, and Hitler. Hence the term "taming the sovereigns." International institutions, the creations of states, have a moderating influence on the plans and actions of their sovereigns. Without them, as the evidence below suggests, the life of states and the societies they encompass would be more precarious, dangerous, and warlike than it is.

How can we test this proposition? One way is to use our imagination, that is, to explore counter-factuals.[2] What would the lives of ordinary people be like if we had no institution of sovereignty, based on principles of self-government and territorial integrity? What would be the consequences to us if the principle of *pacta sunt servanda* was not a foundation of international law? How would trade proceed in the absence of regulations on subsidies, dumping, tariffs, and embargoes? What would happen if there were no rules governing diplomatic immunities? We might not have to rely solely on fantasy, for such a world – or partial

---

[1] As when Hitler declared to his guests on August 26, 1942, "It is not the Treaty of Versailles we must destroy, but the Treaty of Westphalia" (*Hitler's Tabletalk*, 1953: 66).
[2] A persuasive use of counter-factual analysis, in this case demonstrating how the Reformation was a necessary condition for the emergence of sovereignty, is in Philpott's (2001: 98–102) exploration of the thesis "No Reformation, No Westphalia."

world – existed within the Nazi "new order," *circa* 1942–5. Only a few fanatics could prefer that world to the one we live in today, whatever its shortcomings and problems. That "new order" was one in which territories were exchanged and reconfigured with impunity; diplomats abused and harangued; governments set up by Nazi overlords, with elections and all forms of political activity outlawed; "allies" systematically exploited for raw materials and slave labor; vast camps created for the liquidation of Jews, Gypsies, and other "undesirables"; looting of national treasures; and treaties signed with no intention of meeting their obligations. This was a hierarchical world of non-sovereign satrapies held together primarily through terror and force.

But it could be argued that few societies have thrown up the likes of Adolf Hitler and his Nazi movement and that therefore this one example cannot indicate that a world without international institutions would necessarily resemble the Nazi "new order." The problem is that all other efforts to create alternatives to the society of states have not been much better. Lenin's dream of a world revolution succeeded by a universal workers' republic found practical application in Stalin's system of satellites in Eastern and Central Europe. While this scheme may have produced a semblance of order in an area of historical turmoil, most people vigorously reject the values and practices that it involved. No one pines either for the days of Japan's alternative to the Westphalian system, the "Greater East Asia Co-Prosperity Sphere" that extended from Manchuria in the north to Indonesia in the south. Few outside France came to see Napoleon's empire as more than a system of organized pillage and political domination. So we have several examples of "worlds" without international institutions. While we can perhaps imagine more pleasant alternatives, these would represent the triumph of hope over experience.

Historical states systems all had rudimentary international institutions (usually confined to various forms of diplomatic immunities and a few norms regarding the use of force), but most did not have prototypes of sovereignty, territoriality, and codified international law. Their polities regularly engaged in trade and war, but we find no historical counterparts to the Lieber Code and its numerous imitations and descendants, or to the modern institutional arrangements governing commercial relations between societies. Perhaps the most compelling way to answer the "so what?" question is to examine the record of warfare in several states systems that had only rudimentary international institutions.

War in systems of states

The system of states in China during the "Spring and Autumn" and "Warring States" periods, 771–221 BC had as one of its cardinal features the persistence of war between the independent units. The outcome of such wars usually led to the destruction and/or annexation of the defeated unit. The state of Ch'i was one of the more successful expansionary units. In 664 it "brought Chang to terms." Four years later it "removed" Yang. In 567 it "extinguished" Lai and T'ang and eighteen years later "seized" Chieh-ken (Walker, 1953). Prior to the re-establishment of the Chinese Empire, the great powers of Ch'i, Ch'un, Ch'u, Wu, Sung, and Yueh were in almost constant warfare, with Ch'in finally emerging in 221 as the conqueror of all (cf., Ferguson and Mansbach, 1996: 188). There are no exact chronicles of all the wars fought in the five centuries of the Chinese states system, but the existing record indicates that war was ubiquitous and conquest the usual outcome of it. Although historians disagree as to the number of states in the system, an average of several competing numbers would be about 170 at the beginning of the "Spring and Autumn" period (771 BC), while by the end of the "Warring States" period (404–221 BC), the number had declined to about one dozen. This suggests that about 160 disappeared, most through conquest or forced annexation, while some may have amalgamated through purchase, marriage, and other peaceful arrangements.

If we move next to the Italian city-states of the fifteenth century, a similar portrait emerges. Until 1498, this was a largely self-contained system of states that regularly interacted through formal diplomatic institutions eventually copied throughout Europe. Despite this institution and the common culture, language, and religion of the area, the states engaged in almost perpetual war, and their diplomacy was geared more to espionage and subversion than to the peaceful resolution of conflicts. The states constantly interfered in each other's domestic arrangements and frequently sought to overthrow regimes of their disliking. Any account of the international relations of the era indicates a field of activity punctuated by chronic distrust, insecurity, the preparation and waging of war, and the hatching of plots (cf., Bayley, 1961). An attempt to bring some order to these relationships through the Peace of Lodi (1454) had little effect. The scope of violence receded somewhat, but there was no growth of institutional arrangements for peaceful coexistence and insecurity remained the backdrop to all diplomatic relations (cf., Mattingly, 1955: 61, 94–6).

Table 10.2 *Incidence of interstate wars (central system), 1495–2003*[a]

Period	Average no. of states in central system	No. of central system interstate wars	Interstate wars per state per year
1495–1600	18	40	0.021
1648–1714	20	22	0.017
1715–1814	19	36	0.019
1815–1914	21	29	0.015
1918–1941	30	25	0.036
1945–1990	145	38	0.006
1991–2003	181	8[b]	0.003

[a] Excludes European imperial expansion wars, wars among or against non-members of the central state system (e.g., Boxer rebellion, nineteenth-century wars in Latin America), post-1945 wars of "national liberation," and internal wars. The list includes armed interventions resulting in significant loss of life.
[b] The 1991 Gulf War, Yugoslavia–Croatia, Yugoslavia–Bosnia, Kosovo, Eritrea–Ethiopia, Nagorno-Karabakh, Afghanistan, and US coalition–Iraq.
Source: Adapted and amended from Wright (1965: 641–2); Holsti (1996: 24).

Europe prior to Westphalia had a similar profile. War occurred with a frequency seen only once since, during the era of serial aggressions of the 1930s. In the period 1495 to 1600, Quincy Wright (1965: 641–2) recorded forty wars between states in Europe. The great powers of the day were the main participants. Jack Levy (1983: table 4.1, pp. 88–9) counts thirty-six wars in which one or more great powers were involved. This works out to about one new war every 2.6 years. Figures for war frequency do not decline in all subsequent periods – in fact they increase dramatically in the 1918–41 period – but we must take into account the increase in the number of states. If we control for this growth, then the record of warfare shows a steady decline since Westphalia, with only one period – 1918–41 – showing a reversion to pre-Westphalian patterns.[3] Table 10.2 summarizes the figures.

We cannot of course impute direct causality between the incidence of war and the proliferation and solidifying of international institutions. Other explanations for these variations would have to be entertained as

---

[3] Levy (1983: Fig. 6.1, p. 119) demonstrates that there has been a long-term decline in the incidence of interstate war regardless of the number of states in the system. Two recent studies, using different statistics, also demonstrate the long-run secular decline of interstate wars, but an increase in domestic armed conflicts. See Gleditsch (2002) and Sarkees et al. (2003).

well. However, there is one pattern that lends force to causality: every historical period in which anti-Westphalian actors rampaged across the diplomatic and military landscapes was also a period of extremely high war incidence. The numerous wars during the heyday of the Reformation are a reflection of the wild contest between those who were committed to some version of state sovereignty and those who sought to uphold imperial and church authority in a neo-medieval political system. The second peak of war activity is during Napoleon's grand project of creating a Paris-based European empire. And the final anomalous pattern of war incidence is during the onslaught of anti-Westphalian dictators in the 1930s and 1940s. In eras when there were no prominent and powerful anti-Westphalians, war incidence has been significantly lower. It is at these times that sovereignty, territoriality, and international law were observed by most states most of the time.

While average people today face a variety of threats to their individual security, including often their own governments, terrorists, and civil wars of various kinds, death at the hands of foreign soldiers and the prospect of foreign conquest have significantly diminished since Westphalia. Perhaps the most telling number in Table 10.2 is the dramatic growth in the number of states. This is a pattern directly opposite to that in the ancient Chinese states system, where the fate of most independent polities was to be conquered, annexed, and/or destroyed. In contrast, conquest since 1945 has almost disappeared as a form of state activity, and as we have seen in the chapter on territoriality, the incidence of territorial revision through the use of armed force has declined steeply since the end of World War II. A visitor from the sixteenth century would surely find the contemporary international system exotic in its comparative pacifism.

The socialization of states?

Further evidence of the influence of institutions comes from the experience of revolutionary states. Going back to the French Revolution (and to a lesser extent, the American Revolution), through the Bolshevik, Nazi, Chinese, and Iranian revolutions in the twentieth century, most of the parties in power disavowed in one way or another the main norms and rules of international law, diplomacy, and other domains. This was part of their strategy for "de-linking" from the international system of the time, and also for promoting their revolutions abroad (cf., Halliday, 1999: ch. 10). Those tasks could not be undertaken successfully within the context of the major international institutions of the day. We have already quoted Hitler's determination to destroy the institutional framework associated with Westphalia. The Bolsheviks repudiated tsarist debts and some treaties, refused initially to observe the main protocols of diplomatic exchange, and openly sent "people's representatives" abroad, ostensibly as diplomats, but charged with the main task of promoting revolution in other countries. They violated the rules of diplomatic immunity and in general condemned "bourgeois" international law. Initially, the Chinese, Cuban, Libyan, and Iranian revolutions all had components that directly challenged norms such as non-intervention, legal equality, sovereignty and state responsibility. While the Chinese and Cubans made various attempts to export their revolutions, Libya and Iran added to the repertoire the organization and funding of terrorist activities abroad.

David Armstrong (1993) has demonstrated how all these regimes, faced with the prospect of international isolation, eventually adapted to or even embraced most of the norms and rules of the institutions we have explored in this study. He uses the term "socialization" to imply that as within small social groups, the structures of conformity eventually overcome the deviant inclinations of individuals. They eventually learn that if they wish to survive, they must act within the parameters established by the group. But in international political relationships, the means by which deviant revolutionary states "learn" to adapt to the society of states and its prescriptions may be less benign than the term "socialization" suggests. In most instances, revolutionary regimes have had to confront direct attack and attempts at subversion from the major states of the system. This was the case for the Bolsheviks, China, and Cuba, but absent in Libya and Iran. However, even in the latter, various forms of coercion, including economic sanctions and diplomatic boycotts compelled the regimes to change their ways. It was not for the admiration of Western political institutions or international codes that Libya eventually gave up its sponsorship of foreign terrorist activities, but rather the enormous economic costs it bore consequent to the international application of economic sanctions against the regime. In some other instances, through regular cost–benefit analysis, sponsors of foreign revolution eventually find that the economic promises they make to their own populations cannot be achieved if they are dubbed "rogue" states, with all the attending external pressures that category provokes. In brief, revolutionary regimes may ultimately have to choose whether to save the revolution at home or continue exporting revolution abroad. Though not in rhetoric, the Bolsheviks accommodated themselves to many of the norms of the society of states and chose "socialism in one country" over "world revolution." In the case of Iran, much of its early post-revolution rhetoric about exporting the revolution abroad and "liberating" oppressed peoples – Muslims in particular – has diminished substantially. There are only two cases where revolutionary regimes systematically assaulted the main norms of the system and failed to adapt to them: revolutionary France and its Napoleonic aftermath, and Nazi Germany. Both involved major assaults on Westphalian principles, and in both cases large coalitions gathered to defend them through war.

It is evidence such as this that allows us to infer that the foundational institutions of the society of states stand as major constraints on the range of options governments can consider when they pursue their interests. Today, war is the last option; three hundred years ago it was among the first. But equally important, the main modes of conduct consistent with the institutions of sovereignty, territoriality, and the fundamental principles of international law generally have a "taken for granted" quality which means that their norms and rules have largely been internalized. The consequence is that actions tend to become increasingly routine and predictable. We take it for granted, for example, that states will exchange ambassadors who will then staff permanent residencies in each other's capitals. This is routine; it was not so in the seventeenth century when some nascent states almost went to war over questions of diplomatic representation and rank. Governments today consider raising tariffs only under extreme circumstances or in response to the political clout of domestic groups, whereas increasing them regularly one hundred years ago was considered not only normal but solely the prerogative of governments, without any resulting international scrutiny. Similarly, royal governments in the sixteenth and seventeenth centuries regularly interfered in the foreign "family matters" of death and succession quarrels, whereas today most states most of the time do not interfere overtly in the domestic political arrangements of their neighbors and more distant colleagues. That the American proclivity for violating the non-intervention norm has been so often publicized and condemned attests to its robustness. Were most states most of the time imitating American practices, we could not argue that there even was such a norm.

The idea of the international community

One of the legacies of the medieval era was the notion of a common European community that transcends its component units. This *respublica christiana* was largely a religious and cultural identity, buttressed to a certain extent by family ties among the monarchs of the era. The Westphalia settlement tended to emphasize the ancient rights and titles of individual polities, but in the provisions that sought to establish a semblance of a balance of power and authorized Sweden and France to guarantee the peace treaties there is the rudimentary notion of a state responsibility that overlays the interests of individual dynasts. The political discussions that surrounded negotiation of the Treaty of Utrecht (actually, an ensemble of bilateral and multilateral treaties) incorporated constant references to the "repose of Europe" and to the mutual responsibilities of the treaty partners to craft their policies in such a manner as not to disturb that "repose." Eighteenth-century political discourse is filled with references to the "Republic of Europe," to the "Republic of Christian princes," and similar phrases that invoke notions of responsibilities that transcend the vital interests of individual states. *Raison d'état* became tempered by, if not subordinated to, an intersocietal consensus principle that legitimated the system-wide social order (cf., Osiander, 1994; Hall, 1999: 66). Numerous wars, partitions, and conquests characterized the eighteenth century, but there were also cases of self-abnegation, caution, and modesty that were explained by concerns of social ostracism. Hans Morgenthau (1985: 236–8) painted this rather overdrawn portrait of the European states system between Westphalia and the French revolutionary wars:

> The princes and their advisers took the moral and political unity of Europe for granted and referred as a matter of course to the "republic of Europe," the "community of Christian princes" or "the political system of Europe." These men knew Europe as "one great republic" with common standards of "politeness and cultivation" and a common system of arts, and laws, and manners. The common awareness of these common standards restrained their ambitions by the "mutual inference of fear and shame," imposed "moderation" upon their actions and instilled in all of them "some sense of honor and justice." In consequence, the struggle for power on the international scene was in the nature of "temperate and undecisive [sic] contests."

At the Congress of Vienna (1815), three of the main negotiators (Metternich, Alexander, and Castlereagh) had ideas about managing the post-war European states system, or as the various treaties of the era termed it, "the tranquility of Europe." Implicit in all the negotiations, proposals, treaties, and formulas was the notion of the *good of all* taking precedence over the interests of each. The fundamental idea was to establish a management system that would help to maintain this coveted "tranquility" or "repose." Peace was preferable to war, and increasingly those who might resort to the sword would have to find compelling arguments to make it legitimate. The Concert of Europe was a diplomatic arrangement that incorporated a variety of norms that guided the actions of the great powers (Holsti, 1992). To a large extent they were effective constraints on behavior until at least 1854 and occasionally observed subsequently. It is significant that in the dark wartime days of 1916 and 1917 when individuals and groups around the world were drafting their proposals for a post-war international organization, most of them incorporated ideas, norms, and mechanisms of the Concert in its early days.

The idea of community interests and responsibilities was incorporated into both the League of Nations Covenant and the Charter of the United Nations. The prohibitions against the use of force and conquest were not simply orders of "thou shalt not" addressed to the members of the organization, but norms that were essential for the task of "maintaining international peace and security." The pre-eminent task of both organizations was to maintain this august state of affairs, while simultaneously protecting the sovereignty and territorial integrity of each member. The two tasks are organically linked. International peace and security cannot be maintained if *any* state becomes the victim of aggression and conquest. The stake in Iraq in 1990–1 – despite the cynics who maintained that it was all about oil – was not only the fate of a small, Middle East sheikdom (Kuwait), but international peace and security, and through it, the security of all states. Had Saddam Hussein successfully hung on to his conquest, a critical precedent would have been set. Others would follow, each citing Kuwait. To acquiesce to conquest would be to destroy the entire concept of "international peace and security," the main reason why we have international organizations such as the United Nations. The other cases of conquest – India's invasion of Goa (1962), the forced reunification of Vietnam, Indonesia's invasion of East Timor (1975), and Israel's military victories in 1967 and 1983 – had very particular reasons why the international community accepted them (including in two cases, the utterly marginal interest in the victims). In the case of Israel, the territories in question are "occupied," meaning that their status is temporary. That Israel has not annexed them attests to the power of the non-conquest norm. No country would recognize such annexation as legitimate.

The contemporary term "international community" is used frequently and in many contexts to denote a notion of general responsibility that transcends the interests of particular states at particular times. Obviously, many governments, when the perceptions of the two sets of interests are incompatible, will pursue or defend their narrower concerns, notwithstanding extreme criticism from more community-minded actors. But there is a *presumption* that the two should coincide or that the general welfare should be assessed in terms that are consistent with long-range individual gains. This is exactly why the George W. Bush administration received so much criticism. Many of its foreign policy actions were self-serving at the expense of larger community projects designed to benefit all. The abrogation of the ABM Treaty, withdrawal from the draft protocol for verification of the Biological Weapons Convention, withdrawal from the Kyoto accords on earth warming, rejection of the Comprehensive Test Ban Treaty, attempts to subvert the fledgling International Criminal Court, failure to ratify agreements such as those dealing with children's rights, the 2002 threat to veto future peacekeeping operations unless American troops were exempted from potential war crimes prosecutions, and predatory trade practices were major assaults on community projects. President Bush's national security advisor, Condoleezza Rice, made the classical statement justifying the pursuit of such short-term national gains at the expense of community interests when she wrote that "to be sure there is nothing wrong with doing something that benefits all humanity, but that is, in a sense, a second-order effect . . . Foreign policy in [the Bush] administration will proceed from the firm ground of national interest, not from the interests of an illusory international community" (Rice, 2000: 47, 62). The actions taken to fulfill this vow have led to strong denunciations both within the United States and abroad. Indeed, some in Europe even branded the United States a "rogue" state. Rogue states are precisely those that systematically and frequently violate the main norms of the international institutions we have discussed, and fundamentally challenge notions of a nascent "international community" interest.

This detour into the realm of an idea – the international community – is intended to underline the distinction between a mere "system of states" and a "society of states." Hedley Bull (1977) introduced the distinction, but failed to answer questions such as when a system becomes a society and what the dynamics of change are. The substantive chapters of this study do not address these questions directly, but by examining the development of the major norms dealing with sovereignty, territoriality,

316

and the use of force we can at least propose that systems, while they may have some procedural institutions (usually diplomacy), are bereft of the elements of society. These include at minimum some notions of sovereignty and independence, territorial integrity, legal and status equality, the sanctity of contracts, restraints on the use of force, and some notion of community responsibility.

The institutional foundations of the society of states were laid in the late seventeenth and early eighteenth century (sovereignty, legal equality, *pacta sunt servanda*, diplomacy), but in my opinion the post-Westphalia system of states did not become a society of states until at least the post-Napoleonic period. It was at this time that the first norms prohibiting territorial revision and conquest emerged. Development of the norms of self-rule and national self-determination later in the century provided strong normative support for a more general norm outlawing the use of force for *any* purposes except self-defense. The League of Nations Covenant (particularly Article X), in international law, and the Kellogg–Briand Pact, in rhetoric, perhaps represented best the markers for transition from a system of states to a society of states. These indicated that the institutions of sovereignty, territoriality, and major rules of international law were of sacral status.

The serial aggressions of the dictators in the 1930s were a throwback to sixteenth-century behavior, but their long-term consequence was to establish firmly the illegitimacy of aggressive war, conquest, and forced territorial change. By 1945 the major purposes of all other international institutions (e.g., diplomacy, trade, and the use of force) included the maintenance of international peace and security. Theorists of the day and their contemporaries argued that the reduction of trade barriers was not only a question of increasing global welfare, but also a means of reducing conflicts between states. This view is a staple of all the contemporary discourse on economic globalization and free trade. Similarly, among the main functions of diplomats is the maintenance of peace and finding formulas for peaceful change. Few today conceive of diplomacy in fifteenth-century Italian city-state terms, as primarily a mechanism for espionage and subversion. In our day, force is not only – or even in a major way – the primary instrument for the defense and advancement of state interests. It is to be used primarily under the authority of Security Council decisions, in the name of the international community. This is one of the reasons why so many military establishments around the world are being reconfigured for peacekeeping tasks and for maintaining or restoring *internal* order in weak or collapsing states.

To a large extent the sovereigns have tamed themselves through the construction of international institutions. They have done so only imperfectly but the trajectories are in the direction of increased peaceful coexistence between distinct political communities. For most states most of the time, sovereignty and peace are compatible. Hobbes and Rousseau predicted permanent insecurity and war as the predominant consequence of sovereignty. Institutional development since they wrote has proved them wrong. International peace and security, defined as the respect for state sovereignty and territorial integrity, is at least on the road to being achieved as the normal condition in the relations between states and the societies they represent. There will be detours and relapses, but the major problem of the contemporary society of states is no longer aggression, conquest, and the obliteration of states. It is, rather, the collapse of states, humanitarian emergencies, state terror against segments of local populations, civil wars of various types, and international terrorist organizations. This is a new agenda, an agenda about statehood, governance, human rights, political philosophy, the place of religion in public affairs, and economic inequality. It is a menu of difficult and sometimes intractable problems, punctuated by wars – particularly domestic – of the worse kind. But at least they can be attended to within the context of the generally peaceful relations between states.

Some reflections on the nature of change in international politics

The audacious attacks on the United States on September 11, 2001 caused one of America's greatest tragedies of the past half-century. The strike on Pearl Harbor was the signal for America's entry into World War II, but it came from a long-recognized adversary and enemy, and it involved its armed forces. During the Cold War, the threat to the United States was visible and palpable. It could be "seen" and through the normal processes of diplomacy, Soviet intentions and purposes could be plumbed and explored. Terrorist threats are, in contrast, largely invisible, unpredictable, and all encompassing. Everyone, not just soldiers, is a potential victim. Mikkel Rasmussen (2002: 333) has called this condition "ontological insecurity," or the fear of the inability to maintain order. American president George Bush constructed the "new" threat as one emanating from everywhere and anywhere, and directed against civilization itself.

The shock effects of the "9/11" incident were so great, particularly in the United States, that we can understand the common response that "everything has changed" and that "we live in a new system" (cf., Friedman, 2000: xxi). Among other things, it led to a significant alteration in American security policy, from deterrence to pre-emptive attack. Among his many justifications for invading Iraq in 2003, the American president vowed that his pre-eminent duty as president was to protect the American people and that he would use any and all means to secure that promise, including measures that are highly questionable in both American constitutional law and international law. At least for Americans, "9/11" was a "big bang" event that was to lead to significant domestic and foreign policy modifications.

However, the American scurry to find threats everywhere at home and abroad does not in itself herald a change of an entire system and its component institutions. The United States is not the only country to suffer traumas at the hands of unseen adversaries. Both the Israelis and Palestinians live with them every day and continue to do so, but their plight, while a serious and debilitating problem on the international agenda, has not led to system transformation or to the obsolescence of most "old" institutions. For most people in the world, 2001 was not a "monster" year and it may be that within a decade or less much of the "ontological threat" of terrorism will abate. There will be significant residues of the "9/11" incident, to be sure, but they are not likely to be transformative or transcendent for the system as a whole. A great deal in international politics, and particularly in its institutional foundations, has not changed as a result of it. But if the nineteen hijackers and their four airplane-bombs did not change the entire world, what events, trends, and circumstances can count as major markers of change?

In my view, the change from a system of states that developed between the fifteenth and eighteenth centuries to a society of states is best symbolized by two documents: the final treaty of the Congress of Vienna (1815) and the Covenant of the League of Nations (1919). At Vienna, the participants, in the final treaty, began the long process of undermining the right of conquest, one of the hallmarks of sovereignty and a right deriving implicitly from the Westphalia treaties. They did not declare it illegal, but they claimed that any conquest or territorial redistribution gained through force *would require the consent of the great powers.* That is, the ultimate test of Westphalian statehood, the right to go to war for the conquest of neighboring territory, was now to be subject to community approval. Article X of the League of Nations Covenant finished the job: "The Members of the League undertake to respect and preserve as against external aggression the territorial integrity and existing political independence of all Members of the League." Although more a statement of aspiration than a description of typical state behavior, this single article best summarizes the basic idea underlying a society of states: all states have an interest in, and a commitment to, the continued sovereignty and territorial integrity of its members. It is at once supportive and subversive of the Westphalian states system. It subverts the corollary of sovereignty, the right to pursue state interests uninhibited by external constraints. But it also provides at least a rhetorical guarantee for the territorial integrity and continued political independence of states. So, simultaneously, the relevant articles of the Vienna Treaty and Article X of the League of Nations Covenant are conservative and revolutionary.

Most of the institutions of international politics have undergone various forms of change, some slowly, others more dramatically. Most have taken the form of increased complexity, while others like trade are novel. But if there is any quality that sets the texture of international politics in an era, it is the fear of war and impending conquest. The de-legitimization of conquest, both as a right of sovereignty and as a norm of international law, is in my view the most important change in the international system since the early days of the states system in the seventeenth century. The Napoleonic wars of the early nineteenth century and the two great world wars of the twentieth century were in many ways catastrophic. The lessons learned from them were that the search for conquests brings untold misery to humankind, rather than the hoped-for glory and renown. The institution of sovereignty and the universal norm of self-government are powerful underpinnings for the obsolescence of conquest. If there is any single candidate for the claim that "everything has changed," the obsolescence of conquest is my choice.

It was not the result of any single event or of a technological innovation. Devastating wars were largely but not exclusively involved. Changes in ideas, beliefs, and sensibilities were no less important. Major norm entrepreneurs, like the nineteenth-century peace societies, were largely responsible for undermining the common eighteenth-century and later nineteenth-century Darwinist views that wars are ennobling, glorifying, and healthy antidotes to domestic corruption and social lassitude. It required more than a century to move public and government thought away from sanctifying conquest as an inherent right of sovereignty (and an indicator of royal glory) to constructing aggressive war as a crime against humanity. Change was slow and non-linear, and a complex blend of alterations of ideas, beliefs, and norms. But it was ultimately reflected in practice: conquest as a form of state behavior has not disappeared but it has become an increasingly rare event.

But what about globalization, that set of processes or conditions that so many have pointed to as the source of revolutionary changes such as the "death of Westphalia" and the "erosion" of sovereignty? Is this not a major and unprecedented source of institutional change? I have explored this theme in the institutional analyses and concluded that whatever its other consequences for international politics, institutional change resulting from globalization has been confined primarily to the domain of trade and commerce. Thanks in part to the necessities of lowering transaction costs, creating larger markets, and liberalizing trade, some of the elements of globalization have been powerful promoters of trade institutionalization. But in my view the consequences of technological and transportation innovations were not more important than the great revolution in ideas that undermined mercantilism and promoted free trade. Today decisions have to be made more rapidly, transnational networks and lobby groups are more prominent in the various international political games that are played, amateur diplomats are more notable by their presence, and many states face more external constraints. All of these sociological and economic trends are notable, but they have their historical analogies and antecedents, none of which ever justified the claim that "we live in a new world."

This study has sought to show from at least a medium-range perspective (not the *longue durée*) what areas have undergone which sorts of change. We have seen examples of obsolescence and reversion, as well as novelty. But for most of the institutions of international politics, growing complexity has been the most prominent form of change. Complexity incorporates more density of transactions, proliferation of rules and norms, reinterpretation of older ways of doing things, additional functions, some new or reinvented ideas, and modernization of practices. But these do not necessarily add up to transformation or revolution as far as the texture of international politics is concerned. One could make the case, indeed, that from the perspective of the large picture, the most significant trend that could warrant the term "revolution" has been the universalization of the territorial state as the sole format for organizing political life of diverse communities. Statehood has had its share of problems, particularly among its post-colonial variants, but for every case of state collapse or failure, there have been dozens of relative successes. We may focus attention on the dramatic failures of a Kampuchea, Rwanda, Somalia, or Congo, but that should not blind us from seeing and studying the more numerous Botswanas, Mauritius, Barbados, Kuwaits, and Malaysias of the world. Daniel Philpott (2001) has made a compelling argument that both the Reformation, its consequences seen in Westphalia, and the processes of de-colonization entail similar "logics of freedom," the choice of communities to be free of commands (and exploitation) from above. The institutions of international politics are the major mechanisms by which the newly free sovereigns, whether Westphalian or post-colonial states, can escape Rousseau's insight that the price of freedom (sovereignty) is perpetual insecurity.

We should acknowledge, then, that the society of states is, in historical perspective, revolutionary in itself. Compared with its analogues and antecedents, it has many unique features, mostly prominently the institutionalization of sovereignty, territoriality, international law, diplomacy, and trade. These are major human achievements that have notably rendered the Hobbesian vision of international politics, of a war of all against all against a backdrop of all-pervading insecurity, increasingly irrelevant. Admittedly, the Westphalian system was a war system (as were its predecessors) with many rough edges, but the statistics on the decline of war indicate that war and insecurity are not necessary consequences of anarchy. Karl Deutsch (1954) proved satisfactorily more than four decades ago that anarchy and peaceful relations can coexist in the form of "pluralistic security communities." That vast swathes of the world today are "no war" zones suggests that revolutionary change and transformation of the Westphalian system are not necessary conditions for reasonably harmonious relations between independent states. This is not to suggest that all is well in the world. Far from it. But the study illustrates that changes such as obsolescence (colonialism) and novel institutionalization (trade) can have many benefits for the human condition. Transformation is not the only panacea. Increased institutionalization within a society of states has to remain as a major alternative to the various dystopias and utopias that have been proposed as an alternative to it. Not all sovereigns will be tamed in all places at all times. But in the past three centuries, the sovereigns have at least begun to enmesh themselves in normative networks that substantially "tame" them and make their peaceful coexistence reasonably secure. For those who place value on tolerance of diversity, the moral worth of independent and distinct political communities, and the imperfectly peaceful relations between them, a world of tamed sovereigns has a good deal to commend it.

References

Adler, Emmanuel, and Beverly Crawford, eds. (1991). *Progress in Postwar International Relations*. New York: Columbia University Press

Aldecoa, Francisco, and Michael Keating, eds. (1999). *Paradiplomacy in Action: The Foreign Relations of Subnational Governments*. London: Frank Cass

Alderson, Kai (2000). "Beyond the Linguistic Analogy: Norm and Action in International Politics." Vancouver: Institute of International Relations, University of British Columbia, Working Paper No. 31

(2001). "Making Sense of State Socialization." *Review of International Studies* 27, 3: 415–34

Anderson, M. S. (1993). *The Rise of Modern Diplomacy, 1450–1919*. London: Longman

Anderson, Malcolm (1996). *Frontiers: Territory and State Formation in the Modern World*. Cambridge: Polity Press

Anderson, Perry (1979). *Lineages of the Absolute State*. London: Verso

Ansell, Christopher K., and Steven Weber (1999). "Organizing International Politics: Sovereignty and Open Systems." *International Political Science Review* 20, 1: 73–94

Ansprenger, Franz (1989). *The Dissolution of the Colonial Empires*. London: Routledge

Ardant, Gabriel (1975). "Financial Policy and Economic Infrastructure of Modern States and Nations." In Charles Tilly, ed., *The Formation of Nation States in Western Europe*. Princeton: Princeton University Press, pp. 164–242

Armstrong, David (1993). *Revolution and World Order: The Revolutionary State in International Society*. Oxford: Clarendon Press

Ashley, Richard, and R. B. J. Walker (1990). "Reading Dissidence/Writing the Discipline: Crisis and the Question of Sovereignty in International Studies." *International Studies Quarterly* 34, 3: 367–416

Ayoob, Mohammed (1995). *The Third World Security Predicament: State-Making, Regional Conflict and the International System*. Boulder, CO: Lynne Rienner

Badie, Bertrand (1999). *Un monde sans souveraineté: les états entre ruse et responsabilité*. Paris: Fayard

Badie, Bertrand, and Marie Claude Smouts (1999). *Le retournement du monde: Sociologie de la scène internationale*. Paris: Presses de la Fondation Nationale des Sciences Politiques

Bain, William (2001). "The Idea of Trusteeship in International Society: Unity, Progress, and the Perfection of Mankind." PhD dissertation, University of British Columbia

Barber, Peter (1997). "Maps and Monarchs in Europe 1550–1800." In Robert Oresko, G. C. Gibbs, and H. M. Scott, eds., *Royal and Republican Sovereignty in Early Modern Europe: Essays in Memory of Ragnhild Hatton*. Cambridge: Cambridge University Press, pp. 75–124

Barker, J. Craig (2000). *International Law and International Relations*. London: Continuum

Barnett, Michael (1996). "Sovereignty, Nationalism, and Regional Order in the Arab States System." In Thomas Biersteker and Cynthia Weber, eds., *State Sovereignty as Social Construct*. Cambridge: Cambridge University Press, pp. 148–89

Bartelson, Jens (1995). *A Genealogy of Sovereignty*. Cambridge: Cambridge University Press

Bassiouni, Cherif (1997). "Organized Crime and New Wars." In Mary Kaldor and Basker Vashee, eds., *Restructuring the Global Military Sector*, Vol. I: *New Wars*. London and Washington, DC: Frances Pinter for the United Nations University, pp. 34–54

Bayley, C. C. (1961). *War and Society in Renaissance Florence*. Toronto: University of Toronto Press

Bayley, David H. (1975). "The Police and Political Development in Europe." In Charles Tillly, ed., *The Formation of National States in Western Europe*. Princeton: Princeton University Press, pp. 328–79

Bean, Richard (1973). "War and the Birth of the Nation State." *Journal of Economic History* 33 (March): 203–21

Bereciartu, Gurutz J. (1994). *Decline of the Nation-State*, trans. William A. Douglass. Reno and Las Vegas: University of Nevada Press

Best, Geoffrey (1994). *War and Law since 1945*. Oxford: Oxford University Press

Betts, Raymond F. (1985). *Uncertain Dimensions: Western Overseas Empires in the Twentieth Century*. Minneapolis: University of Minnesota Press

Biersteker, Thomas J. (1992). "The 'Triumph' of Neoclassical Economics in the Developing World: Policy Convergence and Bases of Governance in the International Economic Order." In James N. Rosenau and Ernst-Otto Czempiel, eds., *Governance without Government: Order and Change in World Politics*. Cambridge: Cambridge University Press, pp. 102–31

Bojicic, Vesna, and Mary Kaldor (1997). "The Political Economy of War in Bosnia-Herzegovina." In Mary Kaldor and Basker Vashee, eds., *Restructuring the Global Military Sector*, Vol. I: *New Wars*. London and Washington, DC: Frances Pinter for the United Nations University, pp. 137–76

Braudel, Fernand (1988). *The Identity of France*, Vol. I: *History and Environment*, trans. Sian Reynolds. London: Collins

References

Braun, Rudolf (1975). "Taxation, Sociopolitical Structure, and State-Building: Great Britain and Brandenburg-Prussia." In Charles Tilly, ed., *The Formation of National States in Western Europe*. Princeton: Princeton University Press, pp. 243–327

(1996). "Staying on Top: Socio-cultural Reproduction of European Power Elites." In Wolfgang Reinhard, ed., *Power Elites and State Building*. Oxford: Clarendon Press, pp. 235–59

Brawley, Mark R. (1993). *Liberal Leadership: Great Powers and their Challengers in Peace and War*. Ithaca and London: Cornell University Press

Brewin, Christopher (1982). "Sovereignty." In James Mayall, ed., *The Community of States*. London: George Allen & Unwin, pp. 34–48

Brown, J. Scott (1934). *Vitoria and his Law of Nations*. Oxford: Clarendon Press

Brownlie, Ian (1984). "The Expansion of International Society: The Consequences of the Law of Nations." In Hedley Bull and Adam Watson, eds., *The Expansion of International Society*. Oxford: Clarendon Press, pp. 357–69

Bruce, Ian (2002). "Guns for hiring and firing." *The Herald* (United Kingdom), February 19

Bull, Hedley (1977). *The Anarchical Society: A Study of Order in World Politics*. London: Macmillan

(1980). "The Great Irresponsibles? The United States, the Soviet Union, and World Order." *International Journal* 35: 437–47

(1984). "European States and African Political Communities." In Hedley Bull and Adam Watson, eds., *The Expansion of International Society*. Oxford: Clarendon Press, pp. 99–114

Busch, Marc (2000). "Democracy, Consultation, and the Paneling of Disputes under GATT." *Journal of Conflict Resolution* 44, 4: 425–46

Butler, Peter F. (1978). "Legitimacy in a States-System: Vattel's Law of Nations." In Michael Donelan, ed., *The Reason of States: A Study in International Political Theory*. London: George Allen & Unwin, pp. 45–63

Buzan, Barry (1993). *States and Fear: The National Security Problem in International Relations*. Chapel Hill, NC: University of North Carolina Press

Buzan, Barry, and Eric Herring (1998). *The Arms Dynamic in World Politics*. London: Lynne Rienner

Buzan, Barry, and R. J. Barry Jones, eds. (1981). *Change and the Study of International Relations: The Evaded Dimension*. London: Frances Pinter

Byers, Michael (1999). *Custom, Power and the Power of Rules: International Relations and Customary International Law*. Cambridge: Cambridge University Press

Cameron, Maxwell (1998). "Democratization of Foreign Policy: The Ottawa Process as a Model." *Canadian Foreign Policy* 5, 3: 147–65

Carr, E. H. (1946). *The Twenty Years Crisis, 1919–1939: An Introduction to the Study of International Relations*, 2nd edn. London: Macmillan

Chaliand, Gerard (1994). *The Art of War in World History*. Berkeley: University of California Press

Chayes, Abram, and Antonia Chayes (1993). "On Compliance." *International Organization* 47, 2: 175–205

Cheater, A. P. (1998). "Transcending the State? Gender and Borderline Construction of Citizenship in Zimbabwe." In Thomas M. Wilson and Hastings Donnan, eds., *Border Identities: Nation and State at International Frontiers.* Cambridge: Cambridge University Press, pp. 191–214

Checkel, Jeffrey T. (1997). "International Norms and Domestic Politics: Bridging the Rationalist–Constructivist Divide." *European Journal of International Relations* 3, 4: 473–95

Claessen, Henri J. M. and Peter Skalnik, eds. (1978). *The Early State.* The Hague: Mouton

Clapham, Christopher (1996). *Africa and the International System.* Cambridge: Cambridge University Press

  (1998). "Degrees of Statehood." *Review of International Studies* 24, 2: 143–58

  (1999). "Sovereignty and the Third World State." In Robert Jackson, ed., *Sovereignty at the Millennium.* Oxford: Blackwell, pp. 100–115

Clark, Ann Marie, Elisabeth J. Friedman, and Kathryn Hochstetler (1998). "The Sovereign Limits of Global Civil Society: A Comparison of NGO Participation in UN World Conferences on the Environment, Human Rights, and Women." *World Politics* 51, 1: 1–35

Clark, George Norman (1947). *The Seventeenth Century.* Oxford: Clarendon Press

Clark, Ian (1997). *Globalization and Fragmentation: International Relations in the Twentieth Century.* Oxford: Oxford University Press

Cohen, Raymond (1987). *Theatre of Power: The Art of Diplomatic Signalling.* London and New York: Longman

  (1997). *Negotiating across Cultures: International Communication in an Interdependent World,* rev. edn. Washington, DC: United States Institute for Peace Press

Cohen, Raymond, and Raymond Westbrook, eds. (2000). *Amarna Diplomacy: The Beginnings of International Relations.* Baltimore, MD: The Johns Hopkins University Press

Cook, Tanya (2002). "Dogs of War or Tomorrow's Peacekeepers?: The Role of Mercenaries in the Future Management of Conflict." *The Culture Mandala: Bulletin of the Centre for East–West Cultural and Economic Studies* 5, 1: 1–12

Crawford, Neta C. (2002). *Argument and Change in World Politics: Ethics, Decolonization, and Humanitarian Intervention.* Cambridge: Cambridge University Press

Crouch, Colin, and Wolfgang Streeck, eds. (1997). *Political Economy of Modern Capitalism: Mapping Convergences and Diversity.* London: Sage Publications

Crutwell, C. R. M. F. (1937). *A History of Peaceful Change in the Modern World.* London: Oxford University Press

Cutler, A. Clair (1999). "Private Authority in International Trade Relations: The Case of Maritime Transport." In A. Clair Cutler, Virginia Haufler, and Tony Porter, eds., *Private Authority and International Affairs.* Albany: State University of New York Press, pp. 283–332

References

Danish Institute of International Affairs (1999). *Humanitarian Intervention: Legal and Political Aspects*. Copenhagen: Danish Institute of International Affairs

David, Charles-Philippe (2000). *La guerre et la paix: Approches contemporaines de la sécurité et de la stratégie*. Paris: Presses de la Fondation Nationale des Sciences Politiques

Deibert, Ronald J. (1997). "*Exorcismus Theoriae*: Pragmatism, Metaphors and the Return of the Medieval in IR Theory." *European Journal of International Relations* 3, 2: 167–92

   (1999). "Harold Innis and the Empire of Speed." *Review of International Studies* 25, 2: 273–90

Der Derian, James (1997). "Post-Theory: The Eternal Return of Ethics in International Relations." In Michael Doyle and John Ikenberry, eds., *New Thinking in International Relations Theory*. Boulder, CO: Westview Press, pp. 54–76

Deutsch, Karl W. (1954). *Political Community at the International Level: Problems of Definition and Measurement*. Garden City, NY: Doubleday

De Waal, Alex (1997). "Contemporary War in Africa." In Mary Kaldor and Basker Vashee, eds., *Restructuring the Global Military Sector*, Vol. I: *New Wars*. London and Washington, DC: Frances Pinter for the United Nations University, pp. 286–332

Donelan, Michael (1984). "Spain and the Indies." In Hedley Bull and Adam Watson, eds., *The Expansion of International Society*. Oxford: Clarendon Press, pp. 75–85

Doyle, Michael (1986). *Empires*. Ithaca, NY: Cornell University Press

Driessen, Henk (1998). "The 'New Immigration' and the Transformation of the European-African Frontier." In Thomas M. Wilson and Hastings Donnan, eds, *Border Identities: Nation and State at International Frontiers*. Cambridge: Cambridge University Press, pp. 96–116

Duffy, Christopher (1987). *The Military Experience in the Age of Reason*. London: Routledge & Kegan Paul

Dunne, Tim (1998). *Inventing International Society: A History of the English School*. London: Macmillan

Durand, Jean-Louis (2000). "Peace and the New World Order: A Study of Norms, Identity, Community and Intersubjectivity." PhD dissertation, Department of Government, University of Queensland, Brisbane

Duyvesteyn, Isabelle (2000). "Contemporary War: Ethnic Conflict, Resource Conflict, or Something Else?" Paper presented at the 41st Annual Meetings of the International Studies Association, Los Angeles, March 14–18

Eckstein, Harry (1988). "A Culturalist Theory of Political Change." *American Political Science Review* 82: 789–804

The Economist (2001). *The World in 2002*. London: The Economist Newspaper
   (2002). *The World in 2003*. London: The Economist Newspaper

Ellingsen, Tanja (2000). "The New World Order: Global Village or Civilization?" Paper presented at the 41st Annual Meetings of the International Studies Association, Los Angeles, March 14–18

Ellis, Geoffrey (1991). *The Napoleonic Empire*. Basingstoke: Macmillan Education

Ertman, Thomas (1997). *Birth of the Leviathan: Building States and Regimes in Mediaeval and Early Modern Europe*. Cambridge: Cambridge University Press

Evans, Peter (1997). "The Eclipse of the State?" *World Politics* 50 (October): 62–87

Fabry, Mikulas (1998). "Is World Politics Returning to the Middle Ages? The New Medievalism and the Problem of Authority and Change in International Relations Theory." MA thesis, University of British Columbia

(2002). "The Idea of National Self-Determination and the Recognition of New States at the Congress of Berlin (1878)." Paper presented at the 43rd Annual Meetings of the International Studies Association, New Orleans, March 24–27

(forthcoming). "International Society and the Establishment of New States: The Practice of State Recognition in the Era of National Self-Determination." PhD dissertation, Department of Political Science, University of British Columbia

Falk, Richard (1993). "Sovereignty." In Joel Krieger, ed., *The Oxford Companion to Politics of the World*. New York: Oxford University Press, pp. 851–54

(1997). "The United Nations, the Rule of Law and Humanitarian Intervention." In Mary Kaldor and Basker Vashee, eds., *Restructuring the Global Military Sector*, Vol. I: *New Wars*. London and Washington, DC: Pinter for the United Nations University, pp. 108–33

Fenwick, Charles G. (1965). *International Law*. 4th edn. New York: Meredith Publishing

Ferguson, Yale H. and Richard W. Mansbach (1996). *Polities: Authority, Identities, and Change*. Columbia, SC: University of South Carolina Press

(1999). "Global Politics at the Turn of the Millennium: Changing Bases of 'Us' and 'Them.'" *International Studies Review* 1, 2: 77–108

Finer, Samuel E. (1975). "State- and Nation-Building in Europe: The Role of the Military." In Charles Tilly, ed., *The Formation of National States in Western Europe*. Princeton: Princeton University Press, pp. 84–163

Finlayson, Jock A., and Mark W. Zacher (1982). "The GATT and the Regulation of Trade Barriers: Regime Dynamics and Functions." In Stephen D. Krasner, ed., *International Regimes*. Ithaca: Cornell University Press, pp. 273–314

(1988). *Managing International Markets: Developing Countries and the Commodity Price Regime*. New York: Columbia University Press

Finnemore, Martha (1996). *National Interests in International Society*. Ithaca: Cornell Univeresity Press

Finnemore, Martha, and Katherine Sikkink (1998). "International Norm Dynamics and Political Change." *International Organization* 52, 4: 887–917

Ford, Jane (2002). "A Social Theory of Trade Regime Change: GATT to WHO." *International Studies Review* 4, 3: 115–38

Fowler, Michael Ross, and Julie Marie Bunck (1995). *Law, Power, and the Sovereign State: The Evolution and Application of the Concept of Sovereignty*. University Park, PA: University of Pennsylvania Press

Freedman, Lawrence (1998–9). "The Changing Forms of Military Conflict." *Survival* 20, 4: 39–56

Frey, Linda S., and Marsha L. Frey (1999). *The History of Diplomatic Immunity.* Columbus, OH: Ohio State University Press

Friedman, Thomas L. (2000). *The Lexus and the Olive Tree: Understanding Globalization.* rev. edn. New York: Anchor Books

Fukuyama, Francis (1989). "The End of History?" *National Interest* (summer): 3–18

Galtung, Johan (1971) "A Structural Theory of Imperialism." *Journal of Peace Research* 8: 387–417

Gann, L. H., and Peter Duignan (1967). *Burden of Empire: An Appraisal of Western Colonialism in Africa South of the Sahara.* Stanford: Hoover Institution Press

Gelb, Leslie (1994). "Quelling Teacup Wars." *Foreign Affairs* 73, 6: 2–6

George, Jim (1995). *Discourses of Global Politics: A Critical (Re)Introduction to International Relations.* Boulder, CO: Lynne Rienner

Giddens, Anthony (1987). *The Nation-State and Violence.* Berkeley and Los Angeles: University of California Press

Gilboa, Eytan (2000). "Mass Communication and Diplomacy: A Theoretical Framework." *Communication Theory* 10, 3: 275–309

Gilliard, David (1984). "British and Russian Relations with Asian Governments in the Nineteenth Century." In Hedley Bull and Adam Watson, eds., *The Expansion of International Society.* Oxford: Clarendon Press, pp. 87–97

Gilpin, Robert (1981). *War and Change in World Politics.* Cambridge: Cambridge University Press

(1987). *The Political Economy of International Relations.* Princeton: Princeton University Press

(2001). *Global Political Economy: Understanding the International Economic Order.* Princeton: Princeton University Press

Glamann, Kristof (1977). "European Trade 1500–1750." In Carlo M. Cipolla, ed., *The Fontana Economic History of Europe,* vol. II: *The Sixteenth and Seventeenth Centuries.* Sussex: Harvester Press, pp. 427–526

Gleditsch, Nils Petter (2002). *The Future of Armed Conflict.* Ramat Gan, Israel: The Begin–Sadat Center for Strategic Studies

Goff, Patricia (2000). "Invisible Borders: Economic Liberalization and National Identity." *International Studies Quarterly* 44, 4: 53–62

Goldgeier, James, and Michael McFaul (1992). "A Tale of Two Worlds: Core and Periphery in the Post-Cold War Era." *International Organization* 46, 1: 467–92

Gong, Gerrit W. (1984). *The Standard of "Civilization" in International Society.* Oxford: Clarendon Press

Gros, Jean-Germain (1996). "Towards a Taxonomy of Failed States in the New World Order." *Third World Quarterly* 17, 3: 455–71

Guetzkow, Harold (1955). *Multiple Loyalties.* Princeton: Princeton University Press

Guillen Pierre (1984). *L'expansion 1881–1898*. Paris: Imprimerie nationale

Haas, Peter (1990). *Saving the Mediterranean: The Politics of Environmental Cooperation*. New York: Columbia University Press

Hall, John A., ed. (1986). *States in History*. Oxford: Basil Blackwell

Hall, Rodney Bruce (1999). *National Collective Identity: Social Constructs and International Systems*. New York: Columbia University Press

Halliday, Fred (1999). *Revolution and World Politics: The Rise and Fall of the Sixth Great Power*. Durham, NC: Duke University Press

Hamilton, Bruce (1963). *Political Thought in Sixteenth-Century Spain*. Oxford: Clarendon Press

Hamilton, Keith, and Richard Langhorne (1995). *The Practice of Diplomacy*. London: Routledge

Harbeson, John, Donald Rothchild, and Naomi Chazan eds. (1994). *Civil Society and the State in Africa*. Boulder, CO and London: Lynne Rienner

Harding, Sandra (1986). *The Science Question in Feminism*. London: Milton Keynes

Held, David and Anthony McGrew (1998). "The End of the Old Order? Globalization and the Prospects for World Order." *Review of International Studies* 24 (Special Issue, December): 219–44

Held, David, Anthony McGrew, David Gordblatt, and Jonathan Perraton (1999). *Global Transformations: Politics, Economics and Culture*. Stanford: Stanford University Press

Heraclides, Alexis (1990). "Secessionist Minorities and External Involvement." *International Organization* 44, 3: 341–78

  (1997). "The Ending of Unending Conflicts." *Millennium: Journal of International Studies* 26, 3: 678–707

Hinsley, F. H. (1967). "The Concept of Sovereignty and the Relations between States." *Journal of International Affairs* 21, 2: 242–52

Hirst, Paul (1997). "The Global Economy: Myths and Realities." *International Affairs* 73, 3: 409–25

Hitler's Tabletalk 1941–1944 (1953). Trans. Norman Cameron and R. H. Stevens. Oxford: Oxford University Press

Hitti, Nassif (1994). "The Internationalization of the State in the Middle East." In Yoshikazu Sakamoto, ed., *Global Transformation: Challenges to the State System*. Tokyo: United Nations University Press

Hocking, Brian (1999). "Patrolling the 'Frontier': Globalization, Localization and the 'Actorness' of Non-Central Governments." In Francisco Aldecoa and Michael Keating, eds., *Paradiplomacy in Action: The Foreign Relations of Subnational Governments*. London: Frank Cass, pp. 17–39

Hoffmann, Stanley (1977). "An American Social Science: International Relations." *Daedalus* 106, 3: 41–60

Holland, R. F. (1985). *European Decolonization: An Introductory Survey*. New York: St Martin's Press

Holsti, K. J. (1967). *International Politics: A Framework for Analysis*. Englewood Cliffs, NJ: Prentice-Hall

(1991). *Peace and War: Armed Conflicts and International Order 1648–1989.* Cambridge: Cambridge University Press

(1992). "Governance without Government: Polyarchy in Nineteenth-Century European International Politics." In James N. Rosenau and Ernst-Otto Czempiel, eds., *Governance without Government: Order and Change in World Politics.* Cambridge: Cambridge University Press, pp. 30–57

(1994). "The Post-Cold War 'Settlement' in Comparative Perspective." In Douglas T. Stuart and Stephen F. Szabo, eds., *Discord and Collaboration in a New Europe: Essays in Honor of Arnold Wolfers.* Washington, DC: The Paul H. Nitze School of Advanced International Studies, pp. 37–70

(1996). *The State, War, and the State of War.* Cambridge: Cambridge University Press

(1997). "International Relations Theory and War in the Third World: The Limits of Relevance." In Stephanie Neuman, ed., *International Relations Theory and the Third World.* New York: St. Martin's Press, pp. 103–32

(2000) "The Political Sources of Humanitarian Emergencies." In Wayne Nafziger, Francis Stewart, and Raimo Väyrynen, eds, *War, Hunger, and Displacement: The Origins of Humanitarian Emergencies,* Vol. I: *Analysis.* Oxford: Oxford University Press, pp. 239–81

(2001). "The Changing Nature of International Institutions: The Case of Territoriality." *Studia Diplomatica* 53, 5: 41–66

(2002). "The Problem of Change in International Relations Theory." In Yale H. Ferguson and R. J. Barry Jones, eds., *Political Space: Frontiers of Change and Governance in a Globalizing World.* Albany, NY: State University of New York Press, pp. 23–44

Holton, R. J. (1998). *Globalization and the Nation-State.* New York: St. Martin's Press

Howard, Michael (1976). *War in European History.* London: Oxford University Press

(1979). "*Temperamenta Belli*: Can War be Controlled?" In Michael Howard, ed., *Restraints on War: Studies in the Limitation of Armed Conflict.* Oxford: Oxford University Press, pp. 1–16

Howard, Peter, and Reina Neufeldt (2000). "Canada's Constructivist Foreign Policy: Building Norms for Peace." Paper presented at the 41st Annual Meetings of the International Studies Association, Los Angeles, March 14–18

Hueglin, Thomas O. (1989). "Better Small and Beautiful than Big and Ugly? Regionalism, Capitalism, and the Postindustrial State." *International Political Science Review* 10, 3: 209–21

Hull, Cordell (1948). *The Memoirs of Cordell Hull.* 2 vols. New York: Macmillan

Huntington, Samuel (1993). "The Coming Clash of Civilizations?" *Foreign Affairs* 72: 22–49

Hurd, Ian (1999). "Legitimacy and Authority in International Politics." *International Organization* 53, 2: 379–408

Hurrell, Andrew (1993). "International Society and the Study of Regimes: A Reflective Approach." In Volker Rittberger, ed., *Regime Theory and International Relations*. Oxford: Clarendon Press, pp. 49–72

(1996). "Vattel: Pluralism and its Limits." In Ian Clark and Iver B. Neumann, eds., *Classical Theories of International Relations*. London: Macmillan, pp. 233–54

Ignatieff, Michael (1998). *The Warrior's Honour: Ethics, War and the Modern Conscience*. Toronto: Viking Press

Inayatullah, Naeem (1996). "Beyond the Sovereignty Dilemma: Quasi-States as Social Constructs." In Thomas Biersteker and Cynthia Weber, eds., *State Sovereignty as Social Construct*. Cambridge: Cambridge University Press, pp. 50–80

Ingebritsen, Christine (2002). "Norm Entrepreneurs: Scandinavia's Role in World Politics." *Cooperation and Conflict* 37, 1: 11–23

International Commission on Intervention and State Sovereignty (ICISS) (2001). *The Responsibility to Protect*. Ottawa: International Development Research Centre

Isaacs, Ann Katherine and Maarten Prak (1996). "Cities, Bourgeoisies, and States." In Wolfgang Reinhard, ed., *Power Elites and State Building*. Oxford: Clarendon Press, pp. 207–34

Jackson, Robert H. (1990). *Quasi States: Sovereignty, International Relations and the Third World*. Cambridge: Cambridge University Press

(1993). "The Weight of Ideas in Decolonization: Normative Change in International Relations." In Judith Goldstein and Robert O. Keohane, eds., *Ideas and Foreign Policy: Beliefs, Institutions, and Political Change*. Ithaca: Cornell University Press, pp. 111–41

(1998). "Surrogate Sovereignty? Great Power Responsibility and 'Failed States.'" Vancouver: Institute of International Relations, University of British Columbia, Working Paper No. 25

(2000). *The Global Covenant: Human Conduct in a World of States*. Oxford: Oxford University Press

Jackson, Robert H. and Alan James, eds. (1993). *States in a Changing World: A Contemporary Analysis*. Oxford: Clarendon Press

Jackson, Robert H. and Mark W. Zacher (1997). "The Territorial Covenant: International Society and the Stabilization of Boundaries." Vancouver: Institute of International Relations, University of British Columbia, Working Paper No. 15

Jahn, Beate (1999). "The State of Nature: The Cultural Origins of a Ruling Ideology." *Review of International Studies* 25, 3: 411–34

James, Alan (1999). "The Practice of Sovereign Statehood in Contemporary International Society." In Robert Jackson, ed., *Sovereignty at the Millennium*. Oxford: Blackwell, pp. 35–51

Janos, Andrew C. (1986). *Politics and Paradigms: Changing Theories of Change in Social Science*. Stanford: Stanford University Press

Jones, Dorothy (1990). *Code of Peace: Ethics and Security in the World of the Warlord States*. Chicago: University of Chicago Press

Jones, R. J. Barry (1981). "Concepts and Models of Change in International Relations." In Barry Buzan and R. J. Barry Jones, eds., *Change and the Study of International Relations*. London: Frances Pinter, pp. 11–29

Kaldor, Mary (1997). "Introduction." In Mary Kaldor and Basker Vashee, eds., *Restructuring the Global Military Sector*, Vol. I: *New Wars*. London and Washington, DC: Frances Pinter for the United Nations University, pp. 3–33

Kaplan, Robert D. (1994). "The Coming Anarchy." *The Atlantic Monthly* (February): pp. 44–76

Kapuscinski, Ryszard (1995). *Imperium*. Toronto: Vintage Canada

Kaufmann, Johan (1996). *Conference Diplomacy: An Introductory Analysis*. 3rd rev. edn. London: Macmillan

Kearney, Michael (1998). "Transnationalism in California and Mexico at the End of Empire." In Thomas M. Wilson and Hastings Donnan, eds., *Border Identities: Nation and State at International Frontiers*. Cambridge: Cambridge University Press, pp. 117–41

Keating, Michael (1998). *The New Regionalism in Western Europe: Territorial Restructuring and Political Change*. Northampton: Edward Elgar

Keene, Edward (2002). *Beyond the Anarchical Society: Grotius, Colonialism and Order in World Politics*. Cambridge: Cambridge University Press

Keens-Soper, Maurice (1972). "The French Political Academy, 1712: A School for Ambassadors." *European Studies Review* 2, 4: 329–55

(1973). "Francois de Callières and Diplomatic Theory." *The Historical Journal* 16, 3: 485–508

Kegley, Charles W., and Gregory A. Raymond (2002). *Exorcising the Ghost of Westphalia: Building World Order in the New Millennium*. Upper Saddle River, NJ: Prentice-Hall

Keohane, Robert O. (1984), *After Hegemony: Cooperation and Discord in the World Political Economy*. Princeton: Princeton University Press

(1998). "International Institutions: Can Interdependence Work?" *Foreign Policy* 110 (Spring): 82–96

Khalidi, Rashid (1997). *Palestinian Identity: The Construction of Modern National Consciousness*. New York: Columbia University Press

Kimble, George H. T. (1960). *Tropical Africa*, Vol. II: *Society and Polity*. New York: Twentieth Century Fund

Kincaid, John (1999). "The International Competence of US States and their Local Governments." In Francisco Aldecoa and Michael Keating, eds., *Paradiplomacy in Action: The Foreign Relations of Subnational Governments*. London: Frank Cass, pp. 111–33

Kindleberger, Charles (1975). "The Rise of Free Trade in Western Europe, 1820–1875." *Journal of Economic History* 35 (March): 20–55

Kingsbury, Benedict (1996). "Grotius, Law, and Moral Scepticism: Theory and Practice in the Thought of Hedley Bull." In Ian Clark and Iver B. Neumann, eds., *Classical Theories of International Relations*. London: Macmillan, pp. 42–70

Klare, Michael (1997). "An Avalanche of Guns: Light Weapons Trafficking and Armed Conflict in the Post-Cold War Era." In Mary Kaldor and Basker Vashee, eds., *Restructuring the Global Military Sector*, Vol. I: *New Wars*. London and Washington, DC: Frances Pinter for the United Nations University, pp. 55–77

Klein, Robert A. (1974). *Sovereign Equality among States: The History of an Idea*. Toronto: University of Toronto Press

Klingenstein, Grete (1997). "The Meaning of 'Austria' and 'Austrian' in the Eighteenth Century." In Robert Oresco, G. C. Gibbs, and H. M. Scott, eds., *Royal and Republican Sovereignty in Early Modern Europe*. Cambridge: Cambridge University Press, pp. 423–78

Knorr, Klaus E. (1944). *British Colonial Theories, 1570–1850*. Toronto: University of Toronto Press

Knutsen, Torbjørn L. (1997). *A History of International Relations Theory*. 2nd edn. Manchester: Manchester University Press

Korman, Sharon (1996). *The Right of Conquest: The Acquisition of Territory by Force in International Law and Practice*. Oxford: Clarendon Press

Koslowski, Rey and Friedrich Kratochwil (1994). "Understanding Change in International Politics: The Soviet Empire's Demise and the International System." *International Organization* 48, 2: 215–48

Krasner, Stephen D. (1999). *Sovereignty: Organized Hypocrisy*. Princeton: Princeton University Press

Kratochwil, Friedrich (1986). "Of Systems, Boundaries, and Territoriality: An Inquiry into the Formation of the State System." *World Politics* 39, 1: 27–52

(1989). *Rules, Norms and Decisions: On the Conditions of Practical Reasoning in International and Domestic Affairs*. Cambridge: Cambridge University Press

Lauterpacht, Hersch (1946). "The Grotian Tradition in International Law." *The British Year Book of International Law*, pp. 1–53

Lebow, Ned (1994). "The Long Peace, the End of the Cold War, and the Failure of Realism." *International Organization* 15, 2: 249–77

Legro, Jeffrey W. (1995). *Cooperation under Fire: Anglo-German Restraint During World War* II. Ithaca: Cornell University Press

Levy, Jack (1983). *War in the Modern Great Power System, 1495–1975*. Lexington, KY: University of Kentucky Press

Li, Dun J. (1965). *The Ageless Chinese: A History*. New York: Charles Scribner's Sons

Licklider, Roy (1998). "Early Returns: Results of the First Wave of Statistical Studies on Civil War." *Civil Wars* (Autumn): 121–32

Lipson, Charles (1982). "The Transformation of Trade: The Sources and Effects of Regime Change." In Stephen D. Krasner, ed., *International Regimes*. Ithaca: Cornell University Press, pp. 233–72

References

Louis, William Roger (1984). "The Era of the Mandates System and the Non-European World." In Hedley Bull and Adam Watson, eds., *The Expansion of International Society*. Oxford: Clarendon Press, pp. 201–16

Luard, Evan (1992). *The Balance of Power: The System of International Relations, 1648–1815*. New York: St Martin's Press

Lynch, Allen (2002). "Woodrow Wilson and the Principle of National Self-Determination: A Reconsideration." *Review of International Studies* 28, 2: 419–36

Maland, David (1966). *Europe in the Seventeenth Century*. London: Macmillan

Malmvig, Helle (2001). "Reproduction of Sovereignties: Between Man and State during Practices of Intervention." *Cooperation and Conflict* 36, 3: 251–72

Mandel, Robert (1999). *Deadly Transfers and the Global Playground: Transnational Security Threats in a Disorderly World*. Westport, CN: Praeger

Mandelbaum, Michael (1998–9). "Is Major War Obsolete?" *Survival* 204, 4: 20–38

Manning, C. A. W. (1975). *The Nature of International Society*. London: Macmillan

Marino, John (1992). "Administrative Mapping in the Italian States." In David Buisseret, ed., *Monarchs, Ministers, and Maps: The Emergence of Cartography as a Tool of Government in Early Modern Europe*. Chicago: University of Chicago Press, pp. 5–25

Mattingly, Garrett (1955). *Renaissance Diplomacy*. London: Jonathan Cape

Mayall, James (1999). "Sovereignty, Nationalism, and Self-Determination." In Robert Jackson, ed., *Sovereignty at the Millennium*. Oxford: Blackwell, pp. 52–80

Mearsheimer, John J. (1990). "Back to the Future: Instability in Europe after the Cold War." *International Security* 15, 1: 5–56

Migdal, Joel (1988). *Strong States and Weak Societies: State–Society Relations and State Capabilities in the Third World*. Princeton: Princeton University Press

Milner, Helen (2002). "International Trade." In Walter Carlsnaess, Thomas Risse, and Beth A. Simmons, eds., *Handbook of International Relations*. London: Sage Publications, pp. 448–61

Minc, Alain (1993). *Le nouveau moyen age*. Paris: Gallimard

Morgenthau, Hans J. (1985). *Politics among Nations: The Struggle for Power and Peace*. 6th rev. edn. Edited by Kenneth Thompson. New York: Alfred A. Knopf

Morris, Christopher W. (1998). *An Essay on the Modern State*. Cambridge: Cambridge University Press

Motyl, Alexander J. (1999). *Revolutions, Nations, Empires: Conceptual Limits, Theoretical Possibilities*. New York: Columbia University Press

Mueller, John (1989). *Retreat from Doomsday: The Obsolescence of Major War*. New York: Basic Books

  (2001). "Does War Still Exist?" Paper delivered at the conference on "The Waning of Major War," at the University of Notre Dame, Indiana, April 6–8

Murphy, Alexander B. (1996). "The Sovereign State as Political-Territorial Ideal." In Thomas Biersteker and Cynthia Weber, eds., *State Sovereignty as Social Construct*. Cambridge: Cambridge University Press, pp. 81–120

Nadelman, Ethan A. (1990). "Global Prohibition Regimes: The Evolution of Norms in International Society." *International Organization* 44, 4: 479–526

Nardin, Terry (1992). "International Ethics and International Law." *Review of International Studies* 18, 1: 19–30

Newman, David (2001). "Boundaries, Borders, and Barriers: Changing Geographic Perspectives on Territorial Lines." In Mathias Albert, David Jacobson, and Yosef Lapid, eds., *Identities, Borders, Orders: Rethinking International Relations Theory*. Minneapolis: University of Minneapolis Press, pp. 137–52

O'Connor, J. J. and E. F. Robertson (1997). "Longitude and the Académie Royale." http://www.history.mcs.st-andrews.ac.uk/history/HistTopics/Longitude1.html

Ohmae, Kenichi (1995). *The End of the Nation State*. New York: The Free Press

Onuf, Nicholas (2002). "Institutions, Intentions and International Relations." *Review of International Studies* 38, 2: 211–28

Onuma, Yasuaki (2000). "When was the Law of International Society Born? An Inquiry of the History of International Law from an Intercivilizational Perspective." *Journal of the History of International Law* 2: 1–66

Oresco, Robert, G. C. Gibbs, and H. M. Scott (1997). "Introduction." In Robert Oresco, G. C. Gibbs, and H. M. Scott, eds., *Royal and Republican Sovereignty in Early Modern Europe*. Cambridge: Cambridge University Press, pp. 1–42

Ortega, Martin C. (1996). "Vitoria and the Universalist Conception of International Relations." In Ian Clark and Iver B. Neumann, eds., *Classical Theories of International Relations*. London: Macmillan, pp. 99–119

Osiander, Andreas (1994). *The States System of Europe, 1640–1990*. Oxford: Clarendon Press

　(2001). "Sovereignty, International Relations, and the Westphalian Myth." *International Organization* 55, 2: 251–87

Papademetriou, Demetrios (2000). Presentation at the conference on "Rethinking the Line: The Canada–United States Border," Vancouver, Canada, October 25

Parrot, David (1997). "A *prince souverein* and the French Crown: Charles de Nevers." In Robert Oresco, G. C. Gibbs, and H. M. Scott, eds., *Royal and Republican Sovereignty in Early Modern Europe*. Cambridge: Cambridge University Press, pp. 149–87

Parry, J. H. (1971). *Trade and Dominion: The European Overseas Empires in the Eighteenth Century*. London: Weidenfeld & Nicolson

Patterson, Thomas E. (1998). "Time and News: The Media's Limitations as an Instrument of Democracy." *International Political Science Review* 19, 1: 55–68

Paul, Darel E. (1999). "Sovereignty, Survival and the Westphalian Blind Alley in International Relations." *Review of International Studies* 25, 2: 217–31

References

Pegg, Scott (1998). *International Society and De Facto States*. Aldershot: Ashgate

Pettigrew, Pierre (2001). "Some Reflections on Globalization." Notes for an address at the International Congress of Young Lawyers on International Trade Agreements, Montreal, August 20. Department of Foreign Affairs and International Trade, Canada, *Statement* 2001/28

Philpott, Daniel (1997). "Ideas and the Evolution of Sovereignty." In Sohail H. Hashmi, ed., *State Sovereignty: Change and Persistence in International Relations*. University Park, PA: Pennsylvania State University Press, pp. 15–48

(1999). "Westphalia, Authority, and International Society." In Robert Jackson, ed., *Sovereignty at the Millennium*. Oxford: Blackwell, pp. 144–67

(2001). *Revolutions in Sovereignty: How Ideas Shaped Modern International Relations*. Princeton: Princeton University Press

Poggi, Gianfranco (1978). *The Development of the Modern State*. Stanford: Stanford University Press

Polanyi, Karl (1944). *The Great Transformation*. Boston: Beacon Press

Power, Thomas F. (1966). *Jules Ferry and the Renaissance of French Imperialism*. New York: Octagon Books

Puchala, Donald J. (1993). "Western Europe." In Robert H. Jackson and Alan James, eds., *States in a Changing World: A Contemporary Analysis*. Oxford: Clarendon Press, pp. 69–92

Rasmussen, Mikkel Vedby (2002). "A Parallel Globalization of Terror: 9–11, Security and Globalization." *Cooperation and Conflict* 37, 3: 323–49

Raustiala, Kal, and Anne-Marie Slaughter (2002). "International Law, International Relations, and Compliance." In Walter Carlsnaess, Thomas Risse, and Beth A. Simmons, eds., *Handbook of International Relations*. London: Sage Publications, pp. 538–58

Reineicke, Wolfgang H. (1998). *Global Public Policy: Governing Without Government*. Washington, DC: The Brookings Institution Press

Reinhard, Wolfgang, ed. (1996). *Power Elites and State Building*. Oxford: Clarendon Press

Reus-Smit, Christian (1997). "International Society and the Nature of Fundamental Institutions." *International Organization* 51, 4: 555–89

Rice, Condoleezza (2000). "Promoting the National Interest." *Foreign Affairs* 79, 1: 45–62

Richardson, James L. (2000). "International Relations and Cognate Disciplines: From Economics to Historical Sociology." In Robert M. A. Crawford and Darryl S. L. Jarvis, eds., *International Relations – Still an American Social Science?* Albany, NY: State University of New York Press, pp. 277–98

Riordan, Shaun (2003). *The New Diplomacy*. Cambridge: Polity Press

Robinson, Ronald, and John Gallagher (1965). *Africa and the Victorians: The Official Mind of Imperialism*. London: Macmillan

Ron, James (2000). "Boundaries and Violence: Repertoires of State Action along the Bosnia/Yugoslavia Divide." *Theory and Society* 29: 609–49

Rosenau, James N. (1990). *Turbulence in World Politics: A Theory of Change and Continuity*. Princeton: Princeton University Press

(1995). "Signals, Signposts, and Symptoms: Interpreting Change and Anomalies in World Politics." *European Journal of International Relations* 1 (March): 113–22

(1997). *Along the Domestic–Foreign Frontier: Exploring Governance in a Turbulent World*. Cambridge: Cambridge University Press

(2003). *Distant Proximities: Dynamics Beyond Globalization*. Princeton, NJ: Princeton University Press

Rowen, Herbert, ed. (1968). *From Absolutism to Revolution, 1648–1848*. New York: Macmillan

Ruggie, John G. (1982). "International Regimes, Transactions, and Change: Embedded Liberalism in the Postwar Economic Order." In Stephen D. Krasner, ed., *International Regimes*. Ithaca: Cornell University Press, pp. 195–232

(1989). "International Structure and International Transformation: Space, Time, and Method." In James N. Rosenau and Ernst-Otto Czempiel, eds., *Global Change and Theoretical Challenges*. Lexington, MA: Lexington Books, pp. 21–35

(1998). *Constructing the World Polity: Essays on International Institutionalization*. London: Routledge

(1993). "Territoriality and Beyond: Problematizing Modernity in International Relations." *International Organization* 47, 4: 139–74

Sahlins, Peter (1998). "State Formation and National Identity in the Catalan Borderlands during the Eighteenth and Nineteenth Centuries." In Thomas M. Wilson and Hastings Donnan, eds., *Border Identities: Nation and State at International Frontiers*. Cambridge: Cambridge University Press, pp. 31–61

Said, Edward ([1978] 1995). *Orientalism: Western Conceptions of the Orient*. First published London: Routledge & Kegan Paul. Penguin edition with new Afterword

Sakamoto, Yoshikazu, ed. (1994a), *Global Transformation: Challenges to the State System*. Tokyo: United Nations University Press

(1994b). "A Perspective on the Changing World Order: A Conceptual Prelude." In Yoshikazu Sakamoto, ed., *Global Transformation: Challenges to the State System*. Tokyo: United Nations University Press, pp. 15–56

Salter, Mark B. (2002). *Barbarians and Civilization in International Relations*. London: Pluto Press

(2003). *Papers Please: A Genealogy of the Passport*. London: Lynn Rienner

Sarkees Meredith, Frank Wayman, and J. David Singer (2003). "Inter-State, Intra-State, and Extra-State Wars: A Comprehensive Look at their Distribution over Time." *International Studies Quarterly* 47, 1: 49–70

Sassen, Saskia (2002). "A New Cross-Border Field for Public and Private Actors." In Yale H. Ferguson and R. J. Barry Jones, eds., *Political Space: Frontiers of Change and Governance in a Globalizing World*. Albany, NY: State University of New York Press, pp. 173–88

Saurin, Julian (1996). "The End of International Relations? The State and International Theory in the Age of Globalization." In Andrew Linklater and John Macmillan, eds., *Boundaries in Question: New Directions in International Relations*. London: Pinter Publishers, pp. 244–61

Scholte, Jan (1997). "The Globalization of World Politics." In John Baylis and Steve Smith, eds., *The Globalization of World Politics*. New York: Oxford University Press, pp. 13–30

Seiler, D. L. (1989). "Peripheral Nationalism between Pluralism and Monism." *International Political Science Review* 10, 3: 191–207

Shannon, Vaughn P. (2000). "The Political Psychology of Norm Violation." *International Studies Quarterly* 44, 2: 293–316

Sharp, Paul (2001). "Making Sense of Citizen Diplomats: The People of Duluth, Minnesota, as International Actors." *International Studies Perspectives* 2, 2: 131–50

Sharpe, L. J. (1989). "Fragementation and Territoriality in the European State System." *International Political Science Review* 10, 3: 223–38

Singer, Max, and Aaron Wildavsky (1993). *The Real World Order: Zones of Peace/Zones of Turmoil*. Chatham, NJ: Chatham House Publishers

Smith, Thomas W. (2002). "The New Law of War: Legitimizing Hi-Tech and Infrastructural Violence." *International Studies Quarterly* 46, 3: 355–74

Smith, Woodruff D. (1982). *European Imperialism in the Nineteenth and Twentieth Centuries*. Chicago: Nelson-Hall

Snyder, Louis L. (1962). *The Imperialism Reader: Documents and Readings on Modern Expansionism*. Princeton: D. Van Nostrand

Sørensen, Georg (1999). "Sovereignty: Change and Continuity in a Fundamental Institution." In Robert Jackson, ed., *Sovereignty at the Millennium*. Oxford: Blackwell, pp. 168–82

   (2001). *Changes in Statehood: The Transformation of International Relations*. Basingstoke: Palgrave

Spruyt, Hendrik (1994). *The Sovereign State and its Competitors*. Princeton: Princeton University Press

   (2000). "The End of Empire and the Extension of the Westphalian System: The Normative Basis of the Modern State Order." *International Studies Review* 2, 2: 65–92

Stankiewicz, W. J., ed. (1969). *In Defense of Sovereignty*. New York: Oxford University Press

Stivachtis, Yannis A. (1998). *The Enlargement of International Society: Culture versus Anarchy and Greece's Entry into International Society*. London: Macmillan

Strang, David (1996). "Contested Sovereignty." In Thomas Biersteker and Cynthia Weber, eds., *State Sovereignty as Social Construct*. Cambridge: Cambridge University Press, pp. 22–49

Strange, Susan (1996). *The Retreat of the State: The Diffusion of Power in the World Economy*. Cambridge: Cambridge University Press

Strayer, Joseph R. (1970). *On the Mediaeval Origins of the Modern State*. Princeton: Princeton University Press

Stremlau, John, and Greg Mills, eds., (1999). *The Privatization of Security in Africa.* Johannesburg: South African Institute of International Affairs

Suganami, Hidemi (1990). "Grotius and International Equality." In Hedley Bull, Robert Kingsbury, and Adam Roberts, eds., *Hugo Grotius and International Relations.* Oxford: Clarendon Press, pp. 221–56

Taylor, Peter (1994). "The State as Container: Territoriality in the Modern World-System." *Progress in Human Geography* 18, 2: 151–62

  (1999). "The United Nations in the 1990s: Proactive Cosmopolitanism and the Issue of Sovereignty." In Robert Jackson, ed., *Sovereignty at the Millennium.* Oxford: Blackwell, pp. 116–43

Thakur, Ramesh (2001). "Global Norms and International Humanitarian Law: An Asian Perspective." *International Review of the Red Cross* 83, 841: 19–44

Thakur, Ramesh, and William Maley (1999). "The Ottawa Convention on Landmines: A Landmark Humanitarian Treaty in Arms Control?" *Global Governance* 5, 3: 273–302

Thompson, J. (1993). "Norms in International Relations: A Conceptual Analysis." *International Journal of Group Tensions* 23: 67–83

Thomson, Janice E. 1994. *Mercenaries, Pirates, and Sovereigns: State-Building and Extraterritorial Violence in Early Modern Europe.* Princeton: Princeton University Press

Thornton, A. P. (1959). *The Imperial Idea and its Enemies.* London: Macmillan

Tilly, Charles (1975). "Reflections on the History of European State-Making." In Charles Tilly, ed., *The Formation of National States in Western Europe.* Princeton: Princeton University Press, pp. 3–83

  (1990). *Coercion, Capital and European States AD 990–1990.* Oxford: Basil Blackwell

Towle, Philip (2000). *Democracy and Peacemaking: Negotiations and Debates, 1815–1973.* London and New York: Routledge

Tracy, James D., ed. (1990). *The Rise of Merchant Empires: Long-Distance Trade in the Early Modern World, 1350–1750.* Cambridge: Cambridge University Press

Tuck, Richard (1999). *The Rights of War and Peace: Political Thought and the International Order from Grotius to Kant.* Oxford: Oxford University Press

Ullman, Walter (1949). "The Development of the Medieval Idea of Sovereignty." *English Historical Review* 64, 210: 1–33

Underhill, Geoffrey R. D. (1997). "Transnationalizing the State in Global Financial Markets: Cooperative Regulatory Regimes, Domestic Political Authority, and Conceptual Models of the State." Paper presented at the joint meetings of the Asociacion Mexicana de Estudios Internacionales and the International Studies Association, Manzanillo, Mexico, December 11–13

Vann, James (1992). "Mapping the Austrian Hapsburgs." In David Buisseret, ed., *Monarchs, Ministers and Maps: The Emergence of Cartography as a Tool of Government in Early Modern Europe.* Chicago and London: University of Chicago Press, pp. 153–67

Vasquez, John A. (1993). *The War Puzzle*. Cambridge: Cambridge University Press

Väyrynen, Raimo (1997). *Global Transformation: Economics, Politics, and Culture*. Helsinki: The Finnish National Fund for Research and Development, Sitra
  (2000). "Enforcement of International Norms: Why, How, and by Whom?" Paper presented at the 41st Annual Meetings, International Studies Association, Los Angeles, March 15–18

Vincent, John (1974). *Non-Intervention and World Order*. Princeton: Princeton University Press
  (1984). "Racial Equality." In Hedley Bull and Adam Watson, eds., The *Expansion of International Society*. Oxford: Clarendon Press, 239–54

Von Glahn, Gerhard (1992). *Law Among Nations*. 6th edn. New York: Macmillan

Walker, R. B. J. (1993). *Inside/Outside: International Relations as Political Theory*. Cambridge: Cambridge University Press

Walker, Richard (1953). *The Multi-State System of Ancient China*. Hamden, CT: The Shoe String Press

Wallace, William (1999). "The Sharing of Sovereignty: The European Paradox." In Robert Jackson, ed., *Sovereignty at the Millennium*. Oxford: Blackwell, pp. 81–99

Wallensteen, Peter, and Margareta Sollenberg (1997). "Armed Conflicts, Conflict Termination, and Peace Agreements, 1989–1996." *Journal of Peace Research* 34: 339–58

Walter, Andrew Wyatt (1996). "Adam Smith and the Liberal Tradition in International Relations." In Ian Clark and Iver B. Neumann, eds., *Classical Theories of International Relations*. London: Macmillan, pp. 142–72

Waltz, Kenneth N. (1979). *Theory of International Politics*. Reading, MA: Addison-Wesley

Wan, Marilyn (1992). "Naturalized Seeing/Colonial Vision: Interrogating the Display of Races in Late Nineteenth Century France." MA thesis, Department of Fine Arts, University of British Columbia

Warner, Carolyn M. (1999). "The Political Economy of 'Quasi-Statehood' and the Demise of 19th Century African Polities." *Review of International Studies* 25, 2: 233–55

Watson, Adam (1984). "European International Society and its Expansion." In Hedley Bull and Adam Watson, eds., *The Expansion of International Society*. Oxford: Clarendon Press, pp. 13–32
  1992. *The Evolution of International Society: A Comparative Historical Analysis*. New York: Routledge

Weiss, Herbert (1995). "Zaire: Collapsed Society, Surviving State, Future Policy." In William Zartman, ed., *Collapsed States: The Disintegration and Restoration of Legitimate Authority*. Boulder, CO: Lynne Reinner, pp. 157–70

Weiss, Linda (1998). *The Myth of the Powerless State: Governing the Economy in a Global Era*. Cambridge: Polity Press

Wendt, Alexander (1992). "Anarchy is What States Make of It: The Social Construction of Power Politics." *International Organization* 46, 2: 391–425

Wendt, Alexander, and Raymond Duvall (1989). "Institutions and International Order." In James N. Rosenau and Ernst-Otto Czempiel, eds., *Global Changes and Theoretical Challenges.* Lexington, MA: Lexington Books, pp. 51–73

Wesseling, H. L. (1997). *Imperialism and Colonialism: Essays in the History of European Expansion.* Leiden: Leiden University Press

Wight, Martin (1978). *Power Politics.* Leicester: Leicester University Press

Wilson, Charles (1957). *Profit and Power: A Study of England and the Dutch Wars.* London and New York: Longmans, Green and Co

Wilson, Thomas M. and Hastings Donnan (1998). "Nation, State and Identity at International Borders." In Thomas M. Wilson and Hastings Donnan, eds., *Border Identities: Nation and State at International Frontiers.* Cambridge: Cambridge University Press, pp. 1–30

Wolf, Martin (2001). "Will the Nation-State Survive Globalization?" *Foreign Affairs* 80 (January–February): 178–90

Wolfe, Robert (1998a). *Diplomatic Missions: The Ambassador in Canadian Foreign Policy.* Kingston, Ontario: School of Policy Studies

Wolfe, Robert (1998b). "Still Lying Abroad: On the Institution of the Resident Ambassador." *Diplomacy and Statecraft* 9, 2: 23–54

Wright, Quincy (1955). *The Study of International Relations.* New York: Appleton-Century-Crofts

   (1964). *A Study of War.* abridged edn. Chicago: University of Chicago Press

   (1965). *A Study of War.* 2nd edn. Chicago: University of Chicago Press

Young, Crawford (1994). "In Search of Civil Society." In John Harbeson, Donald Rothchild, and Naomi Chazan, eds., *Civil Society and the State in Africa.* Boulder, CO and London: Lynne Reinner, pp. 33–50

Zacher, Mark W. (1993). "The Decaying Pillars of the Westphalian Temple: Implications for International Order and Governance." In James N. Rosenau and Ernst-Otto Czempiel, eds., *Governance without Government: Order and Change in World Politics.* Cambridge: Cambridge University Press, pp. 58–101

   (2001). "The Territorial Integrity Norm: International Boundaries and the Use of Force." *International Organization* 55, 2: 215–50

Zartman, I. William, ed. (1995). *Collapsed States: The Disintegration and Restoration of Legitimate Authority.* Boulder, CO and London: Lynne Reinner

Index

CAMBRIDGE STUDIES IN INTERNATIONAL RELATIONS